T0214368

Lecture Notes in Artificial Intelligence 9086

Subseries of Lecture Notes in Computer Science

More information about this series at http://www.springer.com/series/1244

Yves Demazeau · Keith S. Decker
Javier Bajo Pérez · Fernando De la Prieta (Eds.)

Advances in Practical Applications of Agents, Multi-Agent Systems, and Sustainability

The PAAMS Collection

13th International Conference, PAAMS 2015
Salamanca, Spain, June 3–4, 2015
Proceedings

 Springer

Editors
Yves Demazeau
Centre National de la Recherche Scientifique
Grenoble
France

Keith S. Decker
University of Delaware
Newark
Delaware
USA

Javier Bajo Pérez
Universidad Politécnica
Madrid
Spain

Fernando De la Prieta
Universidad de Salamanca
Salamanca
Spain

ISSN 0302-9743   ISSN 1611-3349   (electronic)
Lecture Notes in Artificial Intelligence
ISBN 978-3-319-18943-7   ISBN 978-3-319-18944-4   (eBook)
DOI 10.1007/978-3-319-18944-4

Library of Congress Control Number: 2015938728

LNCS Sublibrary: SL7 – Artificial Intelligence

Springer Cham Heidelberg New York Dordrecht London

Printed on acid-free paper

Springer International Publishing AG Switzerland is part of Springer Science+Business Media
(www.springer.com)

Preface

Research on Agents and Multi-Agent Systems has matured during the last decade and many effective applications of this technology are now deployed. An international forum to present and discuss the latest scientific developments and their effective applications, to assess the impact of the approach, and to facilitate technology transfer, has become a necessity and has been created a few years ago.

PAAMS, the International Conference on Practical Applications of Agents and Multi-Agent Systems, is the international yearly tribune to present, to discuss, and to disseminate the latest developments and the most important outcomes related to real-world applications. It provides a unique opportunity to bring multi-disciplinary experts, academics, and practitioners together to exchange their experience in the development and deployment of agents and multi-agent systems.

This volume presents the papers that were accepted for the 2015 edition of PAAMS. These articles report on the application and validation of agent-based models, methods, and technologies in a number of key application areas, including: Agents and the Energy Grid, Agents and the Traffic Grid, Affective Computing and Agent Development, Ambient and Contextual Agents, Social Simulation and Social Networks, and Other Agent-based Applications. Each paper submitted to PAAMS went through a stringent peer review by three members of the international committee composed of 111 internationally renowned researchers from 26 countries. From the 48 submissions received, 10 were selected for full presentation at the conference; another 9 papers were accepted as short presentations. In addition, a demonstration track featuring innovative and emergent applications of agent and multi-agent systems and technologies in real-world domains was organized. Seventeen demonstrations were shown, and this volume contains a description of each of them.

We would like to thank all the contributing authors, the members of the Program Committee, the sponsors (IEEE SMC Spain, IBM, AEPIA, AFIA, AAAI, APPIA, ARIA, ATIA, BNVKI, SADIO, SBC, GI, University of Salamanca, and CNRS), and the Organizing Committee for their hard and highly valuable work. Their work has helped to contribute to the success of the PAAMS'15 event. Thanks for your help – PAAMS'15 would not exist without your contribution.

June 2015

Yves Demazeau
Keith S. Decker
Javier Bajo Pérez
Fernando De la Prieta

Organization

General Co-chairs

Yves Demazeau   Centre National de la Recherche Scientifique, France
Keith S. Decker   University of Delaware, USA
Javier Bajo Pérez   Polytechnic University of Madrid, Spain
Fernando De la Prieta   University of Salamanca, Spain

Advisory Board

Frank Dignum   Utrecht University, The Netherlands
Toru Ishida   Kyoto University, Japan
Jörg P. Müller   Technische Universität Clausthal, Germany
Juan Pavón   Universidad Complutense de Madrid, Spain
Michal Pěchouček   Czech Technical University in Prague, Czech Republic
Franco Zambonelli   University of Modena and Reggio Emilia, Italy

Program Committee

Carole Adam   University of Grenoble, France
Emmanuel Adam   University of Valenciennes, France
Frederic Amblard   University of Toulouse, France
Francesco Amigoni   Politecnico di Milano, Italy
Luis Antunes   University of Lisbon, Portugal
Matteo Baldoni   University of Turin, Italy
Cristina Baroglio   University of Torino, Italy
Jeremy Baxter   QinetQ, UK
Michael Berger   DocuWare AG, Germany
Olivier Boissier   Ecole Nationale Superieure des Mines de Saint Etienne, France
Vicente Botti   Polytechnic University of Valencia, Spain
Bruno Bouchard   University of Québec at Chicoutimi, Canada
Lars Braubach   Universität Hamburg, Germany
Stefano Bromuri   University of Applied Sciences, Western Switzerland
Sven Brueckner   AXON AI, USA

Longbing Cao	University of Technology, Sydney, Australia
Javier Carbó	University Carlos III of Madrid, Spain
Luis F. Castillo	University of Caldas, Colombia
Wei Chen	Intelligent Automation Incorporated, USA
Pierre Chevaillier	University of Brest, France
Caroline Chopinaud	MASA, France
Brad Clement	NASA JPL, USA
Helder Coelho	University of Lisbon, Portugal
Rosaria Conte	Institute of Cognitive Science and Technology, Italy
Vincent Corruble	University of Paris 6, France
Frank Dignum	Utrecht University, The Netherlands
Jürgen Dix	Clausthal University of Technology, Germany
Alexis Drogoul	Institut de Recherche pour le Développement, Vietnam
Julie Dugdale	University of Grenoble, France
Ed Durfee	University of Michigan, USA
Amal El Fallah	University of Paris 6, France
Jöhannes Fähndrich	Technical University of Berlin, Germany
Jose Luis Fernandez-Marquez	University of Geneva, Switzerland
Maksims Fiosins	Clausthal University of Technology, Germany
Rubén Fuentes Fernández	Universidad Complutense de Madrid, Spain
Javier Gil-Quijano	Commissariat a l'énergie Atomique, France
Sylvain Giroux	University of Sherbrooke, Canada
Marie-Pierre Gleizes	University of Toulouse, France
Daniela Godoy	University of Tandil, Argentina
Jorge J. Gómez-Sanz	Universidad Complutense de Madrid, Spain
Vladimir Gorodetski	University of Saint Petersburg, Russia
Charles Gouin-Vallerand	Télé-Université du Québec, Canada
Kasper Hallenborg	University of Southern Denmark, Denmark
Salima Hassas	University of Lyon, France
Vincent Hilaire	University of Belfort-Montbeliard, France
Koen Hindriks	University of Delft, The Netherlands
Benjamin Hirsch	Technical University of Berlin, Germany
Martin Hofmann	Lockheed Martin, USA
Tom Holvoet	Catholic University of Leuven, Belgium
Shinichi Honiden	National Institute of Informatics, Tokyo, Japan
Jomi Hübner	Universidade Federal de Santa Catarina, Brazil
Takayuki Ito	Nagoya Institute of Technology, Japan
Michal Jakob	Czech Technical University in Prague, Czech Republic
Vicente Julian	Polytechnic University of Valencia, Spain
Sachin Kamboj	University of Delaware, USA
Achilles Kameas	University of Patras, Greece
Takahiro Kawamura	Toshiba, Japan

Viviane Torres da Silva	Universidade Federale Fluminense, Brazil
Paolo Torroni	University of Bologna, Italy
Rainer Unland	University of Duisburg-Essen, Germany
Domenico Ursino	University of Reggio Calabria, Italy
László Varga	Computer and Automation Research Institute, Hungary
Wamberto Vasconselos	University of Aberdeen, UK
Laurent Vercouter	University of Rouen, France
Jacques Verriet	Embedded Systems Institute, The Netherlands
José R. Villar	University of Oviedo, Spain
Niek Wijngaards	Thales, D-CIS Laboratory, The Netherlands
Gaku Yamamoto	IBM, Japan
Franco Zambonelli	University of Modena and Reggio Emilia, Italy

Organizing Committee

Javier Bajo Pérez (Chair)	Polytechnic University of Madrid, Spain
Fernando De la Prieta (Co-chair)	University of Salamanca, Spain
Juan F. De Paz	University of Salamanca, Spain
Sara Rodríguez	University of Salamanca, Spain
Gabriel Villarrubia González	University of Salamanca, Spain
Javier Prieto Tejedor	University of Salamanca, Spain
Pablo Chamoso	University of Salamanca, Spain
Alberto López Barriuso	University of Salamanca, Spain

PAAMS 2015 Sponsors

Contents

Demo Papers

Invited Speaker

Simulating Sustainability:
Guiding Principles to Ensure Policy Impact

Alex Smajgl[1,2(✉)]

[1] Bangkok-Based Mekong Futures Research Institute (MERFI), Bangkok, Thailand
[2] CSIRO Ecosystems Sciences and Climate Adaptation, University Drive,
Townsville 4810, Australia
alex.smajgl@mekongfutures.com

Abstract. This paper showcases examples for surprising emergent phenomena
from agent-based models developed to support sustainability-focused decision
making. Based on these experiences, ten guiding principles are proposed to minimize the risk of redundancy and inefficacy of agent-based modeling due to
the widening gap between scientific endeavors and policy deliberations. These
guiding principles are not meant to constitute a comprehensive list but to trigger
a debate aiming for a continuous improvement of recommendations for applied
agent-based modeling in sustainability related policy contexts.

Keywords: Emergent phenomena · Agent-based modeling

1 Introduction

For nearly thirty years the sustainability paradigm has been guiding policy design and
decision making [18]. Many decisions are now being assessed against triple-bottom-
line outcomes. Triple bottom line accounting introduces substantial metric interde-
pendencies, creating a substantial push for agent-based modeling (ABM) due to its
ability to consider highly complex relationships of multiple variables, including human behavior [3], [8], [11]. In particular ABM's capacity to incorporate social dimensions created a methodological advantage over most other modeling techniques [6]. In
an applied policy context sustainability-focused simulation often requires the implementation of multiple variables and to account for their mostly non-linear relationships
[6], [12], [15], [32]. Associated with this complexity emerges a critical conundrum
[20], [27]. On the one hand the modeling can reveal unexpected results, suggesting
high utility. On the other hand the cognitive gap between science advances and relatively static policy imperatives widens substantially; the nonalignment renders the
modeling effort potentially redundant. It is vital to understand and manage these
process-related risks for applied agent-based modeling.

   This paper showcases examples for surprising emergent phenomena from agent-
based models developed to support sustainability-focused decision making. Based on
these experiences, ten guiding principles are proposed to minimize the risk of redundancy and inefficacy of agent-based modeling due to the widening gap between scientific

© Springer International Publishing Switzerland 2015
Y. Demazeau et al. (Eds.): PAAMS 2015, LNAI 9086, pp. 3–12, 2015.
DOI: 10.1007/978-3-319-18944-4_1

endeavors and policy deliberations. These guiding principles are not meant to constitute a comprehensive list but to trigger a debate aiming for a continuous improvement of recommendations for applied agent-based modeling in sustainability related policy contexts.

2   Unexpected Modeling Results and Policy Impact

Deforestation in East Kalimantan, Indonesia

Indonesia subsidizes fuel, which by 2005 had created a substantial macro-economic burden. Hence, fuel subsidies were reduced. However, in preparation of new elections a policy debate started pushing for a reduction of fuel prices to reduce poverty levels. A research project assessed the possible outcomes of such a central government decision in combination with various response strategies of local governments. The policy details and the agent-based modeling is described in [21], [25], [22], [26] and [4].

Understanding the efficacy of agent-based modeling requires sophisticated monitoring and evaluation. At the core of the monitoring of this work stand beliefs, following psychological understanding of what underpins behavior and decision making [24], [28]. Table 1 lists two of the beliefs the agent-based model contradicted for the policy context in East Kalimantan, Indonesia.

Table 1. Recorded stakeholder and modelling results for East Kalimantan

Stakeholder beliefs	Agent-based model suggestions
Fuel price reductions decrease poverty.	Fuel prices reductions triggered increasing natural resource use (i.e. fish and honey), which increases rural poverty.
Employment in mining reduces poverty.	Mining activities demand skills that are not available in present population, which triggers import of labor. Immigrating mining workers are likely to bring their families that engage in natural resource based livelihoods increasing the pressure on existing users.

All stakeholders expected fuel price reductions to reduce the expenditure of households and thereby reduce poverty. The modeling revealed for the rural context that this direct effect is likely to be vanquished by an indirect effect, which emphasizes the complexity of sustainability. High fuel prices limit the number of households engaging in fishing and small-scale logging to the households living in close proximity to natural resources. Reducing fuel prices enables other potential users to travel, which diminishes the return for the initial users, in particular for fishing and high value non-timber forest products (NTFP) like wild honey. The emerging pattern from modeling indicates a high risk for overall poverty in rural areas to increase because of declining natural resource stocks.

Many local Governments indicated that in case of increasing poverty they would increase the number of mining licenses to create more employment. The ABM assessment suggests that the counter-intuitive outcome of such a strategy would be that poverty increases. Figure 1 depicts the principle logic of this emerging pattern. New mining operations require more labor but this labor is largely sourced from outside of Kalimantan. The in-migration of labor implies that most workers bring their families as most mining operations run over several years. Most of accompanying family members engage in the use of natural resources, which contributes to the depletion of natural resource stocks, such as fish and high value NTFP. Overall poverty increases until a threshold where many rural households lost their livelihood basis and cannot adapt by further livelihood diversification. Then, these households or some of their members move into the peri-urban context to find employment in the manufacturing or service industries. Given the mismatch of skills the long-term outcome is often a spatial shift of poverty, and an overall increase of poverty.

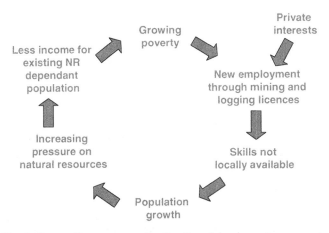

Fig. 1. Cause-effect conceptualisation for mining impacts on poverty

Immediately after presenting such contradicting results all stakeholders articulated a strong resistance. In anticipation of such a rejection of research evidence all results were presented as preliminary drafts and participants were invited to improve model assumptions. Additionally, diagrams such as Figure 1 were presented to reveal the more complex ripple effect causing the overall policy outcomes. Workshop participants were asked to trace the mistake by focusing on each step of the poverty cycle shown in Figure 1. However, stakeholders validated all steps and the overall effect was widely accepted and caused legislation for mandatory training of local population and revived the debate on a logging moratorium.

In-depth interviews with decision makers revealed that presenting results as draft and inviting participants to validate the individual steps of the emerging phenomenon were essential characteristics of the engagement process. Fundamental was also that the research was conducted with and presented by Bappenas, the Ministry for central planning.

Irrigation in the Nam Ngum Basin, Lao PDR

International development debates often argue for the replication of strategies that were successful in a specific country. Often this replication is not combined with an adequate assessment of sustainability related outcomes. Investment in irrigation infrastructure is one of these blanket solutions often recommended to developing countries. An agent-based assessment for the Nam Ngum catchment in Lao PDR suggests that poverty decreases only in a few small areas [24],[27],[28],[29], [30]. Technical details of the agent-based model are provided in [23].

Recorded statements during a series of workshops confirm the initial belief of poverty alleviating effects of irrigation infrastructure (Table 2). The agent-based model, however, suggests that poverty remains largely unaffected. The simple reason behind this phenomenon is that most people under the poverty line do not own land. Hence providing irrigation water would not affect their income. Also indirect effects through increasing demand for farm labor cannot be observed because most farmers would cover also the second rice crop by barter arrangements with other villagers. In low-lying areas, however some income effects can be observed leading to lower levels of poverty, which shows that irrigation cannot be rejected per se as a poverty alleviating strategy.

Table 2. Recorded stakeholder and modelling results for the Nam Ngum Basin

Stakeholder beliefs	Agent-based model suggestions
Irrigation reduces poverty	Irrigation reduces poverty in some low-lying areas with already low poverty but not in mountainous areas with high poverty because most poor people do not own land.
Irrigation increases agricultural production and farm income	Irrigation increases farm income but disproportionately more for large landholders widening the income gap

Participating decision makers responded with immediate rejection of the key results. However, in this case the initial contradiction was easy to overcome because the main message could be communicated without referring to very complex relationships. Participants emphasized that the model results were found valid because they co-designed the broader project and co-developed the model. Ownership was identified as a critical ingredient that prevented stakeholders to disengage when initial beliefs were contradicted.

Payment for Ecosystem Services in Xishuangbanna, China

Xishuangbanna is one of the world's most biodiverse areas. However, climate conditions have fueled the cultivation of rubber, turning large portions of primary forest into monoculture plantations. The central Government aims to halt the expansion of rubber and focuses on financial incentives, which have proven to be promising in other countries. The policy intervention aimed at paying rubber farmers a compensation for replacing 20% of their trees by native species to transform rubber monocultures into an area of agroforestry and safeguard biodiversity.

The research team was invited by the local government to assess the potential impact of such a payment for ecosystem service approach. Agent-based modeling was selected due to the relevance of household responses. Details of this process are documented in [24] and technical model details are provided in [23].

The policy debate was not if PES was an effective instrument for improving biodiversity values (Table 3). The debate was only about by how much rubber farmers need to be compensated to achieve the partial land use change. Hence it came unexpected to all participants that the proposed PES scheme would actually increase the area under rubber. The reason for this unexpected result is that many farmers live on marginal land; land that is likely to be of lower productivity and does not guarantee a successful cultivation of rubber. The PES payment incentivizes these farmers to plant rubber (not as a rubber monoculture though). Clearly, the underlying assumption of the initial belief was that effective monitoring and enforcement exist to ensure the efficacy of the proposed PES scheme. The behavioral responses (informed by 1,000 household interviews) clearly suggest that this monitoring and enforcement is not evident.

Table 3. Recorded stakeholder and modelling results for Xishuangbanna

Stakeholder beliefs	Agent-based model suggestions
PES is an effective conservation instrument	PES can expand rubber, needs effective monitoring and enforcement to help conservation

All stakeholders immediately rejected these results. However, also in this case results were presented as preliminary results and stakeholders were invited to help debugging the logic. However, when revealing the individual steps causing a further expansion of rubber most stakeholders confirmed that households responded in many other cases of government payments in similar ways. This shifted the policy debate to focus on effective monitoring and enforcement as the underpinning prerequisite for any incentive scheme.

3   Discussion: Lessons Learnt – 10 Guiding Principles

First: Never Assume Results Are Correct

It empowers the stakeholders if modeling results are presented as drafts and if uncertainty is emphasized. This empowerment puts the stakeholder into a position that enables the continuation of the discussion. This implies for the modeler that the only validation that counts is the validation done by stakeholders.

Second: Stakeholders Need to Own the Research Process

Stakeholders who co-design and co-develop research activities including the modeling demonstrate a much higher willingness to engage with more controversial results [20]. The lack of any participation leads mostly to an immediate rejection of results that contradict beliefs. If beliefs held by some stakeholders are rejected while other stakeholders' beliefs are confirmed the research is likely to further fuel the conflict instead of translating scientific evidence into a sustainable policy outcome. This implies that in situations with conflicting stakeholders these agencies need to own the process from the beginning.

Third: Simplify Complexity

Technical documents that explain model assumptions are only useful for other researchers. To bridge the policy-science gap complex ripple effects need to be translated into simple cause-effect relationships. Over-simplification is likely to constitute new false panaceas as beliefs.

Fourth: Start and Maintain an Honest Engagement Process

Most sustainability-focused situations involve multiple stakeholders with partly competing interests. In situations in which competing interests meet complex situations it is crucial to establish an effective science-policy interface. Many empirical agent-based modeling initiatives have experienced this requirement and developed participatory approaches [2]. The work described above followed the Challenge and Reconstruct Learning framework, ChaRL [27].

Fifth: Start the Model Design to Address Stakeholder Needs

Many observations confirm that modelers often use an existing model as a starting point for the design of a new applied project. This allows researchers to build on past work and implement an existing model to a new policy context. Such a starting point introduces a substantial risk to having any policy impacts because the research outputs are likely to be suboptimal for stakeholders [2], [5], [16], [31]. This risk can be mitigated if the genuine starting point is the stakeholder needs and if the various stakeholders are invited to specify the assessment context. As a result agent-based modeling might not be the most effective method for a particular policy situation, which creates a risk for the individual modeler. However, this seems favorable to investing years of model development and implementation without any policy impact.

Sixth: Allow the Multidisciplinary Team to Understand the Agent-based Modeling

Sustainability requires trans-disciplinary research [10],[13]. Agent-based modeling can be a very effective modeling platform for integrating many different disciplines. However, this can introduce tension within the research team if the methodological integration process is not made sufficiently transparent. Research team members need to understand the agent-based approach and need to be actively involved in model development to avoid friction and risks to effectively deliver towards stakeholder needs.

Seventh: Combine ABM and Results other Disciplinary Methods

In many cases hydrological, agricultural, social, or economic research methods need to be implemented to inform the agent-based model [9]. Investing in a comprehensive analysis of these disciplinary approaches instead of only utilizing them as inputs for the ABM can create multiple benefits. For instance, stakeholders are trained in understanding results from many disciplinary methods. Presenting disciplinary results before more complex models prepares the systematic understanding of the decision making situation at hand and makes it more likely that more complex results are actually understood and accepted even if they contradict initial beliefs.

Eighth: Utilise Existing Models Stakeholders are Familiar with

For most contexts disciplinary models are already available. Often, key stakeholders are very familiar with these models, the model results and how results are presented. It can be critical for the validation process during the stakeholder engagement process to demonstrate explicitly similarities and differences. Considering the challenges of validating agent-based results [1],[14],[25], such cross-model benchmarking can provide fundamental support to the overall validation strategy.

Ninth: Consider Spatial Representations

The experience from many policy initiatives suggests that a key effect of empirical agent-based modeling in sustainability related contexts is that stakeholders start perceiving a higher level of heterogeneity of the system then before the research process. This applies to all dimensions, including, for instance land use, water flow and people. From a sustainability perspective the spatial understanding of heterogeneity is often of critical importance to fine-tune policies [7],[17],[21]. Hence, the policy impact and the sustainability outcomes thereafter can be improved if results are presented spatially explicit.

Tenth: Develop Communication Material with Stakeholders

Science communication is critical for creating policy impacts. However, messages need to reflect the understanding of stakeholders that participated in conducting the research. Otherwise external communication can damage the science policy interface.

4   Conclusions

Agent-based modeling has proven to be a very effective method as higher levels of complexity can be analyzed to reveal critical ripple effects. For these insights to have policy impact they need to be validated by the relevant decision makers, which requires careful design of the engagement process. Some recommended engagement principles help mitigating the risk of policy failure. These are especially relevant for policy situations characterized by contested values, factual uncertainty and high complexity, which are characteristics of most sustainability-related policy debates.

References

1. Amblard, F., Bommel, P., Rouchier, J.: Assessment and validation of multi-agent models. In: Phan, D., Amblard, F. (eds.) Agent-based modelling and simulation in the social and human sciences, pp. 93–114. The Bardwell Press, Oxford (2007)
2. Barreteau, O., Bots, P.W.G., Daniell, K.A.: A Framework for Clarifying "Participation" in Participatory Research to Prevent its Rejection for the Wrong Reasons. Ecology and Society 15(2), 1 (2010)
3. Barreteau, O., Smajgl, A.: Designing Empirical Agent-based models: An issue of matching data, technical requirements and stakeholder expectations. In: Smajgl, A., Barreteau, O. (eds.) The Characterisation and Parameterisation of Empirical Agent-based models, vol. 1, pp. 217–229. Springer, New York (2013)
4. Bohensky, E., Smajgl, A., Herr, A.: Calibrating behavioural variables in agent-based models: insights from a case study in east kalimantan, indonesia. Paper Presented at the International Congress on Modelling and Simulation (MODSIM 2007), Virginia Beach, VA (2007)
5. d'Aquino, P., Bah, A.: A participatory modeling process to capture indigenous ways of adaptability to uncertainty: outputs from an experiment in West African drylands. Ecology and Society 18(4), 16 (2013). doi:10.5751/ES-05876-180416
6. Edmonds, B., Hernández, C., Troitzsch, K. (Eds.). Social Simulation: Technologies, Advances and New Discoveries: IGI Global (2007)
7. Ernst, A.: Using Spatially explicit Marketing Data to Build Social Simulations. In: Smajgl, A., Barreteau, O. (eds.) Empirical Agent-based Modelling - Challenges and Solutions: Volume 1, The Characterisation and Parameterisation of Empirical Agent-based Models, vol. 1. Springer, New York (2014)
8. Gilbert, N.: Agent-based models. SAGE Publications, Los Angeles (2008)
9. Gray, R., Fulton, E.A., Little, R.: Human-Ecosystem Interactions in Large Ensemble-Models. In: Smajgl, A., Barreteau, O. (eds.) Empirical Agent-based Modelling - Challenges and Solutions: Volume 1, The Characterisation and Parameterisation of Empirical Agent-based Models, vol. 1. Springer, New York (2014)
10. Hirsch Hadorn, G., Bradley, D., Pohl, C., Rist, S., Wiesmann, U.: Implications of transdisciplinarity for sustainability research. Ecological Economics 60(1), 119–128 (2006). doi:10.1016/j.ecolecon.2005.12.002
11. Janssen, M., Ostrom, E.. Empirically Based, Agent-based models. Ecology and Society, 11(2) (2006). Art.37: http://www.ecologyandsociety.org/vol11/iss32/art37/
12. Kay, J.J., Regier, H.A., Boyle, M., Francis, G.: An ecosystem approach for sustainability: addressing the challenge of complexity 560. Futures 31, 721–742 (1999)

13. Lang, D., Wiek, A., Bergmann, M., Stauffacher, M., Martens, P., Moll, P., Thomas, C.: Transdisciplinary research in sustainability science: practice, principles, and challenges. Sustainability Science **7**, 25–43 (2012). doi:10.1007/s11625-011-0149-x
14. Moss, S.: Alternative Approaches to the Empirical Validation of Agent-Based Models. Journal of Artificial Societies and Social Simulation **11**(1), 5 (2008)
15. O'Connor, M., Faucheux, S., Froger, G., Funtowicz, S.O., Munda, G., Costanza, R., Martinez-Alier, J.: Emergent complexity and procedural rationality: post-normal science for sustainability 761 Getting Down to Earth: Practical Applications of Ecological Economics. Island Press, Washington D.C. (1996)
16. Pahl-Wostl, C.: The implications of complexity for integrated resources management. Environmental Modelling and Software **22**(5), 561–569 (2007)
17. Perez, L., Dragicevic, S.: Modeling mountain pine beetle infestation with an agent-based approach at two spatial scales. Environmental Modelling & Software **25**(2), 223–236 (2010)
18. Pregernig, M.: Transdisciplinarity viewed from afar: science-policy assessments as forums for the creation of transdisciplinary knowledge. Science and Public Policy **33**(6), 445–455 (2006). doi:10.3152/147154306781778867
19. Reaney, S.M.: The use of agent based modelling techniques in hydrology: determining the spatial and temporal origin of channel flow in semi-arid catchments. Earth surface processes and landforms. **33**(2), 317–327 (2008)
20. Smajgl, A.: Challenging beliefs through multi-level participatory modelling in Indonesia. Environmental Modelling and Software **25**(11), 1470–1476 (2010)
21. Smajgl, A., Bohensky, E.: Behaviour And Space In Agent-Based Modelling: Poverty Patterns In East Kalimantan, Indonesia. Environmental Modelling and Software **45**, 8–14 (2013). doi:10.1016/j.envsoft.2011.10.014
22. Smajgl, A., Carlin, G. D.: Simulating impacts of energy prices on poverty in east kalimantan, indonesia. Paper Presented at the Combined IMACS World Congress/Modelling and Simulation Society-of-Australia-and-New-Zealand (MSSANZ)/18th Biennial Conference on Modelling and Simulation Cairns (2009)
23. Smajgl, A., Egan, S., Kirby, M., Mainuddin, M., Ward, J., Kroon, F.: The Mekong region simulation (Mersim) model - Design Document Townsville: CSIRO Climate Adaptation Flagship (2013)
24. Smajgl, A., Foran, T., Dore, J., Ward, J., Larson, S.: Visions, beliefs and transformation: Exploring cross-sector and trans-boundary dynamics in the wider Mekong region. Ecology and Society (in print)
25. Smajgl, A., House, A., Butler, J.: Implications of ecological data constraints for integrated policy and livelihoods modelling: an example from East Kalimantan. Indonesia Ecological Modelling **222**, 888–896 (2011). doi:10.1016/j.ecolmodel.2010.11.015
26. Smajgl, A., Prananingtyas, S. D.: Adaptation dynamics shaped by multiple tiers of governance: climate change and deforestation in indonesia. Paper Presented at the Combined IMACS World Congress/Modelling and Simulation Society-of-Australia-and-New-Zealand (MSSANZ)/18th Biennial Conference on Modelling and Simulation, Cairns (2009)
27. Smajgl, A., Ward, J.: A framework for bridging Science and Decision making. Futures **52**(8), 52–58 (2013). doi:http://dx.doi.org/doi:10.1016/j.futures.2013.07.002
28. Smajgl, A., Ward, J.: A design protocol for research impact evaluation: Development investments of the Mekong region. Journal of Environmental Management, Evaluating participatory research: Framework, methods and implementation results (in print)

29. Smajgl, A., Ward, J., Egan, S.: Designing a simulation-supported learning process for decision makers in the mekong region. Paper Presented at the ModSim 2013, Adelaide (2013a)
30. Smajgl, A., Ward, J., Egan, S.: Validating simulations of development outcomes in the mekong region. Paper Presented at the ModSim 2013, Adelaide (2013b)
31. Voinov, A., Bousquet, F.: Modelling with stakeholders. Environmental Modelling and Software **25**(11), 1168–1281 (2010)
32. Wuelser, G., Pohl, C., Hirsch Hadorn, G.: Structuring complexity for tailoring research contributions to sustainable development: a framework. Sustainability Science **7**(1), 81–93 (2012). doi:10.1007/s11625-011-0143-3

Regular Papers

Evaluating the Social Benefit
of a Negotiation–Based Parking Allocation

Francesco Barile[1], Claudia Di Napoli[2], Dario Di Nocera[1][(✉)], and Silvia Rossi[3]

[1] Dipartimento di Matematica e Applicazioni, Università degli
Studi di Napoli "Federico II", Napoli, Italy
{francesco.barile,dario.dinocera}@unina.it

[2] Istituto di Calcolo e Reti ad Alte Prestazioni, C.N.R., Napoli, Italy
claudia.dinapoli@cnr.it

[3] Dipartimento di Ingegneria Elettrica e Tecnologie dell'Informazione,
Università degli Studi di Napoli "Federico II", Napoli, Italy
silvia.rossi@unina.it

Abstract. Smart parking systems usually support drivers to select parking spaces according to their preferences among competitive alternatives, which are well known in advance to the decision maker, but without considering also the needs of a city. In this paper a decision support system for selecting and reserving optimal parking spaces to drivers is presented, where the concept of optimality is related to the city social welfare including the level of satisfaction of both drivers and the city. It relies on an automated software agent negotiation to accommodate the different needs coming from the different actors involved in the parking allocation process. A simulator of such a system is evaluated with respect to a case of complete information sharing among agents, and a case of no shared information. Different metrics to evaluate the social benefit of the parking allocation in terms of both agents utilities, and allocation efficiency are considered.

Keywords: Social welfare · Agent negotiation · Resource allocation · Smart parking

1 Introduction

The problem of allocating parking spaces to drivers is becoming a challenge in big cities, and different solutions are being investigated to provide them with smart parking applications. Most of parking applications, proposed in the literature, are based on Parking Guidance and Information (PGI) systems that provide drivers with dynamic information on parking within controlled areas, and direct them to vacant parking spaces. Shortcomings of PGI systems are due to the competition for parking spaces leading to the possibility of not finding a vacant

D. Di Nocera—Ph.D. scholarship funded by Media Motive S.r.l, POR Campania FSE 2007-2013.

© Springer International Publishing Switzerland 2015
Y. Demazeau et al. (Eds.): PAAMS 2015, LNAI 9086, pp. 15–26, 2015.
DOI: 10.1007/978-3-319-18944-4_2

space, so forcing re–planning the search. In addition, these systems are designed to increase the probability of finding a parking space, but without considering the possibility to find a better solution. Finally, and more importantly, from a traffic city authority point of view, these systems do not allow for a better utilization of parking spaces, but sometimes they may cause even more congestion in the monitored areas.

In this context, our purpose is to design a decision support system helping drivers to select and reserve optimal parking spaces, where the concept of optimality is related to the city *social welfare*, intended as the overall satisfaction level of all the actors involved in a parking system that are: drivers, parking owners, authorities taking into account city needs coming from city regulations (in terms of permitted parking areas, traffic congestion, car emission limitations), or special events. The system is designed to find a parking space within car parks, and it uses an agent–based negotiation approach to accommodate the different needs that have to be fulfilled when selecting parking spaces. While in parking systems competitive alternatives are well–known in advance and shared by drivers, the proposed negotiation mechanism relies on the possibility to selectively show the information concerning the parking spaces to propose to the drivers. This allows to incentive the selection of parking spaces that represents a viable compromise for conflicting needs.

In the present work, a simulator of the decision support system is evaluated by considering a set parking requests to be served. We are interested in evaluating how an agent negotiation approach may be used to improve the well–being of a society as a whole, that is not attainable without negotiation. The evaluation carried out takes into account both agents' utilities, and an efficient allocation of parking spaces. To globally evaluate the social benefit of the overall allocation problem, different metrics are considered that evaluate the negotiation outcome not at the single agent level, as reported in [3], but at the global agent society level, as single negotiations may influence the overall global system behavior.

2   Accommodating Different Needs in Parking Allocation

Smart parking applications are designed to help drivers in finding a parking space that meets their requirements usually regarding cost, and location. Nevertheless, the problem of finding a vacant parking space in densely populated urban areas is a more challenging problem involving different entities: drivers who want to find a vacant parking space that meets their requirements; car parks owners, both public and private, who want to maximize their economic income by selling as many parking spaces as possible; city managers who want to avoid car circulation in specific areas of the city and to have a fair distribution of parking spaces among requesting drivers to limit traffic congestion in the proximity of car parks.

In this context, the problem of finding a parking space is not merely a selection problem, but rather the possibility to find an agreement accommodating the different needs coming from drivers, parking owners, a city manager aware of city needs. For this reason, an automated negotiation mechanism is a viable approach to drive the selection of a parking space. In fact, negotiation allows to find an agreement that satisfies different and sometimes conflicting needs of the entities involved in the selection process, and to manage the dynamic nature of these needs depending on changeable conditions affecting the decision mechanism of both drivers and city managers.

In order to find an agreement among the different entities involved when selecting a parking space in urban car parks, we propose to model the decision support system of a smart parking application as a multi–agent system. The selection of a parking space upon a driver's request is modeled as the result of an agent automated negotiation process occurring among a set of Driver Agents (DAs), each one acting on behalf of a driver looking for a parking space, and a Parking Manager Agent (PMA) responsible for assigning parking spaces. The model extends the one presented in [3], where automated software agent negotiation was used to support users to find a parking space, preventing them to park in specific areas of a city, but without evaluating the overall parking allocation for a set of drivers.

The PMA acts on behalf of the entity responsible for re–selling a set of parking spaces located in different car parks of a city. It takes into account the economic needs of car parks owners that try to fill their car parks as much as possible to improve their profit, and, at the same time, the social needs of a city manager that tries to limit traffic congestion mainly in city centers, and to distribute drivers in different car parks to limit the concentrations of cars in specific or more required city areas. The Driver Agent is the entity acting on behalf of a driver that wants to reserve a parking space located in a specific city destination for a required time, and not exceeding a given cost. The allocation of a required parking space occurs if an agreement between the PMA and the DA can be found as the result of an automated negotiation process.

3   The Negotiation Process

The adopted negotiation protocol is an iterated contract–net interaction protocol [5] occurring between the PMA and a set of DAs issuing parking space requests. The PMA manages a set of available parking spaces and it has the goal to allocate them trying to satisfy all the different requests.

A request (park_req) is characterized by a geographical location, representing the required destination for the driver, located in an urban area, an hourly cost the driver would prefer to pay for the space, and a time interval the parking space is required for. The urban area is split in concentric rings (named *city sectors*) starting from the city center that are used to localize the considered car parks with respect to the city center.

A car park is characterized by static and dynamic attributes. A static attribute is its location within a ring, i.e. with respect to the city center, while a dynamic attribute is the number of available parking spaces at the time a parking space request is issued. The hourly static price for a parking space is assigned according to the criteria that car parks far from city centers are cheaper, so the adopted metric is to discount the price of a factor depending on the quadratic car park distance from the city center. In fact, it is assumed that car parks located in city centers are more expensive since they are located in the most requested and hence most densely populated city areas.

A negotiation process consists of all negotiations taking place between the PMA and each DA that issued a request over a set time window. Requests are collected and processed by the PMA, one by one according to their arrival order.

At the first negotiation iteration, a DA sends a `park_req` to the PMA that replies with an offer (x_j), if any, or with a `decline` message.

An offer has the form $x_j =< j, p_{1,j}, p_{2,j} >$, where j is a selected car park, $p_{1,j}$ is the static hourly cost (`static_price`) of the corresponding parking space, $p_{2,j}$ is the travel distance (`travel_dist`) between the car park location and the destination specified in the request. The travel distance is evaluated in terms of the time necessary to reach the destination from the car park location either by walking, for distances within 500m, or by public or other alternative means of transportation for longer distances.

It should be noted that that the PMA uses a Google Map service to compute the travel distance, but it is assumed that additional city services providing information on specific events that may influence the time necessary to cover such a distance, are made available from a city administration.

The DA replies to an offer with either an `accept` or a `reject` message according to its evaluation of the offer, i.e. if the selected parking space satisfies the driver's requirements. If an agreement is reached with the offer sent at iteration t, the negotiation ends successfully at that iteration, otherwise the offer is rejected and, if $t + 1 \leq t_{MAX}$, the negotiation continues with the PMA proposing another offer until the negotiation deadline t_{MAX} is reached (where t_{MAX} is the number of allowed iterations in the negotiation). The maximum number of iterations is the same as the number of car parks selected by the PMA, and it is not known to the DA. Note that a parking place offered at round t is not considered available at round $t + 1$ to model the possibility to assign a rejected parking space to another driver. So, the negotiation occurs in an incomplete information configuration from the driver agent side, since the information on all the available car parks is known only to the PMA agent. In fact, car parks attribute values may vary in time, so their sharing would require computationally expensive updates. The incomplete information setting leads to the possibility of accepting a sub–optimal agreement.

3.1   Agents Utility Functions

In automated agent negotiation, agents are assumed to have preferences, which represent (partial) orderings on outcomes. Agent preferences can be mapped into values of utility, using an utility function that is simply a mapping from a space of outcomes onto utility values, so providing a measure of the satisfaction level associated to a given offer for the agent.

Both the PMA and the DA have their own private multi–dimensional utility functions, allowing them to evaluate the offers in terms of their own preferences, where each dimension relates to an attribute of the specific parking space.

In general, the utility of an offer x_j at round t is evaluated as follows:

$$U_i(x_j) = \begin{cases} 0 & if\ t = t_{MAX}\ and\ not\ (\textbf{agr}) \\ v_i(x_j)\ if & t \leq t_{MAX}\ and\ (\textbf{agr}) \end{cases} \quad (1)$$

where, $v_i(x_j)$ is the agent's evaluation function. The evaluation function is a weighted sum of the parking attributes (normalized in the range $[0, 1]$), assuming the independence of each attribute. The attributes for the PMA and the DA are different, since they have different preferences regarding a parking solution. Of course, an agreement between them is possible if their respective acceptable regions have a not–empty intersection, i.e. a parking space with attribute values acceptable for both of them.

In the proposed negotiation approach, only the PMA may actually negotiate the values of these parameters, since it may propose a new offer, i.e. a new parking space with different attribute values, at each negotiation iteration. On the contrary, the DA does not issue a counterproposal, since it can only accept or reject the received offer.

Upon receiving a DA request, the PMA selects the set of car parks located in the city sectors within a given radius (named *tolerance*) and centered in the driver's specified location. The tolerance value is private to the PMA, and it can be dynamically set by the PMA according to both the location specified by the driver, and the city needs. In fact, if the destination is very close to the city center, or to an area that for the time specified by the driver should be avoided, the considered radius value may increase to allow for more car parks to be selected, so having more alternatives to provide to the driver. The PMA evaluates each selected car parks according to its own private evaluation function, and it orders them in a descending order of their utility values. The PMA strategy to issue a counterproposal, i.e. a new offer, is to concede in its utility at each negotiation iteration, by offering one parking space at each iteration, in the same descending evaluation order, so applying a monotonic concession strategy.

The adopted evaluation function models the main objectives of the PMA that are: to incentivize drivers to park outside the city center, in order to limit car circulation in most crowded city areas, and to fill the less occupied car parks to allow for a better distribution of the traffic, and profit.

Hence, the evaluation function is the weighted sum of terms modeling the PMA preferences that are: the car park availability $(q_{1,j})$, i.e., the number of free parking spaces at the time the request is processed, and the car park distance from the city center $(q_{2,j})$, calculated as distance of two GPS–located points.

$$v_{PMA}(x_j) = \sum_{k=1}^{2} (\alpha_k * \frac{q_{k,j} - \min(q_{k,j})}{\max(q_{k,j}) - \min(q_{k,j})}) \quad j \in \{1, \ldots, n\} \quad (2)$$

where, α_k are weights associated to each parameter (with $\sum_{k=1}^{2} \alpha_k = 1$), and n is the number of car parks selected for the request. Both terms of the summation are normalized w.r.t. the minimum $(\min(q_{k,j}))$, and the maximum $(\max(q_{k,j}))$ values of each parameter among all the selected car parks. The weights are used to take into account the possibility for the PMA to privilege one parameter or the other in its evaluation according to the specific city needs at the moment the request is processed.

An offer includes attributes of a parking space that are relevant for the DA, i.e. its hourly cost $(p_{1,j})$, and its travel distance from the destination specified by the user $(p_{2,j})$. Upon receiving an offer, the DA evaluates it according to its own parameters using an evaluation function given by the weighted sum of these parameters as follows:

$$v_{DA}(x_j) = 1 - \sum_{k=1}^{2} \beta_k * \frac{p_{k,j} - c_k}{h_k - c_k} \tag{3}$$

where, β_k are weights associated to each parameter (with $\sum_{i=1}^{2} \beta_k = 1$), c_k is the DA preferred value over the k–th parameter, h_k are constant values introduced for normalizing each term of the formula into the set $[0, 1]$.

The weights are used to model different type of drivers:

- **business**, i.e. drivers that consider very important the location of the parking space w.r.t. the location they need to reach, also being available to spend more money to get it $(\beta_1 < \beta_2)$,
- **tourist**, i.e. drivers that are available to choose a parking space not so close to their preferred destination, provided that they can save money $(\beta_1 > \beta_2)$.

The DA strategy is to accept an offer if its utility value is above a *threshold value* (DA_{att}) representing a measure of its attitude to be flexible on its preferred values for the considered parking space attributes. Since the utility function is normalized, its values may range in the interval $[0, 1]$. It should be noted that at each negotiation iteration, the DA utility varies according to the received offer, so it is not monotonic as the PMA one. This means that by keeping on negotiating does not guarantee the DA to find a better parking space in terms of its utility. In addition, the DA is not aware of the car parks available, so it could end up without reserving any parking space if he keeps on negotiating.

Currently, two DA profiles are considered:

- **strict**, i.e. drivers who are quite strict on their preferences, i.e. they are characterized by a high threshold value,
- **flexible**, i.e. drivers who are more flexible on their preferences, i.e. they are characterized by a low threshold value.

4   Computing the Social Benefit of a Parking Allocation

Both the DA and the PMA try to maximize their individual utility when negotiating with each other. The designed negotiation mechanism, proposed in [3],
aims at finding an agreement between the conflicting needs of a DA and the
PMA, leading to an outcome that is a viable compromise.

Here, a set of parking space requests to be globally processed are considered,
each one processed through a negotiation process. The problem can be assimi-
lated to a distributed indivisible resource allocation problem, where the selection
of resources to be allocated for a specific request is carried out through a bilateral negotiation without considering the other requests. In our case, given a set
of available resources $\mathcal{R}$ (i.e., parking spaces), and a set of driver agents $\mathcal{DA}$,
the overall process is to assign a single resource to each request (if available), in
order to best match the DA request and, at the same time, to fulfill as many
requests as possible. In resource allocation problems the *social welfare* is used as
a metric to evaluate the efficient allocation of resources [4]. Hence, social welfare,
computed for all requests, including the not fulfilled ones, can be used also as a
metric to evaluate an efficient allocation of parking spaces as follows.

Given a set $\mathcal{DA}$ of agents requesting a parking space, an optimal allocation of
available spaces is the one that maximizes the social welfare of the driver agents,
given by the sum of the individual outcomes (i.e. utilities) for all requests, fulfilled
or not. So, $SW_{DA} = \sum_{i \in \mathcal{DA}} U_i(x_{agr})$, where U_i depends only on the agent i
and on the selected parking space (agr). Hence, the overall utility of a set $\mathcal{DA}$
correspond to the sum of the individual utilities. In order to get a global utility
value that does not depend on the cardinality of $\mathcal{DA}$, a normalized version of
the social welfare is used:

$$SW_{DA} = \frac{\sum_{i \in \mathcal{DA}} U_i(x_{agr})}{|\mathcal{DA}|} \qquad (4)$$

Equation 4 accounts for the social welfare of driver agents and for the allocation problem in the sense that an high number of fulfilled requests with an high
average utility will result in a high SW_{DA} value. However, in order to evaluate
the social benefit of a global parking space allocation, the social welfare should
include also the utility of the PMA. In fact, there could be two parking spaces
that have the same utility for the DA, but one is more beneficial for the city
welfare, i.e., it has a greater utility for the PMA, so being a Pareto optimal solution with respect to the other one. For this reason, a global social welfare (SW_+)
should include also the PMA utility, so it is obtained, for each negotiation, as
the sum of DA and PMA utilities, normalized in $[0, 1]$.

$$SW_+ = \frac{\sum_{i \in \mathcal{DA}} (U_i(x_{agr}) + U_{PMA}(x_{agr}))/2}{|\mathcal{DA}|} \qquad (5)$$

A fair outcome of the negotiation is an agreement that maximizes the global
social welfare.

While in multi–agent literature the definition of SW is taken for granted,
the economic literature provides different definitions and interpretations.

The adopted definition of social welfare does not account for situations with an imbalanced distribution of utilities among agents. In order to detect these situations the Nash Social Welfare definition [10] can be used, defined as follows:

$$SW_* = \frac{\sum_{i \in \mathcal{DA}}(U_i(x_{agr}) \cdot U_{PMA}(x_{agr}))}{|\mathcal{DA}|} \qquad (6)$$

Equations 4, 5, and 6 are used to evaluate the outcome of negotiation for the parking spaces allocation problem.

5   Negotiation Simulations

In order to assess if the proposed negotiation mechanism is able to push drivers to select a parking space that is beneficial for the different involved entities, an experimentation was carried out simulating a set of drivers' requests sequentially processed in a time window. The experiments are aimed to evaluate the percentage of the allocated parking spaces with respect to the number of processed requests, the available car parks, and the corresponding PMA and DAs utilities, when negotiation is used.

The evaluation is carried out against two baseline cases without negotiation, named *DA-Best* and *PMA-Best*. In the first case, the availability and locations of all parking spaces are known to the DA (i.e., there is a complete knowledge), and the DA selects the parking space (x_i) with the highest utility $(x_i = argmax(U_{DA}(x_j)), \forall j)$, and it reserves it if this utility is above its threshold $(U_{DA}(x_i) > DA_{att})$. In the second case, the PMA selects the parking space with the highest utility $(x_i = argmax(U_{PMA}(x_j)), \forall j)$ to offer, and the DA accepts it if its own utility for that offer is above the threshold $(U_{DA}(x_i) > DA_{att})$, otherwise it rejects the offer.

All requests specify a random destination in a city center that is located in the first city sector with a radius of $500m$. The considered car parks are located in city sectors ranging within a radius of $5km$ from the city center and none located in the first sector that is assumed to be a pedestrian area.

The requests are issued by four different types of users as follows:

- **Flexible business**: $DA_{att} = 0.5$, $\beta_1 = 0.3$, and $\beta_2 = 0.7$;
- **Strict business**: $DA_{att} = 0.7$, $\beta_1 = 0.3$, and $\beta_2 = 0.7$;
- **Flexible tourist**: $DA_{att} = 0.5$, $\beta_1 = 0.7$, and $\beta_2 = 0.3$;
- **Strict tourist**: $DA_{att} = 0.7$, $\beta_1 = 0.7$, and $\beta_2 = 0.3$.

The PMA instead has the same preferences on the attributes included in its utility function, i.e. $\alpha_1 = \alpha_2 = 0.5$ Two sets respectively of 50 and 100 requests are considered, and the number of total available parking spaces is 100 equally distributed over 20 car parks. The requests are processed one by one, and if a request is satisfied the corresponding assigned parking space is reserved and it is not available for the other requests. If a request is not satisfied it is discarded and not processed anymore. We recall that the deadline of a negotiation (t_{MAX}) may vary for each requests according to the number car parks with available places for that request.

5.1   Experimental Results

The overall DAs and PMA utility values (U_{DA} and U_{PMA}), and the percentage of successful allocations (%all.), normalized w.r.t. the number of requests, obtained by simulating 50 and 100 requests, are reported in Table 1. Such utilities are evaluated for the negotiation case (Negotiation), and for the two baseline cases without negotiation, i.e., when the best parking space respectively for the DA (DA–best), and the PMA (PMA–best) are selected.

Table 1. DAs and PMA utilities in different settings

	50 req./100 spaces			100 req./100 spaces		
	U_{DA}	U_{PMA}	%all.	U_{DA}	U_{PMA}	%all.
Negotiation	0.68	0.64	94%	0.67	0.55	91%
DA–best	0.66	0.38	86%	0.60	0.38	79%
PMA–best	0.31	0.37	46%	0.32	0.39	48%

The results show that with negotiation a better parking space allocation is obtained (94% and 91%), with an increased overall utility for the DAs (0.68 and 0.67). Furthermore, the results confirm that with negotiation also the PMA utility increases, so potentially finding an allocation that is more beneficial for the city as well (0.64 and 0.55). As expected, when privileging only the PMA needs (PMA–best) the PMA utility does not increases, compared to the negotiation case, because of the high number of failures in the allocation process for both 50 and 100 requests, that is respectively 44% and 42%, i.e. the complement to the percentage of success.

Table 2. SW_{DA}, SW_+, and SW_* values for 50 and 100 requests

50 Req./100 spaces						
	SW_{DA}	$max(SW_{DA})$	SW_+	$max(SW_+)$	SW_*	$max(SW_*)$
Negotiation	0.68	0.76	0.67	0.73	0.44	0.53
DA–best	0.66	0.66	0.52	0.71	0.29	0.57
PMA–best	0.31	0.36	0.34	0.35	0.25	0.26

100 Req./100 spaces						
	SW_{DA}	$max(SW_{DA})$	SW_+	$max(SW_+)$	SW_*	$max(SW_*)$
Negotiation	0.67	0.72	0.64	0.69	0.40	0.47
DA best	0.60	0.60	0.49	0.65	0.29	0.51
PMA best	0.32	0.38	0.36	0.37	0.27	0.28

In Table 2 the social welfare values (SW_{DA}, SW_+, and SW_*), evaluated respectively with Equation 4, 5, and 6, are reported along with their corresponding maximum values ($max(SW_{DA})$, $max(SW_+)$, and $max(SW_*)$) for the cases of 50 and 100 requests. It should be noted that the definition of Equation 4 is exactly the overall DAs utility ($SW_{DA} = U_{DA}$).

As already highlighted in Table 1, a better overall utility for the DAs is obtained with negotiation, also compared with the DA–best baseline case. This unexpected result is due to the fact that negotiation leads to an increased percentage of parking spaces allocation, and hence, while the average value of the utilities is sub–optimal (i.e., it is less than $max(SW_{DA})$, $0.68 < 0.76$ and $0.67 < 0.72$), it is greater than the optimal value achieved in the case DA–best ($0.68 > 0.66$ and $0.67 > 0.60$). So, even though this negotiation simulation does not lead to an optimal social welfare, it still improves the social welfare with respect to the case of shared information.

When including the PMA utility in the social welfare (SW_+), the values obtained with the negotiation are greater than both baseline cases. In addition, these values are now closer to their respective optimal values ($max(SW_+)$), i.e., the negotiation leads to near optimal global outcomes.

Finally, negotiation allows for a better balancing of utilities among the involved agents, as showed by the values reported for SW_* ($0.44 > 0.29$ and $0.40 > 0.29$). Nevertheless, the values of $max(SW_*)$ with and without negotiation represent an opposite behavior, apparently showing that utilities could be more balanced without negotiation. But this is not the case, since the values of $max(SW_*)$ are not comparable with each other. In fact, the maximum values are considered only at local level for each selection step, but they do not represent the global maximum values for the overall selection process, that should instead be evaluated for all the possible permutations of allocations.

6   Related Works

Multi-agent negotiation has already been used in Intelligent Transportation System applications. In [2] negotiation is used to find better and cheaper parking spaces from the driver point of view, while in [1] cooperative agent negotiation is used to optimize traffic management relying on shared knowledge between drivers and network operators about routing preferences.

In [11] the authors presented, as in our case, a smart parking application that tries to find a trade–off between benefits of both drivers and parking providers. To balance the needs of involved parties, they use a dynamic parking price mechanism as an incentive, as also used in [7], for the drivers to balance the convenience and cost in terms of parking price and the convenience in terms of parking distance from the user's destination. Differently from our approach, in [11] all the information is available and the parking selection is obtained as a maximization of drivers' utilities. In our approach, we showed that a negotiation process is more effective, in terms of social welfare maximization, than a one–sided utility maximization. Dynamic price mechanisms were also explored in [8], where the objective was to set up prices for available parking spaces in a such a way to propose the most efficient parking allocation, in terms of social welfare, intended as the total utility value of all agents for which a parking space is allocated. The social welfare in our approach is a result of a mediation of the conflicting needs of drivers and the city management.

The optimal allocation of cars in car parks was also studied in [9], where the authors propose a semi–centralized approach for optimizing the parking space allocation, and improving the fairness among parking zones by balancing their occupancy–load. In this approach, parking coordinators are used to distribute the optimization allocation problem that is not manageable in a centralized way. In [6] the parking space allocation strategy, is also implemented as a global optimization problem, through the use of a Mixed Integer Linear Program. It is based on a user's objective function that combines proximity to destination and parking cost, while ensuring that the overall parking capacity is efficiently utilized. A set of requests are collected in a given time window, and they are processed by a software module producing an overall allocation that tries to optimize ad hoc function describing both driver–specific requirements, and system–wide objectives. In our case, the use of negotiation allows to model the parking space allocation problem not as a global optimization problem, but as the possibility to find a feasible compromise accommodating different needs.

7   Conclusions

Smart parking applications provide drivers with dynamic information on parking availability within controlled areas and direct them to vacant parking spaces by taking into account their preferences that, as reported in literature, mainly regard parking cost and location. These applications do not take into account that the problem of finding a parking space is not only a user–driven selection problem, but it may impact the well–being of the city causing traffic congestion, and an overbooking of specific and better located car parks. In this context, the parking allocation problem cannot depend only on drivers' needs, but also on needs coming from parking owners, trying to maximizing their profit, and city managers trying to consider the global benefits for the city limiting traffic congestion, or car circulation in specific city areas (e.g., pedestrian areas, or areas car prohibited for special events).

So, we model the parking allocation as a multi–agent negotiation process to find an agreement among different and sometimes conflicting needs. Negotiation occurs among Driver Agents acting on behalf of drivers requesting to reserve a parking space that satisfies their own criteria, and a Parking Manager Agent acting on behalf of a city authority that tries to allocate parking spaces by accommodating city needs.

We already showed in a previous work [3] that negotiation is a viable approach to push drivers to select parking spaces that are also beneficial from a city point of view, in the case of a single parking request. In the present work, we show that also when considering the global parking allocation problem for a set of requests, negotiation leads to better utilities for both the DAs and the PMA, and it allows to improve percentage of fulfilled parking requests with respect to the cases without negotiation.

In order to provide a measure of the social benefit of an allocation that takes into account different needs, the negotiation was evaluated in terms of the obtained social welfare of the global outcome of all negotiations occurring for the received parking requests. Different types of social welfare were evaluated by taking into account: the distribution of parking spaces with respect to only drivers needs, the same distribution with respect to both drivers and city manager needs, and finally the same distribution with respect to how the drivers and city needs are balanced. The results of the experiments carried out confirm that negotiation leads in average to better allocations and utilities for all the adopted measures when compared to experiments carried out without negotiation.

Acknowledgments. This research has received funding from the EU FP7-ICT-2012-8 under the MIDAS Project, Grant Agreement no. 318786, and the Italian Ministry of University and Research and EU under the PON OR.C.HE.S.T.R.A. project (ORganization of Cultural HEritage for Smart Tourism and Real-time Accessibility).

References

1. Adler, J.L., Blue, V.J.: A cooperative multi-agent transportation management and route guidance system. Transportation Research Part C: Emerging Technologies 10(56), 433–454 (2002)
2. Chou, S.Y., Lin, S.W., Li, C.C.: Dynamic parking negotiation and guidance using an agent-based platform. Expert Systems with Applications **35**(3), 805–817 (2008)
3. Di Napoli, C., Di Nocera, D., Rossi, S.: Agent Negotiation for Different Needs in Smart Parking Allocation. In: Demazeau, Y., Zambonelli, F., Corchado, J.M., Bajo, J. (eds.) PAAMS 2014. LNCS, vol. 8473, pp. 98–109. Springer, Heidelberg (2014)
4. Endriss, U., Maudet, N., Sadri, F., Toni, F.: Negotiating socially optimal allocations of resources. J. Artif. Intell. Res. (JAIR) **25**, 315–348 (2006)
5. FIPA: Fipa iterated contract net interaction protocol specification. http://www.fipa.org/specs/fipa00030/ (2001)
6. Geng, Y., Cassandras, C.: New smart parking system based on resource allocation and reservations. IEEE Transactions on Intelligent Transportation Systems **14**(3), 1129–1139 (2013)
7. Longfei, W., Hong, C., Yang, L.: Integrating mobile agent with multi-agent system for intelligent parking negotiation and guidance. In: 4th IEEE Conference on Industrial Electronics and Applications, pp. 1704–1707 (2009)
8. Meir, R., Chen, Y., Feldman, M.: Efficient parking allocation as online bipartite matching with posted prices. In: Proceedings of the 2013 International Conference on Autonomous Agents and Multi-agent Systems, pp. 303–310 (2013)
9. Mejri, N., Ayari, M., Kamoun, F.: An efficient cooperative parking slot assignment solution. In: The Seventh International Conference on Mobile Ubiquitous Computing, Systems, Services and Technologies, pp. 119–125. IARIA (2013)
10. Ramezani, S., Endriss, U.: Nash Social Welfare in Multiagent Resource Allocation. In: David, E., Gerding, E., Sarne, D., Shehory, O. (eds.) AMEC 2009. LNBIP, vol. 59, pp. 117–131. Springer, Heidelberg (2010)
11. Wang, H., He, W.: A reservation-based smart parking system. In: IEEE Conference on Computer Communications, pp. 690–695 (2011)

Load Management Through Agent Based Coordination of Flexible Electricity Consumers

Anders Clausen[1]([✉]), Yves Demazeau[2], and Bo Nørregaard Jørgensen[1]

[1] University of Southern Denmark, Odense, Denmark
ancla@mmmi.sdu.dk, bnj@iti.sdu.dk
[2] CNRS, LIG Laboratory, Grenoble, France
yves.demazeau@imag.fr

Abstract. Demand Response (DR) offers a cost-effective and carbon-friendly way of performing load balancing. DR describes a change in the electricity consumption of flexible consumers in response to the supply situation. In DR, flexible consumers may perform their own load balancing through load management (LM) mechanisms. However, the individual amount of load balancing capacity exhibited by the majority of flexible consumers is limited and as a result, coordinated LM of several flexible electricity consumers is needed in order to replace existing conventional fossil based load balancing services. In this paper, we propose an approach to perform such coordination through a Virtual Power Plant (VPP)[1]. We represent flexible electricity consumers as software agents and we solve the coordination problem through multi-objective multi-issue optimization using a mediator-based negotiation mechanism. We illustrate how we can coordinate flexible consumers through a VPP in response to external events simulating the need for load balancing services.

Keywords: Demand response · Load balancing · Load management · Multi-agent systems · Distributed coordination · Virtual power plant

1 Introduction

The amount of electricity being generated by renewable energy sources is increasing in order to reduce carbon emission [2]. This leads to a more fluctuating electricity production [3] which requires additional regulation capacity and ancillary services for load balancing [4]. In this context Demand Response (DR) is emerging as a cost-effective and carbon friendly load balancing alternative [5]. DR describes changes in electricity consumption in response to changes in electricity price or incentive payments, which reflects changes in the supply situation[1]. Consumers participate in DR programs by performing load management (LM) through either load shedding, load shifting or valley filling [6]. However, DR programs are generally aimed at large consumers due to the complexity of enrolling

---

[1] http://www.ferc.gov/industries/electric/indus-act/demand-response/
dem-res-adv-metering.asp

© Springer International Publishing Switzerland 2015
Y. Demazeau et al. (Eds.): PAAMS 2015, LNAI 9086, pp. 27–39, 2015.
DOI: 10.1007/978-3-319-18944-4_3

consumers. A virtual power plant (VPP) can make smaller consumers attractive as a DR resource. A VPP coordinates the consumption of several consumers and exposes them as a single, controllable entity [1]. The coordination of resources in a VPP is well known in literature. VPPs such as the ones proposed in [7] and [8] rely on centralized coordination, where the problem is formulated as a combinatorial optimization problem. In these approaches, the VPP calculates viable schedules for each unit in the VPP which conforms to an external service request. In this case, the complexity of the search space becomes highly dependent on the number of units in the VPP as this reflects local constraints of each unit. Decentralized coordination of resources provides each unit in the VPP with some decision-making capabilities which forms a multi-agent system (MAS). In [9] a self-organizing MAS is proposed where software agents represent units in the VPP and the problem is solved as a combinatorial problem. Agents selects schedules from a local set of feasible schedules in order to adhere to global requirements. In [10] a hierarchical MAS approach is used to achieve global goals through selection of appropriate schedules of operation from each of the agents. However, these approaches impose constraints on the size of the search space. In both cases the search space is constituted through a finite set of schedules presented by the agents. The work of [9] has been extended by [11] where a method is proposed to handle global and local constraints. The software agents in the proposed solution coordinate autonomously in order to meet service requirements. Each software agent contains a model that produces a feasibility region used to constrain the search space. A comparable approach is used in [12] where a MAS is created with unit agents and broker agents. These approaches assume convex problems, which is a limitation, as most non-trivial real-world energy consuming processes constitute non-convex problem domains. Furthermore, neither the architecture presented in [11], or in [12] supports pursuing multiple global goals simultaneously. We present an approach which allows for a dynamic adaption from consumers to the request for DR services, while providing a single point of interaction towards buyers of DR capacity. The approach revises Controleum [13][14][15] a software framework for multi-objective multi-issue negotiation to enable support for coordination of flexible electricity consumers. We employ a strategy in which each consumer provides a proposal for electricity allocation to the VPP. Previous work has shown how to facilitate Controleum as a mechanism to generate this proposal in non-convex domains [14]. The Controleum VPP generates counterproposals as modified versions of the initial proposals that reflect requirements for DR services and takes into account the perceived flexibility of the consumers. Using Controleum, several DR services can be provided simultaneously and the quality of the DR services can reflect the current capabilities of the consumers.

The rest of the paper is structured as follows: Section 2 gives a brief introduction to Controleum and explains the design of the proposed extensions. Section 3 presents the experimental scenario, the experiments conducted and presents the outcome. Section 4 presents a discussion of the results and describes future work and finally section 5 concludes on the paper.

2   Agent-Based Coordination of Flexible Electricity Consumers

2.1   Multi-objective Multi-issue Negotiation

Controleum acts as a foundation for the software developed in this paper. Controleum is a multi-objective multi-issue negotiation framework applicable to a broad range of problems. The framework defines a *context* as a problem domain in which a set of N *concerns agents*, $(a_1, a_2, \ldots, a_N)$, performs negotiation over a set of M *issues*, $(s_1, s_2, \ldots, s_M)$. A *contract* is defined as a vector of dimension M of *issue values*, $\mathbf{s} = [s_1, s_2, \ldots, s_M]$. A contract represents an option in the decision making process which assigns values to each issue if chosen. Issue values may be either scalars or vectors. The agent addresses issues by responding with a *cost* to a contract proposed by a *mediator agent*. The cost of agent $a_n \in N$ for a contract $\mathbf{s}_c$, defined as q_{a_n, s_c}, is the summarized values of that agent's cost for each issue $s_{j \in M}$ addressed by that agent. The cost assigned by an agent to each issue may depend on variables defined by external preferences. The cost function is specified to suit the domain in which the framework is applied. The mediator agent starts a negotiation by generating random contracts. Each contract is presented to each agent who responds with a cost. This yields a cost vector for each contract $\mathbf{s}$ defined by $\mathbf{q}_s = [q_{a_1, s}, \ldots, q_{a_N, s}]$. The mediator agent uses the Pareto criterion on each of these vectors to select contracts for a new generation, P. This approach allows for multiple solutions representing local optimums to be found, allowing Controleum to handle non-convex domains, in which trade-offs are often present. When the algorithm terminates, due to reaching a generation limit or time constraint, the mediator agent selects a contract, $\mathbf{s}_f$, from the final generation P_f using the selection strategy specified in equations 1 and 2 where $\mathbf{1}$ is a 1xN sum vector[2], $\mathbf{q}'_s$ is the normalized cost vector for contract $\mathbf{s}$ and $q'_{a_n, s}$ is the normalized cost for agent n for contract $\mathbf{s} \in P_f$.

$$\mathbf{s}_f = \min_{\mathbf{s} \in P_f} (\mathbf{1}^T \mathbf{q}'_s)$$
$$\mathbf{q}'_s = [q'_{a_1, s}, \ldots, q'_{a_n, s}, \ldots, q'_{a_N, s}] \tag{1}$$

$$q'_{a_n} = \frac{q_{a_n, s} - q_{a_n, min}}{q_{a_n, max} - q_{a_n, min}} \tag{2}$$
$$q_{a_n, min} = \min_{\mathbf{s} \in P_f} q_{a_n, s} \quad q_{a_n, max} = \max_{\mathbf{s} \in P_f} q_{a_n, s}$$

2.2   A Controleum Virtual Power Plant

We propose a VPP based on Controleum that includes consumers' preferences for electricity allocation in the negotiation with an aggregation party. Based on proposals for electricity allocation made by consumers in the VPP, counterproposals are created which adapt the combined allocation to adhere to requirements

---

[2] http://stattrek.com/matrix-algebra/sum-of-elements.aspx

for DR services. These counterproposals are created based on the flexibility of each consumer in order to offer counterproposals which the consumers are likely to comply with. In cases where insufficient flexibility is available to meet the requirement for DR services, the Controleum VPP will ensure that the counterproposals falls within the flexibility range for as many consumers as possible. A set of abstractions, which are unique to aggregation mechanism in a VPP has been designed and implemented as specialization of existing concepts in the Controleum framework. The design of these abstractions is described below.

Consumer Concern Agent: A Consumer Concern Agent (CCA) is a specialization of the concern agent. A CCA represents a consumer in a Controleum VPP. The goal of a CCA is to ensure that sufficient electric power is allocated to the consumer it represents. Each CCA is associated with a Consumption Schedule Issue and a Consumption Schedule. A CCA introduces a Consumption Schedule Issue in the negotiation to get counterproposals for electricity allocation. The final value of the Consumption Schedule Issue is the counterproposal made by the VPP to the consumer represented by the CCA. The Consumption Schedule contains the initial request for allocation made by the consumer and is used by the CCA to evaluate suggested values for the Consumption Schedule Issue during negotiation. The concept is reflected in figure 1. The Consumption Schedule Issue defines the range in which counterproposals for the consumer may be defined. The Consumption Schedule Issue for agent a_k is defined as a vector $v_k = [v_{1,k}, v_{2,k}, \ldots, v_{t,k}]$ where t defines the number of time slots defined in the Consumption Schedule Issue and $k \in K$ where K is the number of CCAs in the context. The Consumption Schedule for agent a_k is defined as $c_k = [c_{1,k}, c_{2,k}, \ldots, c_{t,k}]$. The range of elements $v_{x,k} \in \epsilon_k$ and $c_{x,k} \in \epsilon_k$ in v_k and c_k is defined as a range $[a_k, b_k] = \{\epsilon | a_k \leq \epsilon_k \leq b_k\}$ whose limits is defined according to the domain specific need for - and capability to define - operating levels for the consumer represented by a_k. Note that we distinguish between operating levels which is an abstract term and consumption levels which specifies a consumption level in Watt. The Consumption Schedule and Consumption Schedule Issue uses operating levels to define steps in consumption levels, but do not assume anything about the corresponding Watt consumption as this is a domain property. Each CCA receives a proposal for allocation from the consumer site as a Consumption Schedule. The cost function of the CCA a_k then returns a value which corresponds to the absolute difference of each element in the Consumption Schedule and a proposed value of the Consumption Schedule Issue which represent the counterproposal. This is illustrated in equation 3.

$$q_k = \sum_{x}^{t} |c_{x,k} - v_{x,k}| \tag{3}$$

This model yields contracts on the form $s = [v_1, \ldots, v_K]$ in the negotiation space, as each CCA adds a new Consumption Schedule Issue to the negotiation. This is illustrated in figure 1. Each CCA calculates a flexibility parameter γ, which describes the CCA's flexibility range. The flexibility parameter is designed

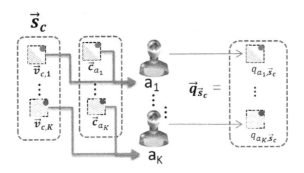

Fig. 1. Illustration showing the concept behind CCAs

to be calculated dynamically, as the flexibility of a consumer may change over time. However, to show the impact of this parameter on the outcome of the negotiation process, we use predefined values in the experiments.

Aggregator Concern Agent: An Aggregator Concern Agent (ACA) represents parties who have an interest in the combined consumption of the consumers in the VPP defined as $z = \sum_k^K v_k$. An ACA represents the need for load balancing services e.g. due to market conditions or capacity constraints. An ACA receives an Aggregated Consumption Schedule which specifies desired consumption levels for the VPP. This proposal, g, spans the range of all CCAs in the aggregate. Thus, the Aggregated Consumption Schedule is defined as $g = [g_1, g_2, \ldots, g_t]$ where the range is $[a_{agg}, b_{agg}] = [\sum_k^K a_k, \sum_k^K b_k]$. The definition of the cost function in the ACA is shown in equation 4.

$$q_{agg} = \sum_x^t \begin{cases} z_x - g_x, & \text{if } z_x > g_x \\ 0, & \text{otherwise} \end{cases} \tag{4}$$

Equation 4 shows that an ACA will attempt to suppress the combined consumer electricity allocation, z, until it is equal to or lower than g. Thus, g reflects the need for load balancing services such as DR requests. This definition of ACAs allow them to calculate a flexibility parameter as well.

Flexibility Selection Strategy: The flexibility range calculated by each agent in the VPP is used in a modified version of the selection strategy presented in equations 1 and 2. Specifically, equation 2 is replaced with the equation shown in equation 5. Here σ is some arbitrarily large number $\gg 1$. Note that the flexibility mechanism spans all agents, including the ACAs. The modified selection strategy ensures that solutions within the flexibility range specified by the agents in the VPP are shifted towards zero, which makes the selection strategy favor these solutions according to equation 1. Besides being used to enable consumers to express their flexibility, we believe that the flexibility parameter can be used to calculate economic incentives, which promotes high flexibility.

$$
q'_{a_n,s} = \begin{cases} \left(\frac{q_{a_n,s} - q_{a_n,min}}{q_{a_n,max} - q_{a_n,min}} \right), & \text{if } q_{a_n,s} > \gamma \\ \left(\frac{\left(\frac{q_{a_n,s} - q_{a_n,min}}{q_{a_n,max} - q_{a_n,min}} \right)}{\sigma} \right), & \text{otherwise} \end{cases} \tag{5}
$$

3   Experiments

We consider a micro grid scenario with one wind turbine based generator plant, one conventional generator plant and 5 consumers. The local generation capacity in the range of 45 to 60 MW where wind turbines constitute 30 MW of the capacity and 20-30 MW is conventional generation capacity. A need for DR arises when the combined production of the wind turbines and the conventional power plant is lower than the planned base-line allocation of the consumers. This scenario yields $K = 5$. Each consumer is assumed to have a maximum consumption of 9 MW controllable in 1 MW intervals, defining $[a, b] = [0, 9]$ and $[a_{agg}, b_{agg}] = [0, 45]$. Allocation is done hourly across 24 hours yielding $t = 24$. All consumers are assumed to have equal initial consumption preferences. This provides cases where all consumers prefer highest consumption in the same time slot. The preferences have been adopted from the overall consumption pattern of Western Denmark on January 1st, 2014[3], and we assume maximum consumption is reached this day. This defines c and z according to equation 6.

$$
c_{pref} = [7\ 6\ 6\ 6\ 6\ 6\ 6\ 6\ 7\ 7\ 7\ 7\ 7\ 7\ 8\ 8\ 9\ 9\ 8\ 8\ 7\ 7\ 6]
$$
$$
\Downarrow
$$
$$
z = [35\ 30\ 30\ 30\ 30\ 30\ 30\ 30\ 30\ 35\ 35\ 35\ 35\ 35\ 35\ 40\ 40\ 45\ 45\ 40\ 40\ 35\ 35\ 30] \tag{6}
$$

We have modeled the problem with a single ACA representing the combined generator capacity, yielding $N = K + 1 = 6$. The wind turbine generator output is varied to reflect historic production of wind turbines in Western Denmark on January 1st, 2014 and we assume that maximum production of the wind turbines in our scenario was reached January 1st 2014 at 24:00, and scale all values accordingly. The maximum amount of electricity generated by the conventional plant between is varied in 4 intervals which gives 4 different values for g as shown in equation 7. This illustrates different complexities in the negotiation, where the amount of fields with conflicts and the difference between the summarized elements vary.

---

[3] Historic data extracted from:
http://www.energinet.dk/EN/El/Engrosmarked/Udtraek-af-markedsdata/Sider/default.aspx (accessed January 5, 2015).

$g_{30MW} =$

[51 52 51 51 51 51 51 50 48 47 48 47 47 47 47 46 46 47 50 51 54 56 58 60]

$g_{25MW} =$

[46 47 46 46 46 46 46 45 43 42 43 42 42 42 42 41 41 42 45 46 49 51 53 55]

(7)

$g_{22MW} =$

[43 44 43 43 43 43 43 42 40 39 40 39 39 39 39 38 38 39 42 43 46 48 50 52]

$g_{20MW} =$

[41 42 41 41 41 41 41 40 38 37 38 37 37 37 37 36 36 37 40 41 44 46 48 50]

The flexibility of the consumers should be utilized to suppress their proposal for allocation of electricity in hours where $g < z$. We have conducted experiments with 3 different consumer flexibilities, $\gamma_1 = 1MW$, $\gamma_3 = 3MW$ and $\gamma_5 = 5MW$ yielding a total consumer flexibility of $\gamma_{1,total} = K \cdot \gamma_1 = 5MW$, $\gamma_{3,total} = 15MW$ and $\gamma_{5,total} = 25MW$ across the VPP. These values will yield cases where sufficient flexibility is available and cases where the available flexibility is insufficient. The ACA exposes no flexibility. We have limited the run-time of each experiment to 600 seconds with a maximum depth of 10000 generations. This means, that a solution is taken from the generation which is present when the algorithm is terminated. The 600 seconds limit enables 6 iterations of negotiations between the VPP domain and the consumer domains in a setting with hourly allocation. The 10000 generations limit is high compared to the expected number of generations that experiments on the Controleum framework typically require to converge. This means that the complete optimal population may have been generated long before the algorithm terminates. We do not measure the degree to which the final generation is optimal. Instead we evaluate the degree to which the chosen contract meets the flexibility specification and analyze how conflicts between allocation and demand are handled. Experiments have been conducted with each of the generator vectors defined in 7. Each set constitutes three experiments which simulate the different values of γ.

3.1 g_{30MW}

These experiments reflect the situation with the generation capacity g_{30MW}. In these experiments, g_{30MW} is larger than z for all elements. The purpose of this experiment is to control that in case of no conflict, the counterproposal generated is $s_f = [v_1, v_2, v_3, v_4, v_5]$ where $v_1, v_2, v_3, v_4, v_5 = c_{pref}$ as the ACA has no intention of changing consumption of any consumers. Figure 2 shows counterproposals generated from the negotiation with 1 MW flexibility. As can be seen each of the allocated values correspond to c_{pref}. This is also the case for the $\gamma_3 =$ and γ_5 experiments.

3.2 g_{25MW}

In these experiments the generation capacity is defined as g_{25MW}. Here a conflict is found where $z_{18} > g_{25MW,18}$. However, as the combined available flexibility of

Fig. 2. Result of negotiation with g_{30MW} and $\gamma_1 = 1MW$. Line depicts c_{pref}

the consumers is between 5 MW and 25 MW and the total difference between g_{25MW} and z differs only by 3 MW, all CCAs should be provided with counterproposals which fall within their flexibility range. Figure 3 show the generated counterproposals. As can be seen three consumers are suppressed by 1 level for γ_1. The same is the case for γ_3. Finally with γ_5 one consumer is suppressed by 2 and one is surprised by 1.

3.3 g_{22MW}

These experiments reflect the generation capacity defined by g_{22MW}. Conflicts exist in 4 timeslots as $z_{16} > g_{22MW,16}$, $z_{17} > g_{22MW,17}$, $z_{18} > g_{22MW,18}$ and $z_{19} > g_{22MW,19}$. In total the summed difference in these fields is 13 MW. Hence, insufficient flexibility is available in the γ_1 experiment. Figure 4 shows the outcome of the negotiations. As expected one consumer is pushed excessively beyond its flexibility limit in the γ_1 experiment, as insufficient flexibility is available.

3.4 g_{20MW}

The experiments in this set reflect the generation capacity defined by g_{20MW}. In this scenario conflicts exist in 4 fields with a combined mismatch of 21 MW. Figure 5 shows the outcome of the negotiations. Insufficient flexibility is available in the γ_1 and γ_3 experiments and as expected we can see that the consumers represented by the blue bar in figure 5a and the purple bar in figure 5b are pushed beyond their flexibility limit. However a problem arises in this experiment. As can be seen in figure 6 $s_{17} > g_{17}$ for $s_{f,3MW}$ and $s_{f,5MW}$. Due to the large deviation between g_{20MW} and z the algorithm exhibits suboptimal performance. The resulting counterproposals $s_{f,3MW}$ and $s_{f,5MW}$ implies a deviation from g which should not happen due to the distribution of the cost values returned by the ACA. Further, the combined flexibility of consumers is not used in either case.

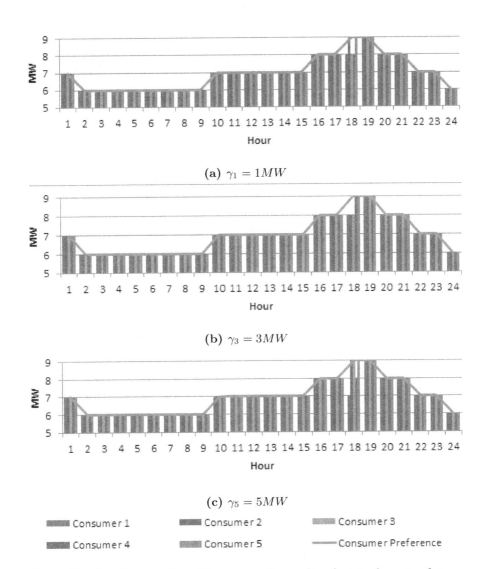

(a) $\gamma_1 = 1MW$

(b) $\gamma_3 = 3MW$

(c) $\gamma_5 = 5MW$

Consumer 1   Consumer 2   Consumer 3
Consumer 4   Consumer 5   Consumer Preference

Fig. 3. Results of negotiation with g_{25MW}. Orange line depicts elements of c_{pref}.

4   Discussion

Our experiments have shown that the Controleum VPP is able to produce counterproposals that utilizes consumer flexibility to meet requirements for DR services. In cases where insufficient flexibility is available, the VPP attempts to
maintain as many consumers as possible within the flexibility range. In these
cases a single consumer gets a counteroffer which exceeded its flexibility parameter considerably. As one consumer is forced outside the range defined by its
flexibility parameter, the normalized cost of the corresponding CCA increases

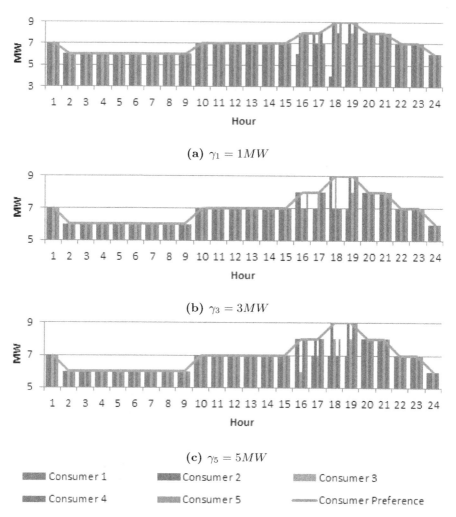

Fig. 4. Results of negotiation with g_{22MW}. Orange line depicts elements of c_{pref}.

significantly. However further deviation do not have a similar impact on the normalized cost, making it more beneficial to impose further deviation on the same consumer. We intend to design an alternative selection strategy in which the counterproposals will exceed the flexibility parameter of more consumers but to a lesser extend, in cases where insufficient flexibility is available. Field experiments will test the selection strategies against each other to determine if a more fair violation of the flexibility parameter yields better results in practice. In the last set of experiments we can see that the outcome of the negotiation was suboptimal as not all flexibility was utilized in the cases of the $\gamma_3 =$ and γ_5 experiments. The consequence is that other parties in the negotiation are forced to make unnecessary compromises. This is a result of a highly complex

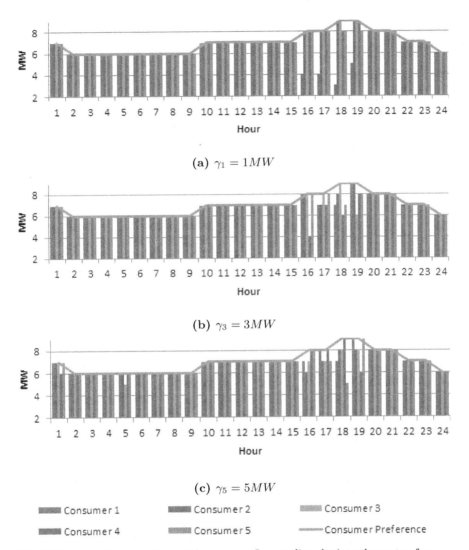

(a) $\gamma_1 = 1MW$

(b) $\gamma_3 = 3MW$

(c) $\gamma_5 = 5MW$

Consumer 1 Consumer 2 Consumer 3

Consumer 4 Consumer 5 Consumer Preference

Fig. 5. Results of negotiation with g_{20MW}. Orange line depicts elements of c_{pref}.

negotiation which includes 5 issues with 24 variables spanning values 0 to 9. Hence, a vast amount of possible tradeoffs exists in negotiations with many conflicts and convergence time increases significantly. In this case, Controleum is unable to produce an optimal generation, and as a result, the selection strategy has to choose from a suboptimal set of contracts. This might be acceptable in the setting of this paper, where counterproposals are produced and a graduate decrease in complexity can be expected over time, as a result of consumers adapting. However, to improve the scalability of the framework in cases of high

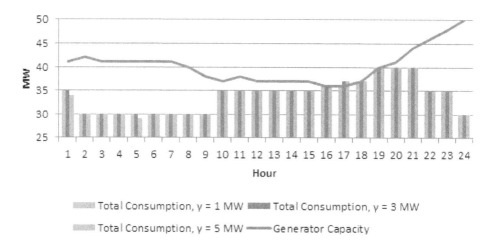

Fig. 6. Combined allocation plotted against the combined capacity. Blue line is elements of g and green, purple and orange bars represent elements of final contracts $s_{f,1MW}$, $s_{f,3MW}$ and $s_{f,5MW}$ respectively.

complexity negotiations we are investigating approaches in which proposed contracts are compared only to a relevant subset of the existing contracts.

5   Conclusion

To utilize LM capabilities of smaller consumers as DR services, their consumption needs to be coordinated. In this paper we present an approach which builds on the idea of a VPP. We have extended the capabilities of Controleum, a multi-objective multi-issue negotiation framework, to encompass abstractions which suit the VPP domain. Further, we have introduced the notion of flexibility which allows concerns to express flexibility in domain specific terms. This is used by a proposed selection strategy to solve conflicts between agents participating in a negotiation which yields counterproposals for electricity consumption that consumers are likely to comply with. In cases where insufficient flexibility is available the selection strategy aims to keep as many consumers as possibly within their flexibility range. The architecture supports employing an arbitrary selection strategy, and we plan to utilize this to employ an alternative selection strategy with the goal of distributing violations of the flexibility parameter more evenly. The negotiation problem increased in complexity when large deviation between the requirement for DR and the initial proposals exists. To avoid situations with suboptimal generations in these cases we are working to improve the scalability of the negotiation algorithm.

References

1. Pudjianto, D., Ramsay, C., Strbac, G.: Microgrids and virtual power plants: concepts to support the integration of distributed energy resources. Proceedings of the Institution of Mechanical Engineers, Part A: Journal of Power and Energy **222**, 731–741 (2008)
2. Banos, R., Manzano-Agugliaro, F., Montoya, F., Gil, C., Alcayde, A., Gómez, J.: Optimization methods applied to renewable and sustainable energy: A review. Renewable and Sustainable Energy Reviews **15**, 1753–1766 (2011)
3. Lund, H., Münster, E.: Management of surplus electricity-production from a fluctuating renewable-energy source. Applied Energy **76**, 65–74 (2003)
4. Ipakchi, A., Albuyeh, F.: Grid of the future. IEEE Power and Energy Magazine **7**, 52–62 (2009)
5. Watson, D.S.: Fast automated demand response to enable the integration of renewable resources (2013)
6. Clausen, A., Ghatikar, G., Jørgensen, B.N.: Load management of data centers as regulation capacity in denmark (2014)
7. Ruiz, N., Cobelo, I., Oyarzabal, J.: A direct load control model for virtual power plant management. IEEE Transactions on Power Systems **24**, 959–966 (2009)
8. Mathieu, S., Ernst, D., Louveaux, Q.: An efficient algorithm for the provision of a day-ahead modulation service by a load aggregator. In: 4th European Innovative Smart Grid Technologies (ISGT 2013) (2013)
9. Hinrichs, C., Sonnenschein, M., Lehnhoff, S.: Evaluation of a self-organizing heuristic for interdependent distributed search spaces. In: ICAART (1), pp. 25–34 (2013)
10. Pournaras, E., Warnier, M., Brazier, F.M.: Local agent-based self-stabilisation in global resource utilisation. International Journal of Autonomic Computing **1**, 350–373 (2010)
11. Hinrichs, C., Bremer, J., Sonnenschein, M.: Distributed hybrid constraint handling in large scale virtual power plants. In: 2013 4th IEEE/PES Innovative Smart Grid Technologies Europe (ISGT EUROPE), pp. 1–5. IEEE (2013)
12. Li, J., Poulton, G., James, G.: Coordination of distributed energy resource agents. Applied Artificial Intelligence **24**, 351–380 (2010)
13. Sørensen, J.C., Jørgensen, B.N., Klein, M., Demazeau, Y.: An agent-based extensible climate control system for sustainable greenhouse production. In: Kinny, D., Hsu, J.Y., Governatori, G., Ghose, A.K. (eds.) PRIMA 2011. LNCS, vol. 7047, pp. 218–233. Springer, Heidelberg (2011)
14. Rytter, M., Sørensen, J., Jørgensen, B., Körner, O.: Advanced model-based greenhouse climate control using multi-objective optimization. In: IV International Symposium on Models for Plant Growth, Environmental Control and Farm Management in Protected Cultivation, vol. 957, pp. 29–35 (2012)
15. Clausen, A., Demazeau, Y., Jørgensen, B.N.: An agent-based framework for aggregation of manageable distributed energy resources. In: Corchado, J.M., et al. (eds.) PAAMS 2014 Workshops. CCIS, vol. 430, pp. 214–225. Springer, Heidelberg (2014)

Agent-Based Distributed Analytical Search

Subrata Das[✉], Ria Ascano, and Matthew Macarty

Machine Analytics, Cambridge, MA, USA
sdas@machineanalytics.com

Abstract. We describe here an agent-based Distributed Analytical Search (DAS) tool to search and query distributed "big data" sources regardless of data's location, content or format. DAS semantically analyzes natural language queries from a web-based user interface. It automatically translates the query to a set of sub-queries by deploying a combination of planning and traditional database query optimization techniques. It then generates a query plan represented in XML and guide the execution by spawning intelligent agents with various types of wrappers as needed for distributed sites. The answers returned by the agents are merged appropriately and return them to the user. We have demonstrated DAS using a variety of data sources that are distributed and heterogeneous. The tool is the prime product of our company with big enterprises as our target market.

1   Introduction

Big data is generally stored in relational databases, such as Oracle, DB2, SQL Server, and MySQL, and in data warehouses such as Terradata. This data is generally heterogeneous and distributed, making it difficult to query accurately and quickly for analytics (Das, 2014). Although big data environments are in the process of migrating to the scalable, fault-tolerant cloud environment, the cloud remains experimental in nature, due to its lack of adequate data security and the unrealized need for a query tools utilizing the Map Reduce paradigm (Dean and Ghemawat, 2008). As a result, data remains distributed in many formats, both structured and unstructured, and only non-essential data is currently stored in the cloud. What is needed is an approach to query distributed sources maintaining autonomy of individual data sources (Widom, 1996). We have developed an agent-based Distributed Analytical Search (DAS) tool to fulfill this gap.

DAS will allow end users to query distributed data sources in natural language without having to know the source formats and locations. In the government space, most distributed archives and databases, such as NASA's DAAC and the DoD's DCGS, are autonomously maintained. Additionally, our personal communications with personnel from big retailers such as Sears and Walmart reveal that their databases are also highly distributed and heterogeneous with less than 10% residing in cloud environments, and that it takes almost a day for an analyst to extract data from relevant sources after the request is placed. Our approach will allow analysts to query data sources directly in natural language and will reduce this one-day turnaround time to within seconds.

© Springer International Publishing Switzerland 2015
Y. Demazeau et al. (Eds.): PAAMS 2015, LNAI 9086, pp. 40–52, 2015.
DOI: 10.1007/978-3-319-18944-4_4

DAS searches distributed structured and unstructured "big data" sources by semantically analyzing natural language queries regardless of data's location, content or format. DAS accepts natural language queries from a web-based user interface, deploying "intelligent agents" to scan unrelated data sources and return answers to support the decision-making process. DAS is format-agnostic. DAS allows users to perform distributed search within the cloud without users needing to already know the format or locations of individual data sources. In addition, it is not necessary for these data stores to be traditional relational, nor do they need to be on the same network. Agent-assembled data is analyzed for underlying trends. This is a non-trivial exercise, with agents building and executing queries based on natural language user input. Secured Agents will build temporary tables from multiple unrelated data sources by taking computations to data sources, thus avoiding large downloads. We are uniquely positioned in this market place.

In summary, DAS answers queries through the following stages:

- Accepts a search query from a user in natural language via a web interface.
- Automatically translates the query to a set of sub-queries by deploying a combination of planning and traditional database query optimization techniques.
- Generates a query plan represented in XML and guide the execution by spawning intelligent agents with wrappers as needed for distributed sites.
- Merges the answers returned by the agents and return them to the user.

Our approach is innovative because no other currently available technology can query distributed data sources, and its extreme need is justified above. Our natural language query translation, using hybrid deep linguistics processing and machine learning, and the plan generation along with XML representation and distributed execution, is unique and is Machine Analytics' trade secrets.

The rest of the paper is organized as follows: Section 1 describes briefly the web-based querying interface and our approach to natural language query translation to SQL. Section 2 describes the query planning and optimization techniques. Section 3 describes in detail the agent-based query execution strategy. We conclude the paper with our future plan with DAS. For the purpose of illustrating DAS functionalities, throughout the paper we will be using a small example database consisting of two tables. Figure 1 shows the tables SALUTE and Mobility, with some sample rows as examples. These example tables are stored at multiple sites. The distributed query execution as described above therefore avoids downloading large volumes of Mobility and SALUTE (size-activity-location-unit-time-equipment) data records from these remote tables to the host site. An example query in this context that we will using throughout the paper is "Show Salute platforms from NAIs with mobility no go."

SALUTE

NAI	FROM	ACTIVITY	EQUIPMENT	TIME	SIZE
47	JSTARS	Milling	Vehicles	14:20	40-60
65	UAV	Emplaced	BMP	18:12	?
91	LRS	Meeting	AK 47	10:30	100-200
20	IMINT	Digging	Truck	05:10	1
...	...	...	...	...	...

NAI-Mobility

NAI	Mobility
47	Slow Go
23	No Go
49	Go
43	Go
...	...

Fig. 1. SALUTE and Mobility tables with some example rows

2   User Interface and Natural Language Querying

Currently the user will find the web-based interface by visiting a URL. For example in a typical installation on one of our servers, the user can access interface and current functionality of DAS via the following URL: `192.168.0.101:8080/Agent7`. The user will be presented with the single page application a screenshot of which can be seen in Figure 2. The screenshot demonstrates the current iteration of the UI with control panel on the left.

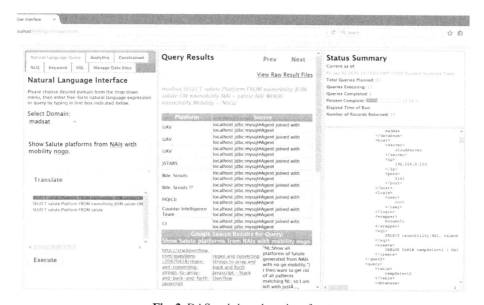

Fig. 2. DAS web-based use interface

The user will select first a domain from a dynamic list of possible domains. This list is populated at load time based on output from the DAS application that the interface accesses via an AJAX call. Once a domain is selected, the user will begin typing a natural language query in the textbox below the domain selection. After a query has been completed the user will click the translate button displayed below the query textbox as shown in Figure 2. This initiates an AJAX call to the DAS translation class, which in turn makes calls to internal dependencies that will translate natural language query into SQL.

DAS automatically translates a natural language query to its equivalent SQL representation to be executed against structured data (e.g. Giordani and Moschitti, 2012). We are making use of the publicly available Stanford parser and the dependency relations (de Marneffe, et al., 2010) that it generates from a given sentence representing a user query in the context of a given database. The algorithm also makes use of the underlying database scheme and its content. The algorithm exploits the structure of the database to generate a set of candidate SQL queries, which we rerank with a heuristics based ranking algorithm developed in-house. In particular we use linguistic dependencies in the natural language question and the metadata to build a set of plausible SELECT, WHERE and FROM clauses enriched with meaningful joins.

Once the translation is complete, possible SQL queries are returned to the user via another AJAX callback. DAS returns all of the possible translations of the original natural-language-like query, using a proprietary algorithm to rank the translations. The list of translated queries that the user is presented with is displayed in rank order as shown in Figure 2. However, the "correct" translation in terms of relevancy is not always ranked highest due to the ambiguity of natural language.

The user can select any translation (first one is by default) by clicking on it and then click the execute button below the list of SQL translations. This action initiates AJAX calls to DAS classes responsible for planning and executing the query using direct cloud based queries to nodes on the network and agent based queries to nodes on the network where this is appropriate. At this point DAS starts by preparing an execution plan whereby subqueries are created and optimized prior to execution. In the UI presentation layer, the user is presented with the XML-based plan that DAS will execute. Figure 2 illustrates a portion of this plan, hiding a significant portion, which the user is able to scroll through both horizontally and vertically if desired to examine the order of execution.

Once the plan has been created by DAS, we will know how many queries will be executed at a maximum, and this number will be presented to the user. In some instances the number of queries planned will not be the same as the number of queries executed. This is primarily due to the fact that some nodes may be unavailable when contacted by an agent. Since it is a basic assumption that nodes will be or become unavailable for querying, DAS can and does continue the execution on available nodes. When this occurs we believe it is relevant to the user to know that not all nodes can be queried at the moment. The user is presented with a new statistic so s/he are alerted to the fact that not all queries will be executed and by extension that some nodes on the network are not available. However should unavailable nodes become available during the course of execution, they will be included in the execution. It should be possible to provide the user with a list of unavailable nodes in future iterations. In Figure 2, in the status summary panel, we can see that 20 queries were planned in this run, but only 8 actually executed, with partial results displayed in the Query Results panel.

Continuous communication between the UI and DAS is maintained via AJAX call throughout the execution process, and as soon as 200 results are available, they are displayed to the user. DAS continues to run and the user is presented with updates on the status of the query. When the user clicks the Next or Prev button a graphic is displayed to indicate that new results are being fetched.

Based on the number of queries that will execute, the user is also presented with a near-real-time "percent complete" statistic and graphic. This graphic and number are replaced with the word "Completed" once all results are available. It should be possible to provide the user with an estimate of time to completion as well. The user is currently given the ability to toggle through results by means of "Next" and "Prev" buttons. Additionally a link is provided to the directory where result files are stored, should the user with to view or download raw result files.

3   Query Planning and Optimization

Query planning (Das et al., 2002 & 2005) involves generating a set of sub-queries from a given user query based on the data source locations that have parts of the required information to answer the query. The optimization process then generates an efficient ordering of execution among these sub-queries. We first create an example to illustrate the concept of query planning and optimization.

Once a natural language query is translated into its equivalent SQL query, we automatically decompose the output SQL query into a query plan composed of subqueries to be executed at distributed sites where data reside. Our implementation makes use of the two tables, Sites and Columns. The table Sites stores the physical location of tables and the table Columns stores the descriptions of columns and the user privileges.

We have focused on planning and optimizing "select-before-join" type of queries as shown below. Below is an example of this type of planning and optimization. The query here (a translation of the original query posed in natural language via the web interface) finds the equipment/vehicles that are operating in a 'no go' named area of interest (NAI):

```
select s.equipment, t.mobility
from s in salute, t in nai-mobility
where s.location = t.location and t.mobility = 'no go'
```

The optimization technique helps to identify the selection sub-query as follows to generate a temporary intermediate relation:

```
select t.mobility
from t in nai-mobility
where t.mobility = 'no go'
```

The executive agent sends an agent to execute the query at the site where terrain mobility information by NAIs is located. The results are then carried by two other agents in a temporary relation to the two sites of the SALUTE databases. The same query that are executed at the two SALUTE data sites are as follows:

```
select s.equipment, temp.mobility
from s in salute
where s.location = temp.location
```

The results are brought back by the agents and merged and presented to the user via the user interface. This kind of optimization avoids downloading the join relations to the user's local environment.

Our target is general query planning and optimization beyond just the limited optimization described above. Consider a family of surveillance platforms (e.g., JSTARS, UAV, and AWACS) and assume that an extraordinary tactical event is reported (e.g., enemy tank T-80 is identified at the named area of interest NAI-68) in the SALUTE format prepared from the UAV mission during the interval (t1, t2). For an analysis through comparison, the analyst needs to access the intelligence data of that location for the interval (t1, t2) from other surveillance platforms as well as the information about terrain and weather during that period. The query involves access from various repositories containing intelligence and environmental data. A high-level user query to retrieve only the intelligence data in this regard will look like the following:

```
select s.*
from s in salute
where s.location = 'NAI-68' and
s.time =< t1 and t2 =< s.time
```

Note that neither the repository nor the wrapper is mentioned in the query. If salute0 and salute1 are the only two tables respectively at repositories r0 and r1 containing SALUTE reports from the surveillance platforms, the above query will be translated as follows:

```
select s.*
from s in union {salute0, salute1}
where s.location = 'NAI-68' and
s.time =< t1 and t2 =< s.time
```

Given the fact that repositories r0 and r1 are at different locations, the following two sub-queries will be generated corresponding to the above query:

```
select s.*                              select s.*
from s in salute0                       from s in salute1
where s.location = 'NAI-68' and         where s.location = 'NAI-68' and
s.time =< t1 and t2 =< s.time           s.time =< t1 and t2 =< s.time
```

The above two sub-queries will be executed in parallel through wrappers w0 and w1 respectively. Not every sub-query will return a result, because the SALUTE report within a repository might not contain a reading of the surveillance platform s at that particular time interval (t1, t2). We generate an efficient query execution order based on several traditional query optimization strategies including a typical "select before join" type

4   Agent-Based Query Execution

The final step in carrying out a user's request for data is performed by the Query Execution module. The Query Execution module controls all aspects of agent creation, migration, data retrieval, and collaboration. These topics will be discussed in the following subsections. The module receives a list of sub-queries from the Planning and Optimization systems and generates a series of mobile agents to carry out these sub-queries. For each agent, the module creates an

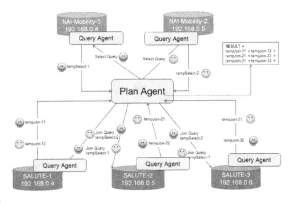

Fig. 3. Plan Agent spawning Query Agents processing information from several databases

itinerary of the various sites to be visited and the data retrieval and processing tasks to be executed at each site. Each mobile agent is then spawned and the system waits for the return of each agent with its associated data. Upon return, the system performs any required data joining, processing, and formatting before displaying the results to the user.

Our mobile agent approach as shown in Figure 3 created multiple Plan Agents and Query Agents as part of the Query Execution module. These mobile agents were built on top of the Aglets 2.02 API along with Tahiti server running on the Java 1.7. But we now have replaced Aglets with our in-house mobile agent platform. Aglets is a Java mobile agent platform and library. An aglet is a Java agent that is able to autonomously and spontaneously move from one host to another. The Plan Agents and Query Agents inherit the properties of an Aglet.

Different types of execution mobilities exist (Jansen and Karygiannis, 1999) corresponding to the possible variations of relocating code and state information, including the values of instance variables, the program counter, execution stack, etc. For example, a simple agent written as a Java applet has mobility of code through the movement of class files from a web server to a web browser. However, no associated state information is conveyed. In contrast, Aglets, developed at IBM Japan, builds upon Java to allow the values of instance variables, but not the program counter or execution stack, to be conveyed along with the code as the agent relocates. A stronger form of mobility allows Java threads to be conveyed along with the agent's code during relocation. DAS design allows relocation of code information and state information.

Detailed architectural diagrams of the Query Execution module will be shown and discussed in the next subsection.

4.1   Query Execution Architecture

Figure 4 (left) shows the diagrams of the Query Execution Module. The two main parts are JSP Server and the Aglets Agent Servers. The Query Execution Module integrates with the Web-based Analyst Interface component and the Planning and Optimization System Module. A user-submitted natural query will be processed by the JSP Server and passed on to the Planning and Optimization systems.

Planning and Optimization systems are customized Java Objects that can process the transformation from a Natural Language Query and produce a plan of action in XML format. The user may then choose a desired transformation SQL and pass it back to the JSP Server to create a plan of action in XML format. The XML file that was created will be processed by the Plan Agent as shown in Figure 4 (right). The figure also shows the roles of the Agents that were customized from the Aglets API. The Plan XML file was read and processed. The Plan Agent creates Query Agents based on the number of queries obtained from the plan XML file. This XML file contains a plan of action created from a catalogue of available databases. Changing the availability of databases in the catalogue will reflect on the plan created in XML.

The Query Agents are then dispatched to the remote computers containing the desired databases. The Query Agents perform all computations locally where the databases reside. Query Agents can be sent to remote machines and process SQL commands to different databases on those machines. The databases that we used for testing were MySQL and Derby. One of the advantages of using agents is that the database needs not be open to outside connection. Since the agent had been sent to the remote machine, the agent has the ability to query the database locally. Query Agent also has the ability to create temporary database tables and carry out any standard SQL command.

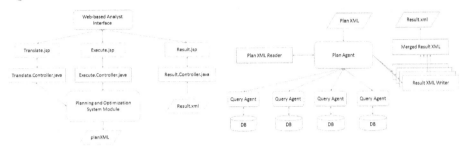

Fig. 4. (left) Query Execution architecture part 1 (JSP Server); (right) Query Execution architecture part 2 (Aglets Agent Servers)

We designed custom codes with the assumption that we have sufficient privileges to modify one or more databases involved in the query as well as permissions to read the corresponding tables across the network. These written codes have automated access to user defined queries obtained from the Planning and Optimization systems. The combined processed results, according to the query plan, from heterogeneous data from multiple sources are sent back to the Plan Agent, who will then save them into an XML format. The resulting XML files are visualized as single or multiple merged results.

4.2   Agent Creation

Plan Agent was created by inheriting the properties of an Aglet. The Aglet class is provided by the Aglets API. Aglets need to be hosted by an agent host such as a Tahiti server. Plan Agent was instantiated within an Aglet Context that performs the role of sending messages to other Agents. The Aglet Context was created by the Tahiti Server which has a network daemon whose job is to listen to the network for other agents. Incoming agents are received and inserted into the context by the daemon. The Context provides all agents with a uniform initialization and execution environment.

One of the challenges faced by mobile agents is that a Tahiti server with the ability to host a query agent needs to be present in the destination database machine. To respond to this challenge we have developed the option for the plan agent to create query agents that will have the ability to query multiple databases without dispatching them to the different machines. Having this additional feature will enable the Plan Agent to combine results from machines that can host Agents as well as machines that cannot host Agents. One of the test scenarios involved multiple databases residing on different servers with different database software. For example we have four servers on machines a, b, c, and d, with MySQL, Derby, CloudBase, and Accumulo, and with different operating systems such as Ubuntu and Windows. Different servers refer to distinct physical machines or multiple virtual machines using different physical hardware. The key point is that there are multiple installations of the database software.

Another challenge that the query agents face includes what to do if the destination machine is temporarily unavailable. Should the program crash, or should it proceed and produce partial results from other available machines? The Query Agents had been designed to detect if the destination machine specified on the plan XML file has become unavailable. The program will complete, produce fewer results, and report to the user that some database sites are unavailable. Destination machines may become unavailable due to loss of network connections, availability of the Tahiti Servers, power outage, or incorrect or change of user access at a particular site, among other reasons. The Query Agent will send a message to the Plan Agent regarding the unavailability of the destination host. The final result will consist of a single result XML file containing the merged results obtained from the available databases. The user interface will display the results on the web browser as a result table. Status reports including availability or unavailability of databases have been made available to the user. Sources of information are also displayed as part of the results.

4.3   Agent Migration

The Plan Agent can create, monitor, coordinate, retract, dispatch, and dispose Query Agents as needed. A Query Agent can be dispatched to a specific host (which itself hosts a database on the network) to visit and perform a specific function, computation, or query. Once an agent completes its tasks, it can send messages to other agents to perform other tasks such as creating temporary database tables or merging query results from different database tables. Agents also send messages to other agents to verify that they have reached their destinations and have completed their tasks. The Plan Agents have the ability to decide what path to take and what actions to perform as they gather data from the nodes that the Query Agent visits.

The Plan Processor reads XML files and stores the information in the form of Serialized objects (Java classes that can be converted into bytes and be sent over the wire). The instance of this class is saved and can be restored upon arrival to a destination. Serialization allows the persistence of an object from memory to a sequence of bits, and deserialization enables the reading of the data to recreate the object.

Plan Agent will create multiple Query Agents that can calculate and carry vital information while "hopping" to and from different machines. The number of Query Agents created depends upon the number of queries in the XML document. Multiple queries can be processed in parallel or sequentially in a distributed manner. Query Agents are deployed to different machines based on the plan XML file to process information from the remote databases. MySQL and Derby Test Databases were configured and used for testing.

4.4   Agent Retrieval

Using agents, it is possible to leave data where it resides and to only extract the required data on demand. The user writes a query in his own words and submits it using the web based user interface. From the user's perspective, one query produces one combined answer and the complexities of the process have been hidden. The original data has not been moved nor modified. Only relevant data had been extracted and passed through the network.

Several databases were loaded with gigabytes of data. A Plan Processor Java Object was designed and implemented to enable carrying huge data streams across the wires. A new scenario was developed and a series of tests were carried out to query new tables containing large amounts of data with a huge number of results that were carried across the wires. The testing was successful and gigabytes of data were obtained from a remote computer.

The Plan Agent has the ability to create Query Agents that can travel autonomously through the network, providing an increased fault tolerance. The agents' ability to travel through the network and carry data along with them enables these agents to individually process queries in parallel and/or in sequence. The query execution module will not crash with a single point of failure and the query process may continue even if individual machines fail or become unavailable.

New computers or new database source may be added to the network. This feature offers better scalability of the module. We have created a data site table stored where users may add or delete existing data sources. The Plan Agent has the ability to automatically increase the creation of Query Agents that can be dispatched to different computers. The ability to have the Query Agents travel through the system and execute their code using the host's resources allows for dynamic load sharing and automatic data processing.

5   Experimental Results

Figure 5 shows the DAS demo implementation environment that we have created. We have set up three database servers to emulate storing and serving big data from a variety of environments, including Hadoop-based cloud and a traditional database server. These servers are connected via a router providing fixed IP addresses to these servers, thus creating local area network. The servers are connected by a common maintenance terminal for configurations.

We have also developed the option to directly query the databases specified on the plan XML document without sending

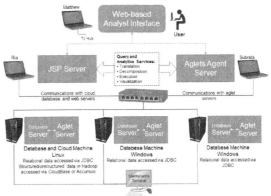

Fig. 5. Agent collaboration

the Agents to the remote locations. A comparison between direct querying and the sending the Agents was developed. Sources of Query Agent delay were found and the code has been restructured to eliminate or minimize runtime inefficiency.

The table below shows a comparison between distributed and centralized database as well as direct parallel querying and sending the Agents to remote locations. It took less than half the time to retrieve 2.1 million records from three distributed databases than the same amount of records from one centralized database. There is not much difference between the direct parallel approaches as opposed to sending the mobile agents remotely.

	Direct	Mobile Agent
Centralized DB (2.1M records returned)	7 min 43 sec	7 min 32 sec
Distributed in 3 DB (0.7M each) (2.1M records returned)	3 min 22 sec	3 min 12 sec

Plan Agents and Query Agents have been configured to run on both Windows and Ubuntu Operating systems. MySQL containing huge amounts of data has also been installed on both platforms. The Ubuntu machine had been expanded from its current capacity of 30 gigabytes storage to 450 gigabytes of space to accommodate big data for traditional SQL databases and Hadoop, CloudBase, and Accumulo. Precautions were taken to ensure that the original data were protected, and the expansion was been carried out without loss of data. Precautionary measures included backing up relevant files and information. Testing is being done on different machines to ensure that the DAS system can operate in a heterogeneous environment.

The ability to have multiple clients querying from different browsers or different machines has been designed and implemented. A unique session directory is created when a user chooses a particular translated query to execute. The plan XML document and all the other relevant documents that are related to this particular query will be contained in this unique session directory. Relevant files include the status XML file and the partial and merged results.

The limits of our system have been continuously subjected to stress testing by sending huge data results across the wires. Gigabytes of data have been loaded across several data sources. Up to 3 million result objects per remote data source have been sent through the wires. There were no issues with using the mobile Agents and we run into heap space issues with the direct approach. Major refactoring was implemented to accommodate the migration of huge data results into different machines. We continue to encounter heap space issues as we increase data and several steps were taken to improve. Memory management is continuously monitored and managed.

The DAS Agents are constructed as lightweight processes, so that each process tests a single vulnerability. As new vulnerabilities are detected and tests for these vulnerabilities are developed, new agents can be added to the test suite. As the system configuration changes, some agents can be retracted or disposed of if they are no longer needed. Test suites can be fine-tuned for each individual node depending on its configuration. This increases the efficiency of the testing as tests are performed only when and where they are needed. A lightweight agent architecture makes the test suite configurable for heterogeneous environments.

6   Conclusions and Future Directions

Our agent-based approach to distributed analytical search offers several advantages: 1) Databases need not be open to outside connections. Since the agent has been sent to the remote machine, it has the ability to query the database locally; 2) Network bandwidth usage is reduced because the Mobile agent moves computation code to where the data resides; 3) The agents do not require a continuous connection between machines and the clients can dispatch an agent into the network when the network connection is healthy, and then it can go off-line. The network connection can be reestablished later when the result from the remote host is ready; and 4) Agents operate asynchronously and autonomously and the user doesn't need to monitor the agent as it roams the internet. This saves time for the user, reduces communication costs, and decentralizes network structure.

Future developments include researching possible security issues. We will investigate the possibility of creating cooperating agents that can help reconfigure the network to deny network services to certain nodes until they have been confirmed to be in a safe state. Query Agents can monitor network events and cooperate with the Plan Agents. For example, if one of the Agents detects suspicious activity on one computer and notifies the rest of the network, the other agents may decide to challenge the nodes by modifying the rights given to those agents.

Real time status reports will be continuously improved. We are researching means to show the user a more detailed report on why data may or may not be available as well as how long it will take to get data. The percentage of completion will be calculated as well as information on particular queries that will be abandoned because of the unavailability of the database or its dependent database. The detailed status report will also show whether an agent was available in the remote machine or a direct query had been implemented.

More testing will be developed to ensure the robustness of the application. New scenarios will be created for testing and more data sources will be explored, including finding data that are publicly available through the internet. Different testing mechanisms will be studied in more detail to enable the system to have flexible capabilities. New scenarios will be considered to test the limits of performance. Simultaneous querying using multiple client machines will be tested and smarter Agents will be designed and developed to operate on both Windows and Ubuntu Systems.

References

Das, S., Shuster, K., Wu, C.: ACQUIRE: agent-based complex QUery and information retrieval engine. In: Proc. of the 1st Int. Joint Conf. on Autonomous Agents and Multi-Agent Systems, Bologna, Italy, July 2002

Das, S., Shuster, K., Wu, C., Levit, I.: Mobile Agents for Distributed and Heterogeneous Information Retrieval. Journal of In Retrieval **8**, 383–416 (2005). Springer Science

Das, S.: Computational Business Analytics. Chapman and Hall/CRC Press (2014)

de Marneffe, M.-C., et al.: Stanford typed dependencies manual: Revised for Stanford Parser v. 1.6.5 (2010)

Dean, J., Ghemawat, S.: Mapreduce: simplified data processing on large clusters. Communication of the ACM **51**(1), 107–113 (2008)

Giordani, A., Moschitti, A.: Generating SQL queries using natural language syntactic dependencies and metadata. In: Bouma, G., Ittoo, A., Métais, E., Wortmann, H. (eds.) NLDB 2012. LNCS, vol. 7337, pp. 164–170. Springer, Heidelberg (2012)

Jansen, W., Karygiannis, T.: Mobile Agent Security, NIST Special Publication 800-19 (1999)

Widom, J.: Integrating Heterogeneous Databases: Lazy or Eager?. ACM Computing Surveys **28** (1996)

Distributed Belief Propagation in Multi-agent Environment

Subrata Das[✉] and Ria Ascano

Machine Analytics, Cambridge, MA, USA
sdas@machineanalytics.com

Abstract. A distributed net-centric environment consist of a large variety of data fusion nodes, where each node represents a sensor, software program, machine, human operator, warfighter, or a combat unit. Fusion nodes can be conceptualized as intelligent autonomous agents that communicate, coordinate, and cooperate with each other in order to improve their local situational awareness (SA), and to assess the situation of the operational environment as a whole. In this paper, we describe how we model this net-centric SA problem using a distributed belief propagation paradigm. A local fusion node maintains the joint state of the set of variables modeling a local SA task at hand using Bayesian network (BN) fragments. Local fusion nodes communicate their beliefs and coordinate with each other to update their local estimates of the situation and contribute to the global SA of the environment. We have implemented the propagation paradigm to determine threat out of terrorist dirty bombs with agents searching unstructured intelligence reports for evidence and assessing local situations via BN fragments. The paradigm is a part of our company's cutting-edge predictive analytics products offering to solve enterprise distributed big data search problem.

1   Introduction

The concept of distributed fusion (Hall et al., 2012) refers to decentralized processing environments consisting of autonomous sensor nodes, and additional processing nodes without sensors, if necessary, to facilitate message communication, data storage, relaying, information aggregation, and assets scheduling. Some of the advantages of distributed fusion are reduced communication bandwidth, distribution of processing load, aggregation of distributed and proprietary knowledge sources, and improved system survivability from a single point failure. The distributed fusion concept naturally fits within the net-centric multi-agent paradigm.

As a concrete example of distributed fusion, consider the decentralized processing environment as shown in Figure 1 (left). In this example, we assume there is a high-value target within a region of interest, and that the designated areas A and B surrounding the target are considered to be the most vulnerable. These two areas must be under surveillance in order to detect any probing activities, which indicate a possible attack threat. The sensor coverage in areas A and B, shown in grey, is by an infrared sensor (MASINT) and a video camera (IMINT), respectively. In addition, a human

© Springer International Publishing Switzerland 2015
Y. Demazeau et al. (Eds.): PAAMS 2015, LNAI 9086, pp. 53–65, 2015.
DOI: 10.1007/978-3-319-18944-4_5

observer (HUMINT) is watching the area in common between A and B. There are two local fusion centers for the two areas to detect any probing activity. The infrared sensor has wireless connectivity with the local fusion center for area A, whereas the video camera has wired connectivity with the local fusion center for area B for streaming video. Moreover, the human observer communicates wirelessly with both local fusion centers. Each of the two local centers fuses the sensor data it receives in order to identify any possible probing activity. The centers then pass their assessments (i.e., higher-level abstraction, rather than raw sensor information, thus saving bandwidth) to another fusion center that assesses the overall threat level, based on the reports of probing activities and other relevant prior contextual information.

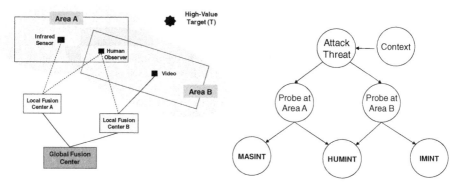

Fig. 1. (left) An example distributed fusion environment; (right) A centralized BN model for situation assessment

In a centralized fusion environment, where observations from IMINT, HUMINT, and MASINT are gathered in one place and fused, a BN model, such as the one in Figure 1 (right), can be used for an overall SA. This model handles dependence among sensors and fusion centers via their representation in nodes and interrelationships. A probing activity at an area will be observed by those sensors covering the area, and the lower half of the BN models this. For example, MASINT and HUMINT reports will be generated due to a probing activity at area A. Similarly, IMINT and HUMINT reports will be generated due to a probing activity at area B. The

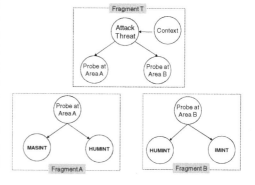

Fig. 2. Distributed parts of the BN models

upper half of the BN models the threat of an attack based on the probing activities at areas A and B, together with other contextual information.

In a decentralized environment, as illustrated in Figure 2, each of the three fusion centers contains only a fragment of the above BN model. Local fusion centers A and B assess probing activities based on their local model fragments, and send their assessments to the global fusion center via messages. The global fusion center then uses its own models to determine the overall attack threat. If the same HUMINT report is received by both local fusion centers, the process has to ensure that this common information is used only once; otherwise, there will be a higher-than-actual level of support for a threat to be determined by the global fusion model. This is called the *data incest problem* in a distributed fusion environment, which is the result of repeated use of identical information. *Pedigree* needs to be traced, not only to identify common information, but also to assign appropriate trust and confidence to data sources. An information graph (Liggins et al., 1997), for example, allows common prior information to be found.

For situation and threat assessment in a distributed net-centric environment, each node is an agent representing (Das, 2010) a sensor, software program, machine, human operator, warfighter, or a unit. A fusion node maintains the joint state of the set of variables modeling a local SA task at hand. Informally, the set of variables maintained by a fusion node is a *clique* (maximal sets of variables that are all pairwise linked), and the set of cliques in the environment together form a clique network to be transformed into a *junction tree*, where the nodes are the cliques. Thus the cliques of a junction tree are maintained by local fusion nodes within the environment. Local fusion nodes communicate and coordinate with each other to improve their local estimates of the situation, avoiding the repeated use of identical information.

A junction tree can also be obtained by transforming (Jensen, 2001) a Bayesian Belief Network (BN) (Pearl, 1988; Jensen, 2001; Das, 2008b) model representing a global SA model in the context of a mission, thereby contributing to the development of a Common Tactical Picture (CTP) of the mission via shared awareness. Each clique is maintained by a local fusion node. Inference on such a BN model for SA relies on evidence from individual local fusion nodes. We make use of the message-passing inference algorithm for junction trees that naturally fits within distributed NCW environments. A BN structure with nodes and links is a natural fit for distributing tasks in a NCW environment at various levels of abstraction and hierarchy. BNs have been applied extensively for centralized fusion (e.g., Jones et al., 1998; Wright et al., 2002; Das et al., 2002a; Mirmoeini and Krishnamurthy, 2005; Su et al., 2011) where domain variables are represented by nodes.

2   Related Work

There are approaches along these lines, namely Distributed Perception Networks (DPN) (Pavlin et al., 2006) and Multiply Section Bayesian Networks (MSBN) (Xiang et al., 1993), but the proposed approach leverages existing algorithms and reduces the overall message flow to save bandwidth. Please refer to Paskin and Guestrin (2004) for a more detailed account of a junction tree-based distributed fusion algorithm along the lines of the one presented here. The algorithm presented later in the paper, in addition, optimizes the choice of junction tree to minimize the communication and computation required by inference.

There is an abundance of work in the area of distributed agent-based target tracking and, more generally, in the area of distributed fusion. In general, a distributed processing architecture for estimation and fusion consists of multiple processing agents. Here we mention only some of them.

Horling et al. (2001) developed an approach to real-time distributed tracking, where the environment is partitioned into sectors to reduce the level of potential interaction between agents. Hughes and Lewis (2009) investigated the Track-Before-Detect (identify tracks before applying thresholds) problem using multiple intelligent software agents. Martin and Chang (2005) developed a tree based distributed data fusion method for ad hoc networks, where a collection of agents share and fuse data in an ad hoc manner for estimation and decision making.

Graphical Bayesian belief networks have been applied extensively by the fusion community to perform situation assessment (Das et al., 2002). A network structure, modeling a situation assessment problem, with nodes and links is a natural fit for distributing tasks at various levels of abstraction and hierarchy, where nodes represent agents with message flows between agents along the links. An approach along these lines has been adopted by Pavlin et al. (2006). Mastrogiovanni et al. (2007) developed a framework for collaborating agents for distributed knowledge representation and data fusion based on the idea of an ecosystem of interacting artificial entities. Mobile agents have also been employed for distributed fusion.

Mobile agents are able to travel between nodes of a network in order to make use of resources that are not locally available. Mobile agents enable the execution code to be moved to the data sites, thus save the network bandwidth and provide an effective way to overcome network latency. Qi et al. (2001) developed an infrastructure for Mobile-agent-based Distributed Sensor Networks (MADSNs) for multisensor data fusion. Bai et al. (2005) developed a Mobile Agent-Based Distributed Fusion (MADFUSION) system for decision making in Level 2 Fusion. The system environment consists of a peer-to-peer ad-hoc network in which information may be dynamically distributed and collected via publish/subscribe functionality. Jameson's Grapevine architecture (2001) for data fusion integrates intelligent agent technology, where an agent generates the information needs of the peer platform it represents. Gerken et al. (2003) embedded intelligent agents into the Mobile Commander's Associate (MCA) decision aiding system to improve the situational awareness of the commander by monitoring and alerting based on the information gathered.

2.1   Implementation

Our approach to complex analytics[1] in our product is to make use of a computational model and its mobile agent-based distributed belief propagation presented in this paper. Figure 3 presents a Bayesian network model to help in assessing the level of a dirty-bomb threat from a rogue nation. In our model, the site maintaining the root node (for example) continually updates the state (i.e., the probability distribution) of an overall threat based on evidence it receives from its child node, representing terrorism indication and warning, which in turn receives evidence of indications and warnings from its four children, namely, planning, acquisition, making, and deployment. The state of these nodes can be maintained by various sites based on the evidence received from their children nodes. This hierarchical breakdown process continues, and model fragments are determined. A fragment is defined here as a connected

---

[1] Analytics and data fusion are two sides of the same coin (Das, 2014)

sub-network of the entire belief network model. For the purpose of our demonstration we assume all the fragments are two levels deep as shown in Figure 3.

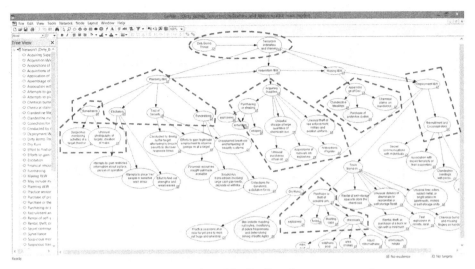

Fig. 3. Some fragmented models distributed across remote sites

The specific strategy for evaluating a fragment at a remote site is determined based on the site's capability of accumulating evidence from multiple sources. Figure 4 shows the current state of the interface for controlling and monitoring the distributed execution, with nine list components for the following nine purposes respectively:

1. Text area where the analyst poses a full or partial analytics query in key words.
2. Lists all the model fragments stored in a directory such as the ones from the BN in Figure 3, filters the models based on the analyst query, and lets user select one.
3. The selected dependent model fragments based on the user selection that are to be distributed and maintained across remote sites.
4. Publishes available http addresses of the remote sites running Aglets servers to host computation.
5. Lists search nodes of the fragments (same as the list of model fragments above).
6. Provides probability distributions corresponding to the search nodes as model fragments.
7. Graphically display a selected fragment from the library.
8. Displays messages that are received and also the evidence that are found.
9. Overall assessment of threat which is 0.25 based on evidence searched so far.

Users can dispatch fragments individually by selecting a fragment from the area marked 3 to a remote site selected from the area marked 4 by pressing the Dispatch Agent button. Users can also dispatch all fragments at once just by pressing the Random Dispatch button. Evidence on a child node at a remote site can be set by selecting the node in the area marked 6 and then by pressing the button Set Evidence. Various messages will be passed among fragments as described earlier in the section on complex analytics. These messages will be displayed in the area marked 8. The probability distributions of each child node will be updated in areas marked by 6. To start execution of the analytics model, a user dispatches all fragments at once by pressing the Random Dispatch button in the analytics interface.

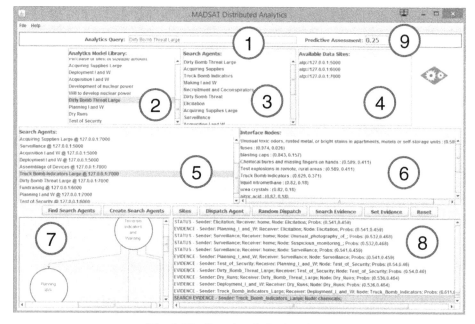

Fig. 4. Distributed analytics interface

3   Distributed Fusion Environments

As shown in Figure 5, a typical distributed fusion environment is likely to contain a variety of fusion nodes that do a variety of tasks:

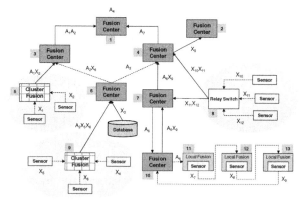

Fig. 5. A typical distributed fusion environment

- Process observations generated from a cluster of heterogeneous sensors (e.g., the local fusion centers A and B in Figure 1, and nodes labeled 5 and 9 in Figure 5).

- Process observations generated from a single sensor (e.g., nodes labeled 11, 12, and 13 in Figure 5).

- Perform a task (e.g., Situation Assessment (SA) and Threat Assessment (TA), Course of Action (COA) generation, planning and scheduling, Common Tactical Picture (CTP) generation, collection management) based on information received from other sensors in the environment and from other information stored in databases (e.g., nodes labeled 1, 2, 3, 4, 6, 7, and 10 in Figure 5).
- Relay observations generated from sensors to other nodes (e.g., the node labeled 8 in Figure 5).

As shown in Figure 5, a fusion node receives values of some variables obtained either from sensor observations (X variables) or via information aggregation by other nodes (A variables). Such values can also be obtained from databases. For example, the fusion center labeled 6 receives values of the variables A2, X5, and X6 from the cluster fusion node labeled 9, and values of the variable X3 from a database. Note that an arrow between two nodes indicates the flow of information in the direction of the arrow as opposed to a communication link. The existence of an arrow indicates the presence of at least a one-way communication link, though not necessarily a direct link, via some communication network route. For example, there is a one-way communication link from node 3 to node 1. A reverse communication link between these two nodes will be necessary in implementing our message-passing distributed fusion algorithm to be presented later.

Each node (fusion center, cluster fusion, relay switch, or local fusion) in a distributed fusion environment has knowledge of the states of some variables, called *local variables*, as shown in Figure 6 (ignore red cross for now). For example, the fusion node labeled 6 has knowledge of the X variables X3, X5, and X6, and A variables A2 and A3. The node receives values of the variables A2, X5, and X6 from the node labeled 9, and the variable X3 from a database. The node generates values of the variable A3 via some information aggregation operation. On the

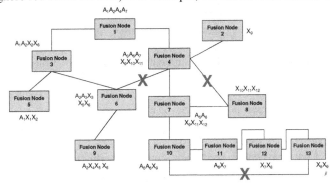

Fig. 6. Network of distributed fusion nodes

other hand, fusion node 9 receives measurements X4, X5, and X6 from a cluster of sensors and generates A2; fusion node 8 relays values of the variables X10, X1, and X12 to other nodes; and fusion node 12 obtains measurements of X8 from a single sensor.

There are four possible distributed fusion environments: centralized, hierarchical, peer-to-peer, and grid-based. In a *centralized* environment, only the sensors are distributed, sending their observations to a centralized fusion node. The centralized node combines the sensor information to perform tracking or SA. In a *hierarchical* environment, the fusion nodes are arranged in a hierarchy, with the higher-level nodes processing results from the lower-level nodes and possibly providing some feedback. The hierarchical architecture will be natural for applications where situations are assessed with an increasing level of abstraction along a command hierarchy, starting with the tracking of targets at the bottom level. Considerable savings in communication effort can be achieved in a hierarchical fusion environment. In both *peer-to-peer* and *grid-based* distributed environments, every node is capable of communicating with every other node. This internode communication is direct in the case of a peer-to-peer environment, but some form of "publish and subscribe" communication mechanism is required in a grid-based environment.

4   Algorithm for Distributed Belief Propagation

As mentioned in the introduction, there are two ways in which we can accomplish SA in a distributed environment: 1) each local fusion node maintains the state of a set of variables; 2) there is a BN model for global SA.

In the first case, we start with a distributed fusion environment such as the one shown in Figure 5. Our distributed SA framework in this case has four steps: 1) Network formation; 2) Spanning tree formation; 3) Junction tree formation; and 4) Message passing. The nodes of the sensor network first organize themselves into a network of fusion nodes, similar to the one shown in Figure 6. Each fusion node has partial knowledge of the whole environment. This network is then transformed into a *spanning tree* (a spanning tree of a connected, undirected graph, such as the one in Figure 6, is a tree composed of all the vertices and some or all of the edges of the graph), so that neighbor nodes establish high-quality connections. In addition, the spanning tree formation algorithm optimizes the communication required by inference in junction trees. The algorithm can recover from communication and node failures by regenerating the spanning tree. Figure 6 with (red crosses indicating link severed) describes a spanning tree obtained from the network in Figure 5. The decision to sever the link between nodes 4 and 6, as opposed to between nodes 3 and 6, can be mitigated using the communication bandwidth and reliability information in the cycle of nodes 1, 3, 6, and 4.

Using pairwise communication-link information sent between neighbors in a spanning tree, the nodes compute the information necessary to transform the spanning tree into a junction tree for the inference problem. Finally, the inference problem is solved via message-passing on the junction tree.

During the formation of a spanning tree, each node chooses a set of neighbors, so that the nodes form a spanning tree where adjacent nodes have high-quality communication links. Each node's clique is then determined as follows. If i is a node and j is a neighbor of i, then the variables reachable to j from i, R_{ij}, are defined recursively as

$$R_{ij} = D_i \bigcup_{k \in nbr(i) - \{j\}} R_{ki}$$

where D_i is the set of local variables of node i. A base case corresponds to a leaf node, which is simply a collection of a node's local variables. If a node has two sets of reachable variables to two of its neighbors that both include some variable V, then the node must also carry V to satisfy the running intersection property of a junction tree. Formally, node i computes its clique C_i as

$$C_i = D_i \bigcup_{\substack{j,k \in nbr(i) \\ j \neq k}} R_{ji} \cap R_{ki}$$

A node i can also compute its *separator set* $S_{ij} = C_i \cap C_j$ with its neighbor j using reachable variables as $S_{ij} = C_i \cap R_{ji}$.

Figure 7 shows the junction tree obtained from the spanning tree in Figure 6. The variables reachable to a leaf node, for example, fusion node 9, are its local variables A_2, X_4, X_5, X_6. The variables reachable to an intermediate node,

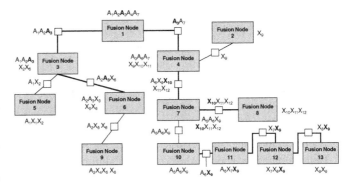

Fig. 7. A junction tree from the distributed fusion environment

for example, fusion node 1, from its neighboring nodes 3 and 4 are

$$R_{31} = \{A_1, A_2, A_3, X_1, X_2, X_3, X_4, X_5, X_6\}$$
$$R_{41} = \{A_3, A_5, A_6, A_7, X_7, X_8, X_9, X_{10}, X_{11}, X_{12}\}$$

The local variable of the fusion node 1 is $D_1 = \{A_1, A_2, A_4, A_7\}$. Therefore, its clique is $C_1 = \{A_1, A_2, A_3, A_4, A_7\}$. The formation of a suitable junction tree from a BN model for SA is the only part of our distributed fusion approach that is global in nature.

4.1   Junction Tree Construction and Inference

The *moral graph* of a BN is obtained by adding a link between any pair of variables with a common "child," and dropping the directions of the original links in the BN. An undirected graph is *triangulated* if any cycle of length greater than 3 has a chord, that is, an edge joining two nonconsecutive nodes along the cycle. The nodes of a junction tree for a graph are the *cliques* in the graph (maximal sets of variables that are all pairwise linked).

Once we have formed a junction tree from either of the above two cases, such as the one in Figure 7, a message-passing algorithm then computes prior beliefs of the variables in the network via an initialization of the junction tree structure, followed by evidence propagation and marginalization. The algorithm can be run asynchronously on each node responding to changes in other nodes' states. Each time a node i receives a new separator variables message from a neighbor j, it recomputes its own clique and separator variables messages to all neighbors except j, and transmits them if they have changed from their previous values. Here we briefly discuss the algorithm, and how to handle evidence by computing the posterior beliefs of the variables in the network.

A junction tree maintains a joint probability distribution at each node, cluster, or separator set in terms of a belief *potential*, which is a function that maps each instantiation of the set of variables in the node into a real number. The belief potential of a set of variables $\mathbf{X}$ will be denoted as φ_X, and $\varphi_X(x)$ is the number onto which the belief potential maps x. The probability distribution of a set of variables $\mathbf{X}$ is just the special case of a potential whose elements add up to 1. In other words,

$$\sum_{x \in X} \varphi_X(x) = \sum_{x \in X} p(x) = 1$$

The marginalization and multiplication operations on potentials are defined in a manner similar to the same operations on probability distributions.

Belief potentials encode the joint distribution $p(\mathbf{X})$ of the BN according to the following:

$$p(\mathbf{X}) = \frac{\prod_i \phi_{C_i}}{\prod_j \phi_{S_j}}$$

where φ_{C_i} and φ_{S_j} are the cluster and separator set potentials, respectively. We have the following joint distribution for the junction tree in Figure 7:

$$p(A_1, ..., A_9, X_1, ..., X_{12}) = \frac{\phi_{C_1} \phi_{C_2} ... \phi_{C_{13}}}{\phi_{S_{13}} \phi_{S_{14}} \phi_{S_{24}} \phi_{S_{35}} ... \phi_{S_{12\,13}}}$$

where C_i represents the variable in clique i and $S_{ij} = C_i \cap C_j$ represents the separator set between nodes i and j. It is imperative that a cluster potential agrees with its neighboring separator sets on the variables in common, up to marginalization. This imperative is formalized by the concept of local consistency. A junction tree is *locally consistent* if, for each cluster $\mathbf{C}$ and neighboring separator set $\mathbf{S}$, the following holds: $\sum_{C \backslash S} \phi_C = \phi_S$. To start initialization, for each cluster $\mathbf{C}$ and separator set $\mathbf{S}$, set the following: $\phi_C \leftarrow 1$, $\phi_S \leftarrow 1$. Then assign each variable X to a cluster $\mathbf{C}$ that contains X and its parents $pa(X)$. Then set the following: $\phi_C \leftarrow \phi_C p(X \mid pa(X))$.

When new evidence on a variable is entered into the tree, it becomes inconsistent and requires a global propagation to make it consistent. The posterior probabilities can be computed via marginalization and normalization from the global propagation. If evidence on a variable is updated, the tree requires re-initialization. Next, we present initialization, normalization, and marginalization procedures for handling evidence.

As before, to start initialization, for each cluster **C** and separator set **S**, set the following: $\phi_C \leftarrow 1$, $\phi_S \leftarrow 1$. Then assign each variable X to a cluster **C** that contains X and its parents $pa(X)$, and then set the following: $\phi_C \leftarrow \phi_C p(X \mid pa(X))$, $\lambda_X \leftarrow 1$, where λ_X is the likelihood vector for the variable X. Now, perform the following steps for each piece of evidence on a variable X:

–   Encode the evidence on the variable as a likelihood λ_X^{new}.
–   Identify a cluster **C** that contains X (e.g., one containing X and its parents).
–   Update as follows: $\phi_C \leftarrow \phi_C \dfrac{\lambda_X^{new}}{\lambda_X}$, $\lambda_X \leftarrow \lambda_X^{new}$

Now perform a global propagation using the two recursive procedures *Collect Evidence* and *Distribute Evidence*. Note that if the belief potential of one cluster **C** is modified, then it is sufficient to unmark all clusters and call only *Distribute Evidence*(**C**). The potential φ_C for each cluster **C** is now $p(C,e)$, where e denotes evidence incorporated into the tree. Now marginalize C into the variable as $p(X,e) = \sum_{C \setminus \{X\}} \phi_C$. Compute posterior $p(X \mid e)$ as follows:

$$p(X \mid e) = \frac{p(X,e)}{p(e)} = \frac{p(X,e)}{\sum_X p(X,e)}.$$

To update evidence for each variable X on which evidence has been obtained, first update its likelihood vector. Then initialize the junction tree by incorporating the observations. Finally, perform global propagation, marginalization, etc.

5   Conclusions

We have presented an agent based approach to distributed belief propagation in net-centric environments. The approach provides the foundation of the company's predictive analytics products. We are currently enhancing the product with agent-based approach distributed semantic search to find evidence to propagate in Bayesian network fragments. We are investigating the best way to make use of any types of local model fragments such as rules, neural networks, and decision trees.

References

Bai, L., Landis, J., Salerno, J., Hinman, M., Boulware, D.: Mobile agent-based distributed fusion (MADFUSION) system. In: Proceeding of the 8th International conference on Information Fusion, Philadelphia (2005)

Chong, C.-Y., Mori, S.: Graphical models for nonlinear distributed estimation. In: Proceedings of the Conference on Information Fusion, vol. I, pp. 614–621 (2004)

Das, S., Grecu, D.: COGENT: cognitive agent to amplify human perception and cognition. In: Proc. of the 4th Int. Conf. on Autonomous Agents, Barcelona, June 2000

Das, S., Grey, R., Gonsalves, P.: Situation assessment via bayesian belief networks. In: Proc. of the 5th Int. Conference on Information Fusion, Annapolis, Maryland (2002a)

Das, S., Shuster, K., Wu, C.: ACQUIRE: agent-based complex query and information retrieval engine. In: Proceedings of the 1st International Joint Conference on Autonomous Agents and Multi-Agent Systems, Bologna, Italy (2002b)

Das, S.: Foundations of Decision-Making Agents: Logic, Probability, and Modality. World Scientific/Imperial College Press, Singapore/London (2008a)

Das, S.: High-Level Data Fusion. Artech House, Norwood (2008b)

Das, S.: Agent-based information fusion. Guest Editorial, Information Fusion, Elsevier Science **11**, 216–219 (2010)

Das, S.: Computational Business Analytics. Chapman & Hall/CRC Data Mining and Knowledge Discovery Series (2014)

Gerken, P., Jameson, S., Sidharta, B., Barton, J.: Improving army aviation situational awareness with agent-based data discovery. In: American Helicopter Society 59th Annual Forum, Phoenix, Arizona (2003)

Hall, D., Liggins, M., Chong, C. (eds) Distributed Data Fusion for Network-Centric Operations. CRC Press (2012)

Horling, B., Vincent, R., Mailler, R., Shen, J., Becker, R, Rawlins, K., Lesser, V.: Distributed sensor network for real time tracking. In: Proceedings of the 5th International Conference on Autonomous Agents, Montreal, pp. 417–424 (2001)

Hughes, E., Lewis, M.: An intelligent agent based track-before-detect system applied to a range and velocity ambiguous radar. In: Electro Magnetic Remote Sensing Defence Technology Center (EMRS DTC) Technical Conference (2009)

Jameson, S.: Architectures for distributed information fusion to support situation awareness on the digital battlefield. In: Proc. of the 4th Int. Conf. on Data Fusion, pp. 7–10 (2001)

Jensen, F.V.: Bayesian Networks and Decision Graphs. Springer, NY (2001)

Lichtblau, D.E.: The critical role of intelligent software agents in enabling net-centric command and control. In: Command and Control Research and Technology Symposium, The Power of Information Age Concepts and Technologies, San Diego, CA (2004)

Liggins, M.E., Chong, C.-Y., Kadar, I., Alford, M.G., Vannicola, V., Thomopoulos, S.: Distributed fusion architectures and algorithms for target tracking. Proceedings of the IEEE **85**(1), 95–107 (1997)

Martin, T., Chang, K.: A distributed data fusion approach for mobile ad hoc networks. In: Proceedings of the 8th Int. Conference on Information Fusion, pp. 25–28 (2005)

Mastrogiovanni, F., Sgorbissa A., Zaccaria, R.: A distributed architecture for symbolic data fusion. In: Proceedings of the 20th International Joint Conference on Artificial Intelligence (IJCAI), Hyderabad, India (2007)

Mirmoeini, F., Krishnamurthy, V.: Reconfigurable bayesian networks for adaptive situation assessment in battlespace. In: Proceedings of the IEEE Conference on Networking, Sensing and Control, pp. 810–815 (2005)

Paskin, M., Guestrin, C.: Robust probabilistic inference in distributed systems. In: Proceedings of the 20th Conference on Uncertainty in Artificial Intelligence (UAI), Banff, Canada (2004)

Pavlin, G., de Oude, P., Maris, M., Hood, T.: Distributed perception networks. In: Proc. of the International Conference on Multisensor Fusion and Integration for Intelligent Systems, Heidelberg, Germany (2006)

Pearl, J.: Probabilistic Reasoning in Intelligent Systems: Networks of Plausible Inference. Morgan Kaufmann, San Mateo (1988)

Qi, H., Wang, X., Iyengar, S., Chakrabarty, K.: Multisensor data fusion in distributed sensor networks using mobile agents. In: Proceedings of 5th International Conference on Information Fusion, pp. 11–16 (2001)

Su, X., Bai, P., Du, F., Feng, Y.: Application of Bayesian Networks in Situation Assessment. In: Chen, R. (ed.) ICICIS 2011 Part I. CCIS, vol. 134, pp. 643–648. Springer, Heidelberg (2011)

Waldock, A., Nicholson, D.: Cooperative decentralised data fusion using probability collectives. In: Proc. of the 1st Int. Work. on Agent Technology for Sensor Networks (2007)

Wright, E., et al, T.: Multi-entity bayesian networks for situation assessment. In: Proceedings of the 5th International Conference on Information Fusion, pp. 804–811 (2002)

Xiang, Y., Poole, D., Beddoes, M.: Multiply sectioned Bayesian networks and junction forests for large knowledge based systems. Computational Intelligence **9**(2), 171–220 (1993)

Situated Artificial Institution to Support Advanced Regulation in the Field of Crisis Management

Maiquel De Brito[1]([✉]), Lauren Thevin[2], Catherine Garbay[2],
Olivier Boissier[3], and Jomi F. Hübner[1]

[1] PPGEAS/Federal University of Santa Catarina, Florianópolis, Brazil
maiquel.b@posgrad.ufsc.br
[2] LIG/Université de Grenoble, Grenoble, France
[3] Laboratoire Hubert Curien UMR CNRS 5516, Institut Henri Fayol,
MINES Saint-Etienne, Saint-Etienne, France

Abstract. This paper highlights the use of Situated Artificial Institution (SAI) within an hybrid, interactive, normative multi-agent system to regulate human collaboration in crisis management. Norms regulate the actions of human actors based on the dynamics of the environment in which they are situated. This dynamics result both from environment evolution and actors actions. Our objective is to couple norms to environment state to provide a context aware crisis regulation. Introducing a constitutive level between environmental and normative states provides a loosely coupling of norms with the environment. Norms are thus no more referring to environmental facts but to status functions, i.e. institutional interpretation of environmental facts through constitutive rules. We present how this declarative and distinct SAI modelling succeeds in managing the interpretation of the events while taking into account organizational context.

Keywords: Situated Artificial Institutions · Normative system · Tangible interaction · Crisis management

1 Introduction

Crisis management aims at organizing a response to disasters, within natural or artificial accidents, to limit material and human damages. It corresponds to a complex decentralized collaborative activity involving various actors and organizations (e.g. firefighters, police, citizens). They act and coordinate altogether in a highly dynamic and uncertain environment in order to take efficient and consistent actions related to multiple missions (e.g. information, security, supply, lodging).

Crisis management collaborative platforms are increasingly used in such a context. In this direction, we are currently developing such a platform based on tangible tables to mediate the opportunist interaction among the involved distant actors. In order to consider and enact crisis management policies and norms

Y. Demazeau et al. (Eds.): PAAMS 2015, LNAI 9086, pp. 66–79, 2015.
DOI: 10.1007/978-3-319-18944-4_6

used to coordinate the collective actions of the actors, we have proposed a normative multi-agent based approach to define a socio-technical system [20] where humans and software agents cooperate with each other (i.e. *hybrid system*) by combining physical, digital and virtual interactions (i.e. *mixed interaction*) that are regulated by norms and organisations (i.e *normative system*). These three pillars are well adapted to tackle with the challenges raised by crisis management systems.

This paper addresses an additional and important feature to develop such a system. It deals with the coupling of the norm-based regulation in the physical environment in which the crisis takes place. Situating norms and regulation in the environment should be realised in a flexible and easy-to-change way in order to face the complex and changing crisis situations. Indeed, two problems may occur: (*i*) discrepancies in the interpretation of events issued of the environment, depending on context, role or actors organization, (*ii*) inconsistencies of the human intervention due to inconsistencies between the systems of norms for different organizations. This is why we turn to *Situated Artificial Institution* (SAI) as proposed in [6] that offers as explained and illustrated in the following sections the right abstractions and constructs to resolve this problem. In this paper we do not present a complete running application but an application prototype showing what SAI (situating norms into the environment through constitutive rules) could bring to the development of the real crisis management application.

Section 2 sets up the applicative context by shortly describing a crisis management use case and lists the requirements driving the developed application. Section 3 defines Situated Artificial Institution. Section 4 presents how SAI has been used and embedded within the Multi-Agent based Crisis management System presented in section 2. Section 5 describes use case execution on the realised implementation. Before concluding, comparisons with related works (cf. Sec. 6) are provided.

2   Principles and Requirements

2.1   Use Case Example

We will consider a simplified use case where the goal is to evacuate a zone. The actors, in this activity, are organized in three groups: a *Communal Command Post (CCP)* under the responsibility of the *Mayor*, a *Logistic Cell (LC)* controlled by the *CCP*, and the *Firefighters (FF)*. Unprofessional people can deal with the evacuation of *secure* zones (*Mayor* commanding and *LC* executing). The *insecure* zones require professional stakeholders such as *FF* to realize evacuations. The actors work under two successive phases – preventive and emergency – managed under dedicated policies. The *Mayor* asks to the *LC* the evacuation of the *secure zones* during the *preventive* phase. *FF* are responsible to organize evacuation when a *risky situation* exists, and during the *emergency* phase, in which the zone is considered as *insecure*.

These actors work under several policies and norms. A first policy specifies that there must be only one group of actors at a time to manage evacuation. Depending on the phase (preventive or emergency), and on the status of the zone (secure, insecure), it is the duty of either LC or FF to intervene. However, qualifying a zone as being secure or risky may appear conflicting. For the actors belonging to the CCP, e.g. the *Mayor*, a zone is considered as *secure* as long as the *phase* is *preventive* and the number of inhabitants is less than a threshold. Contrarily, for the actors belonging to the FF group, the security of a zone depends on the fact that the phase is *preventive* and that there is no *electrical risk* in that zone, whatever the number of inhabitants is. Suppose now that we are in a preventive phase, that the number of inhabitants exceeds the threshold and that there is no *electrical risk*. In this case, the *Mayor* will consider that the FF are responsible of the evacuation, while the FF will consider the reverse: the *Mayor* is responsible of evacuating the zone.

This small example illustrates the possible existence of discrepancies in the interpretation of events coming from the environment, depending on context, role or organization; it also shows inconsistencies of the human intervention due to inconsistencies between sets of policies from different organizations.

Suppose in addition that due to flood evolution, the phase moves from *preventive* to *emergency* phase. This will result in an evolution of the current policies. As a consequence, the validity of some facts like *the asks for the evacuation of the zone* will change. This illustrates an additional issue related to the potential evolution of norms.

2.2   Hybrid, Mixed and Normative Dimensions

As seen before, crisis management is a collaborative activity where the actions of human actors have to be efficient and flexible to tackle the unpredictable evolution of the situations. From the analysis of existing approaches both in crisis management, groupware, multi-agent systems (MAS) the system needs to rely on *hybrid*, *mixed* and *normative* pillar dimensions.

– **Hybrid Multi-Agent System.** Crisis management is a complex collaborative activity where multiple actors and organizations participate. They act and coordinate to take efficient actions related to multiple missions (e.g. information, security, supply, lodging), in a highly dynamic and uncertain environment. Given the inherent distributed and decentralized nature of crisis management, a multi-agent approach is well suited: human and artificial actors are considered as agents interacting with each other in a shared environment under the control of regulation and coordination policies that are organization and context dependent.

– **Tangible/Mixed Interactions.** To tackle the distributed dimension inherent to crisis management, the system is deployed on a network of TangiSense tables [12] through which human actors interact. These tables can detect and locate tangible objects equipped with RFID tags. Their surface is further equipped with a liquid-crystal display (LCD) allowing a virtual display of complex simulations as well as virtual feedback connected to tangible objects. The choice of this technology is motivated by its ability to support flexible and opportunistic activity. To support *organizational context awareness* [10], the possibility for actors to perceive the roles, missions and norms of the other actors, we furthermore exploit feedbacks to figure out the inconsistencies and conflicts that may arise during collaboration w.r.t. the regulation and coordination policies.

– **Normative System.** Collaboration is challenging in crisis management due to the lack of resources, changes in the situations, and decentralized inter-organizational activity [7]. Such a complexity requires that the different actors act according to certain behavioural expectations. Norms and normative systems as defined in [2] provide the right abstractions and mechanisms to express this expected behaviour, regulating thus the decentralized activities in dynamic and unpredictable environments. Beyond regulating human *coordination* activity, norms manage the agent's degree of autonomy and regulate task allocation among the human/agent community. This may be useful to make the system evolve from a mere educative one (most tasks left to the human agents) to a monitoring one (full support from the system). Finally, norms drive man-machine interaction, describing what are the permitted actions for human actors (*production activity*) and how to proceed to feedback generation (*communication activity*).

From these three pillars, we can envision a crisis management system where humans interact with the digital world through tangible interactions and feedbacks. Humans and agents interact with each other in a hybrid system, under the regulation of the norms that define the global expected behaviour in the management of the crisis, agents being there to check and warn humans about norms violations/fulfilment.

2.3 Supporting Human Mediated Collaboration in a Situated Way

Norms regulate the *production, coordination* and *communication* activity spaces in the conceived system (Table 1). Tangible inputs are interpreted as patterns of activity that may be valid or not regarding the production activity specification (Table 1 - line 1). These patterns are then interpreted (Table 1 - line 2) as institutional facts that may be valid or not regarding the coordination activity specification (e.g. is this activity permitted as regards the current mission and role of the actor?). Finally, based on both interpretations (Table 1 - line 3), a virtual fact is generated and transmitted according to the feedback rules (e.g. where and how to transmit some virtual feedback?).

Our objective is to anchor norms into the environment while keeping their definition the more independent as possible. To this end, we introduce an intermediate level formalized by interpretation rules tying the physical and the institutional dimensions. To illustrate the declarative power of our model, we focus on the coordination space (Table 1 - line 2) and consider the potential discrepancies between the *Mayor* and *FF*'s interpretation of the notion of *secure* zone. This may be modelled by means of two different constitutive rules, while keeping the normative specification independent of these discrepancies. As regards now the potential evolution of norms, from preventive to emergency phases, the proposed modelling allows evolving the way to manage a situation (actors roles), while keeping its interpretation stable.

Table 1. Anchoring production, coordination and communication norms in the environment

	Space/Level	*Facts*	*Interpretation rules*	*Interpreted facts*	*Norms*
1	Production	Tangible input	Pattern recognition rules	Pattern	Pattern validity
2	Coordination	Pattern	Constitutive rules	Institutional fact	Institutional fact validity
3	Communication	Pattern Institutional fact validity	Virtualization rules	Virtual fact	Feedback rules

3   Situated Artificial Institution

The model of Situated Artificial Institution (SAI) is based on: *environmental elements*, *status functions*, and *constitutive rules* and *norms*, arranged to allow the regulation of MAS based on facts occurring in the environment (Figure 1(a)) [6]. As in the normative system pillar, norms define what the agents are obliged, permitted, and forbidden to do. Norms refer to an abstract level that is not directly related to the environment. For example, the norm stating that *"the winner of an auction is obliged to pay its offer"* does not specify neither who is the winner that is obliged to fulfil the norm nor what the winner must concretely do to fulfil it. The effectiveness of a norm depends on its connection to the environment as its dynamic (activation, fulfilment, etc) is result of facts occurring there. We will see below how SAI addresses this point through the components described in the section 3.1.

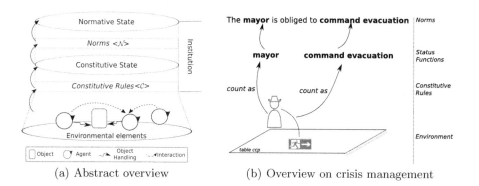

(a) Abstract overview   (b) Overview on crisis management

Fig. 1. SAI overview

3.1 SAI Formal Model

Environmental elements. The environmental elements are represented by $\mathcal{X} = \langle \mathcal{A}_\mathcal{X}, \mathcal{E}_\mathcal{X}, \mathcal{S}_\mathcal{X} \rangle$ s.t. (i) $\mathcal{A}_\mathcal{X}$ is the set of agents possibly acting in the system, (ii) $\mathcal{E}_\mathcal{X}$ is the set of events that may happen in the environment, and (iii) $\mathcal{S}_\mathcal{X}$ is the set of properties used to describe the possible states of the environment.

Status functions. The status functions of a SAI are formally represented by $\mathcal{F} = \{\mathcal{A}_\mathcal{F} \cup \mathcal{E}_\mathcal{F} \cup \mathcal{S}_\mathcal{F}\}$, where (i) $\mathcal{A}_\mathcal{F}$ is the set of agent-status functions (i.e. status functions assignable to agents), (ii) $\mathcal{E}_\mathcal{F}$ is the set of event-status functions (i.e. status functions assignable to events), and (iii) $\mathcal{S}_\mathcal{F}$ is the set of state-status functions (i.e. status functions assignable to states).

Status functions are functions that the environmental elements (agents, events, and states) perform from the institutional perspective [18]. An agent becomes the winner of an auction if the institution assigns so (it does not depend exclusively on the skills of the agent). Similarly, the institution may consider the event of an agent uttering "I offer \$100" as "bid" or "counter-proposal" in an auction. The same applies to environmental states (e.g. "more than twenty people are inside a room at Friday 10am" may mean, in the institution, the minimum quorum for an auction).

Constitutive rules. A constitutive rule $c \in \mathcal{C}$ is a tuple $\langle x, y, t, m \rangle$ meaning that $x \in \mathcal{F} \cup \mathcal{X} \cup \{\varepsilon\}$ counts as (i.e. x has the status function) $y \in \mathcal{F}$ when the event $t \in \mathcal{E}_\mathcal{F} \cup \mathcal{E}_\mathcal{X} \cup \top$ has happened and while the state m holds in the environment or in the institution.[1] If a status function y is assigned to x, it is possible to say that x *constitutes* y.

Norms. Norms in SAI are a tuple $\langle c, a, d, i, o, \rho \rangle$ where (i) c is the condition where the norm is active, expressed by event- and state-status functions; (ii) a is the agent-status function that points to the agents targeted by the norm; (iii) $d \in \{obliged, prohibited, permitted\}$ is the deontic operator of the norm; (iv) i is the aim of the norm expressed by either event- or state-status functions; (v) o is the optional event- or state-status function that is constituted as consequence of the non-compliance of the norm and (vi) ρ is the optional event- or state-status function pointing to the deadline for the norm fulfilment.

A language proposed to specify SAI is proposed in [6]. The Section 4.5 shows a specification according to that language.

4 SAI for Crisis Management Application

The use case described in Section 2 is realized with the hybrid normative MAS deployed on top of a network of tangible tables to support mixed interactions.

---

[1] ε represents that the element is not present in the constitutive rule. The constitutive rule, in this case, determines a *freestanding assignment* [6,18]. When $t = \top$, the assignment does not depend on any event.

The environment on which agents interact corresponds thus to the events and states produced by the actions of human actors on the tables. Since the acting of the agents on the environment does not have per se any meaning in the crisis management, SAI constitutive rules enable to *institutionalize* facts occurring in the environment, and to give them the proper meaning in the particular application (e.g. the tangible B in the position (C, D) counts as a command to evacuate the downtown). Such institutionalization is important to the regulation of the scenario that is, ultimately, the regulation of the activities of the agents in the environment (Figure 1(b)). The Section 4.1 describes the relevant aspects of the environment in the proposed use case. The sections 4.2 to 4.4 explain how the SAI elements provide meaning to the tangible interactions enabling their regulation.

4.1   Crisis Management SAI Environment

The environment is composed of the whole set of (possibly distributed) tangible equipments involved in the application. From the SAI perspective, the agents are also part of the environment. In despite of the possible complexity of the environment, the relevant aspects here are the events occurring and the states holding on it.

Among all the events possibly occurring in the environment, the relevant ones here are (i) *checkin(AgentID, TableID)*, triggered when the agent *AgentID* checks into the table *TableID*, and (ii) *putTangible(TableID,TangiID,X,Y,AgentID)*, triggered when the agent *AgentID* puts a tangible *TangiID* on the coordinates (X, Y) of *TableID*.

The relevant environmental properties that compose the environmental state, provided by databases, GIS, etc, are (i) *nbInhabitants(ZoneID,X)* holding when the *ZoneID* has X inhabitants and (ii) *security_phase(ZoneID, Phase)* holding when the *ZoneID* is on security phase $Phase \in \{preventive, emergency\}$.

4.2   Crisis Management SAI Status Functions

The environmental dynamics described in the Section 4.1 animates the institutional dynamics when it gives rise to the constitution of the status functions. The specification of Section 4.5 specifies the relevant status functions in the presented use case, as follows:

- The **agent-status functions** define that agents act in the scenario as (i) *mayor* of the town, (ii) member of the CCP (*ccp_member*), (iii) member of the LC (*logistic_cell*) or (iv) *firefighter*.
- The **event-status functions** define that events occurring in the environment can mean in the institution (i) the ask to an *Evacuator* to evacuate a *Zone* (*ask_for_evacuation(Zone,Evacuator)*), and (ii) the evacuation of a *Zone* (*evacuate(Zone)*).

– The **state-status functions** define that the system can be in states where, from the institutional perspective, (*i*) a *Zone* is considered secure for security procedures (*secure(Zone)*), (ii) a *Zone* is insecure (*insecure(Zone)*), and (iii) a *Zone* is electrical risky (*electrical_risky(Zone)*).

4.3 Crisis Management SAI Constitutive Rules

As for the status functions, three sets of constitutive rules are considered:

- Agent Status Function Constitutive Rules. The rules 1 to 3 shown in the Section 4.5 specify that the agent-status functions of *mayor*, *logistic_cell*, and *firefighter* are constituted by the *Agent* that checks into the proper *Table* producing the event *checkin(Table,Agent)*. The *while* clause of the rule 1 still ensures that the status function of *mayor* is assigned only to a single agent at a time as it defines that the agent keeps carrying such status function while it is not assigned to another agent or while it is assigned to the *Agent* itself. The rule 4 states the agent carrying the status function of *mayor* carries also the status function of *ccp_member*.

- Event Status Function Constitutive Rules. The rules 5 to 7 shown in the Section 4.5 define that some tangible interactions mean, in the institution, the asking for an evacuation (rule 5) and the execution of an evacuation (rules 6 and 7). This meaning is conditioned to the tangible object used in the interaction and also to the *Actor* that performs the interaction.

- State Status Function Constitutive Rules. By the rule 8 shown in the Section 4.5, the property *security_phase(Zone,preventive)* holding in the environment counts as the *Zone* being secure for unprofessional people to deal with the security. By the first part of the *while* clause, such relation between environmental and institutional state holds while the *Zone* does not pose electrical risks. Besides, by the remainder part of the *while* clause, such relation holds when the *Zone* has, at most, 500 inhabitants or if it is already secure. Thus (i) if the property *security_phase(Zone,preventive)* starts to hold when the zone has more than 500 inhabitants, the zone is not considered secure and (ii) a zone remains secure even if its number of inhabitants changes exceeding the threshold. Notice that, if *security_phase(Zone,preventive)* does not hold in the environment, it cannot carry the status function *secure(Zone)*. The rules 9 and 10 define an *insecure* zone from the institutional perspective. The rule 11 defines what constitutes an electrical risky zone. The rule 11 specifies a *freestanding* assignment since there is not a concrete element in the environment to carry the status functions.

4.4 Crisis Management SAI Norms

The norms of the Section 4.5 define permissions, prohibitions and obligations related to the asking for evacuations and to the evacuations. Notice that the norms do not refer directly to the environment. Rather, they refer to status functions. For example, the norm 2 specifies when the agent carrying the status function of *mayor* is permitted to produce any event that means, in the institution, the ask for the *LC* perform an evacuation.

4.5 SAI Specification

The SAI specification for the proposed use case is shown below:

```
status_functions:
  agents: mayor, ccp_member, logistic_cell, firefighter.
  events: ask_for_evacuation(Zone,Evacuator), evacuate(Zone).
  states: secure(Zone), insecure(Zone), electric_risky(Zone).
norms:
  /*The mayor is prohibited to ask Logistic Cell to evacuate insecure zones*/
  1: insecure(Zone): mayor prohibited ask_for_evacuation(Zone,logistic_cell).
  /*The mayor is permitted to ask Logistic Cell to evacuate secure zones*/
  2: secure(Zone): mayor permitted ask_for_evacuation(Zone,logistic_cell).
  /*Firefighters are obliged to evacuate insecure zones*/
  3: insecure(Zone): firefighter obliged evacuate(Zone).
  /*Firefighters are prohibited to evacuate secure zones*/
  4: secure(Zone): firefighter prohibited evacuate(Zone).
constitutive_rules
               /*** Agent-Status Functions constitutive rules ***/
  /*Actors carry the status functions according to their check in the tables*/
  1: Agent count-as mayor
        when checkin(table_ccp,Agent) while not(Other is mayor)|Other==Agent.
  2: Agent count-as logistic_cell when checkin(table_logistic_cell,Agent).
  3: Agent count-as firefighter when checkin(table_fire_brigade,Agent).
  4: mayor count-as ccp_member.

               /*** Event-Status Functions constitutive rules ***/
  /*Mayor putting tangibleObject1 on (15,20) means the asking to the LC evacuate the downtown*/
  5: putTangible(_,tangibleObject1,15,20,Actor)
        count-as ask_for_evacuation(downtown,logistic_cell) while Actor is mayor.
  /*LC putting tangibleObject2 on (15,20) means the LC evacuating the downtown*/
  6: putTangible(_,tangibleObject2,15,20,Actor) count-as evacuate(downtown)
        while Actor is logistic_cell.
  /*FF putting tangibleObject3 on (15,20) means the FF evacuating the downtown*/
  7: putTangible(_,tangibleObject3,15,20,Actor) count-as evacuate(downtown)
        while Actor is firefighter.

               /*** State-Status Functions constitutive rules ***/
  /*A zone in preventive phase is secure if it does not poses electrical risks
    and if it has at most 500 inhabitants*/.
  8: security_phase(Zone,preventive) count-as secure(Zone)
        while not(electric_risky(Zone)) &
              ((nbInhabit(Zone,X)& X<=500) |
               (phase(Zone,preventive) is secure(Zone)))
  /*A zone in preventive phase is insecure if it poses electrical risks*/.
  9: security_phase(Zone,preventive) count-as insecure(Zone)
        while electric_risky(Zone).
  /*A zone in emergency phase insecure*/
  10: security_phase(Zone,emergency) count-as insecure(Zone).
  /*The downtown is electric risky if the firefighter puts the tangible tangibleObject4 on (15,20)*/
  11: count-as electric_risky(downtown)
        when putTangiNote(_,tangibleObject4,15,20,Actor) while Actor is firefighter.
```

5 Contributions of the SAI Regulation to Complex Crisis Management Issues

To illustrate SAI in practice in our crisis management application, we suppose a system composed of three tangible tables: *ccp*, *logistic_cell*, and *fire_brigade*, possibly remotely placed, used by the *CCP*, *LC*, and *FF* respectively. The regulation of the application follows the specification illustrated in Section 4.5, unless stated otherwise.

Human actors representing the *Mayor*, *LC*, and *FF* have checked in the system, carrying then the proper agent-status functions according to the constitutive rules 1 to 4. They collaborate over a zone containing 300 inhabitants. Upon start, they are in *preventive* phase. The following examples illustrate how the SAI allows situating the regulation in front of discrepancies in the constitutive rules, inconsistencies in the norms, environmental evolutions, or increase in the system autonomy.

5.1 Example 1: Changing the Constitutive Rules (Without Changing the Norms)

In the presented crisis management scenario, while different actors and organizations can have different views about the same institutional fact, they need to have the same interpretation for each situation to distribute efficiently their efforts. Suppose that, for the *Mayor*, a zone is *secure* whenever it is in preventive phase and its number of inhabitants is below a certain threshold. For the *FF*, conversely, a zone is *secure* whenever it is in preventive phase and posing no risk, such as an electrical one. That is to say, a *secure* zone is differently constituted in *Mayor* and *FF* perspectives:

```
/* Mayor's view */
security_phase(Zone,Phase) count-as secure(Zone)
while Zone is preventive & ((nbInhabit(Zone,X)& X<500) |
        (security_phase(Zone,Phase) is secure(Zone))).
/* Firefighters' view */
security_phase(Zone,Phase) count-as secure(Zone)
while not(electric_risky(Zone)) & Zone is preventive &
        (security_phase(Zone,Phase) is secure(Zone))).
```

In this example, as the *Mayor*'s and the *FF*'s conditions `nbInhabit(Zone, X)&` `X<500` and `not(electric_risky(Zone))` do not overlap, interpretation inconsistencies will occur, since one will consider the zone as *secure* and the other as the contrary. Consequently the same action can be considered permitted by an actor and prohibited by other (norms 1 and 2).[2] These inconsistencies can be solved by aggregating these two constitutive rules, generating the constitutive rule 8, that expresses the *institutional* conception of a *secure* zone, independent of the particular view from the actors about what a secure zone is.

5.2 Example 2: Changing the Norms (Without Changing the Constitutive Rules)

The contrary is also possible: norms can be changed without changing the constitutive rules. Consider for example norm 1. It states that the *Mayor* is prohibited to ask the *LC* to evacuate a *Zone* when it is *insecure*, which means for him: it is in emergency phase or there is some electrical risk or it has more than 500 inhabitants (constitutive rules 8 to 10). The institutional rules could evolve to consider electrical risk as the only condition prohibiting the mayor to command the evacuation. To reflect this evolution, the constitutive rules could remain as they are and the norm 1 can be changed to:

```
electric_risky(Zone): mayor prohibited ask_for_evacuation(Zone, logistic_cell).
```

---

[2] Note that there is not a conflict among the norms (there is not, for example, a same entity deeming an action as simultaneously permitted and prohibited [21]). The conflicts are in the interpretation of the conditions that change the normative state.

5.3   Example 3: Contextualize Evolution of the Active Norms

Norms can evolve automatically, depending on context. As already mentioned, in preventive phase, the *Mayor* is permitted to perform evacuation. When the phase changes to emergency, the *Mayor* becomes forbidden to perform evacuation and it is mandatory for the *FF* to do it. In preventive phase, the environmental property *security_phase(Zone, preventive)* always holds. If *Zone* is not electrical risky and has at most 500 inhabitants, then the status-function *secure(Zone)* is constituted by the constitutive rule 8. As a consequence, the norm 2 becomes active. When moving to emergency phase, the previous environmental property is modified to *security_phase(Zone, emergency)*. The status-function *secure(Zone)* is not constituted anymore. Thus, the norm 2 is deactivated while the norm 1 is activated.

As may be seen, by changing the context (*preventive* to *emergency*), even if the facts are interpreted with the same set of constitutive rules, the active norms will change.

5.4   Example 4: Increasing the System's Autonomy

As mentioned in Section 2, the system may change from a purely educative application, where human actors undertake all actions, to a more autonomous crisis monitoring one, where the system can be more autonomous and automatize some actions.

Suppose that the *Mayor* has been informed about a flood in a given zone. In this context, the *Mayor* is mandatory to realize the constitution of the event status function: "ask for evacuation in X,Y". In an educative context, the following constitutive rule would specify how the Mayor can undertake the required action through a tangible interaction:

```
putTangible(_,tangibleObject1,X_zone,Y_zone,Actor)
count-as ask_for_evacuation(Zone, logistic_cell) while Actor is mayor.
```

In a monitoring context, on the contrary, the task "ask for evacuation in X,Y" would be undertaken autonomously by the system if the constitutive rule is defined as follows:

```
get_information(flood, Zone, Agent)
count-as ask_for_evacuation(Zone, logistic_cell) while Agent is mayor.
```

6   Related Work and Discussions

This paper highlights the use of Situated Artificial Institution (SAI) within an hybrid, mixed, normative MAS to regulate human collaboration in crisis management. The proposed design draws on considerations from several research fields. We first of all rapidly recall the specificities of human collaboration in crisis management, and sketch some answers from the field of Computer Supported Collaborative Work (CSCW). We then show its relation to some major issues in distributed, situated and social cognition. We finally discuss the added value of normative multi-agent design, more specifically considering the field of Situated Artificial Institutions.

Crisis management is a complex collaborative activity where multiple actors and organizations participate, potentially distributed in time and space, with local perceptions, goals and policies that may diverge [14]. They must act and coordinate under degraded environment and critical constraints, with clear rules. The lack of mutual knowledge of these rules makes it difficult to ensure a consistent response of the rescue actors.

Current platforms often provide simple communication tools (e.g. Google Wave or Wiki) giving a response to contexts clearly defined and closely supervised. Their adaptation within a crisis management context is only possible for well-defined emergency routines and is not tolerant to exceptions [9]. In CSCW applied in this field [15], particular attention is paid on context awareness, with a focus on the policies that drive distributed work [17], on sharing a common physical environment [19]. Our proposal is based on shared physical environment and shared organizational norms. The used tangible environment supports flexible and opportunistic activity. Virtual feedbacks point out potential gaps or inconsistencies between policies, thus supporting *organizational* context awareness [20]. A hybrid, mixed and normative multi-agent approach is well suited to support such principles. We also have proposed several modelling spaces to cope with the physical dimension, namely production and communication, and the organizational dimension, namely coordination.

Among the different issues on norms applied to CSCW systems, such as normative design and reasoning [8,13,22], we deal with the grounding of the norms within the physical environment, bridging the gap between environmental elements and the semantics of the institution [1]. Such a institutional situatedness is addressed by some related work. In [5], it is proposed to relate environmental facts to the dynamics of the regulative elements rather than to the meaning of the institutional concepts. While it could allow to specify a tangible interaction as counting as, for example, a norm violation, it is not possible, as we do, to specify it as counting as an evacuation. Another proposal [3,4,16] is to address situatedness as a problem related to interoperability between environment and institution, however limited to interfaces to observe the environment informing the regulative elements about *what should happen* in the institution. A third approach, proposed in [1], in line with [11], relates environmental elements to the institutional concepts but not to the semantics of such concepts. In this case, for example, while it is possible to state that something in the environment counts as an *evacuation*, it is not clear if *evacuation* is an event, an agent, or something else. Compared to this approach, SAI provides institutional meaning to the environmental elements relating them also to the semantics of the norms.

As shown from the application examples, the proposed approach answers the 2 issues encountered when designing a tool for crisis management: clear coordination [7] but flexibility, that is necessary but may appear irreconcilable [9]. It allows more precisely to cope with a number of issues among which interpretation discrepancies, norm inconsistencies, context evolution and level of autonomy of the system. This is easily operated thanks to the existence of two distinct modelling levels [1], expressed in a declarative way, by means of modifications at the constitutive level, or at the norm level. More generally, the proposed modelling brings context adaptation to the normative processing, thus solving the flexibility-declarativity compromise: changes in the physical environment will rise the triggering of appropriate constitutive rules, which will in turn activate the corresponding norms.

Future work would involve modelling the full spaces of norms, considering the production and communication activities, thus leading to the design of situated hybrid normative-SMA for mixed interaction, in which situated organizational context awareness is the core.

Acknowledgments. The authors acknowledge the collaboration of members from IRMa (Institut des Risques Majeurs de Grenoble) and the support given by CAPES-PDSE 4926145, CNPq (grants 448462/2014-1 and 306301/2012-1) and ARC 6 Region Rhône-Alpes (ARC-13-009716-01).

References

1. Aldewereld, H., Napagao, S.Á., Dignum, F., Vázquez-Salceda, J.: Making norms concrete. In: van der Hoek, W., Kaminka, G.A., Lespérance, Y., Luck, M., Sen, S. (eds) AAMAS 2010, pp. 807–814 (2010)
2. Boella, G., van der Torre, L., Verhagen, H.: Introduction to the special issue on normative multiagent systems. Autonomous Agents and Multi-Agent Systems **17**(1), 1–10 (2008)
3. de Brito, M., Hübner, J.F., Bordini, R.H.: Programming institutional facts in multi-agent systems. In: Aldewereld, H., Sichman, J.S. (eds.) COIN 2012. LNCS, vol. 7756, pp. 158–173. Springer, Heidelberg (2013)
4. Campos, J., López-Sánchez, M., Rodríguez-Aguilar, J.A., Esteva, M.: Formalising situatedness and adaptation in electronic institutions. In: Hübner, J.F., Matson, E., Boissier, O., Dignum, V. (eds.) COIN 2008. LNCS, vol. 5428, pp. 126–139. Springer, Heidelberg (2009)
5. Dastani, M., van der Torre, L., Yorke-Smith, N.: Monitoring interaction in organisations. In: Aldewereld, H., Sichman, J.S. (eds.) COIN 2012. LNCS, vol. 7756, pp. 17–34. Springer, Heidelberg (2013)
6. de Brito, M., Hübner, J.F., Boissier, O.: A conceptual model for situated artificial institutions. In: Bulling, N., van der Torre, L., Villata, S., Jamroga, W., Vasconcelos, W. (eds.) CLIMA XV. LNCS, vol. 8624, pp. 35–51. Springer, Heidelberg (2014)
7. Dugdale, J., Bellamine-Ben Saoud, N., Pavard, B., Pallamin, N.: Simulation and emergency management. In: Van de Walle, B., Turoff, M., Hiltz, S.R. (eds.) Information Systems for Emergency Management. Advances in Management Information Systems 2010. Part IV. Systems Design and Technology (Chap. 10), vol. 16. M.E. Sharpe (2010)
8. Ferraris, C., Martel, C.: Regulation in groupware: the example of a collaborative drawing tool for young children. In: CRIWG 2000, pp. 119–127 (2000)

9. Franke, J., Charoy, F.: Design of a collaborative disaster response process management system. In: 9th International Conference on the Design of Cooperative Systems (2010)
10. Garbay, C., Badeig, F., Caelen, J.: Normative multi-agent approach to support collaborative work in distributed tangible environments. In: Poltrock, S.E., Simone, C., Grudin, J., Mark, G., Riedl, J. (eds.) CSCW 2012, pp. 83–86. ACM (2012)
11. Grossi, D., Aldewereld, H., Vázquez-Salceda, J., Dignum, F.: Ontological aspects of the implementation of norms in agent-based electronic institutions. Computational & Mathematical Organization Theory **12**(2–3), 251–275 (2006)
12. Kubicki, S., Lepreux, S., Kolski, C.: Rfid-driven situation awareness on tangisense, a table interacting with tangible objects. Personal and Ubiquitous Computing **16**(8), 1079–1094 (2012)
13. Oh, J., Meneguzzi, F., Sycara, K., Norman, T.J.: An agent architecture for prognostic reasoning assistance. In: IJCAI 2011, pp. 2513–2518. AAAI Press (2011)
14. Oomes, A.H.J.: Oragnization awareness in crisis management. In: ISCRAM (2004)
15. Pipek, V., Liu, S.B., Kerne, A.: Crisis informatics and collaboration: a brief introduction. CSCW **23**(4–6), 339–345 (2014)
16. Piunti, M., Boissier, O., Hübner, J.F., Ricci, A.: Embodied organizations: a unifying perspective in programming agents, organizations and environments. In: MALLOW 2010, CEUR, vol. 627 (2010)
17. Robert, J.M.: Cognition située, cognition distribuée et cognition socialement partagée. Cours (2012)
18. Searle, J.: Making the Social World: The Structure of Human Civilization. Oxford University Press (2009)
19. Shaer, O., Hornecker, E.: Tangible user interfaces: Past, present, and future directions. HCI **3**, 1–137 (2010)
20. Thévin, L., Badeig, F., Dugdale, J., Boissier, O., Garbay, C.: Un système multi-agent normatif pour la collaboration et l'interaction mixte. In: JFSMA 18, pp. 1–10 (2014)
21. Vasconcelos, W.W., Kollingbaum, M.J., Norman, T.J.: Normative conflict resolution in multi-agent systems. Autonomous Agents and Multi-Agent Systems **19**(2), 124–152 (2009)
22. Zhang, S., Gu, N., Yang, J.: An norm-driven state machine model for cscw systems. Expert Systems with Applications **31**(4), 800–807 (2006)

Trusting Information Sources Through Their Categories

Rino Falcone, Alessandro Sapienza$^{(\boxtimes)}$, and Cristiano Castelfranchi

ISTC-CNR of Rome, Rome, Italy
rino.falcone@istc.cnr.it

Abstract. In this paper we want to focus our attention on the importance of categories for trust in information sources (TIS). We analyze an interactive cognitive model for searching information in a world where each agent can be considered as belonging to a specific category. We also consider some kind of variability within the canonical categorial behavior and their consequent influence on the trustworthiness of provided information. The introduced interactive cognitive model also allows to evaluate the trustworthiness of a source both on the basis of its category and of the past direct experience with it, selecting the more adequate source with respect to the informative goals to achieve. We present some selected simulation scenarios together with the discussion of their more interesting results.

1   Trust and Information Sources

Starting from our previous works about the socio-cognitive trust model and its application to information sources [1,2,8,12], we want to focus on the importance of categories for information sources' trust evaluation. Many dimensions of Trust in Information Sources (TIS) are quite sophisticated, given the importance of information for human activity and cooperation. We will simplify and put aside several of them. First of all, we have to trust (more or less) the source (F) as competent and reliable in the domain of the specific information. Is F both competent and reliable? Is F sincere and honest?

These competence and reliability evaluations can derive from different reasons:

1. **Previous direct experience with F** (how F performed in previous interactions) on that specific information content, or better our "memory" about, and the adjustment that we have made of our evaluation of F in several interactions, and possible successes or failures relying on its information;
2. **Recommendations** (other individuals (Z) reporting their direct experience and evaluation about F) or **Reputation** (the shared general opinion of others about F) on that specific information content; [3,4,6,7];
3. **Categorization of F** (it is assumed that a source can be categorized and that this category is known), by exploiting inference and reasoning: *inheritance* from classes or groups where an agent (Z) is belonging (as a good "exemplar"); *analogy referred to agents*: Z is (as for that) like Y, if Y is good for, then Z too is good for; *analogy referred to tasks*: Z is good/reliable for task1 it should be good also for task2, since task1 and task2 are very similar.

© Springer International Publishing Switzerland 2015
Y. Demazeau et al. (Eds.): PAAMS 2015, LNAI 9086, pp. 80–92, 2015.
DOI: 10.1007/978-3-319-18944-4_7

On this basis it is possible to establish the competence/reliability of F on the specific information content [2,5].

Here we are not interested in presenting the trust model (already presented in [8,10,16]), but rather to emphasize the importance of categories' evaluation for TIS. For sake of simplicity and for focusing on this aspect, in this model we do not take into account recommendations and reputation.

1.1   Relevant Questions About the Categorization

We want to resume some relevant aspects about trusting categories [11,13,14,15]. We will make use both **categories for competence and categories for reliability**, and in particular we have chosen *taxi-driver, policeman, passer-by* and *shopkeeper* as categories for the competence dimension (agents belonging to these categories have common features of competence deriving from the same definition of these categories). We have also chosen three abstract reliability categories: reliability due to the *role* of the agent (for instance, a policeman -for role- has to be sincere and motivated about security information); reliability due to the *individuality* (a reliability feature due to the specific agent, independent from its category: this is a trait of personality); reliability due to the *culture of the environment* in which the agent is absorbed, due to the specific cultural environment that affects all the categories and the agents in that environment. Some features may be typically emerged as traits shared by (or influential on) the entire population. Think of some moral values, or prejudices or habits of a population or territory. An example could be about the difference in perception of the danger of street crime or of the role of women in society and so on.

There could be also **mixed categories**, not only because we have categories for both competence and reliability, but also because we should mix different categories of competence and of reliability: an agent might belong (and generally belongs) to more than one category.

We will also take into account a given **variability on trustworthy features of the agents belonging to the same categories**: are the agents belonging to the same category (for example all the policemen) equally trustworthy with respect to a specific information request? How much? To what extent this variability determines a stable or unstable trustworthiness for that category with respect that informative task?

2   Computational Model

2.1   General Setup

In order to realize our simulations, we exploited the software NetLogo [9].

The simulations were carried out using (except one case) 40 trustees and 1 trustor. In particular, we decided to classify trustees into 4 categories: shopkeepers (Sk); passers-by (Pb); taxi-drivers (Td); policemen (Pm).

As usual with categories, *agents belonging to them inherit with a certain regularity the features attributed to those categories*. In our case given a specific type of required information, the agents belonging to each category can perform differently, in terms of competence and reliability. The variability within each category is ruled by the uncertainty factors (both for competence and reliability). In other words, the agent's performance on a specific task mainly depends from the agent's category (both its category of competence and its category of reliability) and secondarily from the specific features of that agent (that express its variability within the category).

As later said (§3.5), it is also important to model not only the top-down link (inheritance) but also the reverse process: how the evaluated trustworthiness of a given member of a category bottom-up builds or affects our opinion on its category. We might have a given evaluation on categories by reputation, recommendation, or analogy, or higher categories; but we also build or adjust it on the basis of our direct experience; however direct experience is with individuals, as member of that category.

Each category will be characterized by:

- **competence**, in range [0,100];
- **uncertainty on competence**: we fixed this value on 20%;
- **reliability**, in range [0,100];
- **uncertainty on reliability**: we fixed this value on 20%;

The choice of fixing uncertainty to 20% is due to practical reasons. We are not interested in investigating this dimension in this work; according to that, we empirically chose a value able to give flexibility but also validity to categories.

As a consequence of these parameters, each trustee will be characterized by:

- **competence**, in range [0,100], derived from the value of the belonging category;
- **reliability**, in range [0,100], derived from the value of the belonging category, but also influenced by **individual_reliability** and **contextual/cultural atmosphere**;
- **individual_reliability**: given its category, a trustee could be more available than expected (+20% on reliability), neutral (no influence on reliability) or less available (-20% on reliability). This trait is expressed by a visual feature that the trustor can access: it is a perceivable feature of the trustee. We modeled it in NetLogo changing the image of the trustees: happy face, neutral face and sad face;
- **contextual/cultural atmosphere** of trustees: it is an additional parameter that influences the reliability of all the trustees in the same way; we suppose that the influence of this parameter is not fixed, but depends on the criticality required of the information.
- **own trustworthiness** (objtw), in range [0,100], given by the mean of competence and reliability; it represents the objective probability that, concerning a specific kind of required information, the trustee will communicate the right information;
- **past experience**: this value represents how the trustee performed with the trustor concerning a specific kind of required information; this value is obtained through the experience vector;
- **experience vector**: a vector in which the last performances of the trustee are stored; they are boolean values (as in our cases the information can just be true or false, the trustee can just confirm or deny it).
- **evaluation:** trustor's estimation of trustee's performance as fuzzy value. In particular we define the following fuzzy set: *terrible, poor, mediocre, good, excellent* (see figure 1).

For a full description of the computational model, we remand to [8,10]

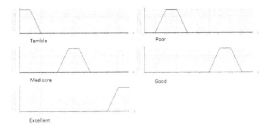

Fig. 1. Representation of the five fuzzy sets

2.2   Category's and Past Experience's Weights

According to the simplification of our model (see §1), we consider just "past experience" and "category/analogy" as dimensions for evaluating a trustee as information source. It is important to assign weights to these dimensions, to establish which of them is more relevant in different situations. In particular, **the past experience weight** depends just on time: it is increased of 1 unit every tick of the simulation, starting from 0 and arriving to a maximum value of 10. This models the fact that, the more the trustor experiences the world, the more its experience acquires importance. In any case if the experience is too old (more than 10 steps), then it will not have any role. Instead, **the category weight** depends on the mean value of uncertainty on the dimensions of each category (to whom the agent belong?): as for each dimension of each category we give an uncertainty of 20%, this weight is fixed to 8 (10 – 2).

2.3   Required Information

It is important to underline that in each simulation the information can be just true or false (and that the correct information is always the true one). Given this assumption, we defined **6** different types or categories of required information (they represent the different tasks to achieve by the trustees), **as of course the trustworthiness of categories and agents is strongly related to it**:

- **ask for x**: to this kind of request just one category of trustee will perform badly, all the others will perform properly;
- **ask for y**: to this kind of request just one category of trustee will perform properly, all the others will perform badly;
- **ask for z**: all the trustees will perform properly (an example could be "ask for hospital"); moreover, trustees are conditioned by cultural/moral factors on reliability;
- **ask for t**: trustees perform all in the same way regardless of the category to which they belong: 100% of trustworthiness and zero uncertainty;
- **ask for j**: to this kind of requests, the performances of the different categories present a variability of response with respect to each informative task less evident that in the previous cases (x and y) and, as a consequence, determine the various behaviors of the belonging trustees (examples could be "ask for street out of the neighborhood", "ask for parking area", "ask for shops' opening hours";);

- **ask for k:** this is a kind of information request in which is unpredictable the performance of the agents' categories, so that the trustor doesn't know how the trustees' categories will perform: it ignores the trustworthiness of all the categories about that specific request of information.

2.4   The Simulations Workflow

In every tick, the trustor moves around the world and meets a number of trustees. It asks about P (the information it needs) just to its neighbors (trustees with distance less than 3 NetLogo patches) and it evaluates them. For the evaluation we use two different approaches, comparing their performance: one uses just past experience; the second one exploits both past experience and category [8,10].

We use some different indexes to understand the result of the simulation:

1.   **Mean error of evaluation (MEV):** for each tick of the simulation, we compute the mean absolute error of neighbors evaluation. The MEV represents the mean of all mean absolute errors of neighbors' evaluation in time. It is computed with both the evaluation's algorithms described above; here is a formula to better explain this:

$$\frac{\sum_{j=1}^{T}\sum_{i=1}^{N_j}|objtw_i - eval_i|}{\sum_{j=1}^{T}N_j} \tag{1}$$

Where: $objtw_i$ is the objective trustworthiness of i-th trustee; $eval_i$ is the evaluation, according to the trustor of i-th trustee; T is the number of current ticks; N_j is the number of neighbors at tick j.

MEV (based on absolute error) is particularly useful to provide an estimation of how much the evaluation produced by the trustor differs from the effective objective trustworthiness of the trustee on average;

2.   **Mean error of evaluation for a given category:** it is the same of MEV, but here we consider just the contribute of a single category;

3.   **Success rate:** it is the percentage of success of a category given a kind of information request.

3   Simulations

3.1   First Simulation: The Relevance of the Memory's Length

We tried to reduce and to increase experience vector length, to understand the effect of this parameter. How does it influence the MEV? Can we identify the limits beyond which we are storing too little information or too many information?

We can say that we have:

- **a too short memory:** when the length of experience vector fails to shape properly the past experience of the trustee; in practice the cumulated experience of the trustee's behavior is not enough for well representing it.

- **a too long memory**: when it memorizes too many old experiences; it could include not more current behaviors of the trustee: this is the case in which the trustee's trustworthiness changes in time.
- **a right memory**: when it memorizes just the needed quantity of information: neither too much nor little; the information included in the experience vector is enough for both representing all of the trustee's behaviors and, at the same time, for taking account for changes of its trustworthiness.

For this simulation we set: 1)kind of information: "ask for street out of the neighborhood", of type "ask for j"[1]; 2)number of trustees: 10 for category; 3)number of ticks: 400;

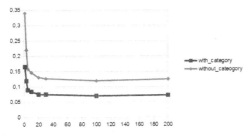

Fig. 2. Representation of MEV and MEV without category

We let the vector size assume the following values: 1, 3, 5, 10, 20, 30, 100, 200. Then for each case we computed MEV with and without category. The results are summarized in the picture below. As we can see, the error of evaluation reaches its maximal value when we set the vector size to 1, then it starts decreasing. Although we increase the length of the past experience vector, there is no improvement after a length value of 100: actually there is a worsening (due to statistical randomness into the model). It means that we reach the minimal error close to 100.

So far we have only considered situations in which the trustworthiness of trustees doesn't change in time. In these cases it is obvious that the more information on past experience I have, the more precise will be my evaluation. Let's now investigate the case in which the trustworthiness changes, considering three different vector size: 3, 10 and 100. We let the trustworthiness changes every 30, 100 and 300 ticks (we called it PTC, i.e. **period of the trustworthiness' change**).

For this simulation we set: 1) kind of information: "ask for street out of the neighborhood", of type "ask for j"[2]; 2)number of trustees: 10 for category; 3)number of ticks: 3000 (since we change trustworthiness, it is necessary to use more time to see its effects);

---

[1] Sk: competence= 30, availability = 30; Pb: competence= 40, availability = 50; Td: competence= 90, availability = 20; Pm: competence= 70, availability = 90; contextual/cultural atmosphere = 0;

[2] Sk: competence= 30, availability = 30; Pb: competence= 40, availability = 50; Td: competence= 90, availability = 20; Pm: competence= 70, availability = 90; contextual/cultural atmosphere = 0;

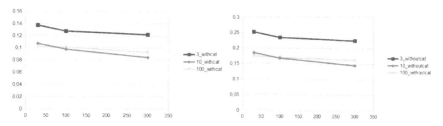

Fig. 3. Representation of MEV and MEV without category. The abscissa represents PTC, while the ordinate represents the MEV for vector sizes 3, 10 and 100.

We can clearly see that the MEV increases when the period decreases: the longer is the size of the vector, the greater is this decrement.

Let's then consider the case in which the trustworthiness gets as possible values just 100 and 0 (limit case). Suppose also that the trustworthiness changes every 30 ticks. We reported results in the following table, were VS stands for Vector Size.

Table 1. MEV and MEV without category when the trustworthiness changes every 30 ticks

	VS = 3 MEV with category	VS = 3 MEV without category	VS = 10 MEV with category	VS = 10 MEV without category	VS = 100 MEV with category	VS = 100 MEV without category
Average	0,1853	0,2992	0,2426	0,3974	0,2775	0,4524

We can clearly notice that in this limit case the shorter is the vector size, the better is the MEV. Then storing a lot of information could become a drawback!

3.2   Second Simulation: Trustworthiness of Mixed Categories

Here the trustor perceives all the agents as "passers-by", while they may also belong to another of the defined categories: trustees perform differently than expected.

We consider that the trustee's competence is the highest among the categories to which the trustee belongs (in fact it has both the competences, so it is natural to use the best one), while the reliability is the one in which the trustee is playing the role.

Let's suppose that trustee Y is a passer-by, but also a policeman. When the trustor asks for information to it (as a passer-by), its reliability will be the same of passers-by, because in that moment it is a passer-by and it will act accordingly. But it is not possible to state the same for its competence. If Y (for the kind of required information) has an higher competence as policeman that as passer-by, its competence will not decrease because of its current role. This is why for mixed categories we consider the competence always as the maximal between the originating ones.

In this scenario we investigate two points:

- what is the difference between a situation in which the trustor perfectly knows the categories of the trustees and the one in which it only perceives partially their categorization (case of the mixed and hidden categories)?
- Accordingly to the trustees' behavior, can the trustor cluster them? Can we rebuild the correlation between these new clusters and the mixed categories?

The setting for these simulations is: 1)kind of information: "ask for y"[3]; 2)number of trustees: 10 for category (mixed categories); 3)number of ticks: 400;

Table 2. Comparison between a simulation with mixed categories and one with normal categories

	MEV with category (mixed categories)	MEV without category (mixed categories)	MEV with category (normal categories)	MEV without category (normal categories)
Average	0,1039	0,1451	0,078	0,1368

We can clearly notice that the MEV is greater in the case of mixed categories, because the information about the behavior of the categories is not always correct. The "MEV without category" is quite the same in both cases, because here it is taken into account just the past experience, that shapes the real behavior of trustees.

Although the trustor sees the trustees as belonging to the same category, by the means of the clustering process it is possible to classify them on the basis of their behaviors. In fact we can clearly see that policemen emerge from the other trustees, having a higher competence on the chosen task.

Table 3. Results of the clustering process

	excellent	good	mediocre	poor	terrible
Pb and Sk	0	3,3%	23,7%	31%	0
Pb	0	6%	20,5%	31,5%	0
Pb and Pm	0	84,9%	34,7%	3,1%	0
Pb and Td	0	5,8%	21,3%	33,9%	0

3.3 Third Simulation: Convergence Speed of the Evaluation's Algorithms

We want to understand which of the two evaluation's algorithm (the one with category and past experience and the one just with past experience) performs better; in other words, which one can provide a better evaluation in the shortest time.

---

[3] Sk: competence= 10, availability = 80; Pb: competence= 10, availability = 50; Td: competence= 10, availability = 80; Pm: competence= 90, availability = 70; contextual/cultural atmosphere = 0;

Here the trustor evaluates the performance of the trustees it meets, memorizing the last three evaluations (here we are talking about the evaluation, not just the performance of the trustee, which only describes success or failure) both for the two evaluation's algorithms. We say that there is convergence with an algorithm on a given trustee when the last three evaluations computed with this algorithm are equal and correct. When there is convergence with one algorithm on a trustee, this trustee is marked, so that it won't be considered for the rest of the run and it is a +1 for the converging algorithm.

The setting for these simulations is: 1)kind of information: "ask for parking area", of type "ask for j"[4]; 2)number of trustees: 10 for category; 3)number of ticks: as many as needed for all trustees to converge.

Table 4. Performance of the two evaluation's algorithms

	Converged without category	Converged with category	Equally converged	Needed ticks
Average	1,7 4,25%	15,8 39,5%	22,5 56,25%	309,4

As expected, we have that the algorithm that exploits both category and past experience performs better than the other one. However there is a special case. Suppose that the categories are equally adequate with respect to the informative task (all good, or mediocre, or bad, and so on). What would happen?

The setting for these simulations is: 1)kind of information: "ask for t"[5]; 2) number of trustees: 10 for category; 3) number of ticks: as many as needed for all trustees to converge.

Table 5. V. Performance of the two evaluation's algorithms

	Converged without category	Converged with category	Equally converged	Needed ticks
Average	0	1 (2,5%)	39 (97,5%)	367,7

In this situation the two algorithm perform quite the same, meaning that the there is no reason to consider the categorical nature of the trustees. In our case this additional information on the trustees is free of cost but in general, one should take into account that accessing to this value could have a cost.

---

[4] Sk: competence= 50, availability = 50; Pb: competence= 50, availability = 50; Td: competence= 50, availability = 50; Pm: competence= 90, availability = 90; contextual/cultural atmosphere = 0;
[5] Sk: competence= 100, availability = 100; Pb: competence= 100, availability = 100; Td: competence= 100, availability = 100; Pm: competence= 100, availability = 100; contextual/cultural atmosphere = 0;

3.4   Fourth Simulation: Corrupted Categories

What if some of the trustees are not representative in the performance with respect to their category? In this simulation we introduce a percentage of 80% of false trustees (non representative of the category) which will have their own trustworthiness increased to 90% in a simulation or decreased to 10% in another simulation.

In a first step the trustor explores the world, making experience with other trustees. It will find good and bad trustees, dependently from the according or less with their categories' values. Then, in a second step, we introduce other new trustees never experienced before. Who will the trustor ask for the information? Will it choose new or old trustees? We made 10 runs (for each of the two simulations). For each run, after the first step, we verified the behavior of the trustor for 10 ticks, checking if it used an old or a new trustee as source of information and why. As reasonable, the result is that the trustor will mostly chose new trustees, in the case of negatively corrupted trustees, and old trustees, in the case of positively corrupted trustees.

We made two simulations, one for negative corrupted trustees and one for positive corrupted trustees. The setting for these simulations is: 1) kind of information: "ask for shops opening hours", of the type "ask for j"[6]; 2) number of trustees: 5 for category (first step); addition of 5 others (second step); 3) number of ticks: 200 for the first step, 200 for the second step. 4) Percentage of false negative/positive trustees: 80%

Table 6. Average of chosen trustees

Kind	New	Old	Why
negatively corrupted trustees	6,6	3,4	- The trustor chooses an old trustee just because it is surrounded by old trustees. - The trustor chooses an old false trustee that it has never experienced. - The trustor chooses an old experienced trustee as it is a good member of its category. - The trustor consciously chooses an old shopkeeper performing badly and seems reliable rather than a new trustee that has a low category value (taxi driver) and is unreliable. - The trustor (wrongly) chooses an old experienced trustee (a shopkeeper) because, even if the past experience is "poor", the evaluation of the category is "excellent".
positively corrupted trustees	1,6	8,4	- The trustor chooses a not experienced trustee given its high category value. - There is just a new trustee nearby. - The trustor chooses a new trustee because the old trustee, even if it is a good element of its category, had a low performance.

---

[6] Sk: competence= 90, availability = 90; Pb: competence= 50, availability = 50; Td: competence= 30, availability = 30; Pm: competence= 50, availability = 70; contextual/cultural atmosphere = 0;

3.5   Fifth Simulation: Trustees Without a Link with Categories

What if it's not possible to access to a category's evaluation? The request of a specific information is could be not directly linked with the categories. How can one deduce the trustworthiness of categories about a task from the bottom, exploiting the performance of each trustee (past experience)?

In this case the trustor asks a new kind of information, without knowing how categories will perform. In order to deduce the category's evaluation from the past experience, the trustor checks the performance of each trustee, computing the success rate (above defined) of each category. So we have that the categories' trustworthiness on these new informative tasks would emerge from the bottom of the interactions between trustor and trustees. The category's evaluation is just the fuzzy value of its success rate.

The setting for these simulations is: 1) kind of information: "ask for k"[7]; 2) number of trustees: 10 for category; 3) number of ticks: 400.

Table 7. Value assigned to categories on the basis of their success rate

	Sk success rate	Pb success rate	Td success rate	Pm success rate
Total	5 x terrible 5 x poor	6 x poor 4 x mediocre	10 x mediocre	10 x good

4   Conclusions

The purpose of this work was to show how the categorical aspect is particularly useful for trust in information sources. In fact, categories could both be designed in a top-down approach and emerge in a bottom-up approach through association of similar structural and functional features. So they represent a relevant guide to define the trustworthiness of the different sources under analysis with respect to the more or less specific informative task.

As showed in the simulations, it is possible to identify categories in both the trustworthy dimensions (competence and reliability); it is possible to exploit the knowledge about the multiple membership of the trustees to different categories; to evaluate the variability of the features of the agents belonging to these categories for understanding how the trustworthiness can change, and so on.

We have also compared the categorical approach to trust information sources with the direct experience with sources, presenting some interesting results and evidences.

Results in fact show that categories allow the trustor to evalutate even unmet trustees (no past experience) or in any case to improve the evaluation of the met ones.

---

[7] Sk: competence= 10, availability = 10; Pb: competence= 30, availability = 30; Td: competence= 50, availability = 50; Pm: competence= 70, availability = 70; contextual/cultural atmosphere = 10;

Acknowledgments. This work is partially supported both by the Project PRISMA (Piatta-foRme cloud Interoperabili per SMArt-government; Cod. PON04a2 A) funded by the Italian Program for Research and Innovation (Programma Operativo Nazionale Ricerca e Competiti-vità 2007-2013) and by the project CLARA—CLoud plAtform and smart underground imaging for natural Risk Assessment, funded by the Italian Ministry of Education, University and Research (MIUR-PON).

References

1. Castelfranchi, C., Falcone, R.: Trust Theory: A Socio-Cognitive and Computational Model. John Wiley and Sons, April 2010
2. Falcone, R., Piunti, M., Venanzi, M., Castelfranchi C.: From Manifesta to Krypta: The Relevance of Categories for Trusting Others. In: Falcone, R., Singh, M. (eds.) ACM Transaction on Intelligent Systems and Technology **4**(2), March 2013
3. Yolum, P., Singh, M.P.: Emergent properties of referral systems. In: Proceedings of the 2nd International Joint Conference on Autonomous Agents and MultiAgent Systems (AAMAS 2003) (2003)
4. Conte, R., Paolucci, M.: Reputation in artificial societies. Social beliefs for social order. Kluwer Academic Publishers, Boston (2002)
5. Burnett, C., Norman, T., Sycara, K.: Bootstrapping trust evaluations through stereotypes. In: Proceedings of the 9th International Conference on Autonomous Agents and Multiagent Systems (AAMAS 2010), pp. 241–248 (2010)
6. Sabater-Mir, J., Sierra, C.: Regret: a reputation model for gregarious societies. In: 4th Workshop on Deception and Fraud in Agent Societies, Montreal, Canada, pp. 61–70 (2001)
7. Jiang, S., Zhang, J., Ong, Y.S.: An evolutionary model for constructing robust trust networks. In: Proceedings of the 12th International Conference on Autonomous Agents and Multiagent Systems (AAMAS) (2013)
8. Castelfranchi, C., Falcone, R., Sapienza, A.: Information sources: Trust and meta-trust dimensions. In: CEUR Workshop Proceedings (2014)
9. Wilensky, U.: NetLogo. Center for Connected Learning and Computer-Based Modeling. Northwestern University, Evanston (1999). http://ccl.northwestern.edu/netlogo/
10. Sapienza, A., Falcone, R., Castelfranchi, C.: Trust on information sources: a theoretical and computational approach. In: Proceedings of the XV Workshop "Dagli Oggetti Agli Agenti" Catania, Italy, 25–26 September (2014)
11. Falcone, R., Castelfranchi, C.: Generalizing trust: inferencing trustworthiness from categories. In: Falcone, R., Barber, S.K., Sabater-Mir, J., Singh, M.P. (eds.) Trust 2008. LNCS (LNAI), vol. 5396, pp. 65–80. Springer, Heidelberg (2008)
12. Castelfranchi, C., Falcone, R., Pezzulo, G.: Trust in information sources as a source for trust: a fuzzy approach. In: Proceedings of the Second International Joint Conference on Autonomous Agents and Multiagent Systems (AAMAS-2003) Melbourne (Australia), pp. 89–96. ACM Press. 14–18 July 2003
13. Burnett, C., Norman, T.J., Sycara, K.: Stereotypical trust and bias in dynamic multiagent systems. ACM Transactions on Intelligent Systems and Technology (TIST) **4**(2), 26 (2013)

14. Fang, H., Zhang, J., Sensoy, M., Thalmann, N.M.: A generalized stereotypical trust model. In: Proceedings of the 11th International Conference on Trust, Security and Privacy in Computing and Communications (TrustCom), pp. 698–705 (2012)
15. Liu, X., Datta, A., Rzadca, K., Lim E.-P.: Stereotrust: a group based personalized trust model. In: Proceedings of the 18th ACM Conference on Information and Knowledge Management, pp. 7–16 (2009)
16. Falcone, R., Castelfranchi, C.: Trust and transitivity: how trust-transfer works. In: Pérez, J.B., Sánchez, M.A., Mathieu, P., Rodríguez, J.M., Adam, E., Ortega, A., Moreno, M.N., Navarro, E., Hirsch, B., Lopes-Cardoso, H., Julián, V. (eds.) Highlights on PAAMS. AISC, vol. 156, pp. 179–188. Springer, Heidelberg (2012)

AGADE Using Personal Preferences and World Knowledge to Model Agent Behaviour

Thomas Farrenkopf[1]([⊠]), Michael Guckert[1], and Neil Urquhart[2]

[1] KITE - Kompetenzzentrum für Informationstechnologie,
Technische Hochschule Mittelhessen, Giessen, Germany
{thomas.farrenkopf,michael.guckert}@mnd.thm.de
[2] School of Computing, Edinburgh Napier University, Edinburgh, Scotland
n.urquhart@napier.ac.uk

Abstract. BDI agents provide a common well established approach for building multi-agent simulations. In this paper we demonstrate how semantic technologies can be used to model agent behaviour. Beliefs, desires and intentions are mapped flexibly to corresponding OWL ontologies structured in layers. This reduces JAVA coding efforts significantly. Reasoning mechanisms and rule evaluation are used to compute agent behaviour by deriving an agent's actions from declaratively formulated rules. An agent's knowledge of its environment and its personal preferences can be expressed and human behaviour can be simulated. The approach is implemented in an integrated tool for running round based agent simulations (AGADE).

Keywords: Multi-agent system · BDI · OWL ontology · Market simulation · Human behaviour

1 Introduction

Multi-agent simulations are a powerful tool for the analysis of complex adaptive systems consisting of independent individuals [9]. These individuals are modelled as agents and their individual behaviour leads to emergent patterns of behaviour in the community of agents. Typical applications are market simulations and predictive investigations of organisational development.

AGADE (Agile Agent Development Environment) a tool for round-based multi-agent simulations where each agent is equipped with world knowledge coded in a layered ontology was developed at Technische Hochschule Mittelhessen. Moreover AGADE allows the specification of a social structure for the community of agents i.e. a sociogram. Agents can e.g. inhabit a community that follows rules of small world networks. Information about this structure is made available to the agents so that they may be aware of their position and their importance in their social environment. A modified version of the page rank algorithm [14] is used to calculate an influence matrix that quantifies mutual influence [7, pp.240–241]. Other social structures can be generated by the tool as well. AGADE is highly configurable and can be used to run different scenarios [7].

© Springer International Publishing Switzerland 2015
Y. Demazeau et al. (Eds.): PAAMS 2015, LNAI 9086, pp. 93–106, 2015.
DOI: 10.1007/978-3-319-18944-4_8

In this paper we address the principal approach of using OWL (Web Ontology Language) ontologies to model agent behaviour i.e. how to code an agent's knowledge and its preferences using OWL and SWRL (Semantic Web Rule Language) and how this corresponds to the BDI model. A major benefit of this approach is the reduction of programming efforts and a clearer separation of concerns in the overall simulation model. The approach is implemented in the tool AGADE mentioned above. Details will be discussed in this paper and examples and demonstrations will be presented.

2 Motivation

This research aims at building stronger connections between semantic technologies and multi-agent systems that can be used and reused flexibly for different scenarios. We demonstrate the use of semantic technologies for modelling realistic purchasing decisions of buyers in simulated market places. Such simulations may be used to enhance business games and potentially within business decision support systems. Thorough literature studies have shown that the idea of using ontologies is not entirely new but up to now these approaches have not lead to a really integrated solution. We refer to [7] for this discussion.

AGADE has been used to run simulations on a model of a mobile phone market where buyers often base their buying decision on social influence. Therefore the agents were modelled to follow the pattern of opinion leadership and the market development indeed developed as predicted and produced the expected statistics [7]. This was a proof of concept and now we aim at modelling more complex scenarios with a more heterogeneous structure of market participants. This presents the challenge of having to model different behavioural patterns into our agents. Besides varying problem solving patterns (How does the agent perform a buying decision?) we also have to model differing personal preferences (What are the agent's personal preferences concerning mobile phones?). This work can be simplified if we separate the agent's Java implementation from the definition of the behavioural patterns.

3 Agents and Ontologies

According to classical definitions an agent is an autonomous software entity which observes its environment, reacts to impulses (internal or external) and acts independently within a defined environment. External stimuli and available information are used to determine an agent's actions. Agents focus these actions on reaching given goals while following available plans. Newell and Simon [13] have already coined the term intelligent agent in 1972 for such an entity. A common paradigm for the development of intelligent agents is the so called BDI concept [5]. The acronym BDI represents three aspects that define the characteristics of an agent: beliefs, desires and intentions. A BDI agent has knowledge about its world (beliefs) and pursues goals (desires) while following given strategies (intentions). Therefore the agent belief base stores everything an agent knows (or believes to know) about the environment it lives and acts in. Here the things that exist and relations between these things can be specified i.e. domain knowledge is made available to the agent. In classical BDI implementations using frameworks like Jadex all aspects have to be coded in Java classes fitting into the hotspots of the framework [4]. While the basic flow of control is left in Java classes we shift certain aspects of the agent so that we can use declarative rule languages. This is described in detail in section 4.

Today we have widely standardised formalisms to represent knowledge in what we call ontologies and we will use the standardised techniques to model BDI agents. Formally an ontology $\mathcal{O}$ is a triple $(\mathcal{C}, \mathcal{R}, \mathcal{I})$ where $\mathcal{C}$ is a set of concepts, $\mathcal{R}$ a set of relations, and $\mathcal{I}$ a set of individuals. Concepts formally denote sets of individuals: sets of individuals are the extension of concepts while concepts are the intentional representation of the corresponding sets of individuals. An individual that belongs to a concept is called an instance of that concept. The elements of $\mathcal{R}$ are relations (also called roles or object properties) having subsets of $\mathcal{C}$ as domain and range. The extension of a role is then a set of pairs (c, d) with $c, d \in \mathcal{I}$. Additionally individuals can have data properties where they get linked to primitive data e.g. strings or numbers. Typically ontologies are formulated by means of description logics with differing levels of expressiveness [2]. Usually description logics are proper subsets of first order logic where typically expressiveness has been traded for decidability. Inference knowledge is implicitly given by the underlying reasoning mechanisms of the available reasoning instruments. Here we use OWL and SWRL both specified by W3C [11],[15]. The sets of beliefs (i.e. knowledge), desires (i.e. goals) and intentions (i.e. plans

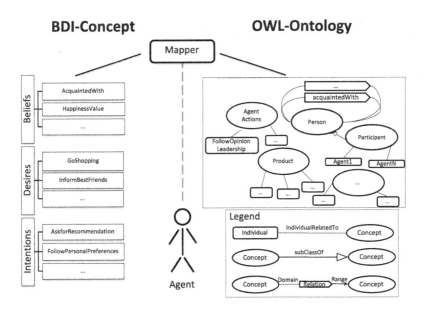

Fig. 1. OWL-BDI-Mapping

of how to reach the goals) of an agent are mapped into a layered OWL ontology. Desires and intentions correspond to OWL individuals of appropriate concepts and beliefs are represented by instantiations of relations (see Fig. 1). A *belief change listener* ensures that beliefs of an agent which are modified in Java operations that are part of the implementation will always be kept up-to-date in the ontology.

The ontology and its inference mechanisms are used to determine the behaviour of an agent e.g. rules are used to determine plans and calculate actions. Each agent has its own private ontology while we make sure that agents have a common understanding of the environment by providing commonly shared elements. We implement this using a layered approach we will discuss in the next section.

4   Layered Ontology

The development of a universally applicable integration of semantic technologies and agent based systems is still a challenge. Our idea is to achieve a blueprint for an architecture that can easily be adapted to various simulation scenarios. We propose a layered ontology (Fig. 2) where domain knowledge can be separated by its degree of generality. We distinguish between the abstract domain layer (ADL), the specific domain layer (SDL) and the individual domain layer (IDL). While ADL contains the most general knowledge elements, SDL can be used for more specific aspects. Individual knowledge is coded in IDL. ADL and SDL are shared by all agents leading to a common understanding of concepts, which realises an ontological commitment that enables communication among the agents. This approach leads to flexibility and a higher degree of reusability as at least ADL can be applied to a wide range of simulations of consumer product market places.

Considering the simulation of markets the abstract domain layer can describe general concepts, relations and individuals which are not restricted to a specific product market. SDL refines ADL by specialising abstract elements of ADL to fit the requirements of a specific market domain. The individuality of each agent

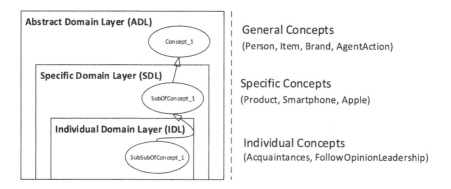

Fig. 2. Three-layer architecture

is expressed in IDL. It contains individual beliefs and definitions of individual behaviour of each agent (e.g. how an agent reacts to a certain stimulus). OWL allows ontologies to import other ontologies. We use this to import the general ontologies into the more specific ones. From a mathematical point of view the set of general concepts is a subset of the specific knowledge available to an agent.

The separation of knowledge into layers allows the general control of the simulation to be independent of specific terms of a given scenario. For example: creating a market simulation of a mobile phone market specific concepts and relations are modelled in SDL e.g. concepts like mobile phone, smartphone or touchphone. The individual aspects of an agent and how it in fact behaves in this market is expressed in the IDL e.g. that it follows opinion leadership.

This layered approach is mirrored into the Java application that implements the BDI concept. We developed an `AbstractOWLAgent` class that describes fundamental elements of an OWL-BDI agent that enable it to participate in AGADE simulations. References and methods to maintain ontologies and trigger plans are implemented here. We equip each agent with its own reasoner and private ontology which is accessed using the OWL API [10]. Subclasses of `AbstractOWLAgent` are on the level of SDL and specify more concrete aspects of an agent (see Fig. 3). Each subclass references an IDL which in turn is the key to the individual behaviour of an agent and describes the type of an agent as well. For example: AGADE has one general market participant class and distinguishes between seller or customer in the individual ontologies used in the prototypical mobile phone market implementation. All available agent actions of the specific market scenario (e.g. plans) have to be expressed as a member of the concept `AgentAction`. Specific plans are relevant for a specific scenario and therefore they are attributable to the SDL.

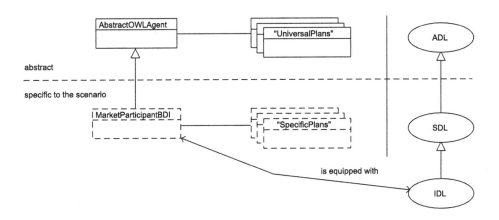

Fig. 3. Layered ontology and agent classes comparison

We decided to use a well established multi-agent framework as underlying technology because it does provide a set of convenience tools (logging, monitoring,...) and fully functioning BDI infrastructure. Jadex was the tool of choice because it is an easily available Java based solution that we achieved to seamlessly connect to the reasoning mechanisms of the ontologies and its reasoners.

In compliance with the Jadex framework possible individual actions have to be implemented as plans. This is done in the Java code that implements the agent. Plans in Jadex can be represented as methods inside the Java class that implements the agent or alternatively as plain Java classes which have to provide a so called plan body method. We recommend to code plans as Java classes to keep the agent behaviour pattern as flexible as possible, because plans written in Java classes can easily be made available to different agents by simply adding `@Plan` annotations to the specific agent class. AGADE can create *plan pools* out of available classes annotated as plans thus making them available in other simulations.

The Java classes annotated as plans find a corresponding member of concept `AgentAction` in the ontology. These links makes facts and rules of the ontology accessible to the agents. The object property `nextAgentAction` (with domain `Person` which is equivalent to the set of agents and range `AgentAction`) together with a rule determines how the agent decides which plan to chose next. The next agent actions are periodically triggered by the round based management of AGADE. Note that the ontology based belief base leads to a very flexible architecture, because important aspects of the agent do not have to be coded statically any more but may be expressed in the rules of the ontology.

Agent knowledge is limited to what is defined in the hierarchy of ontologies possibly differing from what other agents know. An agent may extend its knowledge base during a simulation meaning that it has learning capability. Agents communicate with other agents (e.g. they exchange information about product details) and this communication may refer to knowledge items that belong to the IDL layer. Therefore agents can exchange information which contains concepts that may be totally new for the receiving agent. The agent may then add new facts acquired through this information exchange into its belief base. When incorporating a new concept into its IDL the agent has to obtain all available information relating to that concept. SDL and ADL layers are shared among the agents so that a concept with a direct superclass in SDL or ADL can easily be added to the IDL of the learning agent. Otherwise, if the concept does not have direct ancestors in ADL or SDL the super classes of the sending agent must also be included. Individuals and facts (properties) about individuals can be added directly, if they are instances of a concept defined in ADL and SDL. But agents can also exchange definitions of concepts and information about individuals that are instances of concepts of an IDL. We currently expect that every concept in IDL is a subconcept of concepts in ADL – possibly transitively. This is ensured by a Java routine that performs validation checks on the ontologies. To summarise: Let o_1 and o_2 be individual ontologies. The intersection $o_1 \cap o_2$ is uncritical because it is obviously available to both agents. From the perspective of o_1 the set $o_2 \setminus o_1$ is critical, because it contains elements of $\mathcal{C}$, $\mathcal{R}$ or $\mathcal{I}$ which are relevant for the learning process.

For example: Each product p is represented as an instance of concept *Product*. Let the IDL of an agent a_1 contain product p and further assume that the IDL of agent a_2 does not contain p. If a_1 wants to communicate details of p to a_2 and p is totally new to a_2, the agent a_2 has to add p into its IDL. In this case the corresponding concept hierarchy will be added to the ontology of agent a_2 if necessary.

This learning capability has direct effects on the actions of agents e.g. their buying behaviour. The layered approach enables the learning capability possible described above.

5 Personal Preferences

In general market segments consist of buyers and sellers who demand and offer competing products. A customer will compare these products and try to rank them according to his personal preferences by considering characteristics of available products [3, pp.202-204]. This could possibly be retail prices or any technical features measured quantitatively e.g. camera resolution or battery life span of a mobile phone.

To enable multi criteria comparisons quantifiable attributes are normalised to percentages using the span between the highest and the lowest value that appears among the described products of one kind. For example: let the camera resolution values within a fictive mobile phone market segment range from a minimum value of 4.1 megapixels to a maximum of 20.7 (see Fig. 4). The normalised percentage value of a camera resolution of 15.9 megapixels is then calculated as follows: the actual difference between 15.9 and 4.1 ($15.9 - 4.1 = 11.8$) is divided by the difference between the maximum value of 20.7 and the minimum value of 4.1 ($20.7 - 4.1 = 16.6$): $\frac{11.8}{16.6} = 0.7108 \cdot 100 = 71,08\%$. With this percentage rate a camera resolution with 15.9 megapixels can be estimated to lie in the upper third quantile. But obviously consumers will base their buying decision not only on one attribute. Each consumer weighs different characteristics of a product with different importance. To take these individual preferences into account the criteria get weighted with weighting factors between 0 and 1 which sum up to 1. In our example we may weigh camera resolution with a factor of 0.3 leaving 0.7 for other attributes. The calculated percentage of 71.08 gets multiplied by the individual comparison factor of 0.3: $71.08 \cdot 0.3 \approx 21.33$. To summarise what we have just discussed: Let $a_1, ..., a_n$ be attributes of an object and p_i the corresponding calculated percentage values. The *weighted preference value* of that object is the sum $\sum_{i=1}^{N} w_i \cdot p_i$ where $\sum_{i=1}^{N} w_i = 1$. By definition it lies between 0 and 100.

These are personal preferences, therefore we implement them in the IDL of an agent. Personal preferences are an integral part of the decision process where one product is selected out of many. Another aspect of a buying plan we have to model is the acquisition of information that is input to the calculations of personal preferences.

A simple buying plan of an agent that follows personal preferences may consist of the following actions:

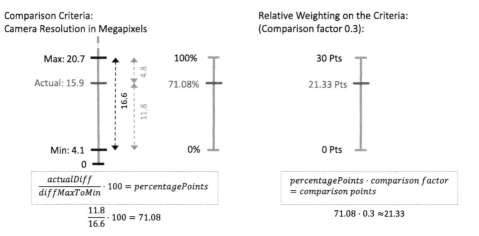

Fig. 4. Calculation of percentage points

1. select *persons* who own a phone
2. ask selected *persons* for all technical data of their phone
3. follow the personal preferences plan and determine the phone with the highest weighted preference value out of the set of phones collected in the step before and select it

In the following we show how such a buying plan can be expressed in the private ontology of an agent. Agents are represented as members of concept **Person** and everything that may be owned in some way or other by a person belongs to the concept **Item** . The properties **hasProduct, knows** and **hasAquaintanceValue** are elements of $\mathcal{R}$ with domain and range **Item** and **Person** respectively.

If an agent a_1 has a **knows** relation to another agent a_2 and a_2 **hasProduct** q and $q \in$ **Item** and q has attributes of a **Phone**, a_1 can conclude that a_2 is a person who owns something that is a phone. a_2 is classified as a member of concept **PersonWithItem** $\subset$ **Person** by using ontology reasoning techniques. Note that q does not have to be defined directly as a phone as the OWL reasoner will conclude this from the properties of q. If the IDL of an agent a does not contain a member of concept **Phone**, an information gathering process will be started. One way to get information about phones is picking agents from the direct social environment which belong to **PersonWithItem** and ask them for advice. As product comparison requires at least two items, information gathering is repeated until the agent knows at least two products. Alternatively agents can delegate a request to one of their neighbours i.e. all agents it is connected with or contact sellers (agents that are members of **Seller**) directly to get available products instead of asking other customers.

Data property relations are used for describing technical data of phones representing numerical values. SWRL math built-ins enable an OWL reasoner to perform mathematical operations and would be suitable for the calculation of personal preference values. However, the support of SWRL built-ins is limited.

Additionally built-ins may cause SWRL rules to become undecidable and therefore we implemented mathematical operations in Java and made them accessible for the ontology [8]. The mathematical operations are triggered by the rule evaluation process during the calculation of an agent's personal preferences. Relevant data will be retrieved from the agent's private ontology and gets updated immediately with the results calculated in Java (see Fig. 5).

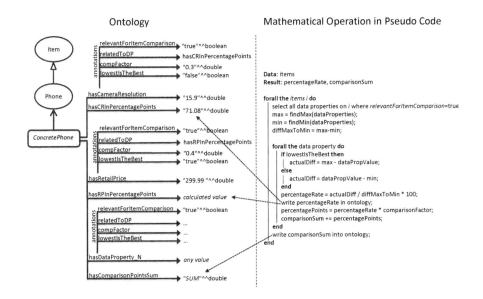

Fig. 5. Mathematical operations performed by a Java routine

The sum of each calculated comparison point is stored in a data property `hasComparisonPointsSum` related to the relevant item. The results are available to the reasoning process immediately. Mathematical operations are controlled by annotations in the ontology. Each element of the ontology can be annotated with instructions of how it will be handled during rule evaluation. In particular we designed *comparison annotations* which can be used to define how data properties will be evaluated during the calculation of personal preferences: `relevant-ForItemComparison`, `compFactor`, `relatedToDP` and `lowestIsTheBest`. They can be used for data properties of individuals of concept `Item`. While `relevant-ForItemComparison` carries a boolean value that indicates whether the property should be included in the calculation, `compFactor` contains the weighting factor. The `relatedToDP` annotation names another data property which stores the calculated percentage points. The `lowestIsTheBest` annotation changes the orientation of the comparisons: a lower value is considered better than a higher value. This applies to attributes as retail price or weight.

After the comparison process is finished, the agent is able to decide which item to buy. Additionally minimal requirements for a phone can be defined e.g.

the phone must have a battery life span that is as least as good as a given value. Such minimal requirements can be easily expressed with SWRL in the IDL layer as they do not require complicated calculations. Only those products which satisfy all given minimal requirements, are classified as members of the concept `ItemAccordingPreferences` and are then ranked according to personal preferences. If there is no item that matches the minimal requirements, the agent can search for further products by starting information gathering or alternatively reduce the minimal requirements. An example of a minimal requirement expressed with SWRL:

$$Phone(?x), double[>= 8.0](?y), hasCameraResolutionInMegapixels(?x, ?y)$$
$$\rightarrow ItemAccordingPreferences(?x)$$

Modelling personal preferences and including them in buying plans show how individual market behaviour can be expressed in an OWL ontology. The ontology is the main basis for the decision-making process of agents. Integration of Jadex agents and elements of the ontology is reached by use of annotations.

6   Results

After successfully simulating a homogeneous crowd of buyers acting in a mobile phone market [7, pp.245–247] where all agents follow a word of mouth decision process and depend on the advice of opinion leaders we modelled a more complex scenario where agents decide according to their personal preferences. Following different information acquisition plans e.g. *follow an expert* or *read test reports* the agents gather detailed information and use that as input to match the phones to their preferences. The agents inhabit a community that models social connections to fellow agents and to agents that represent phone sellers.

We collected data by running online surveys on a restricted group of persons (72 students and staff from Edinburgh Napier University). Among others the survey includes a quantitative analysis of the brand distribution, the brand loyalty of a person and the personal buying behaviour on which we will focus here. According to Holland we intentionally simplified our model by restricting it to a subset of available data [9, pp.45–46]. We aim at clarity and predictability by concentrating on a reduced set of facts.

Survey data is used to set comparison factors and minimal requirements for the products (see section 5). The question "Why did you choose this brand?" had seven possible answers, the following four were named the most often:

1. Decision based on test reports (34 persons)
2. Followed recommendation of friends and family (11 persons)
3. In-store consultation (3 persons)
4. Have many of my friends (socialisation) (2 persons)

Coming from a technically oriented organisation most of the participants used test reports as their main source of information. Test reports typically list all technical features of a product. We briefly describe the four behavioural patterns modelled. Details of the implementation were already discussed in section 5:

Table 1. Behavioural patterns

Buying behaviour	Description
Decision based on test reports	Every phone the agent is aware of is measured by personal preferences with respect to minimal requirements defined and the best is selected. If the agent does only know one phone or none it will gather information about phone models from every agent it is in social contact with and will apply personal preferences then.
Opinion Leadership	The agent will chose the phone that is possessed by the socially most important agent in its community (hub) (see [7])
In-store consultation	Some agents are modelled as phone sellers. An agent following this plan will contact a seller and apply personal preferences to each phone the seller recommends.
Have many of my friends	The agent will chose the phone that most of the agents he is socially connected to possess.

Mark that agents cannot take phone models from test reports as the simulation would converge very fast without influence of the environment. We consider social influence as very important and therefore the test reports are source of detail information only. Modelling these behavioural patterns and respective individual personal preferences resulted in 69 different IDLs. The survey in which participants were asked to order eight available attributes according to its subjective importance for them. The first four attributes were then weighted with the factors 0.4, 0.3, 0.2 and 0.1 meaning that only these four had an effect in the simulation. Non quantifiable factors cannot be used in the computation of the overall comparison factor and were therefore expressed as SWRL rules as the following that states that a phone should have an Android operating system:

$$Android(?y), Smartphone(?x), hasOperatingSystem(?x, ?y)$$
$$\rightarrow ItemAccordingPreferences(?x)$$

If non quantifiable attributes were found among the first four attributes in an individual ordering the weighting factors were shifted so that the highest quantifiable factor received the value 0.4.

The phones modelled were taken from a web portal hosted by a popular German computer magazine [6]. Each brand in the simulation is represented by the product that was ranked highest by that portal (one for each brand). Smartphones are distributed uniformly over all agents at the beginning of the simulation.

We assume that communities generally follow a small world like structure [1]. Therefore we use Barabási's preferential attachment algorithm with slightly modified standard parameterisation to create the social environment the agents live in. The simulation was started with a uniform distribution of 1005 agents (15 for each of the four different buying behaviours listed above).

According to the stimulus-response model [12, p.24] agents need a trigger to start the buying process. We model this by using a so called happiness factor.

It is a numerical value the agent tries to maximise. This factor deteriorates continuously over time. Falling below a given threshold the factor indicates a lack of happiness and the agent gets active following its plans trying to make amends by looking for a new phone.

Fig. 6 shows the brand distribution after a simulation of 100 rounds. While the x-axis describes the number of rounds the y-axis shows the number of phones for a point in time.

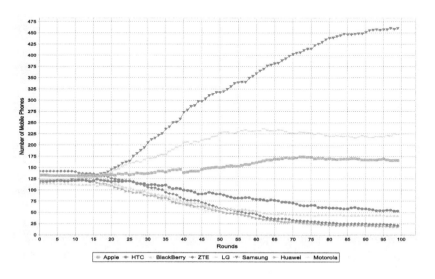

Fig. 6. Brand distribution chart after 100 rounds generated by AGADE

The simulation result and the survey data show significant similarities (Table 2 vs. 3). Looking at Apple, HTC, and LG differences can be observed. We see an explanation in the battery life span where there is a difference in the relevant models. 15 persons chose this attribute among the three most important criteria which caused a relatively high influence on the buying decision. As we simplified reality by only modelling one phone per brand we may have missed details that can cause this effect. Another aspect might be that an apparently rational buying decision based on facts and figures may mask rather subconscious elements of the decision that were not mentioned in the survey. Further research is necessary here.

All in all we have demonstrated that our approach can be calibrated to run realistic simulations on markets. Further research will be invested in even more elaborate behavioural patterns and alternative choices of attributes for the calculation of personal preferences to measure the sensitivity of the model.

Table 2. Brand distribution in survey   **Table 3.** Brand distribution after 100 rounds

Brand	Distribution
Apple	21.74%
BlackBerry	4.35%
HTC	10.14%
Huawei	1.45%
LG	13.04%
Motorola	5.80%
Samsung	40.58%
ZTE	2.90%

Brand	Distribution
Apple	16.52%
BlackBerry	4.28%
HTC	5.27%
Huawei	1.79%
LG	22.29%
Motorola	1.99%
Samsung	45.77%
ZTE	2.09%

7   Conclusion and Future Work

Using ontologies to model agents creates a new perspective for multi-agent simulation scenarios as programming details are reduced and the separation of modelling aspects from coding details is promising as scenarios can be set up with a reduced development effort. The ontology is used as a knowledge base and allows access to powerful standardised inference engines that offer leverage for the agents' decision processes. We define a three-layer ontology thus allowing agents to share knowledge and create a basic common understanding of their environment while enabling reuse of fundamental concepts. The generic approach will allow the simulation of different scenarios. We demonstrated buying behaviour as *personal preferences* can be modelled and how a heterogeneous community of buyers can be simulated with AGADE. The basic architecture with layered ontologies and its integration into the Java BDI application will be further elaborated and standardised. The degree of reuse that can be achieved will be investigated and formalised.

The simulation was run on a quad core CPU and 32GB RAM. We observed that the extensive use of ontologies results in a high memory consumption due to a large number of `String` objects used in the reasoning process and caching mechanisms of the OWL API. We can handle this issue by running simulations distributedly.

References

1. Albert, R., Barabási, A.L.: Statistical mechanics of complex networks. Reviews of Modern Physics **74**(1), 47–97 (2002)
2. Baader, F.: The description logic handbook: theory, implementation, and applications. Cambridge University Press (2003)
3. Baker, M.: The Marketing Book. Taylor & Francis (2012)
4. Bellifemine, F., Caire, G., Greenwood, D.P.A.: Developing Multi-Agent Systems with JADE. Wiley, Chichester (2007)
5. Bratman, M.: Intention, plans, and practical reason. Center for the Study of Language and Information, Stanford and Calif (1999)

6. Chip: Vergleich: Handys im Test. http://www.chip.de/bestenlisten/ Bestenliste-Handys-index/detail/id/900/ (Accessed, 10 January, 2015)
7. Farrenkopf, T., Guckert, M., Hoffmann, B., Urquhart, N.: AGADE. In: Müller, J.P., Weyrich, M., Bazzan, A.L.C. (eds.) MATES 2014. LNCS, vol. 8732, pp. 234–250. Springer, Heidelberg (2014)
8. Feng, Y., et al.: Discovering anomalies in semantic web rules. Secure System Integration and Reliability Improvement 33–42 (2010)
9. Holland, J.H.: Signals And Boundaries. MIT (2012)
10. Horridge, M., Bechhofer, S.: The owl api: A java api for owl ontologies. Semantic Web **2**(1), 11–21 (2011)
11. Horrocks, I., et al.: Semantic Web Rule Language (SWRL). W3C Member Submission (21 May 2004). http://www.w3.org/Submission/2004/ SUBM-SWRL-20040521/
12. Lantos, G.P.: Consumer Behavior in Action: Real-Life Applications for Marketing Managers. M. E. Sharpe Incorporated (2010)
13. Newell, A., Simon, H.A., et al.: Human problem solving, vol. 104. Prentice-Hall Englewood Cliffs, NJ (1972)
14. Page, L., Brin, S., Motwani, R., Winograd, T.: The pagerank citation ranking: Bringing order to the web (1999)
15. W3C OWL Working Group: OWL 2 Web Ontology Language: Document Overview. W3C Recommendation, 11 December 2012. http://www.w3.org/TR/ 2012/REC-owl2-overview-20121211/

Contextualize Agent Interactions by Combining Communication and Physical Dimensions in the Environment

Stéphane Galland[1][(✉)], Flavien Balbo[2], Nicolas Gaud[1], Sebastian Rodriguez[3], Gauthier Picard[2], and Olivier Boissier[2]

[1] IRTES Institute, Université de Technologie de Belfort-Montbéliard, Belfort, France
{stephane.galland,nicolas.gaud}@utbm.fr
[2] Ecole Nationale Supérieure des Mines, 158 Cours Fauriel,
42100 Saint-Etienne, France
{flavien.balbo,gauthier.picard,olivier.boissier}@mines-stetienne.fr
[3] GITIA Laboratory, Facultad Regional Tucumán,
Universidad Tecnológica Nacional, San Miguel de Tucumán, Argentina
sebastian.rodriguez@gitia.org

Abstract. The environment, as a space shared between agents, is a key component of multiagent systems (MAS). Depending on systems, this space may integrate physical, communication or communication dimensions. Each of them has its own process and rules to support agents' interaction. The dimensions of the environment are generally connected either outside of the agents or within each agent, according to the target application. In order to ensure a multiagent control, the relations between dimensions must be explicit outside of the agents. Using these relations between the environment dimensions, the interaction becomes also multi-dimensional. In this paper, rules and mechanisms to make this connection outside of the agents are formalized. The model connects the physical and communication dimensions to realize contextualized interactions. It is implemented using the SARL multiagent programming language, and illustrated with an urban traffic simulation.

Keywords: Environment modeling · Simulation · Programming languages for agents and multi-agent systems · Smart cities

1 Introduction

The environment, as a space shared between agents, is a key component of multi-agent systems [20]. Depending on systems, this space may integrate physical, communication or social dimensions where agents interact. Each dimension of the environment has its own process and rules to support its interaction model. For instance, in the physical dimension, the rules may be based on the location of the agents, i.e. the interaction between agents is allowed according to the distance or any existing obstacle between them. These rules are independent of the agents, i.e. even if it is initiated by the agents, the interaction occurs

© Springer International Publishing Switzerland 2015
Y. Demazeau et al. (Eds.): PAAMS 2015, LNAI 9086, pp. 107–119, 2015.
DOI: 10.1007/978-3-319-18944-4_9

independently of the decision process of the agents, and is performed by the environment. When the environment has several dimensions, the issue is to model and to manage the relations between them. In most systems, the dimensions are considered either independent and connected only through the decision process of the agents. Interactions resulting from the combinations of input information depend of the agent's decision process. The problem is that an agent should not be the place where interaction rules are triggered because the interaction could not rely on its own responsibility. For instance, a rule could be designed to regulate the communication in the social dimension according to information coming from the physical dimension (is the receiver agent physically able to receive the message?). The agent cannot decide by itself. This rule should be triggered by the environment using information coming from the physical and communication dimensions.

This multidimensional point of view on the environment opens new perspectives in the design of contextualized interactions. Interactions could be designed using information coming from different dimensions and interactions between agents are not only the result of the action of an agent in one dimension of the environment but also the potential propagation of the interaction through the other dimensions. For instance, a communication act (an agent sends a message to another) could be influenced by physic conditions. In this case, it may have two effects: an exchange of messages in the communication dimension of the environment, and the propagation of sound in the physical environment. The issue is related to the support in a single model the interaction inside a dimension and the relation between the dimensions. In this paper, a model for combining the communication and physical dimensions of the environment is proposed in order to contextualize interaction between agents. This model is implemented with the SARL[1] agent-oriented programming language that enables to define the different dimensions of the environment based on the same concepts.

This paper is organized as follows. Section 2 describes the services related to the environment and how the interaction is ported inside the dimensions of the environment. The illustrative traffic example is also introduced. Section 3 details the multidimensional model of the environment. Section 4 presents the SARL language, and the implementation key elements of our environment model. Section 5 presents the extension of the model for traffic management and simulation. Section 6 discusses our proposal according to related works. Section 7 concludes and gives perspectives.

2   Dimensions of the Environment

Several researches defined the environment and its role in the design of a multiagent system. Our work is based on the E4MAS[2] (Environment for multi-agent systems) definition of the environment: *The environment is a first-class*

---

[1] http://www.sarl.io
[2] https://distrinet.cs.kuleuven.be/events/e4mas/

abstraction that provides the surrounding conditions for agents to exist and that mediates both the interaction among agents and the access to resources.

Since this definition of the environment being not restrictive, heterogeneous implementations have been proposed. Real or simulated systems are based on a "physical environment" [1,5], where agents and objects have an explicit location and proceed actions that are located too. In these systems, interaction results from these actions. Other systems are based on a "communication environment" [9,17], where agents have a social knowledge about the others, and they interact following different modalities (direct, indirect or awareness). In this paper, the "physical environment" and "communication environment" are considered as two observable and accessible dimensions of the environment. Each of them structures the MAS according to specific models and/or implementations.

An issue is to ensure the management of all the dimensions, and their relations, in a normalized way in order to enable new contextualized interactions. The context is defined as *"any information that can be used to characterize the situation of an entity"* [3]. The design of the interaction based on the analysis of information coming from the different dimensions of the environment is at the heart of this paper: the articulation between the physical and communication dimensions for supporting contextualized interactions.

In order to illustrate our proposal and provide a *proof-of-concept*, a multi-agent traffic simulation, where vehicles are modeled as agents, is implemented (Figure 1). This application aims to reduce the traffic jams by enabling the vehicles to perceive earlier the traffic state through the communication dimension prior the physical dimension, and adapt their driving behaviors. Each vehicle agent communicates with the others and the infrastructure following a cooperative model

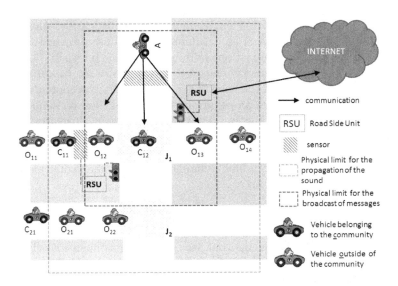

Fig. 1. Traffic simulation example

(V2X communication). Our example focuses on the following scenario: a vehicle requests the priority at junctions. The agent-agent and agent-infrastructure interactions are discussed.

The physical environment is a set of edges, with sensors giving the traffic density, and junctions. Some of these junctions are equipped with Road Side Units (RSU) controlling traffic signals and relaying messages from/to the Internet from/to the vehicles that are equipped with On Board Unit (OBU). The communication environment is composed by vehicles belonging to a community (noted C_x) and vehicles outside of the community (noted O_x). In this community, only emergency vehicles are allowed to request priority by messages and are equipped with a siren, whose sound is propagated following physical laws. The traffic regulation process is based on the dynamic computation of signal plans [2]. An RSU determines the axis with the priority based on the traffic density and existing priority requests. When an emergency vehicle requests the priority, it turns on its siren and sends a priority request at a regular interval. When an RSU receives a priority request, it modifies the traffic plan in order to give a green phase to the vehicle. Its request message, which is completed by an advice, is forwarded by the Internet to all vehicles belonging to the community. There are two junctions in the example. However, only the first, noted J_1, is regulated by an RSU (the second is noted J_2). In the simulation scenario, every vehicle agent slows down when it perceives the sound of a siren without any other information by communication. The agents in the community follow the advice given by the community. Only the vehicle A can request priority.

This simulation scenario illustrates the relations between the dimensions of the environment for interaction in addition of the agent-dimension — or agent-environment — interaction. In the scenario, three cases are considered. The **case a** illustrates when *the interaction in one dimension is constrained by the second*: Coming from the communication environment, the broadcast of the priority request is limited in the physical environment by the V2X propagation model and is extended in the communication environment by the Internet. The **case b** illustrates when *the same interaction has different forms in the two dimensions*: The interaction resulting from the need of the vehicle A has two potential forms: the siren and the message. The propagation of them and their consequences are distinct in each dimension of the environment. The **case c** illustrates when *an interaction initiated by an agent in a dimension generates an interaction in the other dimension*: The priority request in the community is taken into account by the RSU at junction J_1 to adapt dynamically the traffic signal plan in the physical dimension.

3   Environment Model Combining Dimensions

The environment contains elements that are related to its dimensions (Figure 2). Each of these dimensions is associated to a specific model that defines the structure and the dynamics of the environment elements in the dimension.

The physical dimension of the environment contains objects, including the agents' bodies [19]. It can be decomposed into areas, sub-area set, and so on,

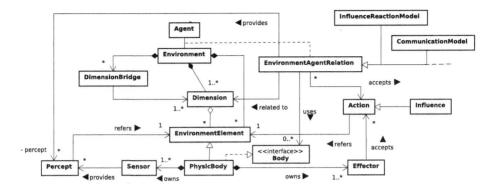

Fig. 2. Environment model combining dimensions, and its relation with the agents

which are connected together thanks to neighborhood links. The communication dimension may take different forms, as blackboard, sugar space, organizational models, etc. In our example, the communication dimension contains the representations of the community members. The underlying model provides the tools for exchanging messages through the Internet between the OBUs, and the OBUs and the RSUs.

It is basically assumed that a dynamic environment can change of state beyond the agents' control. Introducing the concept of dimension implies each dimension belongs its own dynamic process since it is based on the structure and the rules of the related dimension. For example, the RSU entities are part of the endogenous process of the physical dimension. They receive the priority requests and adapt dynamically the traffic signal plan according to the physical environment rules. In addition to the dynamic processes associated with the dimensions, the global behavior of the environment is considered for managing the interaction between the different dimensions.

Each dimension provides an interaction model for defining how agents are able to interact within this dimension. According to the classical definition of the agent, this model should permit the agent to perceive — provides `Percept` — and act — accept `Action` — in the environment dimension. The concrete definition of the interaction model depends on the dimension's model. A suitable concept to manage the interface between the agents and the physical environment is the agent *body*, *i.e.* a component that is attached to each agent for accessing to one dimension of the environment. A body has a collection of sensors and effectors since they are related to the intrinsic nature and structure of the environment. These sensors and effectors contain a collection of filtering mechanisms that permit to restrict the information that is provided to and received from the agents, respectively. In the example, each agent belonging to the community has two bodies: the vehicle for the physical dimension, and the avatar of the connected device on the Internet for the communication dimension.

For supporting joint actions of the agents in a dimension of the environment, the concept of `Action` is specialized to `Influence` according to the Influence-Reaction model [8]. An influence describes a desired change of the state of an

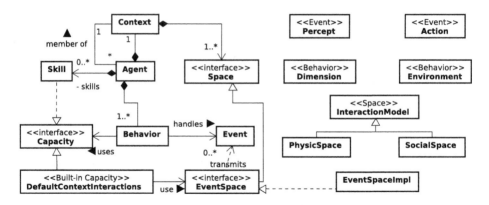

Fig. 3. Major concepts in the SARL metamodel

environment dimension. The influences are gathered by the dimension's model. Conflicts among them are detected and solved. And finally, the dimension model is reacting to the influences by applying the resulting state change.

4 Implementation with the SARL Language

SARL is a general-purpose agent-oriented programming language [15]. This language aims at providing the fundamental abstractions for dealing with concurrency, distribution, interaction, decentralization, reactivity, autonomy and dynamic reconfiguration. SARL provides a reduced set of key concepts that are considered as essential for implementing multi-agent systems: Agent, Space, Capacity and Skill.

Space is the abstraction to define *an interaction space between agents or between agents and their environment.* In the SARL toolkit, a concrete default space, which propagates events, called EventSpace (and its implementation Event-SpaceImpl), is proposed. *An **Agent** is an autonomous entity having a set of skills to realize the capacities it exhibits.* An agent has a set of built-in capacities considered essential to respect the commonly accepted competences of agents, like the autonomy, reactivity, pro-activity and social capacities. The agent has the capacity to incorporate behaviors that will determine its global conduct. *Behavior maps a collection of perceptions represented by Events to a sequence of Actions.* By default, the behaviors of an agent communicate using an event-driven approach. *An Event is the specification of some occurrence in a Space that may potentially trigger effects by a listener. A **Capacity** is the specification of a collection of actions.* This specification makes no assumptions about its implementation. It could be used to specify what an agent can do, what a behavior requires for its execution. Indeed, an action is a specification of a transformation of a part of the designed system or its environment. This transformation guarantees resulting properties if the system before the transformation satisfies a set of constraints. *A **Skill** is a possible implementation of a capacity fulfilling all the constraints of this specification.* Each of these generic concepts of the SARL's metamodel is associated to language statements. These statements are used for implementing the multidimensional environment model.

In order to interact in the physical dimension, agents must have a dedicated capacity. The script 1 describes the features that are accessible to an agent for all physical environments (`AbstractPhysicEnvironmentCapacity`) and more specifically for the environments related to traffic domain (`RoadEnvironmentCapacity`).

```
1  capacity AbstractPhysicEnvironmentCapacity {
2      def getLinearSpeed: double
3      def setPhysicalPerceptionAlterator(filter: PhysicalPerceptionAlterator)
4      def influence(inf: Influence)
5      def killBody
6  }
7  capacity RoadEnvironmentCapacity extends AbstractPhysicEnvironmentCapacity {
8      def getPosition: Pair<Edge,double>
9      def getOrientation: Direction
10 }
```

Script 1. Interaction capacity with physical Environment

The perception mechanism of the agents in the physical environment depends on the agent's body which contains a geometric description of the perception field. The agent can modify this description in order to alter the physical properties of its sensors (`PhysicalPerceptionAlterator`). When the set of perceptible objects has been computed, the agent receives it in a `Perception` event.

```
1  event Influence { var object: EnvironmentElement }
2  event MotionInfluence extends Influence {
3      var linearSpline: double
4      var linearShift: double
5      var path: Edge[]
6  }
7  event Siren extends Influence
8  event Perception { var objects: Percept[] }
```

Script 2. Events related to the physical environment

A space dedicated to the physical environment (`PhysicSpace` and `PhysicSpace-Impl`) allows creating an agent's body, to put it in the physical environment and to notify the corresponding model when there are influences related to the body (Script 3). For each described capacity, a concrete skill must be defined. This skill (`RoadPhysicSpace`) is used to bind the agent to its body in the physical dimension, and to serve as a gateway between the capacity functions and the space functions (Script 3).

```
1  space PhysicSpace {
2      def getBodyFactory: PhysicBodyFactory
3      def putInEnvironment(body: AgentBody, perceptionListener: Agent)
4      def influence(body: AgentBody, influences: Influence*)
5      def destroyBody(body: AgentBody)
6  }
7  class PhysicSpaceImpl extends EventSpaceImpl
8          implements PhysicSpace {
9      val env: Environment
10     def influence(body: AgentBody,influences: Influence*) {
11         for(i: influences) emit(i, new Scope(env))
12     }
13     ...
14 }
15 skill RoadEnvironmentSkill implements RoadEnvironmentCapacity {
16     var body : AgentBody
17     def install {
```

```
18          body = bodyFactory.newInstance
19          getSpace(PhysicSpace).putInEnvironment( body, owner)
20      }
21      def influence(inf: Influence) { getSpace(PhysicSpace).influence(body, inf)}
22      def uninstall { getSpace(PhysicSpace).destroyBody(body) }
23      ...
24  }
```

Script 3. Specification of the physical space

SARL enables to define a special type of space, called `Internet`, which gives a support to social interaction between agents.

The default interaction model proposed by the SARL language (`EventSpace` interface and its implementation `EventSpaceImpl`) uses events as support for the interaction: *a message becomes an event for agents that are receivers*. Then the communication environment can be defined as the specialization of an event space, and that ensures the link to the environment entity.

```
1   space InternetSpace {
2       def emit(e: Message, scope: Scope)
3       def register(agent: Agent): Address
4       def unregister(agentAddress: Address)
5   }
6   class InternetSpaceImpl extends EventSpaceImpl
7           implements InternetSpace {
8       val env: Environment
9       def emit(e: Message, scope: Scope) {
10          e.destination = scope
11          super.emit(e, new Scope(env))
12      }
13  }
```

Script 4. Internet space specification

Script 4 gives the definition of a communication space (`InternetSpace`) and a possible implementation (`InternetSpaceImpl`) based on the SARL tools. In the communication space, the agents communicate by message thanks to the capacity, and the skill described in Script 5.

```
1   event Message {
2       var destination: Scope
3   }
4   capacity InternetCapacity {
5       def emit(e: Message, scope: Scope=null)
6   }
7   skill InternetSkill implements InternetCapacity {
8       def install { getSpace(InternetSpace).register(owner) }
9       def emit(e: Message, scope: Scope=null) { getSpace(InternetSpace).emit(e, scope) }
10      def uninstall { getSpace(InternetSpace).unregister(owner)    }
11  }
```

Script 5. Internet interaction capacity

5   Model Extension for Traffic Simulation

The two dimensions of the environment presented above are supported and combined within a unique entity (`Environment`).

```
1   behavior Environment {
2       var roads : RoadNetwork
3       var physicSpace : Space
4       var communicationSpace : Space
5
6       var rules : List<Pair<
```

```
 7                    (Behavior, Event, Object) => boolean,
 8                    (Behavior, Event, Object) => boolean>>
 9
10       def applyRules(e: Event, o: Object) : boolean {
11           var propagate = true
12           for(pair: rules) {
13               if (pair.left.invoke(this, e, o)) {
14                       var p = pair.right.invoke(this, e, o)
15                       propagate = propagate && p }
16           }
17           return propagate
18       }
19       on Influence {
20           if (applyRules(occurrence, occurrence.object)) {
21               saveInfluenceForEvolve(occurrence)            }
22       }
23       on Message {
24           for(participant: communicationSpace.participants) {
25               if (occurrence.scope.matches(participant)) {
26                   if (applyRules(occurrence, participant)) {
27                       saveMessageFoEvolve(occurrence)
28                   } } }
29       }
30       on Initialize {
31           /* Rule for case a */
32           rules += [ env,e,o | e instanceof  PriorityRequestMessage] =>
33               [ env,e,o | e.scope = Scopes.addresses( env.roads.vehiclesAtDistance( e.
                    source, env.physicSpace.V2X_distance)) ]
34           /* Rule for case b */
35           rules += [ env,e,o | e instanceof Siren] =>
36               [ env,e,o | env.communicationSpace.emit( new PriorityRequestMessage(e.
                    source)) ]
37           rules += [ env,e,o | e instanceof PriorityRequestMessage] =>
38               [ env,e,o | env.physicSpace.influence(  new Siren(e.source)) ]
39           /* Rule for case c */
40           rules += [ env,e,o | e instanceof PriorityRequestMessage] =>
41               [ env,e,o | env.physicSpace.influence(new PriorityRequestInfluence(e.
                    source),Scopes.addresses(env.roads.rsuNear(e.source))
42                   true ]
43           /* Create spaces */
44           physicSpace = currentContext.createSpace(PhysicSpaceSpecification, UUID.random
                , this)
45           communicationSpace = currentContext.createSpace(InternetSpaceSpecification,
                UUID.random, this)
46           /* Create the model of the physical dimension */
47           roads = new RoadNetwork(physicSpace)
48       }
49  }
```

Script 6. Environment behavior

In Script 6 (line 6), the set of combination rules is defined by the attribute rules as a list of pairs, where the left members are the syntactical closures with the following parameters: (i) the abstraction related to each algorithm with a dynamic behavior, including agents; (ii) the event appearing in one of the dimensions of the environment; and (iii) the object related to the event. The syntactical closures are functions returning a Boolean value that is true if the predicate (the rule) can be triggered. The right members are the closures with the same formal parameters as the left member, processing the task related to the rule and returning the Boolean value true if the propagation of the influence or the message in original dimension is authorized.

The applyRules function, the on Influence and the on Message event handlers in Script 6 (lines 10–29) represent the application of rules resulting from the combination of different environments. This arbitration heuristic consists in triggered the first matching rule, and move this rule at the end of the list for giving a chance to be trigger to another rule. The handling functions for the Influence (line 19) and `Message` (line 23) catch the influences in the physical dimension and the messages in the communication dimensions for applying rules on them.

The script 6 (lines 32–42) gives the definition of the rules related to the cases a, b and c of our illustrative example (see Section 2). The SARL notation `[ parameters | statements ]` allows defining the syntactical closures associated with the rules. And the notation `p => f` defines a rule as a pair of a predicate p and a definition f of the state changes in the environment. Rule a (line 32) permits restricting the set of receivers — by setting the scope of the event — of every priority request message to the vehicles that are close to the source of the priority request in the physical dimension of the environment. In other words, when the message `PriorityRequestMessage` is received, its scope is set to the vehicles that are close — according to the V2X propagation distance — to the source vehicle in the physical dimension. Rules b (lines 35 and 37) correspond to an interaction that is shared between the two dimensions. The first (resp. second) rule for the case b permits to emit automatically the `PriorityRequestMessage` message (resp. `Siren` influence) in the communication (resp. physical) dimension when the agent has sent the `Siren` influence (resp. `PriorityRequestMessage` message) in the physical (resp. communication) dimension. Consequently, when an event was sent in a specific dimension, it is automatically sent in the other dimension without change of its content. The rule c (line 40) describes one example of an interaction in a dimension generates interaction in the other dimension.

In our example (illustrated by Figure 1), the regulation of the interactions between the dimensions of the environment following these rules influences the behavior of the agents. The agent A broadcast a priority request that is received by the agents O_{12}, O_{13} thanks to the rule a (line 32) even if they do not belong to the community. The agent C_{12} receives twice the message thanks to the rules a, and the Internet since he belongs to the community. Using the content of the message, the agent O_{12} adapts its behavior because it enters into the junction contrary to the agents O_{13} and C_{12}, who leave the junction. Thanks to the interaction model related to each dimension of the environment, the agent A interacts with other agents in each dimension. In the physical dimension, its siren is, for instance, perceived by the agents O_{22}, O_{14}. Without any other information, they slow down. It is the correct behavior for the agent O_{22} but not for the agent O_{14}. In the communication dimension, the agent C_{21} receives the message by the Internet and adapts its behavior following its position according to the junction and the advice given by the message.

In that way, it is possible to simulate complex situations like unexpected slowdowns and the related risks. For instance, the vehicle O_{14} slows while the vehicles C_{12} and O_{13} will not. Thanks to the rule c (line 40), the interaction in the communication dimension modifies the physical dimension with the modification of the traffic signal plan. The vehicle O_{11} will be stopped even if it receives no information coming from any dimensions of the environment.

6   Related Works

Our inspirations for the physical environment are the models for the simulation of crowds and traffic into virtual environments [5,18]. The Artifact [12], CArtAgO [14] and smart object [19] models are also an inspiration. They propose similar interaction models between agents and objects in the environment, and the definition of the latter.

The problems related to the interaction between an agent, and the physical environment have been treated with different perspectives. One of the models used in our approach is the Influence-Reaction model [8]. It supports the simultaneity of the actions in an environment by considering the interactions initiated by agents as uncertain, and detecting and resolving the conflicts between the interactions. This approach can be compared to the concept of artifact [13], which proposes to model the objects in the environment. They provide a set of actions that can be applied on each of them. A similar model named smart object is proposed for virtual environments [19]. This vision is supported by our model due to events such as Siren. The influences related to spatial travel (MotionInfluence) and those dedicated to trigger actions (Siren) are distinct for enabling a detailed specification of the parameters for each of them. The IODA model and its extension PADAWAN [10] allow modeling the interactions between the agents and the various dimensions of the environment by assuming that every entity is an agent. Our model is partially incompatible with this vision in the context of the physical dimension modeling. Indeed, the bodies of the agents are not agents.

In the communication environment models, the environment is a shared space in which agents drop off or withdraw filters that describe the context of their interactions, in order to manage their multiparty communications [1,17,21]. These filters are managed by the environment. The physical environment is not separated from the communication environment, and filters always involve an agent. Therefore, it is possible to treat the use case a, but not the other two cases explicitly.

Several organizational approaches consider the environment [4,6,11]. In the context of this paper, the key element is the introduction of the concept of space as an abstraction for organizational groups and spatial areas. However, these models do not explicitly propose to consider the physical and communication dimensions jointly, as well as their direct interactions.

7   Conclusion and Perspectives

In this paper, a model for the combination of the physical and communication dimensions of the environment is proposed. It enhances the modeling capabilities of the environment, and provides the tools to define more complex behaviors to agents. The two dimensions of the environment are defined with interaction spaces in the SARL agent-oriented language. These spaces can be considered as points of view on the environment that is combining the different dimensions.

The use of rules provides a general and adaptable tool for different classes of applications. Several concrete definitions of rules for the simulation of traffic are proposed. We think that the social dimension of the environment could be also supported by our model.

A perspective of our work is to relate, map and compare our model to other approaches for modeling the environment: artifacts [13], smart objects [19], holarchies [16], etc. The SARL language should be adapted for facilitating the definition and the description of the environment instances and their rules, like GAML has already done [7].

References

1. Badeig, F., Balbo, F., Pinson, S.: A contextual environment approach for multi-agent-based simulation. In: Filipe, J., Fred, A.L.N., Sharp, B. (eds.) ICAART 2010 - Proceedings of the International Conference on Agents and Artificial Intelligence, Vol. 2 - Agents, Valencia, Spain, pp. 212–217. INSTICC Press, 22–24 January 2010
2. Bhouri, N., Balbo, F., Pinson, S.: An agent-based computational approach for urban traffic regulation. Progress in AI **1**(2), 139–147 (2012)
3. Abowd, G.D., Dey, A.K.: Towards a better understanding of context and context-awareness. In: Gellersen, H.-W. (ed.) HUC 1999. LNCS, vol. 1707, p. 304. Springer, Heidelberg (1999)
4. Ferber, J., Michel, F., Baez, J.: AGRE: integrating environments with organizations. In: Weyns, D., Van Dyke Parunak, H., Michel, F. (eds.) E4MAS 2004. LNCS (LNAI), vol. 3374, pp. 48–56. Springer, Heidelberg (2005)
5. Galland, S., Gaud, N.: Holonic model of a virtual 3D indoor environment for crowd simulation. In: International Workshop on Environments for Multiagent Systems (E4MAS14). Springer, May 2014
6. Gouaïch, A., Michel, F.: Towards a unified view of the environment(s) within multi-agent systems. Informatica **29**(4), 423–432 (2005)
7. Grignard, A., Taillandier, P., Gaudou, B., Vo, D.A., Huynh, N.Q., Drogoul, A.: GAMA 1.6: advancing the art of complex agent-based modeling and simulation. In: Boella, G., Elkind, E., Savarimuthu, B.T.R., Dignum, F., Purvis, M.K. (eds.) PRIMA 2013. LNCS, vol. 8291, pp. 117–131. Springer, Heidelberg (2013)
8. Michel, F.: The IRM4S model: the influence/reaction principle for multiagent based simulation. In: Sixth International Joint Conference on Autonomous Agents and Multiagent Systems (AAMAS07). ACM, May 2007
9. Odell, J.J., Van Dyke Parunak, H., Fleischer, M., Brueckner, S.A.: Modeling agents and their environment. In: Giunchiglia, F., Odell, J.J., Weiss, G. (eds.) AOSE 2002. LNCS, vol. 2585, pp. 16–31. Springer, Heidelberg (2003)
10. Picault, S., Mathieu, P., Kubera, Y.: PADAWAN, un modèle multi-échelles pour la simulation orientée interactions. In: JFSMA, pp. 193–202. Cépaduès (2010)
11. Piunti, M., Ricci, A., Boissier, O., Hübner, J.: Embodying organisations in multi-agent work environments. In: IEEE/WIC/ACM Int. Conf. on Web Intelligence and Intelligent Agent Technology (WI-IAT 2009), Milan, Italy (2009)
12. Ricci, A., Omicini, A., Denti, E.: Activity theory as a framework for MAS coordination. In: Petta, P., Tolksdorf, R., Zambonelli, F. (eds.) ESAW 2002. LNCS (LNAI), vol. 2577, pp. 96–110. Springer, Heidelberg (2003)

13. Ricci, A., Viroli, M., Omicini, A.: Programming MAS with artifacts. In: Bordini, R.H., Dastani, M., Dix, J., El Fallah Seghrouchni, A. (eds.) PROMAS 2005. LNCS (LNAI), vol. 3862, pp. 206–221. Springer, Heidelberg (2006)

14. Ricci, A., Viroli, M., Omicini, A.: CArtAgO: a framework for prototyping artifact-based environments in MAS. In: Weyns, D., Van Dyke Parunak, H., Michel, F. (eds.) E4MAS 2006. LNCS (LNAI), vol. 4389, pp. 67–86. Springer, Heidelberg (2007)

15. Tejchman, J., Kozicki, J.: General. In: Tejchman, J., Kozicki, J. (eds.) Experimental and Theoretical Investigations of Steel-Fibrous Concrete. SSGG, vol. 3, pp. 3–26. Springer, Heidelberg (2010)

16. Rodriguez, S., Hilaire, V., Gaud, N., Galland, S., Koukam, A.: Holonic multi-agent systems, chapter 11. In: di Marzo Serugendo, G., Gleizes, M.P., Karageorgos, A. (eds.) Self-Organising Software From Natural to Artificial Adaptation - Natural Computing, pp. 251–279. Springer, Heidelberg (2011)

17. Saunier, J., Balbo, F., Pinson, S.: A formal model of communication and context awareness in multiagent systems. Journal of Logic, Language and Information, 1–29 (2014)

18. Tamminga, G., Knoppers, P., van Lint, H.: Open traffic: a toolbox for traffic research. In: 3nd International Workshop on Agent-based Mobility, Traffic and Transportation Models, Methodologies and Applications (ABMTRANS14). Springer, June 2014

19. Thalmann, D., Musse, S.R.: Crowd simulation. Springer, London (2007)

20. Weyns, D., Omicini, A., Odell, J.: Environment as a first-class abstraction in multi-agent systems. Autonomous Agents and Multi-Agent Systems. Special Issue on Environments for Multi-agent Systems **14**(1), 5–30 (2007)

21. Zargayouna, M., Balbo, F., Haddad, S.: Data driven language for agents secure interaction. In: Dastani, M., El Fallah Segrouchni, A., Leite, J., Torroni, P. (eds.) LADS 2009. LNCS, vol. 6039, pp. 72–91. Springer, Heidelberg (2010)

"1-N" Leader-Follower Formation Control of Multiple Agents Based on Bearing-Only Observation

Qing Han[1], Tiancheng Li[1(✉)], Shudong Sun[1],
Gabriel Villarrubia[2], and Fernando de la Prieta[2]

[1] School of Mech. Eng., Northwestern Polytechnical University, Xi'an 710072, China
`{hanqing,t.c.li}@mail.nwpu.edu.cn`
[2] Faculty of Science, University of Salamanca, 37008, Salamanca, Spain
`{gvg,fer}@usal.es`

Abstract. A formation control method is proposed for multiple agents of "1" leader and "N" follower where the following N-agents (as called followers) can only observe the bearing information of the leading 1-agent (as called the leader). It is proven that bearing-only observation meets the observability condition required for the "1-N" leader-follower formation system. The unscented Kalman filter is employed to estimate the relative position of the leader, based on which the input-output feedback control law is executed to control the real-time movement of the followers so that the "1-N" leader-followers formation is properly maintained. Simulation results demonstrate the effectiveness of our approach.

Keywords: Multi-agent system · Formation control · Unscented Kalman filter

1 Introduction

Multi-agent systems have matured during the last decade and many effective applications have been deployed in terms of both software and hardware (Carrascosa et al. 2008, Zato et al. 2012). This papers concerns on the formation control of multi-agent of the "1-N" structure where several following agents (as called followers) are self-controlled to follow a leading agent (leader) based on the bearing-only observation from the followers to the leader. That is, the motion of the leader defines the desired motion, while the followers are controlled to follow it. This is particularly related to the multi-robot formation, which is of high interest to underwater or outer space exploration, shop floor transportation, guarding, escorting, and patrolling missions. A variety of formation control methods have been proposed, such as virtual structure approach (Ren et al. 2004), leader-follower approach (Sun et al. 2012; Chen et al. 2009; Shao et al. 2007; Consolini et al. 2008; Cristescu et al. 2012), artificial potential (Kwon 2012), graph theory (Sharma et al. 2012). Among them, the leader-follower formation that consists of "1" leader and "N" followers has been mostly used owing to its universality, scalability and reliability.

The formation control becomes challenging when the observation information between agents is poor. Most of the existing leader-follower approaches as mentioned use both distance and bearing observation. However, in many real-life situations,

© Springer International Publishing Switzerland 2015
Y. Demazeau et al. (Eds.): PAAMS 2015, LNAI 9086, pp. 120–130, 2015.
DOI: 10.1007/978-3-319-18944-4_10

available observations might be only the bearing information, namely bearing-only formation control, which will pose a great challenge to the formation control. This challenging albeit important problem has been executed in Moshtagh et al. (2008), Basiri et al. (2010), Bishop (2011a, 2011b) and Eren (2012) based on special requirements on the number of agents or the form of the formation. A distributed control law is used in Franchi et al. (2012) and Zhao et al. (2014a) to stabilize the formations, based on which angle constraint is further considered in Zhao et al. (2014b). In Mariottini et al. (2009), the observability condition for position estimation by using bearing-only observations is estiblished. In order to utilize the feedback control law, an "off-the-axis" point has to be constructed in Mariottini et al. (2009), Morbidi et al. (2010) and Das et al. (2002). Differently, our approach will rely on neither special requirement for the form of the formation and nor off-the-axis point.

In particular, position estimation of each agent is critical to generate the real time form information that is required to control the movement of the follower. Estimation algorithms available include the extended Kalman filter (EKF) (Mariottini et al. 2009), the extended information filter (EIF) (Sharma et al.2013), the particle filter (PF) (Li et al. 2010) and maximum a posteriori (MAP) (Nerurkaret al. 2009). Most of them except the PF are not well qualified to deal with highly nonlinear systems while the PF is very computationally intensive. In contrast, the UKF sits between them, which handles nonlinearities with higher accuracy than the EKF and requires lesser computational requirement than the PF.

The contribution of this paper is two-fold. Firstly, the observability of the "1-N" multi-agent formation is studied based on the rank of the observability matrix (Section 2). Secondly, an UKF based on bearing-only observations is designed for the state estimation of multi-agents, rendering real-time and reliable movement control of the followers via the input-output feedback control law (Section 3) which gets rid of off-the-axis points. Properly designed simulations are given (Section 4) to demonstrate the validity of our approach. We offer our conclusions (Section 5).

2   Problem Statement and Observability Analysis

2.1   Problem Statement

This section will formulate the "1-N" bearing-only observation model and give the notations used. As shown in Fig. 1, R_1 represents the leader while R_2 is a follower (for simplicity, we only show one here). The control inputs for agents are linear and

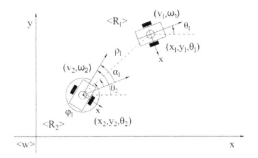

Fig. 1. 1-1 Leader-Follower coordinate definition

angular velocities $[v_i, w_i], i = 1,2, ..., \rho_i$ is the distance from the centroid of the leader to the centroid of the follower. φ_i is the view-angle from the y-axis of the follower to the centroid of the leader-robot. θ_i and θ_j are the orientations of the leader and the follower with respect to the world frame $\langle W \rangle$, respectively, while α_i is the relative orientation between the leader and the follower robot, i.e., $\alpha_i \triangleq \theta_i - \theta_j$.

With reference to Fig. 1, the kinematic model of a 1-1(one leader and one follower) formation can be expressed as follows

$$S_n : \begin{cases} \dot{s} = f(s,u) = F(s)U \\ y = h(s) = \left[h_1^T(s) \right]^T = \left[\varphi_1 \quad \alpha_1 \right]^T \end{cases} \tag{1}$$

where state vector $\mathbf{s} \triangleq [s_1^T]^T$, $s_1 \triangleq [\rho_1 \ \varphi_1 \ \alpha_1]^T$, $\delta_1 = \varphi_1 + \alpha_1$, input vector $\mathbf{u} \triangleq [v_1 \ w_1 \ v_2 \ w_2]^T$, output vector $\mathbf{y} = h(s) = [h_1^T]^T$, $h_1 \triangleq [\varphi_1 \ \alpha_1]^T$ and

$$F(s) = \begin{bmatrix} \cos \delta_1 & 0 & -\cos \varphi_1 & 0 \\ -\sin \delta_1 / \rho_1 & 0 & \sin \varphi_1 / \rho_1 & -1 \\ 0 & 1 & 0 & -1 \end{bmatrix}.$$

The kinematic model of the "1-N" (one leader and n follower) formation can be readily retrieved as an extension of (1),

$$S_n : \begin{cases} \dot{s} = f(s,u) = \left[f_1^T \left(s_1, u_1 \right), \quad \cdots \quad f_{n+1}^T \left(s_n, u_{n+1} \right) \right]^T \\ y = h(s) = \left[h_1^T(s_1), \quad \cdots \quad h_n^T(s_n) \right] \end{cases} \tag{2}$$

where $s = [s_1^T, s_2^T, \cdots, s_n^T]^T \in \mathbb{R}^{3n}$, $U = [u_1^T, u_2^T, \cdots, u_{n+1}^T]^T \in \mathbb{R}^{2(n+1)}, h : \mathbb{R}^{2n} \longmapsto \mathbb{R}^{2n}$, and $f : \mathbb{R}^{3(n+1)} \times \Lambda \longmapsto \mathbb{R}^{3(n+1)}$.

To make the formation control problem solvable, the system must be observable. The system is defined to be observable only if the system output convey an information that is sufficient to allow the follower to obtain correct estimates of the position of the leader; otherwise, the system is not observable. In the following, we will analysis the observability of the "1-N" leader-followers system based on the nonlinear observability rank criteria that is developed in Hermann et al. (1977).

The observability matrix of (2) is defined as

$$M = \left[\nabla L_{f_{v_i}, \cdots, f_{v_j}, f_{a_i}, \cdots f_{a_j}}^p h_k(s) \right] \tag{3}$$

where $i = 1, k = 1, \cdots, n, j=2, \cdots, n+1, p \in \mathbb{N}$, ∇ represents the gradient operator.

Lemma 1: System S_n is (locally weakly) observable if its observability matrix M whose rows are given in (3) has full rank (Hermann et al. 1977), e.g., in our case rank$(M) = 3n$, n refers to the number of followers. `

2.2   Bearing-Only Observability

We analysis the observability based on Lemma 1. For simplicity, we only analysis the 1-1 system of one leader and one follower. This result is readily extendable to the parallel "1-N" system of one leader and multiple followers, since each follower is independent to each other. The function $f(\cdot)$ can be separated into a summation of independent functions in the special case, and each one excited by a different component of the control input vector, (1) can be restated as follows

$$S_n : \begin{cases} \dot{s} = f(s,u) = f_{v_1} v_1 + f_{w_1} \omega_1 + f_{v_2} v_2 + f_{w_2} \omega_2 \\ y = h(s) = \left[h_1^T(s) \right]^T = \left[\varphi_1 \quad \alpha_1 \right]^T \end{cases} \tag{4}$$

where,

$$f_{v_1} = [\cos\delta_1 \quad -\sin\delta_1 / \rho_1 \quad 0]^T \tag{5}$$

$$f_{\omega_1} = [0 \quad 0 \quad 1]^T \tag{6}$$

$$f_{v_2} = [-\cos\varphi_1 \quad \sin\varphi_1 / \rho_1 \quad 0]^T \tag{7}$$

$$f_{\omega_2} = [0 \quad -1 \quad -1]^T \tag{8}$$

Proposition 2 given in Morbidi et al. (2010) indicates that the gradients of the Lie derivatives of $h(s)$ are equal to the same order gradients of the time derivatives of $h(s)$ from. That is, the zeroth-order Lie derivative is:

$$L^0 h_1(s) = h_1(s) = [\varphi_1 \quad \alpha_1]^T \tag{9}$$

and gradient is,

$$\nabla L^0 h_1(s) = \begin{bmatrix} 0 & 1 & 0 \\ 0 & 0 & 1 \end{bmatrix} \tag{10}$$

The first-order Lie derivative of the function $h_1(s)$ with respect to f_v and f_ω are defined as follows,

$$L^1_{f_{v_1}} h_1(s) = \nabla[L^0 h_1(s)] \cdot f_{v_1} = [-\sin(\delta_1)/\rho_1 \quad 0]^T \tag{11}$$

$$L^1_{f_{\omega_1}} h_1(s) = \nabla[L^0 h_1(s)] \cdot f_{\omega_1} = [0 \quad 1]^T \tag{12}$$

$$L^1_{f_{v_2}} h_1(s) = \nabla[L^0 h_1(s)] \cdot f_{v_2} = [\sin(\varphi_1)/\rho_1 \quad 0]^T \tag{13}$$

$$L^1_{f_{\omega_2}} h_1(s) = \nabla[L^0 h_1(s)] \cdot f_{\omega_2} = [-1 \quad -1]^T \tag{14}$$

where "·" denotes the vector inner product, with their gradients given as follows

$$\nabla L^1_{f_{v_1}} h_1(s) = \begin{bmatrix} \sin(\delta_1)/\rho_1^2 & -\cos(\delta_1)/\rho_1 & -\cos(\delta_1)/\rho_1 \\ 0 & 0 & 0 \end{bmatrix} \tag{15}$$

$$\nabla L^1_{f_{\omega_1}} h_1(s) = \begin{bmatrix} 0 & 0 & 0 \\ 0 & 0 & 0 \end{bmatrix} \tag{16}$$

$$\nabla L^1_{f_{v_2}} h_1(s) = \begin{bmatrix} -\sin(\varphi_1)/\rho_1^2 & \cos(\varphi_1)/\rho_1 & 0 \\ 0 & 0 & 0 \end{bmatrix} \tag{17}$$

$$\nabla L^1_{f_{\omega_2}} h_1(s) = \begin{bmatrix} 0 & 0 & 0 \\ 0 & 0 & 0 \end{bmatrix} \tag{18}$$

Substituting the above gradients of Lie derivatives into the observability matrix (3), we have

$$M = \begin{bmatrix} \nabla L^0 h_1(s) \\ \nabla L^1_{f_{v_1}} h_1(s) \\ \nabla L^1_{f_{\omega_1}} h_1(s) \\ \nabla L^1_{f_{v_2}} h_1(s) \\ \nabla L^1_{f_{\omega_2}} h_1(s) \end{bmatrix} = \begin{bmatrix} 0_{2\times1} & & I_{2\times2} \\ \sin(\delta_1)/\rho_1^2 & -\cos(\delta_1)/\rho_1 & -\cos(\delta_1)/\rho_1 \\ 0_{3\times3} & & \\ -\sin(\varphi_1)/\rho_1^2 & \cos(\varphi_1)/\rho & 0 \\ 0_{3\times3} & & \end{bmatrix} \quad (19)$$

It shows that the rank of the observability matrix does not change with the increasing order of the Lie derivatives. The observability matrix can be determined based on the gradients of the first-order and zeroth order Lie derivatives. Then, we have the following two remarks on the observability of the bearing-only leader-follower system as described so far.

Remark 1: rank$(M) = 3$ if

1) $v_1 > 0$, $v_j > 0$, where $j=2, \cdots, n+1$;
2) $\varphi_i \neq 0$, $i=1, \cdots, n$;
3) The leader and the follower move neither in parallel nor straightly.

Proof: Given the above three prerequisite requirements, the M matrix by means of a finite sequence of elementary row operations, can be transformed to a simplified form as given in (20), obtaining rank $(M) = 3$.

$$M \Rightarrow \begin{bmatrix} 1 & 0 & 0 \\ 0 & 1 & 0 \\ 0 & 0 & 1 \\ & O_{7\times3} & \end{bmatrix} \quad (20)$$

Remark 2: rank$(M) = 2$ if

1) $v_1 > 0$, $v_j > 0$, where $j=2, \cdots, n+1$;
2) $\varphi_i = k_1$, $\alpha_i = k_2$, where $i=1, \cdots, n$, and k_1, k_2 is constant , i.e., the leader and the followers move straightly (in parallel).

Proof: Supposing $\varphi_i = k_1$, $\alpha_i = k_2$, k_1, k_2 are constant and the differentiation of the functions φ_i and α_i are zero, we have

$$\nabla h_1^{(0)}(s) = \begin{bmatrix} 0 & 1 & 0 \\ 0 & 0 & 1 \end{bmatrix} \quad (21)$$

$$h_1^{(1)}(s) = h_1^{(2)}(s) = \cdots = h_1^{(n-1)}(s) = 0 \quad (22)$$

$$\nabla h_1^{(1)}(s) = \nabla h_1^{(2)}(s) = \cdots = \nabla h_1^{(n-1)}(s) = \begin{bmatrix} 0 & 0 & 0 \\ 0 & 0 & 0 \end{bmatrix} \quad (23)$$

These lead to a simplified form of M matrix as follows

$$M \Rightarrow \begin{bmatrix} 0 & 1 & 0 \\ 0 & 0 & 1 \\ & O_{8\times3} & \end{bmatrix} \quad (24)$$

i.e. rank $(M) = 2$.

Based on Remark 1 and 2, we have the conclusion that M has full rank (that the system is locally weakly observable) when the agents move along a curvilinear line (moving in neither parallel nor straightly) and rank $(M) = 2$ when the agent move along a straight line (the system is not locally observable).

3   UKF-Based Input-Output Feedback Control

To maintain a desired "1-N" formation, the followers need to know the relative position of the leader, and adjusts their current positions accordingly in real time. In our approach, the former is estimated by UKF while the latter is carried out based on the classical input-output feedback control law. In the following, we will explain how to calculate the control input required for the followers for formation.

To implement UKF, the continuous-time state dynamic (1) needs to be discretized firstly. Assume both the continuous-time state dynamics (25) and the observation equation (26) are affected with additive noises as

$$\dot{s} = F(s)U + O \qquad (25)$$

$$y = Gs + N \qquad (26)$$

where G is the output transition matrix, O and N are white Gaussian noises with zero mean and covariance matrices P_O and P_N, respectively. We assume that $s(0)$, O and N are uncorrelated for simplicity. We apply the Euler forward method with sampling time T_c to discretize the state dynamics (25), obtaining

$$s(k+1) = \Gamma(s(k), u(k)) + T_c O \qquad (27)$$

where $\Gamma(s(k), u(k)) = T_c F(s)U + s(k)$ and $k \in \mathbb{N}$.

By taking the derivative on $\alpha_1 \triangleq \theta_1 - \theta_2$, we have

$$\dot{s}_r = L(s)U_1 + M(s)U_2 \qquad (28)$$

$$\dot{\alpha}_1 = \omega_1 - \omega_2 \qquad (29)$$

where $s_r \triangleq [\rho_1 \ \varphi_1]^T$ is the reduced state-space vector. $L^{2 \times 2}$ and $M^{2 \times 2}$ are the upper-left and right submatrices of F, respectively.

The input-output feedback control law (Slotine et al. 1991, Das et al. 2002) algebraically linearizes a nonlinear system dynamics and then calculates the control put U for the follower to achieve a desired s_r^{ide}.

The control input for our input-output feedback control system is:

$$U_2 \triangleq [v_2 \ \omega_2 \ ]^T = M^{-1}(s)(C - L(s)U_1) \qquad (30)$$

where

$$C = -K(s_r - s_r^{ide}) \qquad (31)$$

and $K = diag[k_1 k_2]$, with $k_1, k_2 > 0$, the superscript "ide" refers to the desired state, and C is auxiliary control parameter. Eq. (30) serves as a feedback linearizing control for Eq. (28). Substituting Eq. (30) into Eq. (28), we have

$$\dot{s}_r = C = -K(s_r - s_r^{ide}) = \begin{bmatrix} k_1(\rho_1^{ide} - \rho_1) \\ k_2(\varphi_1^{ide} - \varphi_1) \end{bmatrix} \tag{32}$$

4   Simulation

In order to demonstrate the validity of the proposed formation control approach, simulations are designed based on the hybrid platform of Webots 7 and Matlab. The leader-followers formation of four agents is formed where followers R_2, R_3 and R_4 follow the leader R_1. The simulation scenario given in Webots 7 is shown in Fig. 2. In the simulation, two typical trajectories are designed for the leader. As stated, to make the system always weakly observable $(rank(M) = 3)$, the trajectories do not include straight and parallel movements for the leader and followers. In scenario 1 (as shown in Fig.3 (a)), the trajectory of the leader is a complete elliptical. In scenario 2 (as shown in Fig.4 (a)), the leader will move straightly (shortly) firstly and then turn right and left in circles. Simulation results are given in subfigures of Fig.3 and 4 for scenario 1 and 2 respectively.

Fig. 2. The simulation scene of mobile agents

4.1   Simulation Setup

In scenario 1, the following velocity inputs are assigned to the leader

$$v_1(t) = 2.0 \ m/s, \omega_1(t) = \pi/5 \ rad/s, t \in [0,10]$$

while in scenario 2, the following velocity inputs are assigned to the leader

$$v_1(t) = 2.0 \ m/s, \omega_1(t) = \begin{cases} 0 \ rad/s, t \in \{[0,2),[8,9)\} \\ -\pi/5 \ rad/s, t \in [9,12) \\ \pi/5 \ rad/s, t \in \{[2,8),[12,14]\} \end{cases}$$

For both scenarios, the initial vectors of the leader and three followers are

$$[x_1(0) \ y_1(0) \ z_1(0)]^T = [0 \ 0 \ 0]^T, [x_2(0) \ y_2(0) \ z_2(0)]^T = [-0.1 \ -0.25 \ 0]^T,$$
$$[x_3(0) \ y_3(0) \ z_3(0)]^T = [-0.1 \ 0.2 \ 0]^T, [x_4(0) \ y_4(0) \ z_4(0)]^T = [-0.1 \ 0.4 \ 0]^T.$$

Parameters required for the input-output state feedback control are set follows. $k_1 = 0.65$, $k_2 = 0.15$. $s(0) = [0.27 \ 4.33 \ 0 \ 0.22 \ 2.03 \ 0 \ 0.41 \ 1.82 \ 0]^T$, $s_r^{ide}(0) = [0.45 \ 3\pi/4 \ 0.45 \ 5\pi/4 \ 0.75 \ 5\pi/4]^T$ where the distances are in meters and angles in radians. For the parameters required by the UKF, $T_c = 0.01s$, $P_0 = diag[h \ h]$, $P_N = diag[h \ h]$, $P = diag[1.13 \ 1.13]$, where $h = 2.11 \times 10^{-2} rad^2$.

4.2   Simulation Analysis

Fig. 3 (a) and 4 (a) give the trajectories of the leader and followers, showing intuitively that the desired formation are properly maintained in both scenarios. This is because the system is observable under the given scenario according to the observability described in Section 2.2. Fig. 3. (b), (c) and (d) present the observation angle estimation error, direction angle estimation error and velocities of the followers respectively. The results show that both the observation and direction angle errors are quite small after the initial stage (the formation becomes stable) and the velocities of the follower agents change slightly during the entire input-output feedback control process. The velocity of the follower agent outside of the leader is larger than the velocity of the leader and inside of the leader is smaller. Similar results are shown in scenario 2. It is shown in Fig. 4. (b) that the observation angle estimation error is very small. Fig. 4. (c) and (d) show that the direction angle estimation error is also very small and the velocities of the follower are relatively stable during the input-output feedback control process. There is an exception. When the leader changes moving direction suddenly, the maximum direction angle error occurs around -0.0126 and the velocities of the followers change significantly. Overall, these results indicate a stable performance of the proposed formation control solution and a quick response to the change as long as the system is observable.

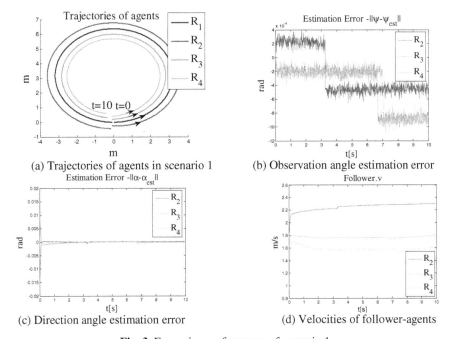

(a) Trajectories of agents in scenario 1   (b) Observation angle estimation error

(c) Direction angle estimation error   (d) Velocities of follower-agents

Fig. 3. Formation performance of scenario 1

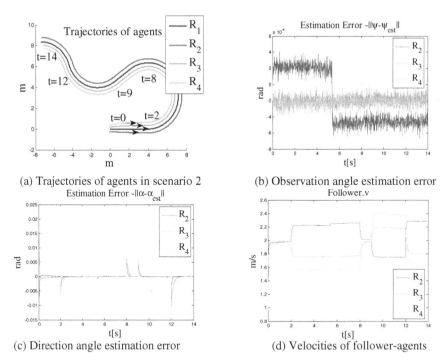

(a) Trajectories of agents in scenario 2

(b) Observation angle estimation error

(c) Direction angle estimation error

(d) Velocities of follower-agents

Fig. 4. Formation performance of scenario 2

5 Conclusion

A leader-follower formation control method is presented for multiple agents of the "1-N" structure where multiple followers follow one leader. The observability of the "1-N" leader-follower formation system is studied, which theoretically shows that the bearing-only observation meet the observability requirement if the leader and followers do not move straightly in parallel. The UKF is employed for the position estimation, which enables the movement control of the followers via input-output feedback control. Simulation results show that the system can rapidly obtain the desired formation and maintain the desired formation accurately and reliably. Further research for multi-agent formation control will consider dynamical obstacles.

Acknowledgements. This work was supported by the National Natural Science Foundation of China (Grant No.51475383, 51075337) and by the project Sociedades Humano-Agente en Entornos Cloud Computing (Soha+C) SA213U13.

References

1. Carrascosa, C., Bajo, J., Julián, V., Corchado, J.M., Botti, V.: Hybrid multi-agent architecture as a real-time problem-solving model. Expert Systems with Applications **34**(1), 2–17 (2008)

2. Zato, C., Villarrubia, G., Sánchez, A., Barri, I., Rubión, E., Fernández, A., Rebate, C., Cabo, J.A., Álamos, T., Sanz, J., Seco, J., Bajo, J., Corchado, J.M.: PANGEA - Platform for Automatic construction of organizations of intElligent Agents. In: 9th International Conference Distributed Computing and Artificial Intelligence (2012)

3. Ren, W., Beard, R.W.: Formation feedback control for multiple spacecraft via virtual structures. IEE Proceedings of the Control Theory and Applications, IET **151**(3), 357–368 (2004)

4. Sun, T., Liu, F., Pei, H., He, Y.: Observer-based adaptive leader-following formation control for non-holonomic mobile robots. IET Control Theory & Applications **6**(18), 2835–2841 (2012)

5. Chen, J., Sun, D., Yang, J., Chen, H.Y.: A leader-follower formation control of multiple nonholonomic mobile robots incorporating receding-horizon scheme. The Int. J. Robotics Research **28**, 727–747 (2009)

6. Shao, J., Xie, G., Wang, L.: Leader-following formation control of multiple mobile vehicles. IET Control Theory & Applications 1(2), 545-552 (2007)

7. Consolini, L., Morbidi, F., Prattichizzo, D., Tosques, M.: Leader-follower formation control of nonholonomic mobile robots with input constraints. Automatica **44**(5), 1343–1349 (2008)

8. Cristescu, S.M., Ionescu, C.M., Wyns, B., DeKeyser, R.: Leader-Follower String Formation using Cascade Control for Mobile Robots. In: 20th Mediterranean Conference on Control and Automation, pp. 1092–1098 (2012)

9. Kwon, J.W., Chwa, D.: Hierarchical formation control based on a vector field method for wheeled mobile robots. IEEE Tran. Robotics 28(6), 1335–1345 (2012)

10. Sharma, R., Beard, R.W., Taylor, C.N., Quebe, S.: Graph-based observability analysis of bearing-only cooperative localization. IEEE Transactions on Robotics 28(2), 522–529 (2012)

11. Moshtagh, N., Michael, N., Jadbabaie, A., Daniilidis, K.: Bearing-only control laws for balanced circular formations of ground robots. In: Proceedings of Robotics: Science and Systems IV. MIT Press (2008)

12. Basiri, M., Bishopand, A.N., Jensfelt, P.: Distributed control of triangular formations with angle-only constraints. Systems & Control Letters **59**(2), 147–154 (2010)

13. Bishop, A.N.: A very relaxed control law for bearing-only triangular formation control. In: Proceedings of the 18th IFAC World Congress, Milano, Italy, pp. 5991–5998 (2011a)

14. Bishop, A.N.: Distributed bearing-only quadrilateral formation control. In: Proceedings of the 18th IFAC World Congress, Milano, Italy, pp. 4507–4512 (2011b)

15. Eren, T.: Formation shape control based on bearing rigidity. International Journal of Control **85**(9), 1361–1379 (2012)

16. Franchiand, A., Giordano, P.R.: Decentralized control of parallel rigid formations with direction constraints and bearing measurements. In: CDC, pp. 5310–5317 (2012)

17. Zhao, S., Lin, F., Peng, K., Chen, B.M., Lee, T.H.: Finite-time stabilisation of cyclic formations using bearing-only measurements. International Journal of Control **87**(4), 715–727 (2014)

18. Zhao, S., Lin, F., Peng, K., Chen, B.M., Lee, T.H.: Distributed control of angle-constrained cyclic formations using bearing-only measurements. Systems & Control Letters **63**, 12–24 (2014)

19. Mariottini, G.L., Morbidi, F., Prattichizzo, D., et al.: Vision-based localization for leader-follower formation control. IEEE Transactions on Robotics **25**(6), 1431–1438 (2009)

20. Sharma, R., Quebe, S., Beard, R.W., Taylor, C.N.: Bearing-only Cooperative Localization. Journal of Intelligent & Robotic Systems **72**(3–4), 429–440 (2013)

21. Li, T., Sun, S.: Double-resampling based Monte Carlo localization for mobile robot. Acta Automatica Sinica **36**(9), 1279–1286 (2010)
22. Nerurkar, E.D., Roumeliotis, S.I., Martinelli, A.: Distributed maximum a posteriori estimation for multi-robot cooperative localization. In: Robotics and Automation, ICRA 2009, pp. 434–439 (2009)
23. Hermann, R., Krener, A.J.: Nonlinear controllability and observability. IEEE Transactions on Automatic Control **22**(5), 728–740 (1977)
24. Morbidi, F., Marottini, G.L., Prattichizzo, D.: Observer design via Immersion and Invariance for vision-based leader-follower formation control. Automatica **46**(1), 148–154 (2010)
25. Wan, E.A., Van Der Merwe, R.: The unscented Kalman filter for nonlinear estimation. In: The IEEE 2000 Adaptive Systems for Signal Processing, Communications, and Control Symposium 2000, AS-SPCC, pp. 153–158 (2000)
26. Slotine, J.J.E., Li, W.: Applied nonlinear control, vol. 46(1). Prentice-Hall, Englewood Cliffs (1991)
27. Das, A.K., Fierro, R., Kumar, V., et al.: A vision-based formation control framework. IEEE Transactions on Robotics and Automation **18**(5), 813–825 (2002)

Echo State Networks for Feature Selection in Affective Computing

P. Koprinkova-Hristova[1], L. Bozhkov[2], and P. Georgieva[3(✉)]

[1] Institute of Information and Communication Technologies,
Bulgarian Academy of Sciences, Sofia, Bulgaria
[2] Technical University of Sofia, Sofia, Bulgaria
[3] DETI/IEETA, University of Aveiro, Aveiro, Portugal
petia@ua.pt

Abstract. The Echo State Networks (ESNs) are dynamical structures designed initially to facilitate learning in Recurrent Neural Networks which are normally applied for time series modeling. In this paper we show that the ESN reservoirs can serve as an effective feature selection procedure that improved the discrimination of human emotion valence from EEG signals, a task that belongs to the research field of affective computing. A number of supervised and unsupervised machine learning techniques provided with the new feature vector extracted from ESN reservoir states were comparatively studied with respect to their discrimination accuracy. This novel application serves as a proof of concept for the possibility of extending the usability of the ESNs in classification or clustering frameworks.

Keywords: Echo state network · Feature selection · Affective computing · EEG data classification and clustering

1 Introduction

Echo State Networks (ESN) represent a class of recurrent neural networks (RNN) where the so called "reservoir computing" approach for training is formulated, [15]. The key idea of this biologically inspired approach is to mimic structures in human brain that seem to be composed by randomly connected dynamic non-linear neurons called reservoir whose output is usually linear combination of the current states of the reservoir neurons. The main advantage of the ESN is the simplified training algorithm since only weights of the connections from the reservoir to the readout neurons are subject to training. Thus instead of gradient descent learning much faster least squares method can be used.

Although the reservoir connections and their weights are randomly generated, in order to prevent improper behavior of ESN, the reservoir needs to possess the so called "echo state property" as formulated in [5]. The basic rule formulation is: the effect of input disturbances should vanish gradually in time, that means the dynamic reservoir must be stable. According to this rule, a reservoir weight matrix with spectral radius below one needs to be generated. However as pointed out in [15] this

© Springer International Publishing Switzerland 2015
Y. Demazeau et al. (Eds.): PAAMS 2015, LNAI 9086, pp. 131–141, 2015.
DOI: 10.1007/978-3-319-18944-4_11

condition will not guaranty ESN stable behavior in general. Therefore, many task-dependent recipes for improvement of reservoir connections were proposed.

Since one of the laws of thermodynamics says that any stable stationary state has a local maximum of entropy [3], it can be expected that maximization of entropy at the ESN reservoir output could increase its stability. This motivated several works proposing ESN reservoir improvement by its entropy maximization [16]. Other authors proposed the biologically motivated algorithm called Intrinsic Plasticity (IP) based on mechanisms of changing neural excitability in response to the distribution of the input stimuli [18], [19]. In [6] we have shown that in fact IP training achieves balance between maximization of entropy at the ESN reservoir output and its concentration around the pre-specified mean value increasing at the same time reservoir stability. During the investigations in [6] another interesting effect was observed: the reservoir neurons equilibrium states were concentrated in several regions. Then a question arose: is it possible to use this effect for classification or clustering purposes too? This initiated development of the proposed here algorithm for multidimensional data classification and clustering.

Since ESN are dynamic structures designed initially for time series modeling, using them for static data classification/clustering might seem odd. However the idea for using RNNs in this way is not new. There are examples in the literature like neural systems possessing multi-stable attractors [2] that perform temporal integration aimed at discrimination between multiple alternatives. In other works [1, 4] unsupervised learning procedures that minimize given energy function were proposed aiming at achievement of network equilibrium states that reflect given data structure.

Concerning ESN applications for classification or clustering, there are only few works available. In [20] it was proposed for the first time to use ESN as feature extraction stage of image classification. Their role was to "draw out" silent underlying features of the data to be used further to train a feedforward neural network classifier. In [17] the idea to exploit equilibrium states of the ESN reservoir in order to design multiple-clusters ESN reservoirs was proposed. It was inspired by complex network topologies imitating cortical networks of the mammalian brain. In [14] it was reported that using another kind of IP algorithm in combination with Spike-time Dependent plasticity (STDP) of synaptic weights changes the connectivity matrix of the network in such a way that the recurrent connections capture the peculiarities of the input stimuli so that the network activation patterns can be separated by an unsupervised clustering technique.

The idea described in this paper was motivated initially from stability analysis of ESN and proposed for the first time in [7]. It exploits similar reservoir properties reported by other works but looking from a different point of view: to consider combinations between steady states of each two neurons in the reservoir as numerous two-dimensional projections of the original multidimensional data fed into the ESN input; next to use these low dimensional projections for classification or clustering of the original multidimensional data. The ESN feature selection methodology proposed in [7] was successfully tested on a number of different data sets [8-13] to solve clustering problems.

In this paper we go further and apply it for the first time to a binary classification problem. We also compare classification and clustering technique for discrimination of positive and negative emotional states of multiple subjects.

2   Echo State Networks Basics

The basic structure of an ESN, presented in Fig. 1, consists of a reservoir of randomly connected dynamic neurons with sigmoid nonlinearities fres (usually hyperbolic tangent):

$$r(k) = f^{res}\left(W^{in}in(k) + W^{res}r(k-1)\right)$$
(1)

and a linear readout f^{out} (usually identity function) at the output:

$$out(k) = f^{out}\left(W^{out}\left[in(k)\quad r(k)\right]\right)$$
(2)

Here k denotes discrete time instant; $in(k)$ is a vector of network inputs, $r(k)$ - a vector of the reservoir neurons states and $out(k)$ – a vector of network outputs; n_{in}, n_{out} and n_r are the dimensions of the corresponding vectors in, out and r respectively; W^{out} is a trainable $n_{out} \times (n_{in}+n_r)$ matrix; W^{in} and W^{res} are $n_r \times n_{in}$ and $n_r \times n_r$ matrices that are randomly generated and are not trainable. In some applications direct connection from the input to the readout is omitted.

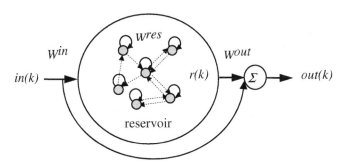

Fig. 1. Echo state network basic structure

The key idea is that having rich enough reservoirs of nonlinearities will allow to approximate quite complex nonlinear dependence between input and output vectors by tuning only the linear readout weights. Hence the training procedure is simplified to solving in one step Least Squares task [5].

Although this idea seems to work well, it appears that initial tuning of reservoir connections to the data that will be fed into the ESN helps to improve its properties. In [18], [19] was proposed a reservoir tuning approach called "intrinsic plasticity" (IP). It is aimed at maximization of information transmission through the ESN that is equivalent to its output entropy maximization. Motivation of this approach is related to known biological mechanisms that change neural excitability according to the distribution of the input stimuli. The authors proposed a gradient method for adjusting the biases and an additional gain term aimed at achieving the desired distribution of outputs by minimizing the Kullback-Leibler divergence:

$$D_{KL}\left(p(r),p_d(r)\right) = \int p(r)\log\left(\frac{p(r)}{p_d(r)}\right) \tag{3}$$

That is a measure for the difference between the actual $p(r)$ and the desired $p_d(r)$ probability distribution of reservoir neurons output r. Since the commonly used transfer function of neurons is the hyperbolic tangent, the proper target distribution that maximizes the information at the output according to [18] is the Gaussian one with a prescribed small variance σ and a zero mean μ:

$$p_d(r) = \frac{1}{\sigma\sqrt{2\pi}}\exp\left(-\frac{(r-\mu)^2}{2\sigma^2}\right) \tag{4}$$

Hence equation (3) can be rearranged as follows:

$$D_{KL}(p(r),p_d(r)) = -H(r) + \frac{1}{2\sigma^2}E\left((r-\mu)^2\right) + \log\frac{1}{\sigma\sqrt{2\pi}} \tag{5}$$

Where $H(r)$ is entropy, the last term is constant and the second one determines the deviation of the output from the desired mean value. Thus minimization of (5) will lead to compromise between entropy maximization and minimization of distance between μ and r.

In order to achieve those effects two additional reservoir parameters - gain a and bias b (both vectors with n_r size) - are introduced as follows:

$$r(k) = f^{res}\left(diag(a)W^{in}in(k) + diag(a)W^{res}r(k-1) + b\right) \tag{6}$$

The IP training is a procedure that adjusts vectors a and b using gradient descent.

3   Affective Computing and Data Set Description

We consider learning to discriminate emotional states of human subjects, based on their brain activity observed via Event Related Potentials (ERPs). ERPs are transient components in the EEG generated in response to a stimulus. ERPs were collected while subjects were viewing high arousal images with positive or negative emotional content. This problem is important because such classifiers constitute "virtual sensors" of hidden emotional states, which are useful in psychology science research and clinical applications [21], [22].

A total of 26 female volunteers participated in the study. The signals were recorded while the volunteers were viewing high arousal images with positive and negative valence. For each image, signals from 21 EEG channels were sampled at 1000Hz and stored (see Table 1). The signals were recorded while the volunteers were viewing pictures selected from the International Affective Picture System (IAPS) repository.

A total of 24 high arousal (IAPS rating> 6) images with positive valence (M=7.29 +/- 0.65) and negative valence (M=1.47 +/- 0.24) were selected. Each image was presented 3 times in a pseudo-random order and each trial lasted 3500 ms: during the first 750 ms, a fixation cross was presented, then one of the images was presented during 500 ms and at last a black screen appeared during 2250 ms. The raw EEG signals were first filtered (band-pass filter between 0.1 and 30Hz.), eye-movement corrected, baseline compensated and segmented into epochs using NeuroScan software. The single-trial signal length is 950 ms with 150ms before the stimulus onset. The ensemble average for each condition (positive/negative valence) was also computed and filtered using a Butterworth filter of 4th order with passband [0.5-15] Hz. Thus, the filtered ensemble average signals cover the frequency band ranges corresponding to Delta ([0.5 -4] Hz), Theta ([4 -8] Hz) and Alpha neural activity ([8 -12] Hz).

Temporal features (amplitudes and latencies) are extracted from the filtered, segmented and ensemble averaged ERP data. Starting by the localization of the first minimum after time t=0s, the features are defined as a sequence of the local positive and negative picks, and their respective latencies (time of occurrence). Twelve temporal features are stored (Table 2) corresponding to the amplitudes of the first three local minimums (A_{min1}, A_{min2}, A_{min3}), the first three local maximums (A_{max1}, A_{max2}, A_{max3}), and their associated latencies (L_{min1}, L_{min2}, L_{min3}, L_{max1}, L_{max2}, L_{max3}).

Table 1. Channels

N°	EEG Channels
1	Ch 1 (FP1)
2	Ch 2 (FPz)
3	Ch 3 (FP2)
4	Ch 4 (F7)
5	Ch 5 (F3)
6	Ch 6 (Fz)
7	Ch 7 (F4)
8	Ch 8 (F8)
9	Ch 9 (T7)
10	Ch 10 (C3)
11	Ch 11 (Cz)
12	Ch 12 (C4)
13	Ch 13 (T8)
14	Ch 14 (P7)
15	Ch 15 (P3)
16	Ch 16 (Pz)
17	Ch 17 (P4)
18	Ch 18 (P8)
19	Ch 19 (O1)
20	Ch 20 (Oz)
21	Ch 21 (O2)

Table 2. Features

N°	Features
1	$A_{min1(A1)}$
2	A_{max1}
3	A_{min2}
4	A_{max2}
5	A_{min3}
6	A_{max3}
7	L_{min1}
8	L_{max1}
9	L_{min2}
10	L_{max2}
11	L_{min3}
12	L_{max3}

As a result, the initial feature set is a matrix X with dimension of 252 columns (21 channels x12 features) and 52 lines (the ensemble averaged positive and negative labeled trials of 26 subjects). The ESN-based features selection discussed in the next section is applied on the normalized feature matrix

$$\overline{X} = \frac{X - mean(X)}{std(X)} \tag{7}$$

4   ESN for Feature Selection

The original feature matrix (7) was processed via ESN reservoir following the procedure developed in [8-13]. The two-step algorithm is outlined in Table 3:

Step 1: IP tuning of the ESN reservoir using original feature data set;

Table 3. Algorithm to obtain the new feature vector as a vector of equilibrium states of neurons in the ESN reservoir

```
in(1:features number,1:examples number)=original_features;
n_in=features number; n_out=1; n_r=chosen number;
esn=generate_esn(n_in, n_out, n_r);
for it=1:number of IP iterations
        for i=1:examples number
                esn=esn_IP_training(esn, in(:,i));
        end
end
for i=1:examples number
        r(0)=0;
        for k=1:chosen number of steps
                r(k)=sim_esn(esn, in(:,i),r(k-1));
        end
        r_e(i)=r(k);
end
esn_features=r_e;
```

The structure of ESN was determined according to the size of the original feature matrix (7) so that the size of the ESN input vector corresponds to the number of the original features (in this case 252 features). Since we explore only the reservoir output, the size of the readout doesn't matter and it was set to one. The size of the reservoir varies starting from 10 up to 500 neurons in order to study its influence on the accuracy of the emotion valence discrimination. Our experimental results with 10, 30, 50, 100, 150, 300 and 500 neurons are visualized in the next section. The IP tuning was done by presenting one by one the feature vector of all training examples to the ESN input over a predefined number of iterations (we used 10 iterations) and adjusting the gain and the bias terms using gradient rules from [18].

Step 2: Calculating of the equilibrium states of all reservoir neurons.

Since it is hard to solve analytically the equation for equilibrium states corresponding to each input data in_c:

$$r_e = \tanh\left(diag(a)W^{in}in_c + diag(a)W^{res}r_e + b\right),$$

the equilibrium states r_e were determined by simulations for a previously chosen number of steps until reaching of steady state (in our experiments 25 steps were enough). The achieved reservoir neurons equilibrium states were kept as the new feature vector called further *esn_features*.

5   Emotion Valence Discrimination – Experimental Results

In this section we use the ESN extracted features (*esn_features*) in order to discriminate the positive and negative emotion valence applying supervised (classification) or unsupervised (clustering) learning techniques. Two approaches related with the new feature space were studied:

Approach 1: Using all possible 2D combinations between equilibrium states $r_e(i)$ and $r_e(j)$ of every two neurons *i* and *j* from the ESN reservoir as a 2D feature vector.

This approach actually maps the original feature data set into a bigger space of reservoir equilibriums, i.e. we first expand the feature data set and then select the best 2D projections among all possible combinations.

Approach 2: Using all reservoir equilibrium states *esn_features* as the new feature vector.

In contrast to the first approach, Approach 2 maps the original feature data set into a smaller size reservoir and thus the new feature set has a smaller dimension. This approach is analog to the PCA (Principal Component Analysis) where a feature reduction is first performed before the classification or clustering.

In the next section Approach 1 and Approach 2 are applied to two basic clustering algorithms, k-means and fuzzy C-means (FCM).

5.1   Data Clustering

In Fig. 2 are summarized the discrimination accuracies of k-means and FCM. It should be noted that Approach 1 produces a variety of 2D feature sets and in Fig.2 are presented the accuracy results only for the best 2D feature sets. Among the huge number of 2D feature combinations, only few of them achieve these results. For comparative purposes we also present the clustering accuracy of k-means and FCM using the original feature matrix (7).

From Fig. 2 it can be concluded that for all reservoir sizes (nr=10, 30, 50, 100, 150, 300, 500) the best clustering was obtained with Approach 1 (a combination of 2D

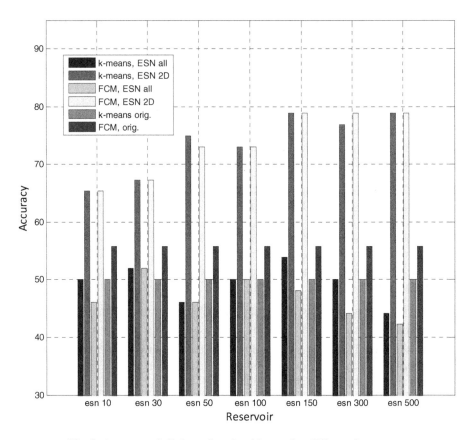

Fig. 2. Accuracy of all clustering algorithms using different features sets

feature sets). The clustering accuracy using all ESN reservoir states (*esn_features*) seems comparable and even worse (especially in the case of bigger reservoir size) than those obtained by direct clustering of the original features. Higher the reservoir size is, better is the clustering accuracy in the 2D feature scenario which goes close to 80%. Another interesting observation is that FCM outperforms k-means clustering when directly applied to the original feature matrix, while using the ESN extracted features seem to make both approaches similar. In the case of using all *esn_features* k-means outperforms slightly FCM while in the case of 2D feature vector both algorithms achieve similar accuracy.

5.2   Data Classification

The same ENS models were tested for the case of supervised learning to discriminate the two emotion valences. In order to eliminate the problem of choosing the "wrong" or the "lucky" model, we applied a number of standard classifiers, namely Linear Discriminant Analysis (LDA), k-Nearest Neighbors (kNN), Naïve Bayes (NB),

Support Vector Machines (SVM) and Decision Trees (DT). Due to the limited number of examples (only 26 subjects), cross validation with leave-one-out subject is adopted. In order to increase the statistical confidence of the obtained results, classification based on the majority votes of the classifiers (LD, kNN, NB, SVM, and DT) was also done. We call this hierarchical classification methodology VOTE.

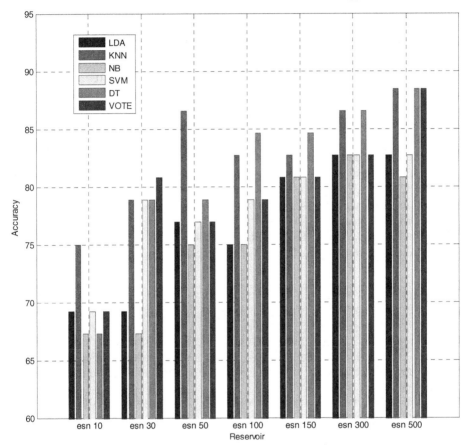

Fig. 3. Accuracy of all classification algorithms using different features sets

The results in Fig.3 show the same tendency of better accuracy for increasing number of neurons in the ENS reservoir. The intuition behind this is that higher the reservoir size, more binary combinations of neurons are produced and thus the probability of getting a good feature selection increases. An interesting observation but difficult to explain is the fact that the VOTE classifier does not always produce the best classification. In previous studies [23] we have obtained quite encouraging results with VOTE classifier in the framework of different feature selection scenarios. However, for bigger reservoir size, VOTE improves and approaches the expected performance.

Another interesting observation is the surprisingly good performance of the kNN and DT classifiers. Finally, comparing the bars in Fig.2 and Fig.3, it can be concluded that the supervised learning (classification) outperforms significantly the unsupervised (clustering) approach, which is not a surprising result.

6   Conclusions

In this paper we propose the ESN as a mechanism for feature selection in two scenarios: i) map the original features into an expanded feature space defined by the number of the reservoir neurons (more neurons than ENS inputs) and choose the best combination of two neurons (2D projection) as the new features; ii) map the original features into a reduced feature space defined by the number of the reservoir neurons (less neurons than ENS inputs) and use all of them as the new features. Both scenarios were tested on the challenging problem of affective computing based on brain neural data (ERPs). In the 2D projection scenario it is always possible to find a combination of features that will cluster or classify the data with reasonable accuracy (close to 80% for the clustering and close to 89% for the classification task).

The computational complexity is however an unavoidable problem particularly when the reservoir size increases. Moreover from the very big number of neuron combinations (for example 124750 combinations for nr=500) only few of them reveal to be the proper choice.

Nevertheless, these proof of concept results encourage us to further test the ESN as a feature selection step prior to data classification/clustering in other applications.

References

1. Ackley, D.H., Hinton, G.E., Sejnowski, T.J.: A learning algorithm for Boltzmann machines. Cognitive Science **9**, 147–169 (1985)
2. Brody, C.D., Romo, R., Kepecs, A.: Basic mechanisms for graded persistent activity: Discrete attractors, continuous attractors, and dynamical representations. Current Opinion in Neurobiology **13**, 204–211 (2003)
3. Haddad, W.M., Chellaboina, V.S., Nersesov, S.G.: Thermodynamics: A Dynamical System Approach. Princeton University Press (2005)
4. Hinton, G.E., Salakhutdinov, R.: Reducing the dimensionality of data with neural networks. Science **313**(5786), 504–507 (2006)
5. Jaeger, H.: Tutorial on training recurrent neural networks, covering BPPT, RTRL, EKF and the "echo state network" approach, GMD Report 159, German National Research Center for Information Technology (2002)
6. Koprinkova-Hristova, P., Palm, G.: ESN Intrinsic Plasticity versus Reservoir Stability. In: Honkela, T. (ed.) ICANN 2011, Part I. LNCS, vol. 6791, pp. 69–76. Springer, Heidelberg (2011)
7. Koprinkova-Hristova, P., Tontchev, N.: Echo State Networks for Multi-dimensional Data Clustering. In: Villa, A.E., Duch, W., Érdi, P., Masulli, F., Palm, G. (eds.) ICANN 2012, Part I. LNCS, vol. 7552, pp. 571–578. Springer, Heidelberg (2012)
8. Koprinkova-Hristova, P., Alexiev, K., Borisova, D., Jelev, G., Atanassov, V.: Recurrent neural networks for automatic clustering of multispectral satellite images. In: Bruzzone, L. (ed.) Proceedings of SPIE, Image and Signal Processing for Remote Sensing XIX, 88920X, vol. 8892 (October 17, 2013) doi:10.1117/12.

9. Koprinkova-Hristova, P., Angelova, D., Borisova, D., Jelev, G.: Clustering of spectral images using Echo state networks. In: 2013 IEEE International Symposium on Innovations in Intelligent Systems and Applications, IEEE INISTA 2013, June 19-21, Albena, Bulgaria (2013). doi:10.1109/INISTA.2013.6577633

10. Koprinkova-Hristova, P., Doukovska, L., Kostov, P.: Working regimes classification for predictive maintenance of mill fan systems. In: 2013 IEEE International Symposium on Innovations in Intelligent Systems and Applications, IEEE INISTA 2013, June 19-21, Albena, Bulgaria (2013) doi:10.1109/INISTA.2013.6577632

11. Koprinkova-Hristova, P., Alexiev, K.: Echo State Networks in Dynamic Data Clustering. In: Mladenov, V., Koprinkova-Hristova, P., Palm, G., Villa, A.E., Appollini, B., Kasabov, N. (eds.) ICANN 2013. LNCS, vol. 8131, pp. 343–350. Springer, Heidelberg (2013)

12. Koprinkova-Hristova, P., Alexiev, K.: Sound fields clusterization via neural networks. In: 2014 IEEE International Symposium on Innovations in Intelligent Systems and Applications, INISTA 2014, June 23–25, Alberobello, Italy, pp. 368–374 (2014)

13. Koprinkova-Hristova, P., Alexiev, K.: Dynamic Sound Fields Clusterization Using Neuro-Fuzzy Approach. In: Agre, G., Hitzler, P., Krisnadhi, A.A., Kuznetsov, S.O. (eds.) AIMSA 2014. LNCS, vol. 8722, pp. 194–205. Springer, Heidelberg (2014)

14. Lazar, A., Pipa, G., Triesch, J.: Predictive Coding in Cortical Microcircuits. In: Kurková, V., Neruda, R., Koutník, J. (eds.) ICANN 2008, Part II. LNCS, vol. 5164, pp. 386–395. Springer, Heidelberg (2008)

15. Lukosevicius, M., Jaeger, H.: Reservoir computing approaches to recurrent neural network training. Computer Science Review 3, 127–149 (2009)

16. Ozturk, M., Xu, D., Principe, J.: Analysis and design of Echo state networks. Neural Computation 19, 111–138 (2007)

17. Peng, X., Guo, J., Lei, M., Peng, Yu.: Analog Circuit Fault Diagnosis with Echo State Networks Based on Corresponding Clusters. In: Liu, D., Zhang, H., Polycarpou, M., Alippi, C., He, H. (eds.) ISNN 2011, Part I. LNCS, vol. 6675, pp. 437–444. Springer, Heidelberg (2011)

18. Schrauwen, B., Wandermann, M., Verstraeten, D., Steil, J.J., Stroobandt, D.: Improving reservoirs using intrinsic plasticity. Neurocomputing 71, 1159–1171 (2008)

19. Steil, J.J.: Online reservoir adaptation by intrinsic plasticity for back-propagation-decoleration and echo state learning. Neural Networks 20, 353–364 (2007)

20. Woodward, A., Ikegami, T.: A reservoir computing approach to image classification using coupled echo state and back-propagation neural networks. In: Proc. of 26th Int. Conf. on Image and Vision Computing, Auckland, New Zealand, November. 29–December 1, 2011, pp. 543–458 (2011)

21. Calvo, R.A., D'Mello, S.K.: Affect Detection: An Interdisciplinary Review of Models, Methods, and their Applications. IEEE Transactions on Affective Computing 1(1), 18–37 (2010)

22. Georgieva, O., Milanov, S., Georgieva, P., Santos, I.M., Pereira, A.T., da Silva, C.F.: Learning to decode human emotions from ERPs. Neural Computing and Applications, Springer, On-line Access (2014). doi:10.1007/s00521-014-1653-6

23. Bozhkov, L., Georgieva, P., Trifonov, R.: Brain Neural Data Analysis Using Machine Learning Feature Selection and Classification Methods. In: Mladenov, V., Jayne, C., Iliadis, L. (eds.) EANN 2014. CCIS, vol. 459, pp. 123–132. Springer, Heidelberg (2014)

Performance Investigation on Binary Particle Swarm Optimization for Global Optimization

Ying Loong Lee[1(✉)], Ayman Abd El-Saleh[1], Jonathan Loo[2], and MingFei Siyau[3]

[1] Faculty of Engineering, Multimedia University, Jalan Multimedia
63100, Cyberjaya, Selangor, Malaysia
lee.ying.loong12@student.mmu.edu.my, ayman.elsaleh@mmu.edu.my
[2] School of Science and Technology, Middlesex University, London NW44BT, UK
j.loo@mdx.ac.uk
[3] BiMEC Research Group, School of Engineering,
London South Bank University, London SE10AA, UK
siyaum@lsbu.ac.uk

Abstract. Binary particle swarm optimization (BinPSO) is introduced as a population-based random search algorithm for discrete binary optimization problems. A number of BinPSO variants have been introduced in the literature and showed performance improvements over the original BinPSO algorithm. However, no detailed performance comparison between these BinPSO variants has been found in the current literature. In this paper, a more thorough performance comparison study on the BinPSO variants in terms of convergence speed, solution quality and performance stability is presented. The BinPSO variants are further compared with a newly adopted cooperative BinPSO variant. The performance evaluation is conducted using De Jong's test functions, several complex multimodal functions, and a real-world engineering problem, namely optimization of the detection performance of cooperative spectrum sensing in cognitive radio networks. Results show that most of the BinPSO variants exhibit excellent performance on solving De Jong's test functions while the cooperative BinPSO variant performs better on the complex multimodal problems and the real-world engineering problem. Overall, the cooperative BinPSO variant shows the most promising performance, especially in terms of solution quality and performance stability.

Keywords: Particle swarm optimization · Binary particle swarm optimization · Convergence · Stability · De Jong's test functions · Multimodal functions

1 Introduction

Particle swarm optimization (PSO) is a population-based random search algorithm inspired from the social behavior of bird flocking [8]. Compared to other evolutionary algorithms, the implementation of PSO algorithms is relatively simple as it requires fewer parameters to adjust. In the past decade, PSO algorithms have been successfully applied to solve many real-world problems, including those requiring autonomous real-time adaptation [5, 13, 16, 18, 21].

© Springer International Publishing Switzerland 2015
Y. Demazeau et al. (Eds.): PAAMS 2015, LNAI 9086, pp. 142–154, 2015.
DOI: 10.1007/978-3-319-18944-4_12

The original PSO algorithm can only be applied to solve optimization problems that are in the continuous-valued (floating-point) domain. In order to solve discrete binary optimization problems, a binary particle swarm optimization (BinPSO) algorithm is proposed in [9]. The BinPSO algorithm retains the same advantages of the original PSO algorithm proposed in [8] and it allows for solving optimization problems of discrete binary nature. The BinPSO algorithm has been modified and implemented to solve several real-world problems [1, 14, 15, 17, 20].

In the literature, various studies have been carried out to continue improving the performance of BinPSO algorithms for global optimization. These studies have led to several new variants such as Novel BinPSO (NBinPSO) [11], Essential BinPSO (EPSO) [2] and Modified BinPSO (MBinPSO) [12]. Most of these studies employ the BinPSO algorithm proposed in [9] as the only benchmark. Comparison between the recent BinPSO variants in various performance aspects is not provided in these studies, hence leaving the progress of the BinPSO development unclear. As such, a performance comparison study on BinPSO would be useful to the readers as it would give insights about the recent development of BinPSO in various aspects.

The objective of this paper is to investigate the performance of various BinPSO variants proposed in the literature in terms of solution quality, convergence speed and performance stability. These BinPSO variants are further compared with a BinPSO algorithm enhanced with the cooperative approach in [19]. This is to investigate the potential of cooperative approaches to improve the BinPSO performance, which may spark researchers' interest to further explore into these approaches. The performance comparison is conducted using De Jong's test functions [3], which consist of several unimodal and simple multimodal optimization problems, and a number of complex multimodal functions, which contain large numbers of suboptimal solutions. In addition, a real-world application problem is used to evaluate the BinPSO variants.

The rest of the paper is organized as follows: Section 2 introduces PSO and reviews several recent BinPSO variants. In Section 3, performance evaluation of the recent BinPSO variants presented and discussed. Finally, Section 4 provides a number of concluding remarks about the performance evaluation and highlights potential future work.

2   Particle Swarm Optimization

2.1   Continuous PSO

In PSO, a group of particles travels through the search space of a given optimization problem to look for the optimal solution. This group of particles is referred to as a swarm. The position of each particle represents a candidate solution for the optimization problem. The basic working principle of the PSO algorithm is to allow all particles travelling in the search space in such a way that the movement of these particles is dependent on their personal and past experiences. In the PSO algorithm, the velocity and position update equations of each particle are given as [8]:

$$v_{ij}(t+1) = v_{ij}(t) + c_1 r_1 \left(y_{ij}(t) - x_{ij}(t) \right) + c_2 r_2 \left(\hat{y}_j(t) - x_{ij}(t) \right) \tag{1}$$

$$x_{ij}(t+1) = x_{ij}(t) + v_{ij}(t+1) \qquad (2)$$

where $x_{ij}(t)$ and $v_{ij}(t)$ are the position and velocity of the i-th particle in the j-th dimension at the t-th iteration respectively, c_1 and c_2 are acceleration constants, r_1 and r_2 are uniformly distributed random values ranging in $[0, 1]$, $y_{ij}(t)$ is the personal best (pbest) position, which is the best position found by the i-th particle in the j-th dimension at the t-th iteration while $\hat{y}_j(t)$ is the global best (gbest) position, which is the best position found by the entire swarm in the j-th dimension at the t-th iteration.

Fig. 1 shows the PSO algorithm for solving a maximization problem, where P denotes the swarm, N_s is the swarm size, n is the number of dimensions (i.e., number of decision variables), $f(.)$ is the objective function of the maximization problem, $x_i = [x_{i1}, x_{i2}, ..., x_{in}]$, $y_i = [y_{i1}, y_{i2}, ..., y_{in}]$ and $\hat{y}_i = [\hat{y}_{i1}, \hat{y}_{i2}, ..., \hat{y}_{in}]$ [19]. Each particle is first initialized at a random position in the search space of the problem. In each iteration, the velocity of each particle is updated using Eq. (1) followed by the position update using Eq. (2). After the updates, the new position of each particle will be evaluated using the objective function. If the solution found by a particle in an iteration provides a better objective function value than the previous iteration, this solution will be updated as the pbest position. Similarly, if the pbest position of a particle at current iteration is better than the gbest position, the gbest position will be replaced by the pbest position. This process is repeated until a certain stopping criterion is met.

```
Create and initialize an n-dimensional cPSO: P
repeat:
    for each particle i ∈ [1..Ns]:
        if f(P.xi) > f(P.yi)
            then P.yi = P.xi
        if f(P.yi) > f(P.ŷi)
            then P.ŷi = P.yi
        Perform PSO updates on P using Eqs. (1) and (2)
    endfor
until the stopping criterion is met
```

Fig. 1. Pseudocode of the PSO algorithm [19]

The topology of particles, i.e., their neighborhood structure can be modified to improve the performance. Various topologies have been proposed such as the global best (Gbest) model and the local best (Lbest) model [10]. In the Gbest model, all particles are neighbors to each other whereas in the Lbest model, each particle has two neighbors only. For further reading of topologies, readers may refer to [10].

2.2   Binary PSO

The first BinPSO algorithm proposed in [9] has a similar pseudocode compared to the original continuous-valued PSO algorithm except that the position update equation is replaced by:

$$x_{ij}(t+1) = \begin{cases} 1 & \text{if } r_3 < \text{sigmoid}\big(v_{ij}(t)\big) \\ 0 & \text{otherwise} \end{cases} \tag{3}$$

where r_3 is a uniformly distributed random value ranging in [0, 1] and the sigmoid function of $v_{ij}(t)$ is defined as [9]:

$$\text{sigmoid}\big(v_{ij}(t)\big) = \frac{1}{1+\exp\big(-v_{ij}(t)\big)} \tag{4}$$

In the BinPSO algorithm, $x_{ij}(t)$, $y_{ij}(t)$ and $\hat{y}_j(t)$ take only the binary values; that is zero or one, while the $v_{ij}(t)$ remains continuous-valued. Unlike the PSO algorithm in [8], $v_{ij}(t)$ in the BinPSO algorithm represents the probability of $x_{ij}(t)$ approaching the value of one. Moreover, $v_{ij}(t)$ is limited by a maximum velocity, V_{max}. The practical value of V_{max} was suggested to be ±4 [7]. It is noteworthy that the sigmoid function in Eq. (4) is used to normalize the $v_{ij}(t)$ so that its value is restricted within the range [0, 1].

In [11], the behavior of the parameters of the BinPSO algorithm is said to be deviated from that of the original PSO algorithm [8], leading to difficulties in choosing the appropriate parameter settings. To address these difficulties, the study in [11] proposed the NBinPSO algorithm in which a set of rules are introduced to update the position and velocity of each particle such that they imitate more closely to those of the original PSO algorithm. In addition, an inertia weight w is added to the particles' velocity to preserve the direction each of them has previously travelled.

The study in [2] exploits another approach for the same issues pointed in [11] by reformulating the particles' velocity and position update equations into probabilistic ones, deriving a new BinPSO variant known as Essential BinPSO (EPSO). Moreover, adopting the concept of ant colony optimization, a queen informant particle is added to further improve the search capability of the EPSO algorithm. As the queen informant particle will leave some pheromones in its previously travelled path in each iteration, this enhances the solution exploration and exploitation at the beginning and the end of the EPSO algorithm operation, respectively. This new EPSO variant is known as EPSOq.

In [12], the MBinPSO algorithm is proposed based on the genotype-phenotype concept where the velocity and the position of the particle are replaced by the so-called genotype and phenotype particle. The genotype particle is updated using Eqs. (1) and (2) with their respective $x_{ij}(t)$ being replaced by the phenotype and genotype particles. The phenotype particle is updated using Eqs. (3) and (4) with $x_{ij}(t)$ being replaced by the genotype particle. This modification allows the new position of each particle to take into account its previous position in the velocity and position update, which is not the case for the original BinPSO algorithm. Moreover, a bit change mutation feature is incorporated into the algorithm to mutate the genotype particle for better solution exploration.

In [19], a cooperative approach is proposed to enhance the ability of the PSO algorithm in solving high-dimensional optimization problems. This cooperative approach can be applied to any PSO algorithm, in fact, not limited to BinPSO. The idea of the cooperative approach is to decompose the candidate solution vector, which consists of all decision variables, into a number of component vectors, denoted by K. Each component vector is optimized by a separate swarm. In order to evaluate a component vector from a particular swarm, a *context vector* function is defined to compose this component vector with other component vectors from other swarms and form a global solution vector. The context vector function, $\mathbf{b}(k, \mathbf{z})$ is defined as follows [19]:

$$\mathbf{b}(k, \mathbf{z}) \equiv \left(P_1.\hat{\mathbf{y}}, ..., P_{k-1}.\hat{\mathbf{y}}, \mathbf{z}, P_{k+1}.\hat{\mathbf{y}}, ..., P_K.\hat{\mathbf{y}} \right) \tag{5}$$

where $P_k.\hat{\mathbf{y}}$ denotes the best component vector found by the k-th swarm where $k = 1$, 2, ..., K, and $\mathbf{z}$ denotes the component vector of the k-th swarm, which is to be evaluated. Using this context vector function, a candidate solution vector is reformed which can then be evaluated by the objective function. By applying the cooperative approach to the BinPSO algorithm, the pseudocode of the cooperative BinPSO (CBinPSO) algorithm can be presented in Fig. 2 where n_b is the number of binary-valued decision variables. It is noteworthy that $K = K_1 + K_2$ swarms are created with each of the first K_1 swarms optimizing $\lceil n_b/K \rceil$ decision variables and each of the next K_2 swarms optimizing $\lfloor n_b/K \rfloor$ decision variables. K_1 and K_2 are separately calculated because n_b may not always be evenly divided by K. Then, each swarm runs the BinPSO algorithm independently and evaluates its solution vectors using Eq. (5).

```
define
    b(k, z) ≡ ( P₁.ŷ, …, Pₖ₋₁.ŷ, z, Pₖ₊₁.ŷ, …, Pₖ.ŷ)
    K₁ = nₒ mod K
    K₂ = K – (nₒ mod K)
    Initialize K₁ ⌈nₒ/K⌉-dimensional PSOs: Pₖ, k ∈ [1..K₁]
    Initialize K₂ ⌊nₒ/K⌋-dimensional PSOs: Pₖ, k ∈ [(K₁+1)..K]
    repeat:
        for each swarm k ∈ [1..K]:
            for each particle i ∈ [1..Nₛ]:
                if f(b(k, Pₖ.xᵢ)) > f(b(k, Pₖ.yᵢ))
                    then Pₖ.yᵢ = Pₖ.xᵢ
                if f(b(k, Pₖ.yᵢ)) > f(b(k, Pₖ.ŷᵢ))
                    then Pₖ.ŷᵢ = Pₖ.yᵢ
                Perform BinPSO updates on Pₖ using Eqs. (1), (3) and (4)
            endfor
        endfor
    until the stopping condition is met
```

Fig. 2. Pseudocode of the CBinPSO algorithm

3   Performance Evaluation

The performance of various BinPSO variants is investigated in terms of solution quality, performance stability and convergence speed. The solution quality achieved by the BinPSO variants implies how well their ability in finding optimal solutions. The performance stability indicates the ability of the BinPSO variants in maintaining consistent performance in such a way that the solutions found in each run do not differ significantly compared to those found in other runs. The convergence speed shows how fast the BinPSO variants can converge to a solution. Intuitively, an effective and efficient optimization algorithm would demonstrate high solution quality, high performance stability and fast convergence speed. Using these performance aspects, the following BinPSO variants have been evaluated and compared: BinPSO [9], BinPSO [11], EPSO [2], EPSOq [2], MBinPSO [12] and CBinPSO [19].

Additionally, two different topologies, i.e., Gbest and Lbest models are applied to the BinPSO, EPSO, EPSOq and Modified BinPSO algorithms.

3.1 Benchmark Functions

In the performance evaluation, De Jong's test functions [3] and three complex multimodal functions [12] are employed as the benchmark problems. These functions are given as follows:

$$f_1(x) = \sum_{j=1}^{n} x_j^2 \tag{6}$$

$$f_2(x) = \sum_{j=1}^{n-1} \left(100(x_j^2 - x_{j+1})^2 - (1 - x_j)^2\right) \tag{7}$$

$$f_3(x) = 6n + \sum_{j=1}^{n} \lfloor x_j \rfloor \tag{8}$$

$$f_4(x) = \sum_{j=1}^{n} jx_j^4 + U(0,1) \tag{9}$$

$$\frac{1}{f_5(x)} = \frac{1}{500} + \sum_{m=1}^{25} \frac{1}{m + \sum_{j=1}^{2} (x_j - a_{jm})^6} \tag{10}$$

$$f_6(x) = 10n + \sum_{j=1}^{n} \left(x_j^2 - 10\sin(2\pi x_j)\right) \tag{11}$$

$$f_7(x) = -20\exp\left(-0.2\sqrt{\frac{1}{30}\sum_{j=1}^{n} x_j^2}\right) - \exp\left(\frac{1}{n}\sum_{j=1}^{n} \cos(2\pi x_j)\right) + 20 + e \tag{12}$$

$$f_8(x) = \frac{1}{4000}\sum_{j=1}^{n} x_j^2 - \prod_{j=1}^{n} \cos\left(\frac{x_j}{\sqrt{j}}\right) + 1 \tag{13}$$

where $a_{jm} = \begin{pmatrix} -32 & -16 & 0 & 16 & 32 & -32 & ... \\ -32 & -32 & -32 & -32 & -32 & -16 & ... \end{pmatrix}$ and n is the number of di-

mensions. Also, it is noteworthy that f_6 - f_8 are minimization problems. To show evaluation consistency with De Jong's test functions, i.e., f_1 - f_5 which are maximization problems, f_6 - f_8 are converted into equivalent maximization problems by multiplying the achieved fitness value with -1 [6].

3.2   Experimental Setup

Since all the decision variables in De Jong's test functions are continuous-valued, they need to be converted to binary-valued variables before being employed by the BinPSO algorithms. In this study, a binary encoding scheme that is commonly used to perform the conversion in genetic algorithms (GAs) is used. In this scheme, a user-defined *resolution factor* (RF), which is the smallest continuous value represented by a bit, is used to determine the number of bits required to represent a continuous-valued decision variable of a given optimization problem. Given an RF, the number of bits per continuous-valued decision variable, N_b can be obtained as:

$$N_b = \left\lceil \log_2 \left(\frac{x_{max} - x_{min}}{RF} \right) \right\rceil \tag{14}$$

where the x_{max} and x_{min} denote the maximum and minimum boundary values of the given search space, respectively. After finding N_b, the conversion between continuous-valued and binary-valued decision variables can be performed using:

$$x_b = \frac{x_c - x_{min}}{RF} \tag{15}$$

where x_c is the value of the continuous-valued decision variable and x_b is the decimal value of the binary equivalent of x_c. Then, x_b is converted to its binary equivalent in the form of bitstring consisting of N_b bits. After that, all the bitstrings are concatenated to a single bitstring, forming a solution vector which consists of $n \times N_b$ binary-valued decision variables. In this study, the RFs chosen for each test function is given in Table 1.

As the CBinPSO algorithm contains multiple swarms while other BinPSO variants contain only one swarm, the number of iterations is not accurate as a processing time measure. This is because, in one iteration, the CBinPSO algorithm spends a number of function evaluations (FEs) equivalent to K swarms multiplied by the number of particles of one swarm whereas other BinPSO variants spend only a number of FEs equivalent to the number of particles of one swarm in one iteration. Thus, the number of FEs is used as the processing time measure for a fair complexity comparison. The total number of FEs is given as $FE = N_t N_s K$ for the CBinPSO algorithm and $FE = N_t N_s$ for other BinPSO variants, where N_t is the number of iterations.

Table 1. Parameter settings of test functions and their global maxima

F	Function Name	n	RF	N_b	n_b	Domain $[x_{min}, x_{max}]^n$	Global Maxima
f_1	Sphere	3	0.01	10	30	$[-5.12, 5.12]^n$	78.64
f_2	Rosenbrock	2	0.001	12	24	$[-2.048, 2.048]^n$	3905.93
f_3	Step	5	0.01	10	50	$[-5.12, 5.12]^n$	55.0
f_4	Noisy Quadric	30	0.01	8	240	$[-1.28, 1.28]^n$	1248.2
f_5	Foxholes	2	0.001	17	34	$[-65.536, 65.536]^n$	500.0
f_6	Rastrigin	30	0.01	10	300	$[-5.12, 5.12]^n$	0
f_7	Ackley	30	0.1	10	300	$[-30, 30]^n$	0
f_8	Griewank	30	0.1	13	390	$[-300, 300]^n$	0

For f_1 - f_5, the simulation parameters are set as follows: N_s, FE and the number of simulation repetitions are set to 20, 4000 and 20, respectively. For f_6 - f_8, N_s, FE and the number of simulation repetitions are set to 40, 40000 and 30, respectively. The mutation rate of the MBinPSO algorithm is set to 0.3, 0.7, 0.5, 0.7, 0.7, 0.0, 0.0 and 0.4 for for $f_1, f_2, f_3, f_4, f_5, f_6, f_7$ and f_8, respectively as in [12]. Additionally, K is set to n of each test function for the CBinPSO algorithm (see Table 1). The rest of the parameters of the BinPSO, NBinPSO, EPSO and EPSOq, and MBinPSO algorithms are set as in [7], [11], [2] and [12], respectively.

3.3   Results and Discussion

Table 2 tabulates the mean and standard deviation of the objective function values achieved by each BinPSO variant on the test functions where the values in bold indicate the best results. Overall, the CBinPSO algorithm attains the best solution quality as it optimizes most of the test functions. The NBinPSO, EPSO and EPSOq algorithms can only obtain optimal solutions for f_1, f_2, f_4 and f_5. Other BinPSO variants do not perform well on all the test functions. As such, the CBinPSO algorithm is generally the best algorithm in terms of solution quality for both unimodal and multimodal optimization problems. On the other hand, the NBinPSO, EPSO and EPSOq algorithms is only suitable for unimodal and simple multimodal problems.

The performance of the EPSOq algorithm (with GBest) on De Jong's test functions is generally more stable compared to other BinPSO variants, as shown in Table 2. Its stability on f_3 is outperformed by only the CBinPSO algorithm. On the other hand, the CBinPSO algorithm demonstrates more stable performance on f_6 and f_8, compared to other BinPSO variants. Additionally, as the CBinPSO algorithm is the only one that finds near-optimal solutions to the multimodal problems, i.e., f_6 - f_8, its comparison against other BinPSO variants in terms of performance stability is thus trivial.

Fig. 3(a)-(e) shows the convergence performance of the BinPSO variants in maximizing the De Jong's test functions. The NBinPSO, EPSO and EPSOq algorithms converge within 300 FEs to the optimal solutions for f_1, f_2, f_4 and f_5, which are the fastest among all the other BinPSO variants. Although these BinPSO variants also converge within 300 FEs for f_3, they converge to a suboptimal solution. This implies that the BinPSO variants are vulnerable to the local optimums of f_3 and likely to be trapped in these values. The CBinPSO algorithm converges slower than the NBinPSO, EPSO and EPSOq algorithms for f_1 - f_5. This is because the CBinPSO algorithm spends more FEs in each iteration. In particular, the CBinPSO algorithm is unable to reach convergence for f_4 because the number of FEs given is insufficient to converge. The BinPSO and MBinPSO algorithms converge to local optimums of all the test functions, thus it is trivial to compare them with other BinPSO variants in terms of convergence speed. In summary, the NBinPSO, EPSO and EPSOq are more time-efficient for solving unimodal and simple multimodal problems.

Table 2. Mean and standard deviation of the achievable fitness scores

PSOs	f_1	f_2	f_3	f_4
BinPSO–Gbest	$77.94\pm8.767\times10^{-1}$	$3749\pm1.116\times10^{2}$	$53.30\pm8.645\times10^{-1}$	$735.5\pm5.623\times10^{1}$
BinPSO–Lbest	$78.12\pm4.897\times10^{-1}$	$3529\pm3.986\times10^{2}$	$53.55\pm1.234\times10^{0}$	$792.6\pm6.779\times10^{1}$
NBinPSO	$\mathbf{78.64\pm1.458\times10^{-14}}$	$\mathbf{3905\pm4.665\times10^{-13}}$	$44.65\pm2.277\times10^{0}$	$1248\pm2.956\times10^{-1}$
EPSO–Gbest	$\mathbf{78.64\pm1.458\times10^{-14}}$	$\mathbf{3905\pm4.665\times10^{-13}}$	$41.50\pm2.856\times10^{0}$	$1248\pm2.938\times10^{-1}$
EPSO–Lbest	$\mathbf{78.64\pm1.458\times10^{-14}}$	$\mathbf{3905\pm4.665\times10^{-13}}$	$41.10\pm2.673\times10^{0}$	$1248\pm2.939\times10^{-1}$
EPSOq–Gbest	$\mathbf{78.64\pm1.458\times10^{-14}}$	$\mathbf{3905\pm4.665\times10^{-13}}$	$42.00\pm2.733\times10^{0}$	$\mathbf{1248\pm2.850\times10^{-1}}$
EPSOq–Lbest	$\mathbf{78.64\pm1.458\times10^{-14}}$	$\mathbf{3905\pm4.665\times10^{-13}}$	$42.10\pm2.593\times10^{0}$	$1248\pm2.887\times10^{-1}$
MBinPSO–Gbest	$74.75\pm1.553\times10^{0}$	$3733\pm8.859\times10^{1}$	$48.00\pm7.255\times10^{-1}$	$554.0\pm2.813\times10^{1}$
MBinPSO–Lbest	$74.02\pm1.851\times10^{0}$	$3736\pm8.318\times10^{1}$	$48.60\pm1.231\times10^{0}$	$543.4\pm2.067\times10^{1}$
CBinPSO	$\mathbf{78.64\pm1.458\times10^{-14}}$	$3901\pm4.181\times10^{0}$	$\mathbf{55.00\pm0.000\times10^{0}}$	$1248\pm1.664\times10^{1}$
PSOs	f_5	f_6	f_7	f_8
BinPSO–Gbest	$\mathbf{499.9\pm3.559\times10^{-6}}$	$-349.8\pm2.881\times10^{1}$	$\mathbf{-20.17\pm6.100\times10^{-2}}$	$-151.5\pm1.640\times10^{1}$
BinPSO–Lbest	$\mathbf{499.9\pm1.416\times10^{-6}}$	$-384.4\pm3.063\times10^{1}$	$\mathbf{-20.14\pm4.670\times10^{-2}}$	$-229.3\pm1.767\times10^{1}$
NBinPSO	$\mathbf{499.9\pm2.916\times10^{-13}}$	$-400.4\pm2.636\times10^{1}$	$\mathbf{-20.62\pm8.200\times10^{-2}}$	$-225.3\pm2.392\times10^{1}$
EPSO–Gbest	$\mathbf{499.9\pm2.916\times10^{-13}}$	$-423.2\pm2.013\times10^{1}$	$-19.99\pm1.475\times10^{-1}$	$-231.2\pm2.682\times10^{1}$
EPSO–Lbest	$\mathbf{499.9\pm2.916\times10^{-13}}$	$-404.1\pm2.683\times10^{1}$	$-19.94\pm2.703\times10^{-4}$	$-231.2\pm2.134\times10^{1}$
EPSOq–Gbest	$\mathbf{499.9\pm2.916\times10^{-13}}$	$-410.7\pm2.275\times10^{1}$	$-20.16\pm2.778\times10^{-1}$	$-233.5\pm1.716\times10^{1}$
EPSOq–Lbest	$\mathbf{499.9\pm2.916\times10^{-13}}$	$-409.7\pm3.073\times10^{1}$	$-19.94\pm7.754\times10^{-4}$	$-224.5\pm2.336\times10^{1}$
MBinPSO–Gbest	$499.9\pm6.199\times10^{-6}$	$-43.88\pm7.944\times10^{0}$	$-15.45\pm3.918\times10^{0}$	$-149.9\pm1.044\times10^{1}$
MBinPSO–Lbest	$499.9\pm6.783\times10^{-6}$	$-378.9\pm1.947\times10^{1}$	$\mathbf{-20.06\pm1.698\times10^{-1}}$	$-147.5\pm1.198\times10^{1}$
CBinPSO	$\mathbf{499.9\pm3.604\times10^{-13}}$	$\mathbf{-0.668\pm2.803\times10^{-1}}$	$\mathbf{-0.875\pm3.760\times10^{-2}}$	$\mathbf{-0.164\pm1.831\times10^{-1}}$

For f_6 - f_8, the NBinPSO, EPSO and EPSOq algorithms prematurely converge within 5000 FEs to solutions at which the achievable fitness scores are significantly lower than their global maximum, as shown in Fig. 3(f)-(g). This indicates that these BinPSO variants suffer from premature convergence for complex multimodal problems and hence they are not suitable for such problems. Though the BinPSO and MBinPSO algorithms achieve better solutions for the complex multimodal functions, they need more FEs to reach convergence. The CBinPSO algorithm converges to near-optimal solutions after around 15000 FEs for f_6 and f_7 and after 5000 FEs for f_8, which is reasonably fast. This shows that the CBinPSO algorithm is more time-efficient for solving complex multimodal functions.

3.4   Real-World Engineering Problem

In this section, the BinPSO variants are tested on a real-world application, which is the cooperative spectrum sensing problem in a cognitive radio network. This problem is to maximize the probability of detecting the occupancy of a primary wireless channel by a group of secondary or cognitive radio users as in [4]. For this problem, the number of cognitive radio users is set to 20, each weighting coefficient is binary-encoded with RF = 0.0001, and the other network parameter settings follow those in [4]. For the CBinPSO algorithm, K is set to 20. For the MBinPSO algorithm, the

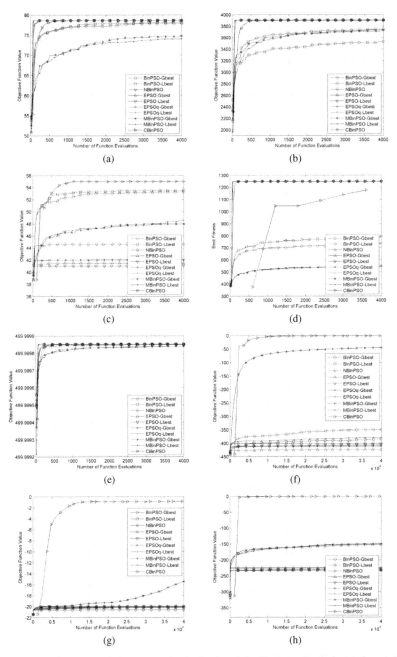

Fig. 3. Convergence performance on (a) f_1, (b) f_2, (c) f_3, (d) f_4, (e) f_5, (f) f_6, (g) f_7 and (h) f_8

mutation rate is set to 0.5. For all the BinPSO variants, N_s, *FE* and the number of simulation repetitions are set to 40, 3000 and 100, respectively. Other BinPSO parameters are the same as in the previous section.

The CBinPSO algorithm is shown to achieve the best solution quality and performance stability, as shown in Table 3. In Fig. 4, the EPSO algorithm attains the highest convergence speed while the CBinPSO and MBinPSO algorithms are the Overall, the CBinPSO algorithm is generally the best performer due to its high solution quality and stability. Although its convergence speed is slow, it almost reaches convergence in the given number of FEs.

Table 3. Mean and standard deviation achieved for the cooperative spectrum sensing problem

PSO	BinPSO		NBin PSO	EPSO		EPSOq		MBinPSO		CBin- PSO
	Gbest	Lbest		Gbest	Lbest	Gbest	Lbest	Gbest	Lbest	
Result	0.591 ± 0.014	0.589 ± 0.014	0.651 ± 0.036	0.751 ± 0.037	0.747 ± 0.038	0.655 ± 0.050	0.655 ± 0.056	0.740 ± 0.037	0.675 ± 0.089	**0.858 ± 0.004**

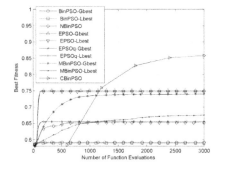

Fig. 4. Convergence performance

4   Conclusion and Future Works

In this paper, we have investigated the performance of various BinPSO variants in terms of solution quality, performance stability and convergence speed. The NBinP-SO, EPSO and EPSOq algorithms are more suitable for solving unimodal and simple multimodal problems due to their high solution quality, stability and convergence speed on such problems, compared to other BinPSO variants. Although the CBinPSO algorithm can also achieve high solution quality on the problems, the NBinPSO, EPSO and EPSOq algorithms are more processing time-efficient. On the other hand, the CBinPSO algorithm is more suitable for solving complex multimodal problems as it achieves high solution quality and stability with reasonably fast convergence, compared to other BinPSO variants. The CBinPSO algorithm also performs well on the cooperative spectrum sensing problem in cognitive radio networks. Overall, the CBinPSO algorithm is the most promising candidate for various types of problems.

Nevertheless, improvement on the convergence speed of CBinPSO algorithm is still required when applied to other real-time applications.

References

1. Chatterjee, A., Tudu, B., Paul, K.C.: Towards optimized binary pattern generation for grayscale digital halftoning: A binary particle swarm optimization (BPSO) approach. J. Vis. Commun. Image R. **23**(8), 1245–1259 (2012)
2. Chen, E., Li, J., Liu, X.: In search of essential binary discrete particle swarm. Appl. Soft Comput. **11**(3), 3260–3269 (2011)
3. De Jong, K. A.: An analysis of the behaviour of a class of genetic adaptive systems. Unpublished doctoral dissertation, University of Michigan, Ann Arbor, MI, US (1975)
4. El-Saleh, A.A., Ismail, M., Ali, M.A.M.: Genetic algorithm-assisted soft fusion-based linear cooperative spectrum sensing. IEICE Electron. Express **8**(18), 1527–1533 (2011)
5. Jin, N., Rahmat-Samii, Y.: Advances in particle swarm optimization for antenna designs: real-number, binary, single-objective and multiobjective implementations. IEEE Trans. Antennas Propag. **55**(3), 556–567 (2007)
6. Kameyama, K.: Particle swarm optimization – a survey. IEICE Trans. Inf. & Syst. **E92-D**(7), 1354–1361 (2009)
7. Kennedy, J., Eberhart, R.: Swarm Intelligence. Morgan Kaufmann Publisher, San Francisco (2001)
8. Kennedy, J., Eberhart, R. C.: Particle swarm optimization. In: Proceedings of the IEEE International Conference on Neural Networks, Perth, WA (1995)
9. Kennedy J., Eberhart, R. C.: A discrete binary version of the particle swarm algorithm. In: IEEE International Conference on Systems, Man, and Cybernetics, Orlando, FL (1997)
10. Kennedy, J., Mendes, R.: Population structure and particle swarm performance. In: Proceedings of the IEEE Congress on Evolutionary Computing, Honolulu, HI, USA (2002)
11. Khanesar, M.A., Teshnehlab, M., Shoorehdeli, M. A.: A novel binary particle swarm optimization. In: Mediterranean Conference on Control and Automation, Athens, Greece (2007)
12. Lee, S., Soak, S., Oh, S., Pedrycz, W., Jeon, M.: Modified binary particle swarm optimization. Prog. Natural Sci. **18**(9), 1161–1166 (2008)
13. Messerschmidt, L., Engelbrecht, A.P.: Learning to play games using a PSO-based competitive learning approach. IEEE Trans. Evol. Comput. **8**(3), 280–288 (2004)
14. Pookpunt, S., Ongsakul, W.: Optimal placement of wind turbines within wind farm using binary particle swarm optimization with time-varying acceleration coefficients. Renew. Energ. **55**, 266–276 (2013)
15. Sarath, K.N.V.D., Ravi, V.: Association rule mining using binary particle swarm optimization. Eng. App. Artif. Intel. **26**(8), 1832–1840 (2013)
16. Schutte, J.F., Groenwold, A.A.: Sizing design of truss structures using particle swarms. Struct. Multidisc. Optim. **25**(4), 261–269 (2003)
17. Tasgetiren, M.F., Liang, Y.: A binary particle swarm optimization algorithm for lot sizing problem. J. Econ. Soc. Res. **5**(2), 1–20 (2003)

18. Van den Bergh, F., Engelbrecht, A.P.: Cooperative learning in neural networks using particle swarm optimizers. South African Comput. J. **26**, 84–90 (2000)
19. Van den Bergh, F., Engelbrecht, A.P.: A cooperative approach to particle swarm optimization. IEEE Trans. Evol. Comput. **8**(3), 225–239 (2004)
20. Yuan, X., Nie, H., Su, A., Wang, L., Yuan, Y.: An improved binary particle swarm optimization for unit commitment problem. Expert Syst. Appl. **36**(4), 8049–8055 (2009)
21. Zhao, Z., Xu, S., Zheng, S., Shang, J.: Cognitive radio adaptation using particle swarm optimization. Wirel. Commun. Mob. Comput. **9**(7), 875–881 (2009)

Contracts for Difference and Risk Management in Multi-agent Energy Markets

Francisco Sousa[1], Fernando Lopes[2]($\boxtimes$), and João Santana[1]

[1] Instituto Superior Técnico, Universidade de Lisboa, INESC-ID, Lisbon, Portugal
{francisco.sousa,jsantana}@ist.utl.pt
[2] LNEG–National Research Institute, Est. Paço do Lumiar 22, Lisbon, Portugal
fernando.lopes@lneg.pt

Abstract. The liberalization process of the power sector has led to competitive wholesale and retail markets. Market participants are exposed to risks associated with price volatility and uncertainties regarding production and consumption. This paper addresses these issues by analyzing and evaluating the role of contracts for difference (CFDs) as a financial product used to hedge against risk. The article presents several key features of software gents able to negotiate CFDs, paying special attention to risk management, notably risk attitude, and price negotiation. It starts with a contextualization of the subject, which is followed by the definition of a model to negotiate CFDs, involving several trading strategies and tactics. It starts with a contextualization of the subject, which is followed by the definition of a model to negotiate CFDs, involving a group of strategies to control the exposure of risk by software agents. Finally, a set of case studies is described to assess the performance of CFDs as a risk management tool and to compare their performance to forward bilateral contracts.

Keywords: Electricity markets · Bilateral contracting · Contracts for difference · Risk management · Trading strategies · Autonomous software agents

1 Introduction

The power sector covers four main activities: generation, transmission, distribution and retail of electricity. The way this sector has been organized changed throughout the last century and is customary to distinguish four main models: a regulated natural monopoly, single buyer, competition in a wholesale market, and competition in both wholesale and retail markets [1]. Two key mechanisms for purchasing and selling electrical energy are electricity pools and bilateral contracting. A pool, or market exchange, involves basically a specific

This work was performed under the project MAN-REM (FCOMP-01-0124-FEDER-020397), supported by both FEDER and National funds through the program "COMPETE−Programa Operacional Temático Factores de Competividade" and "FCT−Fundação para a Ciência e a Tecnologia".

© Springer International Publishing Switzerland 2015
Y. Demazeau et al. (Eds.): PAAMS 2015, LNAI 9086, pp. 155–164, 2015.
DOI: 10.1007/978-3-319-18944-4_13

form of auction, where participants send bids to sell and buy electricity, for a certain period of time. A bilateral contract is an agreement between two parties where one party commits to deliver energy and the other to pay for it. The advantage of this type of agreement is that the terms (such as quantity of energy and price) are custom-made to the parties' needs.

Bilateral contracts can also help to mitigate the position of power of bigger producers in the spot market by not allowing buyers to be dependent on them to fulfill their energy needs and looking elsewhere for a better deal. Another advantage of bilateral contracts is the support given to renewable generation. Renewable energy is characterized by high capital costs and outputs heavily dependent on weather conditions, problems that traditional energy sources do not have. Potential investors require a guaranteed stream of future revenues in order to obtain financing for those resources. Hence, if they engage in bilateral contracts to sell their energy output they have a guaranteed flow of revenue independent of market prices [2].

Electrical energy needs to be consumed within a tenth of second of generation. Consequently, offer has to match demand to ensure efficiency, stability and reliability. Market participants are, therefore, exposed to several risks since they have to work with predictions. These include financial risks related to high volatility of prices due to demand fluctuation which can reach peaks in periods of insufficient generation. Also, important to mention are the risks related to energy volume due to the inherent uncertainty regarding both demand and renewable generation. Risk hedging is essential to market participants and several financial instruments can be used when two parties with opposite views are willing to exchange risk. The most common are future contracts, forward contracts, options contracts and contracts for differences. These contracts can either require the physical delivery of electricity or have a purely financial settlement.

Future contracts include an obligation to buy or sell a specified quantity of energy at a certain future time for a certain price. These contracts have financial daily settlements between the agreed price and the variable spot market price. The parties do not interact directly and a central counter-party guarantees the fulfillment of obligations. The physical delivery is optional. Forward contracts imply a commitment between the parties to sell or buy a specific amount of electricity at a certain future time for a certain price. Unlike future contracts, they involve commitments regarding the date on which the energy is delivered and the payment is done [3]. In these cases, there is no financial settlement and the physical delivery is always required. Option contracts include a right (not an obligation) to buy or sell a specific quantity of an asset at a certain future time for a certain price. A call option gives the right to buy an asset and a put option the right to sell it in a certain future time.

Contracts for difference (CFDs) involve no physical delivery of energy by sellers. The parties fulfill their energy needs in the spot market during the duration of the contract [4]. They establish a bilateral agreement regarding the provision of an amount of energy for a fixed price called the strike price. Also, they come to an agreement regarding the reference price which is used to calculate the differences. If the reference price is higher than the strike price, then the seller will pay the difference to the buyer. Conversely, the buyer pays an amount equal to the difference between the strike price and the reference price. In some cases, contracts for difference can be one way contracts, when the difference payments are made only by one of the parties [3].

Electricity markets are a complex evolving reality—there is now a number of market participants, each one with their own set of objectives, strategies and exposure to risk. One way to model such a complex system is by using autonomous software agents. Software agents are computer systems capable of flexible autonomous action in order to meet their design objectives. They can to respond in a timely fashion to changes that occur in the environment, exhibit goal-directed behavior, and interact with other agents in order to reach their design objectives.

In particular, each agent can be characterized by a set of key features, including [5]:

- A set of beliefs that represent information about the agent and the market;
- A set of goals representing words states to be achieved;
- A library of plan templates to be used in order to reach the goals;
- A set of plans for execution, either immediately, or in the near future.

Against this background, this paper presents several key features of software gents able to negotiate contracts for difference, paying special attention to risk management, notably risk attitude, and price negotiation.

2   Energy Contracts and Bilateral Negotiation

2.1   A Bilateral Negotiation Model

The negotiation model described in this section is based on our previous work in the area of automated negotiation [6–10]. Let $\mathcal{A} = \{a_1, a_2\}$ be the set of autonomous agents participating in negotiation. Let $Agenda = \{x_1, \ldots, x_n\}$ be the negotiating agenda representing the set of issues to be deliberated. Each issue is quantitative and defined over a continuous domain $D = [min, max]$. The price limit of each agent for an issue x is denoted by lim.

One of the key aspects of negotiation is the adoption of a negotiation protocol that settles the rules of trading. In the present case, we consider an alternating offers protocol. The agents determine an allocation of the issues by alternately submitting proposals at times in $\mathcal{T} = \{1, 2, \ldots\}$. This means that only one offer is submitted in each period $t \in \mathcal{T}$, with an agent, say $a_i \in \mathcal{A}$, offering in odd periods $\{1, 3, \ldots\}$, and the other agent $a_j \in \mathcal{A}$ offering in even periods $\{2, 4, \ldots\}$. The agents have the ability to unilaterally opt out of the negotiation when responding to a proposal made by the opponent.

The negotiation process starts with a_i submitting a proposal $p^1_{i \to j}$ to a_j in period $t = 1$. The agent a_j receives $p^1_{i \to j}$ and can either accept the offer (Yes), reject it and opt out of the negotiation (Opt), or reject it and continue bargaining (No). In the first two cases, negotiation comes to an end. Specifically, if $p^1_{i \to j}$

is accepted, negotiation ends successfully and the agreement is implemented. Conversely, if $p_{i \to j}^1$ is rejected and a_j decides to opt out, negotiation terminates with no agreement. In the last case, negotiation proceeds to the next time period $t = 2$, in which a_j makes a counter-proposal $p_{j \to i}^2$. This process repeats until one of the outcomes mentioned above occurs.

Conceptually, each offer is a vector of issue values sent by an agent $a_i \in \mathcal{A}$ to an agent $a_j \in \mathcal{A}$ in period $t \in \mathcal{T}$:

$$p_{i \to j}^t = (v_1, \dots, v_n) \tag{1}$$

where v_k, $k = 1, \dots, n$, is a value of an issue $x_k \in Agenda$. The decision to accept or reject an offer depends on the rating that agents give to each issue taking into account their preferences. Each agent has a multi-issue utility function:

$$U_i(x_1, \dots, x_n) = \sum_{k=1}^{n} w_k \times V_k(x_k) \tag{2}$$

where w_k is the weight for an issue x_k (a number representing the preference of an agent for x_k) and $V_k(x_k)$ is the marginal utility function that gives the score a_i assigns to a value of x_k. This function is used by agents to rate incoming offers and counter-offers. Specifically, offer acceptance will occur when the utility given to a received offer is higher than the utility of the offer that an agent is willing to counter-propose.

2.2   Contracts for Difference and Negotiation

This section extends the above model to simulate typical procedures associated with CFDs. Consider that negotiation involves the prices and quantities of energy for a generic n-rate tariff. Typical tariffs involve two levels (off-peak and on-peak) and three levels (off-peak, mid-peak and on-peak). More refined tariffs backed by legislation can also be imagined and considered if, instead of three rates, suppliers offer four, or even an hour-wise tariff. Accordingly, the agenda includes n energy quantities, i.e., $\{Q_1, \dots, Q_n\}$, where each quantity represents the consumption of a specific part of a day. The agenda also includes n strike prices and n reference prices. In particular, CFDs require that the parties agree on a set of strike prices:

$$Sp = (sp_1, \dots, sp_n) \tag{3}$$

where:

(i) Sp is the vector of strike prices (in €/MWh);
(ii) sp_k, $k = 1, \dots, n$, is the strike price for the specific quantity q_k of Q_k.

CFDs also require that the parties agree on a set of reference prices to be used in the definition of the differences. These prices are represented by:

$$Rp = (rp_1, \dots, rp_n) \tag{4}$$

where:

(i) Rp is the vector of reference prices (in €/MWh);
(ii) rp_k, $k = 1, \ldots, n$, is the reference price associated with a specific block of a day.

With the formalization of these vectors, the differences between prices can be computed, and their multiplication by energy quantities gives the appropriate financial compensations. Specifically, when the strike prices are smaller than the reference prices, the seller agent will pay to the buyer. The total amount will be given by the following expression:

$$C_s = \sum_{k=1}^{n} (rp_k - sp_k) \times q_k \qquad (5)$$

Conversely, it will be the buyer's turn to pay a financial compensation when the strike prices are higher than the reference prices. The total amount will be given by:

$$C_b = \sum_{k=1}^{n} (sp_k - rp_k) \times q_k \qquad (6)$$

3 Bilateral Contracting and Risk Management

3.1 Risk Attitude and Utility

Agents can control their exposure to risk by adopting specific behaviors throughout negotiation. These behaviors depend on their attitude towards risk and the model presented below tries to formalize this dependency.

The expected utility theory states that agents are risk averse when they prefer a prospect with guaranteed outcomes to any other risky prospect that may have better outcomes [11]. Accordingly to this theory, the negotiating agents fit into one of the following categories:

1. *Risk-averse agents*: prefer a setting where they are guaranteed to profit a certain amount to another setting where that profit can be bigger but there is a chance of not getting anything;
2. *Risk-seeking agents*: prefer a setting where there is a chance of making bigger profits (although they are not guaranteed) to another setting where a smaller amount of profit is guaranteed;
3. *Risk-neutral agents*: generally, have no preference over the outcome of negotiation and takes an intermediate stance compared to the two described above.

Negotiation may end with either agreement or no agreement. Risk-averse agents show typically more flexibility to secure a deal, and therefore, concede more to avoid that negotiation ends prematurely without agreement. If an agreement is reached, these agents will probably buy (sell) energy at a higher (lower) price compared to agents that are not averse to risk. Risk-seeking agents

Table 1. Agent classification according to the attitude towards risk

Level of risk aversion	Value of $r(x)$	Interval for λ
Risk-averse	$r(x) > 0$	$\lambda \in]0, 1]$
Risk-neutral	$r(x) = 0$	$\lambda = 0$
Risk-seeker	$r(x) < 0$	$\lambda \in [-1, 0[$

tend to be more rigid and firm, typically conceding less than their opponent. By engaging in this behavior, negotiation may end without an agreement being in place. Despite this, if negotiation ends successfully with agreement, risk-seeking agents will probably benefit more than risk-averse agents in similar situations.

In economy, utility is often considered the price that agents are willing to pay for the fulfillment or satisfaction of their desires [11]. Their preferences can be represented using a utility function $u(x)$ with the following properties:

(1) $U(x) > U(x')$ if agents prefer x to x';
(2) $U(x) = U(x')$ if agents are indifferent between x and x'.

For each $x_1, x_2, \ldots, x_n$, there is a probability $\pi_1, \pi_2, \ldots, \pi_n$, of occurrence. Considering mutual exclusivity, the utility function can be written in the following way:

$$u(x) = \pi_1 u(x_1) + \pi_2 u(x_2) + \cdots + \pi_n u(x_n) \tag{7}$$

which is often referred to as expected utility function or von Neumann-Morgenstern utility function [12]. Typically, for risk-averse agents, the utility function is concave, meaning that the utility of the expected value is greater than the expected utility of wealth. Likewise, for risk-seeking agents, the utility function is convex. For the intermediate case (risk-neutral), the utility function is linear [13].

3.2 Measuring Agents' Risk Aversion

A typical approach to quantify agents' attitude toward risk is through the curvature of the utility function. Considering the second derivative $u(x)''$, it will be negative for a concave function, positive for a convex one, and zero for a linear function. John Pratt [14] proposed the following equation to measure agents' risk aversion:

$$r(x) = \frac{-u''(x)}{u'(x)} \tag{8}$$

The sign of $u''(x)$ equals the sign of $-r(x)$. A negative (positive) sign implies unwillingness (willingness) to accept risk. Also, a negative (positive) sign implies strict concavity (convexity) and, therefore, aversion (propensity) to accept risk. Pratt's work will be used as a basis to measure agents' risk aversion: let λ be a parameter correlated with $r(x)$, with $\lambda \in [-1, 1]$. Given λ, and using the sign stipulation of Pratt, agents can be classified according to table 1.

3.3   Negotiation Strategies and Risk Management

Negotiation strategies can reflect a wide range of behaviors and lead to different outcomes. In this paper, we focus on concession making strategies: negotiators reduce their aspirations to accommodate the opponent. Specifically, the measure of risk aversion (λ) will be used to develop a new group of concession strategies.

For a given price P, we adopt the formulae proposed in [5,9] (for seller and buyer, respectively):

$$P_{k_{new}} = P_{k_{prev}} - C_f\ (P_{k_{prev}} - lim),\ k = 1, \ldots, n \qquad (9)$$

$$P_{k_{new}} = P_{k_{prev}} + C_f\ (lim - P_{k_{prev}}),\ k = 1, \ldots, n \qquad (10)$$

where $P_{k_{new}}$ is the new price for period k, C_f is the concession factor, and lim is the price limit established by the agent. The concession factor C_f varies, in percentage, between 0 and 100. If C_f is null, then agents will not concede during the course of negotiation. If it is equal to 100, then agents make a complete concession on P and thus accept a price equal to their limit.

The concession factor can be simply a positive constant independent of any objective criteria. However, most often it is modelled as a function of a single criterion. Typical criteria include the total concession made on each issue throughout negotiation [5] and the time elapsed since the beginning of negotiation [15]. In this work, we model the concession factor as a function of the attitude towards risk: the bigger the flexibility in negotiation the bigger the concession factor will be. This implies that a risk-averse agent makes concessions at a bigger rate and, therefore, the concession factor will be bigger than the one of a risk-seeking agent that shows unwillingness to concede and less flexibility in negotiation.

The concession factor can be represented by considering either a polynomial or an exponential function. In this work, we consider an exponential function. To keep multi-agent negotiation as close as possible to real-world negotiations, functions that give values for C_f smaller than 5% and larger than 25% were not considered, as these values do not represent reasonable negotiation stances. The general form of the exponential function is as follows:

$$C_f = C_{fn}\ e^{c\,\lambda} \qquad (11)$$

where λ is the value of the agent's risk aversion, C_{fn} is the concession factor for a risk-neutral agent ($\lambda = 0$), and c is a constant that shapes the function's curvature.

Equation 11 represents a family of tactics, one for each pair of values (C_{fn}, c). Accordingly, several simulations were made to define appropriate values for these

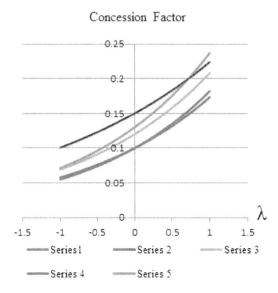

Fig. 1. Concession factor for a given measure of risk aversion

parameters. Table 2 shows the values considered and figure 1 the behavior of the resulting functions. After a detailed analysis, we chosen the following exponential function: $C_f = 0.1 \, e^{0.55 \lambda}$, which gives the following range of values for the concession factor: $[0.057, 0.17]$.

Table 2. Tested exponential functions

Series	Function
1	$C_f = 0.15 \, e^{0.40 \lambda}$
2	$C_f = 0.10 \, e^{0.55 \lambda}$
3	$C_f = 0.12 \, e^{0.55 \lambda}$
4	$C_f = 0.10 \, e^{0.60 \lambda}$
5	$C_f = 0.13 \, e^{0.60 \lambda}$

4   Conclusion

This paper has presented the key features of a negotiation model for bilateral contracting in multi-agent electricity markets, placing emphasis on risk management and contracts for difference. Conceptually, the model incorporates a set of strategies and a set of tactics. The agents negotiate according to their attitude towards risk. Risk-averse agents show typically more flexibility to secure deals, and therefore, are willing to concede more to avoid that negotiation ends prematurely without agreement. Risk-seeking agents are more rigid and firm, typically conceding less than their opponent.

Negotiation tactics are functions that specify the individual moves to be made at each point of the negotiation. Typically, these tactics are modelled as functions of specific criteria (e.g., the time elapsed since the beginning of negotiation). In this paper, we focus on concession making tactics: negotiators reduce their aspirations to accommodate the opponent. They are modelled as exponential functions of the attitude towards risk: the bigger the flexibility in negotiation the bigger the concessions will be. In the future, we intend to perform a number of experiments to empirically evaluate the key component of the agents, notably the concession making strategies and their associated tactics.

References

1. Hunt, S., Shuttleworth, G.: Competition and Choice in Electricity. Wiley, Chichester (1996)
2. Hausman, E., Hornby, R., Smith, A.: Bilateral Contracting in Deregulated Electricity Markets. Report to the American Public Power Association, Synapse Energy Economics (2008)
3. Bajpai, P., Singh, S.: Electricity trading in competitive power market: an overview and key issues. In: International Conference on Power Systems, Kathmandu (2004)
4. Paiva, J.: Redes de Energia Elétrica. IST Press, Lisboa (2007)
5. Lopes, F., Mamede, N., Novais, A.Q., Coelho, H.: A Negotiation Model for Autonomous Computational Agents: Formal Description and Empirical Evaluation. Journal of Intelligent & Fuzzy Systems 12(3), 195–212 (2002)
6. Lopes, F., Mamede, N., Novais, A.Q., Coelho, H.: Negotiation in a multi-agent supply chain system. In: Third Int. Workshop of the IFIP WG 5.7 Special Interest Group on Advanced Techniques in Production Planning & Control, pp. 153–168. Firenze University Press (2002)
7. Lopes, F., Mamede, N., Novais, A.Q., Coelho, H.: Negotiation among autonomous agents: experimental evaluation of integrative strategies. In: 12th Portuguese Conference on Artificial Intelligence, pp. 280–288. IEEE Computer Society Press (2005)
8. Lopes, F., Coelho, H.: Concession behaviour in automated negotiation. In: Buccafurri, F., Semeraro, G. (eds.) EC-Web 2010. LNBIP, vol. 61, pp. 184–194. Springer, Heidelberg (2010)
9. Lopes, F., Coelho, H.: Strategic and Tactical Behaviour in Automated Negotiation. International Journal of Artificial Intelligence 4(S10), 35–63 (2010)
10. Lopes, F., Coelho, H. (eds.): Negotiation and Argumentation in Multi-agent Systems. Bentham Science, The Netherlands (2014)

11. Kahneman, D., Tversky, A.: Prospect Theory: An Analysis of Decision Under Risk. Econometrica **47**(2), 263–292 (1979)
12. von Neumann, J., Morgenstern, O.: Theory of Games and Economic Behavior. Princeton University Press (1953)
13. Varian, R.: Intermediate Microeconomics: A Modern Approach. W. W. Norton & Company, New York (2010)
14. Pratt, J.: Risk Aversion in the Small and in the Large. Econometrica **32**(1/2), 122–136 (1964)
15. Faratin, P., Sierra, C., Jennings, N.: Negotiation Decision Functions for Autonomous Agents. Journal of Robotics and Autonomous Systems **24**(3–4), 159–182 (1998)

Why Are Contemporary Political Revolutions Leaderless? An Agent-Based Explanation

Alessandro Moro[✉]

Department of Economics, Ca' Foscari University,
Cannaregio 873, 30121 Venice, Italy
alessandro.moro@unive.it

Abstract. Modern revolutions, like the recent uprisings in the so-called Arab Spring, seem to be organized by social network technologies and characterized by a lack of a strong political leadership. This feature is in sharp contrast with the previous historical revolutions, often shaped by charismatic figures. The present paper provides an explanation for this radical change into an agent-based framework: simulations show that, without the use of social media, influential leaders are necessary to obtain a huge mass mobilization whereas, in the presence of a social network, it is possible to accomplish this result without the need of a strong political leadership.

Keywords: Political revolutions · Arab Spring · Political leadership · Social network technology · Agent-based modeling

1 Introduction

One of the main aspects of the recent wave of revolutions in the so-called Arab Spring is the absence of a strong political leadership, substituted by an intensive use of social network technologies as a mean to obtain mass mobilization, as noted by Hussain and Howard (2013). This evidence is in sharp contrast with the previous historical experience: in fact, charismatic figures, like Robespierre, Lenin, Mao and Khomeini, have shaped the major revolutions in History.[1] The present paper tries to provide an explanation for this radical change into an agent-based framework.

In particular, this paper presents a model in which a subjugated population of agents decides to rebel or not against a central authority. This decision is made under two different settings: in the absence of a social network, with and without charismatic leaders, in one case; and in the presence of a social network, in the other case. The simulations of the model show that, without the use of social media, influential leaders are necessary to obtain a huge mass mobilization

---

I am grateful to professor Paolo Pellizzari, my thesis supervisor, and to three anonymous referees for their extremely useful comments and suggestions.

[1] Goldstone (2001, pp. 156-158) reviews the main theories about the role of political leadership in different revolutions.

© Springer International Publishing Switzerland 2015
Y. Demazeau et al. (Eds.): PAAMS 2015, LNAI 9086, pp. 165–174, 2015.
DOI: 10.1007/978-3-319-18944-4_14

while, in the presence of a social network, it is possible to observe such a result without the need of a strong political leadership.

The rest of the paper is organized as follows: next section presents a brief survey of the main sociological and economic theories about revolutions as well as the agent-based models that are more related to the present paper; Section 3 describes the details of the model; Section 4 presents the main results emerging from the simulations of the model; finally, Section 5 concludes.

2   Literature Review

For decades the most popular sociological theories of revolution were the Marxian theory (Skocpol, 1979) and the relative deprivation theory (Davies, 1962): the former emphasizes the role of changes in production methods in generating discontent and rebellion while the latter focuses on the gap between expectations and realized economic performances to explain the sense of frustration and, consequently, the riot participation. Both of them establish an automatic link between the structural conditions that generate grievance in the society and the likelihood of revolutions. Moreover, in both theories the participation in revolutionary episodes is motivated by a collective good argument, such as the desire to change the oppressive social order.

By contrast, Tullock (1971) develops an economic approach to explain the participation in revolutions: since the benefit of an extra unit of public good is small relative to the cost of obtaining it through the participation in a rebellion, individuals decide to participate or not according to their private gains or losses. Silver (1974) provides a classification of revolutions based on Tullock's theory. Moreover, Kuran (1989) criticizes the idea of an automatic relationship between social grievance and revolution, arguing that most historical revolutions were unanticipated. He provides an explanation based on the observation that people who dislike their government tend to conceal their political preferences as long as the opposition seems weak. For this reason, regimes that appear absolutely stable might see their support vanish immediately after a slight surge in the opposition's size, even if caused by nearly insignificant events. Furthermore, in line with Kuran's theory, Rubin (2014) argues that cascades of preference revelation are more likely to happen after a big shock in highly centralized regimes because in these political systems citizens have higher incentives to falsify their true political opinions in order to avoid economic or legal sanctions imposed by the central authority.

There are also some game theoretic papers that analyze the economic causes of political change: for instance, following Acemoglu and Robinson's (2001) model of the economic origins of democracy, Ellis and Fender (2011) derive conditions under which democracy arises peacefully, when it occurs after a revolution and when oligarchic governments persist.

Finally, this paper is also greatly influenced by Granovetter's (1978) theory about threshold models of collective behaviors and by Epstein's (2002) agent-based model of civil violence. According to Granovetter, individuals face many situations with multiple alternatives and the costs and benefits associated to the different alternatives depend on how many other individuals have chosen which alternative. For this reason, each individual has a personal threshold and decides to join a collective action, like a riot or a strike, if the number of people who already participate exceeds this threshold. Following this idea, Epstein develops an agent-based model of civil violence in which agents decide to rebel against the government if their level of grievance corrected by the risk of being arrested is higher than their personal threshold. Moreover, Makowsky and Rubin (2013) develop an agent-based model to study how social network technology fosters preference revelation in centralized societies: they show that the presence of a social network makes more likely the destabilization of an autocratic regime and this is the reason why centralized governments attempt to restrict information flows via the media.

3   The Model

The population of agents interacts in a bidimensional torus space and the results of this interaction are followed over time.

Each agent i is endowed with two time-invariant characteristics: a value for the grievance g_i, drawn from a uniform distribution on the $[0, 1]$ interval, and a value for the ability to persuade other agents to rebel, which measures the influential power of the agent, denoted by p_i and drawn again from a uniform distribution on the $[0, 1]$ interval.

Following Granovetter (1978) and Epstein (2002), at each time agents decide to be quiet or active, i.e., to rebel or not against the central authority, according to a threshold-based rule. In the present model, the activation rule involves: i) the level of grievance g_i; ii) the average persuasion agent i is exposed to, indicated with $\bar{p}_{it}$, which depends on the persuasion abilities of the other rebellious agents in the neighborhood, but also on the presence of charismatic revolutionary leaders or on the availability of a social network technology; iii) finally, a deterrence term represented by the probability of being arrested P_{t-1}, which is determined by the aggregate behavior of agents in the previous period.

Combining these quantities, the decision rule can be defined: agent i becomes active if and only if inequality

$$g_i + \beta \bar{p}_{it} - \gamma P_{t-1} > \tau \tag{1}$$

holds, where β, γ and τ are positive parameters. This formula simply states that the likelihood that a player joins the rebellion is positively influenced by the level of personal grievance and by the average intensity of pro-revolutionary propaganda this player is subject to, whereas it is negatively associated to the repression faced by agents in the previous period.

The average persuasion each agent can be exposed to is the result of three potential sources. The first of them is the presence of already active agents in the neighborhood. The neighborhood includes the lattice positions within the vision radius of agents, whose length is parametrized by v: assuming a radius vision equal to one, each agent has four neighbors, in the north, east, south and west position, respectively. The second source is represented by the presence of revolutionary leaders in the neighborhood: this second type of players is characterized by an extraordinary high persuasion ability, indicated by p^l, taking a much higher value compared to the average persuasion of the population of agents. Moreover, leaders are always active, except when they are in jail, as it will be explained below. Finally, the third source of propaganda is the social media technology: in some model simulations, it is assumed that a fraction of agents is connected to a social network and, consequently, it is subject to the persuasion of the other connected rebellious agents, no matter their geographical location. Consequently, the general expression for the average pro-revolutionary persuasion is:

$$\bar{p}_{it} = \frac{\sum_{j \in (N_{it} \cup \bar{N}) \cap A_t} p_j + n_{N_{it} \cap L_t} p^l}{n_{(N_{it} \cup \bar{N}) \cap A_t} + n_{N_{it} \cap L_t}} \tag{2}$$

in which N_{it} is the set of players that are neighbors of agent i at time t, $\bar{N}$ is the set of agents connected to the social medium, A_t is the set of active agents, L_t is the set of active revolutionary leaders, $n_{(N_{it} \cup \bar{N}) \cap A_t}$ is the number of active agents that are neighbors of agent i or they are active agents connected to the social network, and, finally, $n_{N_{it} \cap L_t}$ is the number of active leaders that are neighbors of agent i. The set of neighbors N_{it} is time-varying because agents and leaders can move to an empty random position within their vision radius in each period. On the other hand, the set of connected agents $\bar{N}$ is assumed to be fixed over time: in fact, at the beginning of each simulation, agents are assigned to the social network with a probability equal to c. Therefore, this last parameter measures the degree of connectivity of the society. The two sets of active players, A_t and L_t, are time-varying because active agents and active leaders can be arrested and because agents can turn from quiet to active and vice versa.

In any period t the probability of arrest for a single active player is a decreasing function of the fraction of rebel forces to the overall population:

$$P_t = \frac{exp\left[-\phi\left(\frac{n_{A_t} + n_{L_t}}{n_a + n_l}\right)\right]}{1 + exp\left[-\phi\left(\frac{n_{A_t} + n_{L_t}}{n_a + n_l}\right)\right]} \tag{3}$$

where n_{A_t} is the number of active agents in the population at time t, n_{L_t} is the number of active leaders, n_a and n_l are the numbers of agents and leaders, respectively, in the population, and ϕ is a positive constant; the logistic transformation ensures that the probability lies inside the $(0, 1)$ interval: more precisely, it starts with a value equal to 0.5, when there are no active players, and it decreases up to a value close to zero when a huge rebellion takes place. This expression captures the fact that the arrest probability of a single revolutionary is higher when there are few active players and it declines when more agents decide to join the rebellion, as in Epstein (2002): in fact, if the repression capacities of a state, like the number of cops, are fixed, it is more difficult to arrest a single active agent in a crowd of rebels than when this specific agent protests in isolation. If an agent or a leader is arrested, he turns from active to quiet and the number of periods in jail is drawn from a uniform distribution on the $[0, j_{max}]$ interval, like in Epstein (2002).

Table 1. Values chosen for the fixed parameters of the model

Space Dimensions	n_a	v	β	γ	τ	ϕ	j_{max}	t_0	θ	σ
21x21	360	1	0.8	0.2	0.85	9	30	100	0.05	0.75

Furthermore, it is assumed that at each time only a fraction θ of agents decides to change its status from quiet to active or vice versa. In order to start the revolution, at time t_0 a shock occurs and, starting from this period, a greater fraction of agents, equals to $\theta + \sigma$, decides to change or not its status. In the case of the Arab Spring, this shock may represent the Mohamed Bouazizi's self-immolation, which gave rise to the revolution in Tunisia.

Table 1 shows the values chosen for the parameters of the model that are fixed in all simulations.[2]

4   Results

This section describes the main results obtained by the simulation of the model. In more detail, eight simulations have been performed: i) in the first one, there are no leaders and there is not a social network technology; ii) in the second scenario, the case of a single leader without an extraordinarily high persuasion ability ($p^l = 0.8$) is considered; iii) in the the third simulation the presence of a charismatic leader is analyzed ($p^l = 1$); iv) the fourth simulation adds one influential leader to the previous scenario; v-viii) finally, the last simulations consider the effect of a social network technology connecting, respectively, the 1%, 5%, 10% and 20% of the agent population, without the presence of political leaders. These eight scenarios are described in Table 2.

For each of these simulations three graphs are reported: the time series of the number of quiet, active and jailed agents. These graphs are shown in Figure 1 for the first four simulations, which are characterized by the absence of a social network technology, and in Figure 2 for the remaining cases, which have in common the presence of social media.

In all simulations, the period before the revolution is characterized by small episodes of rebellion involving very few agents because only a small fraction of the population takes into consideration the possibility of rebelling. These riots are immediately suppressed by the government: in fact the probability of arrest is very high since few agents decide to be active.

---

[2] The model has been implemented using NetLogo (Wilensky, 1999) while the time series graphs of the next section have been produced using R (R Core Team, 2014).

Table 2. Eight simulations of the model

Simulation	Leaders (n_l)	p^l	% Connected (c)
1	0	.	0
2	1	0.8	0
3	1	1	0
4	2	1	0
5	0	.	1
6	0	.	5
7	0	.	10
8	0	.	20

At time $t_0 = 100$, a shock happens and a considerable number of agents evaluates the decision to rebel or not against the central authority: this gives rise to the revolution. The following situation depends strongly on the presence of influential political leaders and on the availability of a social network.

In the first simulation, the rebel activity increases after the shock but it remains bounded geographically because the transmission mechanism of the rebellion is only local: population members are more likely to be active if they are located in positions surrounded by active and influential agents. This results in a modest turmoil after the start of the revolution, as shown in the first row of Figure 1.

Introducing one revolutionary leader without an extraordinarily high persuasion ability ($p^l = 0.8$) raises considerably the level of protests in the early periods after the shock: in fact, in the second row of Figure 1, a huge pick of activation is clearly visible immediately after t_0. On the other hand, the number of active players declines rapidly over time.

Results change substantially with an influential leader, whose persuasion ability is equal to the double of the average persuasion of agents ($p^l = 1$). In this scenario, the number of active agents increases after the shock and it persistently remains at an high value for a long period of time (second graph in the third row of Figure 1). With two influential leaders this effect is even reinforced: in fact, the number of active players is anchored to a very high value during the entire observed period after the start of the revolution, as can be seen by the graphs in the last row of Figure 1.

Therefore, the model has been calibrated in order to exhibit successful revolutions in the presence of one or two charismatic leaders: in these two cases, the great mass of active agents immediately lowers the probability of arrest after the shock and this leads to a continuously increasing number of active players which rapidly exceeds the number of quiet agents for long periods of time. These types of rebellions can be associated to the major historical revolutions, such as the French (1789), the Russian (1917), the Chinese (1949), and the Iranian Revolution (1979), in which two charismatic revolutionary leaders, like Robespierre and Danton, Lenin and Trotsky, or even one, such as Mao and Khomeini, were influential enough to inspire huge mass mobilizations.

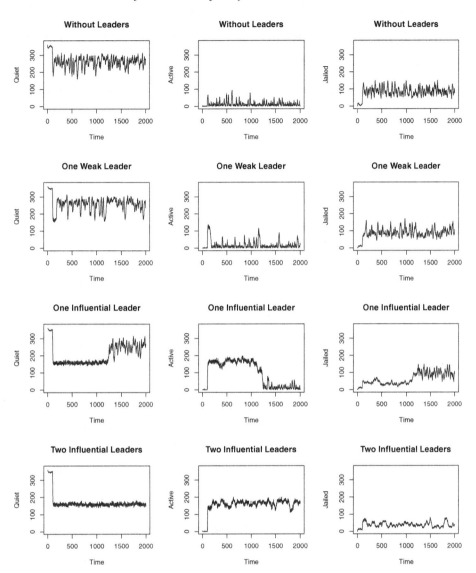

Fig. 1. Time series of the number of quiet, active and jailed agents for different simulations of the model without a social network technology

This last result can be equivalently reached without political leaders, introducing a social network technology connecting a sufficient number of agents. In fact, if the fraction of connected population is very low (1% in the fifth simulation displayed in the first row of Figure 2), the rebel activity is very modest after the shock. On the contrary, if the number of connected agents is slightly higher (5% in the sixth simulation shown in the second row of Figure 2), the

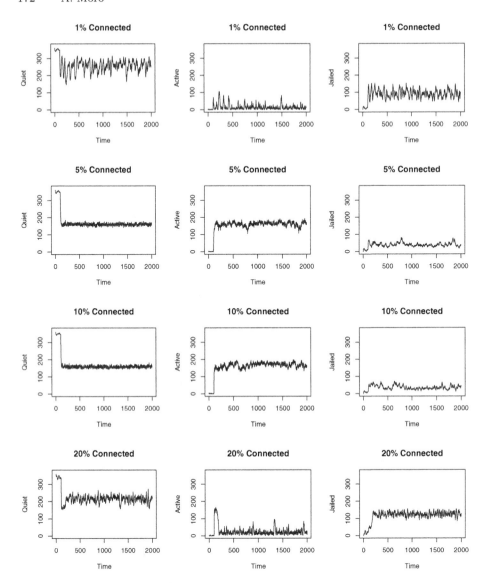

Fig. 2. Time series of the number of quiet, active and jailed agents for different simulations of the model with a social network technology

diffusion mechanism allowed by the social network is able to stimulate massive protests after the shock. The same is true for a percentage of connected agents equal to 10%, as presented in the third row of Figure 2.

However, the effectiveness of the network in stimulating riots is not monotonically increasing in the fraction of connected agents: this result is evident considering the scenario with a 20% connected population (last row in Figure 2).

In this situation, after the initial huge peak, the riot activity immediately drops to a low value. In fact, if the social network is excessively widespread, it also includes agents with a low persuasion ability and this negatively affects the average persuasion of the social medium, undermining the revolutionary potential of the network.

Summarizing the evidence provided by the results in Figure 2, the presence of a social network technology connecting a reasonable number of agents is able to generate massive protest movements by increasing the overall connectivity of the society. This mechanism explains why modern revolutions can be generated by social media without the need of a strong and influential political leadership.

5   Concluding Remarks

The recent uprisings in the Arab World have been characterized by the lack of a strong and universally recognized political leadership and by the intensive use of social network technologies as a mean to obtain consensus and generate massive protests. This represents a sharp discontinuity with the past: the major historical revolutions have been often shaped by charismatic figures with an uncommon influence over the masses of people.

The present paper tries to highlight the mechanisms through which social media can substitute revolutionary leaders in generating mass mobilizations: a widespread network of agents, not endowed with particularly influential capacities, can be as effective as multiple charismatic revolutionary leaders because it allows the geographical diffusion of protests as well as their persistence over time.

The focus is on social network technology rather than standard media, such as television, radio, newspapers, because traditional mass media are often under the strict control of the government in autocratic societies and this explains why they played a little role during the 2011 revolutions in the Arab countries.

The model presented in this paper extends the basic Epstein's (2002) agent-based model of civil violence by incorporating the effects of revolutionary leaders and social media, which are fundamental ingredients in explaining massive protest phenomena. Moreover, it enriches the analysis of Makowsky and Rubin (2013) about the importance of social network technologies in triggering cascades of preference revelation in autocratic societies by explaining the reason why contemporary uprisings are fundamentally different from the historical revolutions, in particular with respect to the mechanisms of mass mobilization.

References

Acemoglu, D., Robinson, J.A.: A Theory of Political Transitions. American Economic Review **91**, 938–63 (2001)

Davies, J.C.: Toward a Theory of Revolution. American Sociological Review **27**, 5–19 (1962)

Ellis, C.J., Fender, J.: Information Cascades and Revolutionary Regime Transitions. Economic Journal **121**, 763–92 (2011)

Epstein, J.M.: Modeling Civil Violence: An Agent-Based Computational Approach. Proceedings of the National Academy of Sciences of the United States of America **99**, 7243–50 (2002)

Goldstone, J.A.: Toward a Fourth Generation of Revolutionary Theory. Annual Review of Political Science **4**, 139–187 (2001)

Granovetter, M.: Threshold Models of Collective Behavior. American Journal of Sociology **3**, 1420–43 (1978)

Hussain, M.M., Howard, P.N.: What Best Explains Successful Protest Cascades? ICTs and the Fuzzy Causes of the Arab Spring. International Studies Review **15**, 48–66 (2013)

Kuran, T.: Sparks and Prairie Fires: A Theory of Unanticipated Political Revolution. Public Choice **61**, 41–74 (1989)

Makowsky, M.D., Rubin, J.: An agent-Based Model of Centralized Institutions, Social Network Technology, and Revolution. PLoS ONE **8**, e80380 (2013)

Core Team, R.: R: A Language and Environment for Statistical Computing. R Foundation for Statistical Computing, Vienna, Austria (2014). http://www.R-project.org/

Rubin, J.: Centralized Institutions and Cascades. Journal of Comparative Economics **42**, 340–357 (2014)

Silver, M.: Political Revolution and Repression: An Economic Approach. Public Choice **17**, 63–71 (1974)

Skocpol, T.: States and Social Revolutions: A Comparative Analysis of France, Russia, and China. Cambridge University Press, Cambridge (1979)

Tullock, G.: The Paradox of Revolutions. Public Choice **11**, 89–99 (1971)

Wilensky, U.: NetLogo. Evanston, IL: Center for Connected Learning and Computer-Based Modeling, Northwestern University (1999). http://ccl.northwestern.edu/netlogo/

Time Machine: Projecting the Digital Assets onto the Future Simulation Environment

Jose Antonio Olvera[(⌐)] and Josep Lluis de la Rosa

TECNIO - Centre EASY, Agents Research Lab, VICOROB Institute,
Univ. of Girona, 17071 Girona, Spain
joseantonio.olvera@udg.edu, peplluis@eia.udg.edu

Abstract. In this paper we present the Time Machine (TiM), an environment that simulates the digital assets onto the future and allows studying what self-preservation behaviors need the digital objects. This is based in computation intelligence and related methods of cost management under their own budget, powered by a social network as an environment that enables their behavior under the policy that preservation is to share. This approach contributes to achieve the following digital preservation requirements: adaption to unexpected situations, scalability, and efficient cost management, through an agent-based simulation. The key differentiation feature of TiM is that digital objects become active actors in their long term digital preservation, which has a digital preservation budget devoted to funding the replication of the objects and other operations such as format migration or finding a safe storage within a social network of users; in all, an environment where they will live. Its design considerations and implementation details are presented and, finally an example to illustrate some of the functionalities of the simulator.

Keywords: Multi-agent system · Simulation · Digital preservation · Computational intelligence

1   Introduction

The need for research into new ways of long term digital preservation (LTDP) has been evident over two decades. Memory institutions and academic organizations have taken the lead in defining solutions to LTDP issues; although the digital preservation (DP) problem is not limited to cultural and scientific information. Legislation is placing an increasingly large burden on commercial, industrial, cultural and governmental organizations to ensure that their digital records are retained, made accessible, and effectively preserved for the long term. The PLANETS project estimated that the value of digital documents produced in the EU that are in danger of digital obsolescence if no action is taken to preserve them, is in excess of 3 billion € per year[1].

The challenge in LTDP of complex objects – consisting of text, video, images, music, 3D information, sensor data, etc. generated throughout all areas of our society – is

---

[1] http://www.planets-project.eu

© Springer International Publishing Switzerland 2015
Y. Demazeau et al. (Eds.): PAAMS 2015, LNAI 9086, pp. 175–186, 2015.
DOI: 10.1007/978-3-319-18944-4_15

real and growing at an exponential pace. An already old study by the International Data Corporation (IDC) found that in 2012 the information created and replicated broke the zettabyte barrier growing by a factor of 9 in just five years [10]. The LTDP of such information will become a pervasive as well as ubiquitous problem that will concern everyone who has digital information to be kept for long time, implying a shift in at least a couple of software and hardware generations.

Currently the level of automation in DP solutions is low. The preservation process currently involves many manual stages but should be approached in a flexible and distributed way, combining intelligent automated methods with human intervention. The scalability of existing preservation solutions has been poorly demonstrated; and solutions have often not been properly tested against diverse digital resources or in heterogeneous environments [20].

We try to meet the following requirements involved in DP:

- Scalability: The exponential growth of digitally born objects requires of scalable solutions from the technological point of view.
- Cost: Associated to the exponential growth because there are limited resources to cope with DP.
- Uncertain future: DP is about heuristics of what results we will get in the future, only.

These problems, together with the rapid obsolescence of software and hardware due to frequent update of private vendors, make DP one of the most challenging application areas for MAS.

As was explained at [18], the prevailing paradigm is centralized, top-down, where institutions are the main players. We propose studying a change of paradigm, mainly bottom-up, where the digital objects *self-preserve*.

Our research is based in studying what self-preservation behaviors need the digital objects (DOs), based in computation intelligence (CI), and related methods of cost management under their own budget, powered by a social network as an environment that enables their behavior under the policy that "preservation is to share". It means that the more you share your DOs, the most likely you will keep them in the future: one computer or server can fail but does not matter because your DO is spread around the world. In this concept, DOs become active actors in their own LTDP, here named the Self-Preserving Digital Object (SPDO) [5], which has a DP budget devoted to funding the replication of the objects and other operations such as format migration or finding a safe storage within a social network of users; in all, a controlled environment where they will "live".

The principle behind is to think of a SPDO as an autonomous entity that interacts with the environment as well as with other SPDOs with which it competes or cooperate and thus creates good living conditions to keep alive as long as possible to have descendants who follow its existence. Under this expectation, the research in this topic will pursue self-organization paradigms, including multi-agent systems (MAS) with interesting emergent behaviors. In this paradigm, three approaches for agentification has been proposed [17]: the SPDOs; the collective cognitive networks on DP: the Sites; and the DP Services [23]. We agentified the first two: the SPDO and Sites.

With the purpose of providing the scientific community with a new tool suitable to carry out analysis of novel digital preservation strategies, in this paper we present the product of an iterative work carried out in the last years, the Time Machine (TiM), a simulation environment for the SPDO, written in Java, and implemented with the purpose of:

- Studying what are the social behaviors that supports the task of preservation of the DOs (rules of collaboration),
- Finding out an efficient cost management of the DOs,
- Analyzing what are the topologies of social networks that back better the DOs.

As a consequence, TiM is a more abstract preservation simulator than other similar-purpose tools. Our simulator does not reach the level of detail of other preservation simulators (i.e. bit preservation, ingest or access). The paper is structured as follows: section 2 presents related work and the differentiation of the current work regarding the literature; section 3 are the design considerations and implementation of the agent-based simulator by presenting the most relevant diagrams; section 4 shows the TiM simulating a concrete case, presenting the Graphical User Interface (GUI) of the simulator and the obtained results; section 5 presents where the digital preservation simulation tool is accessible; finally section 6 is devoted to conclusions and future research.

2   Related Work

There are works that use MAS with the aim to simulate the processes involved in the DP. For instance, the EU FP7 PROTAGE project [23] opened up a novel approach to DP by utilizing agent ecosystems for automation of preservation processes. The dissemination results of the project are [13][14] [15]. Another approach named "Shout and Act" [7], is a type of swarm intelligence for communication and coordination of agents inspired by rescue robots: the files, all digital objects (DOs), that need preservation are called the "victims", and there are teams of preservation agents, whose main goal is to detect files as potential victims that need migration actions and curate them. In addition, a recent work of Pellegrino [12] demonstrates how MAS can either perform an autonomous preservation action or suggest a list of best candidate solutions to the user. It describes an agent-based model aimed to simulate those processes in which a DO faces the risk of obsolescence, a migration process has to be performed and the most appropriate file format has to be adopted.

All the aforementioned works have in common with the current work that use MAS for automation of preservation processes, but none of them agentifies the DO themselves. We claim that, although preservation is currently perceived as being as repository level, in fact it occurs at object level, so mechanisms are required to enable preservation management of objects, and for this to succeed, objects must be self-preserving. Very few works are conducted in this line, among them our previous work [5] and a remarkable recent study with a data-centric perspective through the use of Unsupervised Small World (USW) graph creation algorithm [2], but they focus on

Web Objects (WO), they do only copies but not migrations, as we do, and their networks is of WO whereas our network is composed of sites of users; both of them, have a promising level of success.

As well, there exist works that concretely use simulation principles to analyze digital repositories. In [4], authors presented a simulation tool (ArchSim) able to evaluate a repository system implementation. The focus is on comparing different options such as disk reliability, error detection and preventive maintenance to estimate the Mean Time to a Failure (MTTF) of a whole repository. Similar work was done in [3] where a simulation tool was built to evaluate potential design of the Danish web archive. More recent work was conducted during the PrestoPrime project[2]. In [1] authors describe a tool able to simulate the costs and risks of using IT storage systems for the long-term archiving. The tool is now known as iModel[3]. The main focus of these simulation tools is "bit preservation"; there is a limited support for "logical preservation".

Regarding Rabinovici-Cohen et al. [21], "Bit preservation is the ability to retrieve the bits in the face of physical media degradation or obsolescence, corruption or destruction due to errors or malicious attacks, or even environmental catastrophes such as fire and flooding. Logical preservation involves preserving the understandability and usability of the data, despite unforeseeable changes that will take place in servers, operating systems, data management products, applications and even users. Additionally, logical preservation needs to maintain the provenance of the data, along with its authenticity and integrity so that current and future systems can ensure that only legitimate users access that data".

Within this approach of logical preservation there is the SCAPE simulator [8] that is an environment with a focus on logical preservation, such as migrations, format evolutions, ingest and potential collection change over time, and is also considering aspects such as resources. Our work is more similar to the SCAPE simulator than others explained before. We focus on logical preservation, yet with our goal of not trying to analyze digital repositories as a difference; in our model, the environment is a social network devoted to the DP.

3   Design Considerations and Implementation

There are different digital preservation approaches. Regarding Feeney [9], "*Three approaches to digital preservation have been developed:*

- *Preserve the original software (and possible hardware) that was used to create and access the information. This is known as the technology preservation strategy. It also involves preserving both the original operating system and hardware on which to run it.*
- *Program future powerful computer systems to emulate older, obsolete computer platforms and operating systems as required. This is the technology emulation strategy.*

---

[2] http://www.prestoprime.org/
[3] http://prestoprime.it-innovation.soton.ac.uk/imodel/download/

- *Ensure that the digital information is re-encoded in new formats before the old format becomes obsolete. This is the digital information migration strategy."*

We focus on the third one to simulate DP activities of refreshing and migration while SPDOs sharing using different computational intelligence methodologies. We conceived the migration of SPDO formats as a replication (copies) of files in different formats and refreshing as a copy in the same format [11][18]. The SPDOs will be distributed over a network of computers or devices as an environment that enables the behavior of the SPDOs in an attempt to preserve them.

Migrated copies of SPDOs are created in various formats following a migration strategy to ensure their survival against Software Adoption Waves (SAW), which occur regularly. SAW are defined as massive format changes that DOs suffer throughout their lifetime after the shifts of software and hardware, resulting in the likely "disappearance" of a percentage of the SPDOs when they become unreadable or inaccessible due to the accumulation of technological changes that provokes their obsolescence.

In our model, a network with nodes represents the users' computers (the sites) and the connections among nodes determine which users are friends with who else, resulting in a social network devoted to the DP[6][13].

In all the experiments, DOs travel through the network that is build up out of a social network and distribute copies of them for preservation. These copies maintain links to the parent SPDO because they correspond to a same object. Each node representing a user's computer might only be able to read a specific format of files after suffering a SAW. Formats range from *oldest* to *newest* to simulate the processing of files in a computer when these files can only be read by special software installed in the computer (the site). The files in older formats become *unreadable* when they are no longer compatible with the new software versions installed on a given computer after several migrations. That formats are taken as a representation of pre-web and non-web formats, because there is no danger of forgetting how to read a file format that was in use after web became available, it exist a migration path forward, as David Rosenthal argues[4]. Further details of the model are provided in the following sections.

3.1   The SPDOs Agents

The SPDOs in our experiments are different file types in several formats. For the sake of simplicity and abstraction their representation ranges from 1, the newest, to 5, the oldest.

Initially, a SPDO belongs to a particular user, and lives in his filesystem, i.e., on his computer, a site that is a node in the network structure. Any SPDO has the following behaviors with subtle variations depending upon the CI implemented: make a copy, move on to other nodes in the network, or remain in the site where it is. The aim of the SPDOs and their descendants is traveling from sites all over the net, mak-

---

[4]   http://blog.dshr.org/2013/02/rothenberg-still-wrong.html

ing digital copies of themselves when they can afford to, accordingly the restrictions of the CI algorithm that is applied. The cost for a site to host a SPDO, is directly related with the concrete format of the SPDO: the older, the more expensive (harder to have an adequate software to host it) than if it was newer. Finally, the SPDOs must determine whether the original SPDO or any of its copies are alive in the network.

The following describes the three CI algorithms that have been implemented over the SPDO behaviors, which are not detailed because they are out of the scope of this paper:

- Multi-Population Genetic Algorithm (MPGA),
- Ant Colony Algorithm (ACA),
- and Virus-Based Algorithm (VBA), approach that we implanted it similar to a computer *worm*. SPDOs try to move through the entire network selecting connections randomly but attempting to spread as far away as possible replicating themselves, with some limitations for not collapsing the system.

3.2   The Agents Site

The users have preservation services installed in their own computers for dealing, at some extent, with DP of the SPDOs hosted there. The services are limited in nature and it is represented by a percentage of employment (0%-100%) that describes the capacity of DOs that can be hosted in the user's site and a data structure that indicates the social proximity of several other nodes as users who may be available to help sharing DP efforts, for example, by sharing their SPDOs. The users' computers are connected each other for fulfilling the social and intelligent environment to support the LTDP of the SPDOs. The computers will be named nodes after the creation of a full network of LTDP resources available for SPDOs. Finally, the user's node clearly displays what formats of each file type are supported. All users have a contact list that is represented by nodes (other users' nodes) to which they are connected. These nodes are their friends' computers, resulting in a network through which SPDOs can move onto for new LTDP services, hosting, copies support, or do any other operation. Users can update the formats of their SPDOs when they change format support at the time of their software updates. We will refer to the users' computers as nodes or sites indistinctively.

3.3   Integration of the Agents in the Platform

Fig. 1 shows the framework that has been applied in the presented MAS. In this framework, the communications of the agents are performed through Java methods. The Simulation class can be executed given a certain number of times or a percentage of stability (explained in next section), and contains all the agents within a list. All the agents have a main method, in which they perform their activities in every step of simulation. Finally the platform can be executed via GUI or via console and it has access to the statistics as well agents and Simulation class can save them though the Statistics class.

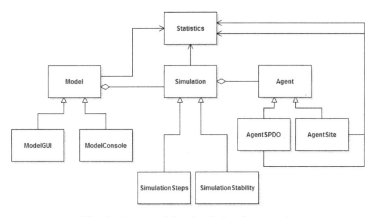

Fig. 1. Excerpt of the simulation framework

4   Simulation Experimentation of Time Machine

4.1   The Measure of Expected Resilience and the Reliability of the Experiments

If we subscribe that *preservation is about sharing*, and knowing that SPDOs when shared might be object of LTDP manipulations, notably migrations for enhancing their *preservability*; here we come with a growing diversity of objects that might contribute with higher resilience in the long-term after suffering several SAWs.

Thus, after acknowledging that these heuristics will be applied to our SPDOs, we need measures of expected resilience that might be explained by the diversity of SPDOs. To do so we use the Shannon entropy (Equation 1) for the evaluation of the results. High entropy indicates high expected *preservation* and resilience after successive SAWs according to our strategy for format migrations. The fact that several copies exist in diversified formats provides better resistance and recovery in the case of a SAW (improved *resilience*).

$$H(x) = -\sum_{i=1}^{n} p_i \cdot \log_2 p_i \tag{1}$$

Equation 2 is the DP application of Equation 1, where n is the total number of original SPDOs, j are the formats SPDOs can migrate from and to (with a value ranging from 1 to 5), and pi,j is the percentage of the copies in format j among the total number of copies of an original SPDO i. Equation 3 defines Pi,j, where k are the formats from 1 to 5.

$$H(x) = \frac{-\sum_{i=1}^{n}\left(\sum_{j=1}^{5} p_{i,j} \cdot \log_2 p_{i,j}\right)}{n} \tag{2}$$

$$p_{i,j} = \frac{f_{i,j}}{\sum_{k=1}^{5} f_{i,k}} \qquad (3)$$

For the reliability of the experiments, the average resulting entropy is calculated after the number of executions is enough to achieve a stabilized result. We measured this reliability of the experiments using Equation 4, which defines $\overline{x}_n$ as the average of the steady entropy value x_n in execution n, such that the sum converges when an increasing number of experiments to yield a reliability of $1 - \varepsilon = 99.3\%$.

$$S_n = \sum_{i=1}^{n} \left(\overline{x_n} - \overline{x_{n-1}} \right) < \varepsilon \qquad (4)$$

4.2   Brief Overview of the Platform Functionality

The multi-agent platform can be executed via GUI or via console and it allows to generate the desired topology of social network or choose some defined by default, to set up the different parameters that act in the simulations, and to see (via GUI) a screen that displays everything that is happening in real time (shown in Fig. 2). The executions via console will get all the input parameters from a file.

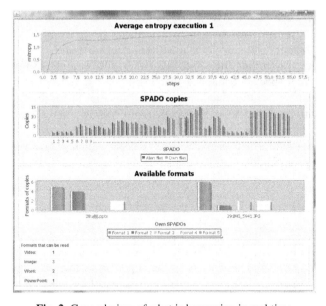

Fig. 2. General view of what is happening in real time

As a result of the simulation, a number of useful statistics are saved in files for future analysis:

- The entropy of each execution and the average entropy of all executions;

- The percentage of accessible SPDOs in each execution and the average accessible SPDOs in all executions – accessible SPDOs means that at the end of the executions maintain at least one copy of themselves ;
- The percentage of readable SPDOs in each execution and the average readable SPDOs in all executions – readable SPDOs means that have a copy with a format compatible of the site they live (they are immediately readable in that node and thus technically straightforward preserved);
- The percentage of occupation of the sites in each execution and the average percentage of occupation in all executions;
- The number of copies of each SPDO in different formats for each execution and the average in all executions;
- The parameters used in the simulation.

4.3   Examples of Experiments

TiM simulations are deployed over 35-year period in which a SAW occurs every 5 years. After every SAW it is the time at which SPDOs show severe symptoms of obsolescence and an urgent need of DP or curation. We use the month as the temporal unit at every step for our simulations, and thus, there is a SAW every 60 steps (12 months × 5 years), and an execution has a total length of 420 steps (12 months x 35 years). The three CI algorithms as a SPDO behaviors have been simulated and Table 1 shows all the parameters of the simulations.

Table 1. Formulation of the parameters used for the TiM experiment

Parameters	MPGA	ACA	VBA
Total simulation time		35 years	
Equivalence of 1 simulation step		1 month	
Total waves		6 (for 35 years)	
Percentage of DOs involved in a SAW		72%	
# DOs associated to any user		Between 1 and 5	
Preservation service for each user		100%	
Percentage of statistical stability		99.3%	
Random seed		123456789	
Percentage of mutation	2% of the population		
Percentage of exchange	2% of the population		
Percentage of nodes of the network where ants can make copies		20%	
Period in which nodes are changed where ants can make copies		3 years	
Maximum number of copies that a DO can have at each site			1

The function watts.strogatz.game() from R package igraph was used to create the small-world graph of 1000 nodes. The graph was checked to ensure that it was simple and connected. The clustering coefficient (CC) resulting from the graph is 0.48 and the average path length (APL) is 4.41. It was added as default network that can be chosen with the simulator.

The results of the experiments are shown in Fig. 3, that show the evolution of the average entropy over the simulation period, where the X axis are the steps of the simulation (months) and the Y axis is the entropy value, explained above. Looking the results obtained with this experiments, in the end of the simulation the highest entropy value is obtained with the ACA, but the period before is also of the same importance (SPDO must be accessible and reproducible by users at any time) and in that case both VBA and MPGA are better solutions than ACA. In this case is difficult to select the best because the three executions have positive entropy values during all the simulation, but the one that have higher entropy as a mean is VBA (high entropy value indicates high expected preservation).

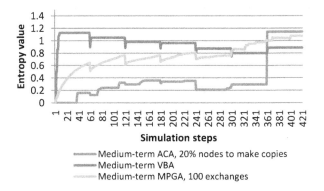

Fig. 3. Comparison of CI algorithms over 35-year period

5   Availability

The software is publicly available at http://timemachine.jaolvera.test.easyinnova.com, along with the documentation, some examples and the source code that can be downloaded. We expect to enrich the site with more source code examples, and illustrative simulation scenarios. Besides, as contributions from the community are welcomed and desired, we plan to encourage the development of new components that can be kept in a public repository.

In this paper we have described the main functionalities of TiM; others have not been mentioned, for example those pertaining to electronic auctions of preservation and curation services for these objects to be preserved, explained at [19], as well as using real social network topologies and the interaction between the users obtained from Facebook, Google+ and Twitter developed in [16]. There are initial classes that implement them, but further development is anticipated in those areas.

6   Conclusions and Future Work

In this paper we have presented the Time Machine (TiM), a simulation environment that projects the digital assets onto the future and allows studying what self-preservation behaviors need the digital objects, based in computation intelligence, and related methods of cost management under their own budget, powered by a social network as an environment that enables their behavior under the policy that preservation is to share. The key differentiation feature of TiM is that digital objects become active actors in their own long term digital preservation. The related work provides several MAS with the aim to simulate the processes involved in the digital preservation as well as well-known digital repositories simulators. Then, TiM design considerations and implementation details are presented. Additionally, an example of experimentation illustrates some of the functionalities of our proposal.

Future work will follow in the direction of studying variations of the CI algorithms that we performed, adding electronic auctions of preservation and curation services for these objects to be preserved and use real social network topologies and make the topology varying with time to have more realistic simulation.

We hope that TiM evolves with the addition of new functionalities both by the authors and the contributions of other developers and that this software becomes a helpful tool for the digital preservation research community.

Acknowledgements. This research is partly funded by the TIN2013-48040-R (QWAVES) Nuevos métodos de automatización de la búsqueda social basados en waves de preguntas, the IPT20120482430000 (MIDPOINT) Nuevos enfoques de preservación digital con mejor gestión de costes que garantizan su sostenibilidad, and VISUAL AD Uso de la Red Social para Monetizar el Contenido Visual, RTC-2014-2566-7 and GEPID Gamificación en la Preservación Digital desplegada sobre las Redes Sociales, RTC-2014-2576-7, the EU DURAFILE num. 605356, FP7-SME-2013, BSG-SME (Research for SMEs) Innovative Digital Preservation using Social Search in Agent Environments, as well as the AGAUR 2012 FI_B00927 awarded to José Antonio Olvera and the grup de recerca consolidat CSI-ref. 2014 SGR 1469.

References

1. Addis, M., Jacyno, M.: D2.1.2 Tools for modeling and simulating migration-based preservation (2010)
2. Cartledge C.L., Nelson M.L.: When should I make preservation copies of myself? In: Digital Libraries 2014, London, UK, September 8-12 (2014)
3. Christensen, N.H.: Preserving the bits of the Danish Internet. In: 5th International Web Archiving Workshop, Vienna (2005)
4. Crespo, A., Garcia-Molina, H.: Modeling archival repositories for digital libraries. In: Borbinha, J.L., Baker, T. (eds.) ECDL 2000. LNCS, vol. 1923, pp. 190–205. Springer, Heidelberg (2000)
5. de la Rosa J.L., Olvera J.A.: First studies on self-preserving digital objects. In: Artificial Intelligence Research & Dev., Procs 15th Intl. Conf. of the Catalan Assoc. for Artificial Intelligence, CCIA 2012, Alacant, Spain, vol. 248, pp. 213–222 (2012)

6. de la Rosa, J.L., Trias, A., Ruusalepp, R., Aas, F., Moreno, A., Roura, E., Bres, A., Bosch, T.: Agents for social search in long-term digital preservation. In: The Sixth International Conference on Semantics, Knowledge and Grid, SKG 2010, Ningbo, China, November 1-3 (2010)

7. de la Rosa, J.L., Trias, A., Aciar, S., del Acebo, E., Quisbert, H.: Shout and act: An algorithm for digital objects preservation inspired from rescue robots. In: Proceedings of the 1st Intl Work. on Innovation in Digital Preservation, Austin, Texas, June 19 (2009)

8. Duretec, K.: Final version of the simulation environment.SCAPE. http://www.scape-project.eu/wp-content/uploads/2014/10/SCAPE_D12.3_TUW_V1.0.pdf

9. Feeney, M.: Towards a national strategy for archiving digital materials. Alexandria **11**(2), 107–121 (1999)

10. Gantz, J., Reisel, D.: The Digital Universe In 2020: Big Data, Bigger Digital Shadows, and Biggest Growth in the Far East, December 2012

11. Garrett, J., Waters, D, (eds.) Preserving Digital Information, Report of the Task Force on Archiving of Digital Information commissioned by The Commission on Preservation and Access and The Research Libraries Group (1996)

12. Jacopo, P.: A Multi-agent Based Digital Preservation Model, Master's Degree Thesis, Department of Physics, University of Turin. (2014)

13. Jin, X., Jiang, J., de la Rosa J.L: PROTAGE: Long-Term Digital Preservation Based on Intelligent Agents and Web Services. ERCIM News **80**, 15–16 (2010)

14. Jin, X., Jiang, J., Min, G., de la Rosa J.L., Quisbert, H., Bengtsson, J.E, Ruusalepp, R.: Towards Computerized Digital Preservation via Intelligent Agent Based Approaches. International Journal of Digital Curation (2011)

15. Jin, X., Jiang, J, Min: A software agent and Web service based system for digital preservation. First Monday, [S.l.], October. 2010. ISSN 13960466

16. McAuley, J., Leskovec, J.: Learning to Discover Social Circles in Ego Networks. In: NIPS (2012)

17. Olvera, J.A., de la Rosa i Esteva, J.L.: An Outline of the Application of Agents to Digital Preservation and an Introduction to Self-Preservation Aware Digital Objects. In: EASSS 2011, Girona, Catalonia, Spain, July 11-15 (2011)

18. Olvera, J.A.: Digital Preservation: A New Approach from Computational Intelligence. In: Joint Conference on Digital Libraries 2013, JCDL Doctoral Consortium 2013, Indianapolis, Indiana, USA, July 22-26 (2014)

19. Olvera, J.A., Carrillo, P.N., de la Rosa, J.L.: Combinatorial and multi-unit auctions applied to digital preservation of self-preserving objects. In: Artificial Intelligence Research and Development - Recent Advances and Applications, vol. 269, pp. 265–268 (2014)

20. Quisbert, H.: On Long-term Digital Information Preservation Systems – a Framework and Characteristics for Development. Ph D Thesis. Luleå University of Technology (2008)

21. Rabinovici-Cohen, S., Baker, M.G., Cummings, R., Fineberg, S., Marberg, J.: Towards SIRF: self-contained information retention format. In: Proceedings of the 4th Annual International Conference on Systems and Storage (SYSTOR 2011), Article 15, 10 pages. ACM, New York (2011). http://doi.acm.org/10.1145/1987816.1987836

22. Rothenberg J.: Avoiding Technological Quicksand: Finding a Viable Technical Foundation for Digital Preservation. Council on Library and Information Resources (1999)

23. Ruusalep R., Dobreva M.: Digital Preservation Services: State of the Art Analysis. www.dc-net.org/getFile.php?id=467

24. The PROTAGE Project: PReservation Organizations using Tools in AGent Environments.

From Goods to Traffic: First Steps Toward an Auction-Based Traffic Signal Controller

Jeffery Raphael[1](✉), Simon Maskell[2], and Elizabeth Sklar[1]

[1] Department of Computer Science, University of Liverpool, Liverpool, UK
{jeffery.raphael,e.i.sklar,s.maskell}@liverpool.ac.uk
[2] Department of Electrical Engineering and Electronics,
University of Liverpool, Liverpool, UK

Abstract. Traffic congestion is a major issue that plagues many urban road networks large and small. Traffic engineers are now leaning towards Intelligent Traffic Systems as many types of physical changes to road networks are costly or infeasible. Multi-Agent Systems (MAS) have become a popular paradigm for exploring intelligent solutions to traffic management problems. There are many MAS approaches to traffic management that utilise market mechanisms. In market-based approaches, drivers "pay" to use the roadways. However, a major issue with many of these solutions is that they require technology that, as yet, does not exist or is not widely available. For example, they rely on a special software agent that resides within the vehicle. This "vehicle agent" is responsible for participating in the market mechanism and communicating with the transportation infrastructure. In this paper, an auction-based traffic controller is proposed which exploits all the benefits of market mechanisms *without the need for a vehicle agent*. Experimental results show that such a controller is better at reducing delay and increasing throughput in a simulated city, as compared to fixed-time signal controllers.

Keywords: Multi-agent systems · Auctions · Traffic signal control

1 Introduction

Traffic congestion occurs when the volume of traffic exceeds the capacity of the infrastructure and causes traffic flow to slow. Over 60% of commuters in England and Wales drive to work [13]. In London, despite having access to an extensive public transportation network, over a quarter of Londoners still choose to drive to work [13]. During *rush hours*, traffic volume often reaches levels that severely strain current traffic management systems. Traffic volume and common work hours are just two of the many factors that can grind traffic to a halt. This type of recurring congestion pattern is responsible for 86% and 32% of traffic congestion in France and Germany respectively [1]. The cost of traffic congestion can be measured both in time and money. According to a report put out by the Centre for Economics and Business Research (CEBR), drivers in London waste around 66.1 hours a year waiting in traffic. All those hours

© Springer International Publishing Switzerland 2015
Y. Demazeau et al. (Eds.): PAAMS 2015, LNAI 9086, pp. 187–198, 2015.
DOI: 10.1007/978-3-319-18944-4_16

add up and across the UK close to €4.94 billion [2] are lost in the form of fuel and the increased cost of delivering goods. Other European countries face similar monetary losses. Traffic congestion costs France, Germany, and Spain € 5.55, € 7.83, and € 5.5 billion respectively [2,8]. The estimated annual cost of congestion in the EU is € 111.3 billion [8]. The staggering cost of traffic congestion and its complexities make it an attractive problem to help solve.

There are many tools at the disposal of transportation departments to manage traffic flow. Traffic lights are probably the most prevalent means of controlling traffic. Other methods include stop signs and roundabouts. Although many traffic lights rely on simple fixed protocols, they are none-the-less a vital component of traffic management [4]. More advanced adaptive Urban Traffic Controllers (UTC), such as RHODES [17], OPAC [11] and SCOOT[1], have been developed in an effort to improve the performance of traffic lights [18,22]. Adaptive UTCs use information about current road conditions and determine, some in real-time, the best signal settings. Adaptive UTCs attempt to harmonise the interplay between all aspects of traffic (private cars, public transportation and pedestrians) in areas ranging in size from a few city blocks to entire cities. The majority of adaptive UTCs employ optimisation algorithms which are costly to develop, maintain and expand [22].

The fundamental nature of traffic flow makes it an ideal problem for *Multi-Agent Systems (MAS)*. Traffic control is geographically distributed, takes place in a dynamic environment and the interactions amongst its components are highly complex [7]. It is easy to see all the vehicles, pedestrians, cyclists and traffic control mechanisms as a collection of autonomous agents interacting in a large space. The MAS paradigm offers a flexible and inexpensive method for designing traffic control solutions [22]. There is a plethora of traffic control solutions that fall under the umbrella of MAS. Our work focuses on those solutions that utilise market-based mechanisms.

Our approach for controlling traffic signals has been greatly influenced by coordination efforts in Multi-Robot Routing (MRR) [9,12,14,19]. *Auctions*, which are a form of market-based mechanism for resource allocation, can produce near optimal results in some MRR scenarios [16]. Traffic control can be viewed as a coordination problem [5] where traffic signals work together to maintain adequate traffic flow and minimise delays. A common theme in the existing literature on auction-based traffic controllers is the need for a *vehicle agent*, which refers to a vehicle-borne software system responsible for tasks as simple as vehicle-to-infrastructure communications to more demanding vehicle navigation and control.

There are two main problems with any system that relies on vehicle agents: the development and deployment of vehicle agents and the current transportation infrastructure. Car manufacturers will have to agree on international communication protocols, physical specifications and the many other aspects of deploying vehicle agents to the millions of vehicles that are currently in use. Second, the communication infrastructure within the traffic system itself currently does not exist. Our overarching goal is to design a system that reaps the benefits of a

---

[1] http://www.scoot-utc.com

market mechanism that is able to take advantage of existing infrastructure but does not require *vehicle agents*.

We demonstrate a simple approach to such a system here. Section 2 discusses other auction-based approaches to traffic control, focussing on the MAS literature. Section 3 presents our approach. Sections 4 and 5 describe our experiments and results. Finally, we close with some discussion (Section 6) and conclusions (Section 7).

2   Related Work

Dresner et al. [10] designed a reservation-based traffic management system to reduce traffic congestion. In a reservation-based system, vehicles request time slots. The time slots are time spans when the vehicle is allowed to occupy the intersection. The reservation-based system functions on a first-come, first-served basis. The reservation-based system relies on vehicle agents (autonomous cars) that have complete control of the vehicle. The authors measured the delay experienced by vehicles passing through the intersection. Dresner et al. [10] compared their reservation-based approach to two other traffic control schemes: *overpass* and traffic light. Overpass simulates a road with absolutely no signals. Traffic light simulates how current signals functions. Dresner et al. [10] found that their reservation-based system outperformed the normal traffic light.

Vasirani et al. [21] expanded on Dresner's work and examined the performance changes to a reservation-based system where time slots were allocated via a combinatorial auction. And they also expanded [10] to include multiple intersections to study the effects of such a market-based reservation system would have on drivers' route choice. They viewed the space within an intersection as a resource and managed that resource using a market-based system. Vasirani et al. [21] looked at the delay experienced by drivers based on the amount they were willing to "pay" to use the intersection under various traffic densities. They were interested in finding out if drivers willing to pay more would experience less delay. They also looked at the delay experienced as traffic volume increased across the intersection. Vasirani et al. [21] found that initially having a willingness to pay does decrease delay, but eventually this levels off. As [21] is an extension of [10] it too relies on vehicle agents.

Carlino et al. [6] described a traffic control system where auctions are run at intersections to determine use. This solution assumes vehicles have an embedded agent bidding on their behalf, which is referred to as the *wallet agent*. A *system agent* also bids in a manner that facilitates traffic flow beneficial to the entire transportation system—while the *wallet agent* is solely concerned with getting its occupants to their destination in the least expensive (and quickest way). Carlino et al. [6] used a second-price sealed bid auction mechanism. They tested four different modes: *FIFO* (this is how your typical intersection works), *Equal* (every driver submits a bid of one, *Static Wallet*), *Auction* (drivers use the *Fair Wallet*, and *Fixed* (drivers always bid the same amount based on the value they've assigned for the trip). FIFO performed the worst.

Schepperle et al. [20] created a *valuation-aware* traffic-control mechanism which allows concurrent use of the intersection through an auction mechanism. In a valuation-aware traffic controller, the intersection takes into account the driver's value of time; but many of these systems do not allow concurrent use of the intersection. Schepperle et al. [20] proposes two auction-based mechanisms: *Free Choice* and *Clocked*. In Free Choice, the auction winner gets to select the time slot it wants from an interval; while in Clocked, time slots are auctioned off. Schepperle et al. [20] concluded that Free Choice reduced the average weighted wait time by up to 38.1%. Clocked reduced the average weighted wait time for only lower degrees of concurrency and high traffic volume. Like other works of this nature, [20] assumes that cars have a vehicle agent and that intersections have an agent as well. Our approach, detailed in the next section, does not involve vehicle agents or other embedded software.

3   Our Approach: Auction-Based Traffic Signalling

In this section, we describe our auction-based mechanism for traffic signalling which does not employ vehicle agents. Instead, we use an *intersection agent* (as an auction manager) and *traffic signal agents* that represent the traffic signals at each intersection—one per pair of opposing-direction traffic flows (i.e., opposing traffic light phases). Thus, at every crossroads, there is an intersection agent working in concert with two traffic signal agents to adapt the signal timing to meet traffic demands. This scheme is illustrated in Figure 1. Each intersection functions on a two-phase traffic light programme: one light phase for north/south bound traffic and the other phase for west/east bound traffic.

Our traffic signal control mechanism employs a first-price, single-item auction. As traffic flows through the intersection, auctions take place at fixed intervals which we call the *auction frequency*. The two traffic signal agents bid against each other to increase the amount of *green time* in their respective phases. The winner is the traffic signal agent with the highest bid. The winning agent gains 5 additional seconds of green time, while the loser's green time decreases by the same amount. The cycle length remains the same, but the amount of green time changes.

Note that the *auction frequency* does not (have to) match the cycle length. An auction may occur in the middle of a cycle or after a series of cycles have passed. Green time is only updated after the current traffic light phase has completed. As a safeguard against *starvation*, traffic signal agents are prevented from having less than 10 seconds of green time. Starvation is defined as the situation where traffic is prevented from flowing in a particular direction. *Gridlock* is defined as the situation where starvation occurs in both directions.

Traffic signal agents use *road sensors* to assess road conditions and generate an appropriate bid. Road sensors include, but are not limited to, inductive-loop vehicle detectors and cameras. The former are loops of wire buried in the road with a current running through it and are the primary sensor used in SCOOT. Vehicles are detected via disruptions in the magnetic field of the wire loop caused

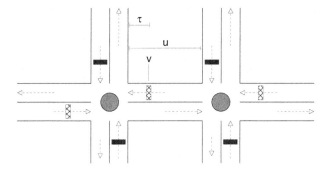

Fig. 1. Traffic Signalling Scheme. The hash-patterned rectangles represent the pre-existing *induction-loop* sensors for the west/east traffic signal agents; black rectangles for the north/south traffic signal agents. Grey circles indicate intersection agents (though they have no physical embodiment in the simulated system). In addition, the following parameters are indicated: **v** is the *volume* of traffic as measured by an induction-loop sensor; **u** is the occupation level between consecutive intersections; and τ is the occupation level between the sensor and the intersection. (See text for further explanation.)

by the metal body of the vehicle. Each induction-loop sensor (the hash-patterned and black rectangles illustrated in Figure 1) computes v, the number of vehicles that have crossed the induction-loop in a fixed time period. The induction-loop sensors are located 20 meters from the intersection.

We have defined two methods of traffic control: **Saturation (SAT)** and **Saturation with Queuing (SATQ)**.

SAT. In the SAT method, the traffic signal agents use the *saturation* of their road segment as a bidding rule. The *saturation* of a road segment is the ratio of the volume of traffic (here, represented as v and measured by the induction-loop sensors) to its estimated capacity c (defined by the physical road network). In the experiments conducted here, the traffic signal agents are only concerned with the single block preceding the junction they manage. For example, the west/east signal agent collects volume data one block west and one block east of its location. Equation 1 defines the bidding rule for the traffic signal agents.

$$bid = v/c \tag{1}$$

SATQ. The SATQ method functions similarly to the SAT method, except that its bidding rule is augmented with road occupation, u, which is an indication of how "full" the road is. This provides a better picture of road conditions (e.g., whether there is a queue of vehicles leading up to the road sensor) than the induction-loop sensor alone. A traffic camera could be used to obtain this data. The modified bidding rule employed by the SATQ method is defined in Equation 2.

$$bid = (v/c) + u \tag{2}$$

4 Experiments

We evaluated our auction-based methods using the *Simulation of Urban MObility (SUMO)* traffic simulator [15]. SUMO is an open source microscopic traffic simulator and is often used in vehicular communications (either vehicle-to-vehicle or vehicle-to-infrastructure) research but it is also used to study route choice and traffic control algorithms [15]. Although it has a GUI front-end, for our experiments we treated it as a back-end server. We developed a client application to control the simulation using SUMO's Traffic Control Interface (TraCI) through a TCP socket.

As a benchmark for evaluating the effectiveness of our auction-based methods, we also tested a **Fixed** method of controlling traffic signals. The Fixed method represented traditional, non-adaptive, traffic lights that display the same light sequence in every cycle. The cycle lengths ranged from 80 to 90 seconds (varying across different intersections), with each traffic signal spending at least 68% of their phase showing green.

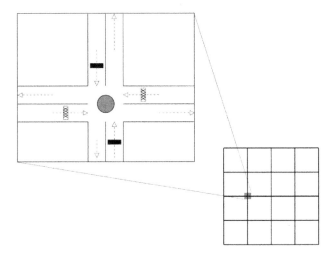

Fig. 2. Grid city

For the purpose of experimentation, to determine the effectiveness of the proposed traffic controller, a simulated "Grid" city was used, following a Manhattan-style road network (shown in Figure 2). Although simple, similar networks have been used in other traffic experiments [3,4]. A single Grid City block measures 200 meters. Grid City contains 25 traffic lights, but only 21 are four-way junctions (the four corners do not have opposing traffic flows). In the simulation, there are four induction-loops at each intersection, one for each traffic flow entering the intersection. The exact positions of the induction-loops are shown in the insets of Figure 2.

During each simulation run, $2,000$ vehicles entered Grid City and travelled across the network. The four corners of Grid City were designated as entrance/exit points. Vehicles entered at one of four entry points and exited at another. For each of the four entry points there was a 90% probability of generating a new vehicle at any given time step. Table 1 presents the vehicle specification settings used. Each simulation run lasted a maximum of $15,000$ seconds (4 hours and 10 minutes); simulations could terminate early if all vehicles reached their destination before the maximum time passed. For each traffic control method tested, 50 simulation experiments were executed.

In addition to comparing the Fixed, SAT and SATQ methods for traffic signal control, we experimented with varying the *auction frequency*. We ran fifteen sets of experiments, varying the auction frequency from 1 to 15 minutes. Note that the auction frequency remained constant throughout an experiment, and that all auctions occurred synchronously (i.e., all bidding and matching took place at the same time). Future work will explore variable auction frequencies within a simulation, as well as asynchronous auctions.

The results from the experiments are presented in Section 5.

Table 1. Vehicle specifications

Parameter	Value
acceleration	$0.8m/s^2$
deceleration	$4.5m/s^2$
size of vehicle (length)	$5m$
maximum velocity	$16.67m/s$
minimum gap between vehicles	$2.5m$

Performance was measured in three ways. The first was in terms of total trip duration: on average, how long it took for all the vehicles to complete their trips, measured in seconds. The second was *throughput* (p) which was measured in terms of *vehicles/hour*. Throughput is the estimated number of vehicles that could pass through the road network in an hour. This was calculated using Equation (3), where: n is the number of cars participating in the simulation and t is the total amount of time (in seconds) it took for all cars to complete their journeys.

$$p = \frac{n}{t} \times 3600 \tag{3}$$

The third metric was *completion rate*: the percentage of the 2000 vehicles entering the system were able to complete their journeys before the maximum simulation time had elapsed.

5 Results

The results of our experiments are presented in Figures 3 and 4. Although SAT sometimes reduced travel times as much as SATQ, Figure 3 shows that

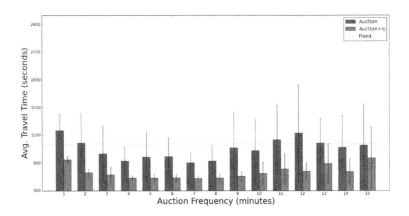

Fig. 3. Average time to complete travel plan

SATQ consistently outperformed the other two traffic control methods. The large amount of deviation seen in SAT reflects the quality of its bidding rule. The bidding rule indirectly provides a representation of the state of traffic at the time an auction is executed. The traffic signal agents select actions that are most appropriate for the traffic conditions it perceives through its bidding rule. Traversing the solution space using the bidding rules developed thus far does not guarantee a sequence of actions that will gradually improve overall travel times from one time step to the next. If there are enough traffic signal agents that fail to accurately capture current traffic trends and act appropriately, the combined effect is an increase in overall network delay. Infrequent auctions can also lead to this disconnect between traffic signal actions and road conditions as evident in the increased deviation experienced by SATQ after the 10 minute mark in Figure 3. The lowest average travel time was achieved when the auction frequency was set to 7 minutes.

Figure 4 further supports the conclusion that SATQ was the best control method. In terms of throughput, SATQ had a statistically significant advantage over the other two methods. SATQ was able to handle nearly 50% more traffic than Fixed. Some simulations did end in gridlock using SAT or SATQ (the Fixed controller always ran to completion). Figure 5 shows the percentage of vehicles that completed their entire trip versus the auction frequency. SATQ reached 100% completion until after the 11 minute mark. Again, we see performance issues emerge with infrequent auction frequencies.

6 Discussion

SATQ produced superior results as compared to a single fixed cycle. In order to get a better picture of how well SATQ worked, we compare it to the *overpass* benchmark employed by Dresner et al. [10].

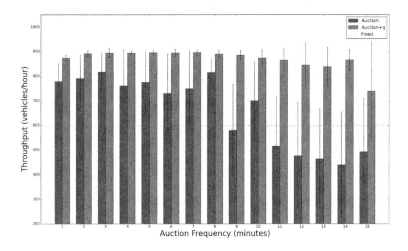

Fig. 4. Estimated throughput

Table 2. Average travel time for all vehicles to complete trip in seconds. Auctions were executed every 5 minutes.

Control Method	Average Travel Time	(std)
Overpass	*301.30*	
Fixed	1108.52	(23.84)
SAT	1054.23	(293.24)
SATQ	**803.27**	**(96.90)**

As shown in Table 2, the minimum average travel time for all vehicles to complete their trip is 301.30 seconds versus SATQ's 818.17. The vehicles using the Fixed method required 3.7 times more time (compared to the the lower bound) to complete their trip, while SATQ required 2.7 times more time. This in itself is impressive considering that no effort was made to optimise any global parameters in the case of SAT and SATQ. In this initial implementation, traffic signal agents behaved rather selfishly: they were concerned with improving travel time solely at their junction. These results support our belief that an appropriately designed market-based MAS can improve traffic flow. Future work will investigate traffic signal agents that consider a *neighbourhood* of intersections, not just their immediate junction.

The most likely reason as to why SATQ outperformed SAT has to do with queue formation and how inductive-loop detectors work. If and when a queue formed at an intersection and that queue surpassed the position of the induction-loop it would register traffic flow as zero. The issue with returning a zero count is that it has two meanings, either there is no traffic on the road at all or traffic is so *backed up* that a vehicle is sitting directly over the sensor. Unfortunately,

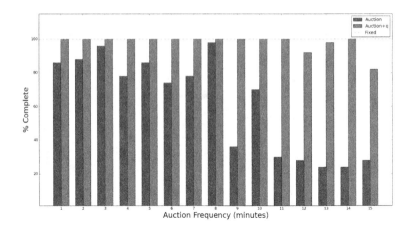

Fig. 5. Completion Rate: percentage of runs where all the vehicles reached their destination by auction frequency

one meaning suggests the signal requires less green time while the other suggests it requires more green time. The u term (Equation 2) clarifies this ambiguity. If the detector returns zero because a queue has formed, then $u \geq \tau$, where τ is the percentage of the road that would be occupied by vehicles if the queue has reached the position of the inductive-loop detector. So, the u term supports the agent's bid for more green time when a queue of sufficient size has formed. If it returns zero because there is no traffic, then $u = 0$. Interestingly, the performance gap between SAT and SATQ is a great example of how multiple sources of road data can be used in tandem to improve a traffic control mechanism.

7   Conclusion

The work presented in this paper demonstrates how an auction-based traffic controller could be implemented without the use of vehicle agents. Our approach takes advantage of road sensor devices that are currently available. We implemented two versions of our mechanism: SAT and SATQ. We tested their effects on traffic flow in a fictitious road network, Grid City. The results show that our mechanism is capable of outperforming a fixed-time signal system. Although acting locally, our *intersection agent* and signal agents are able to minimise the delay and increase the throughput of the road network. If one considers that the majority of adaptive UTCs use complex and time-consuming optimisation techniques, then our method is even more interesting. Our preliminary implementation, although simple, produced results that are quite an improvement on average travel time and throughput. Our mechanism exhibits traits that make it ideal for a real-time adaptive traffic light controller: it has minimal communications overhead, it is highly reactive to changing traffic conditions and its design is uncomplicated.

Future work will focus on the auction mechanism parameters and traffic testing scenarios. We plan to examine how including traffic signal agents from multiple connected intersections in a single auction might effect performance. We will also test our mechanisms against SCOOT in a simulation of an actual city with more intersections and realistic traffic flows.

Acknowledgments. Thanks to Frans Coenen for comments on earlier drafts, Simon Parsons and Liverpool City Council for research advice.

References

1. Managing urban traffic congestion. Technical report, OECD Publishing (2007)
2. The economic costs of gridlock. Technical report, Centre for Economic and Business Research, December 2012
3. Azevedo, T.M.L., de Arajo, P.J.M., Rossetti, R.J.F., Rocha, A.P.C.: JADE, TraSMAPI and SUMO: a tool-chain for simulating traffic light control. In: Proceedings of the Thirteenth International Joint Conference on Autonomous Agents and Multiagent Systems, May 2014
4. Bakker, B., Whiteson, S., Kester, L., Groen, F.C.A.: Traffic light control by multi-agent reinforcement learning systems. In: Babuška, R., Groen, F.C.A. (eds.) Interactive Collaborative Information Systems. SCI, vol. 281, pp. 475–510. Springer, Heidelberg (2010)
5. Bazzan, A.L.C.: A distributed approach for coordination of traffic signal agents. Autonomous Agents and Multi-Agent Systems $10(2)$, 131–164 (2005)
6. Carlino, D., Boyles, S.D., Stone, P.: Auction-based autonomous intersection management. In: Proceedings of the 16th IEEE Intelligent Transportation Systems Conference (ITSC) (2013)
7. Chen, B., Cheng, H.H.: A review of the applications of agent technology in traffic and transportation systems. IEEE Transactions on Intelligent Transportation Systems $11(2)$, 485–497 (2010)
8. Christidis, P., Rivas, J.N.I.: Measuring road congestion. Technical report, European Commission, Joint Research Centre (2012)
9. Dias, M.B., Zlot, R., Kalra, N., Stentz, A.: Market-based multirobot coordination: A survey and analysis. Proceedings of the IEEE $94(7)$, 1257–1270 (2006)
10. Dresner, K.M., Stone, P.: Multiagent traffic management: a reservation-based intersection control mechanism. In: Proceedings of the Third International Joint Conference on AAMAS, pp. 530–537. IEEE Computer Society (2004)
11. Gartner, N.H., Pooran, F.J., Andrews, C.M.: Implementation of the OPAC adaptive control strategy in a traffic signal network. In: IEEE Intelligent Transportation Systems. IEEE (2001)
12. Gerkey, B.P., Mataric, M.J.: Sold!: auction methods for multirobot coordination. IEEE Transactions on Robotics and Automation $18(5)$, 758–768 (2002)
13. Gomm, P., Wengraf, I.: The car and the commute, the journey to work in england and wales. Technical report, The Royal Automobile Club Foundation for Motoring, December 2013
14. Koenig, S., Tovey, C.A., Lagoudakis, M.G., Markakis, E., Kempe, D., Keskinocak, P., Kleywegt, A.J., Meyerson, A., Jain, S.: The power of sequential single-item auctions for agent coordination. In: Proceedings of the 21st National Conference on Artificial Intelligence, AAAI 2006, vol. 2, pp. 1625–1629. AAAI Press (2006)

15. Krajzewicz, D., Erdmann, J., Behrisch, M., Bieker, L.: Recent development and applications of SUMO - simulation of urban MObility. International Journal On Advances in Systems and Measurements **5**(3–4), 128–138 (2012)
16. Lagoudakis, M.G., Berhault, M., Koenig, S., Keskinocak, P., Kleywegt, A.J.: Simple auctions with performance guarantees for multi-robot task allocation. In: Proceedings of the IEEE/RSJ International Conference on Intelligent Robots and Systems, pp. 698–705. IEEE (2004)
17. Mirchandani, P., Wang, F.-Y.: RHODES to intelligent transportation systems. IEEE Intelligent Systems **20**(1), 10–15 (2005)
18. Mladenovic, M., Abbas, M.: A survey of experiences with adaptive traffic control systems in north america. Journal of Road and Traffic Engineering **59**(2), 5–11 (2013)
19. Sariel, S., Balch, T.R.: Efficient bids on task allocation for multi-robot exploration. In: Sutcliffe, G., Goebel, R. (eds.) FLAIRS Conference, pp. 116–121. AAAI Press (2006)
20. Schepperle, H., Böhm, K.: Auction-based traffic management: towards effective concurrent utilization of road intersections. In: CEC/EEE, pp. 105–112. IEEE (2008)
21. Vasirani, M., Ossowski, S.: A market-inspired approach for intersection management in urban road traffic networks. Journal Artificial Intelligence Research **43**, 621–659 (2012)
22. Wang, F.-Y.: Agent-based control for networked traffic management systems. IEEE Intelligent Systems **20**(5), 92–96 (2005)

Social Emotional Model

J.A. Rincon[(✉)], V. Julian, and C. Carrascosa

Departamento de Sistemas Informáticos y Computación (DSIC),
Universitat Politècnica de València,
Camino de Vera s/n, Valencia, Spain
{jrincon,vinglada,carrasco}@dsic.upv.es

Abstract. This article aims to give a first approach of an emotional model, which allows to extract the social emotion of a group of intelligent entities. The emotional model PAD allows to represent the emotion of an intelligent entity in 3-D space, allowing the representation of different emotional states. The social emotional model presented in this paper uses individual emotions of each one of the entities, which are represented in the emotional space PAD. Using a social emotional model within intelligent entities allows the creation of more real simulations, in which emotional states can influence decision-making. The result of this social emotional mode is represented by a series of examples, which are intended to represent a number of situations in which the emotions of each individual modify the emotion of the group.

1 Introduction

Human-Computer Interaction (HCI) is a field that appeared in the 80s decade, with the Personal Computers, giving access to the new digital technologies and converting all the people in potential users without any knowledge about computers. HCI involves information interchange between people and computers using some kind of dialogue, like programming languages and information interchange platforms. These platforms include from input devices such as keyboards and optical mouses to output devices as the own computer screens. Cognitive psychology integration with HCI field lead to adopt new forms of information processing and to better understanding how people did communicate with the devices. Nevertheless, in spite of the accessibility solutions presented by HCIs, user interfaces were very limited. As a result, the discipline adopt other research subjects focused in usability, ergonomics and to try to build new interfaces allowing a more natural interaction between humans and machines.

These research subjects have made appear new interaction paradigms created by the mobile computing, portable and ubiquitous. They have incorporated devices to communicate directly with the physical world such as movement and gestures capture through the *Kinect* [1] and even user biosignals capture through the *MYO* and *Emotiv* devices [2], [3]. The idea is that machines will not only receive orders from users but also they will perceive their emotional states or behaviors using all this information to execute the different actions [4], [5].

© Springer International Publishing Switzerland 2015
Y. Demazeau et al. (Eds.): PAAMS 2015, LNAI 9086, pp. 199–210, 2015.
DOI: 10.1007/978-3-319-18944-4_17

The information increase generated by the new ways of interaction has made appear the need of using other computational toolkits to classify and process information to benefit user. The AI tools such as pattern recognition ones, automatic learning, and multi-agent systems (MAS) allow the development of this kind of tasks, creating environments that adapt to human needs to improve his welfare and life quality.

Human beings manage themselves in different environments, either in the working place, at home or in public places. At each one of these places we perceive a wide range of stimuli, that interfere in our commodity levels modifying our emotional levels. For instance, the high levels of noise or the temperature conditions may produce stress situations. Before each one of these stimuli, humans answer varying our face gestures, body or bio-electrical ones. These variations in our emotional states could be used as information useful for machines. Nevertheless, it is needed that the machines will have the capability of interpreting or recognizing such variations. This is the reason for implementing emotional models that interpret or represent the different emotions.

Emotional models such as *OCC* [6] presented by *Ortony, Clore & Collins* and the *PAD* model [7] are the most used ones to detect or simulate emotional states. Nevertheless, these models don't allow the execution of intelligent decisions based on the emotional state perception. Between these toolkits, we can find MAS, which are able to modify their behavior based on the emotional state perception. This way, it is obtained that the agent being part of the MAS contains an emotional model able of interpreting and/or emulating different emotional states. To detect emotional states, it is needed to include pattern recognition algorithms, automatic learning contributing to the decision making to execute an action. For instance, if an agent detects that the user presents an emotional state of sadness, it is able to counter that emotional state by executing actions trying to modify it. This way a clean and transparent human-machine interaction is obtained. However, this situation is only valid for a lonely entity inside the environment. The incorporation of more entities inside the environment (multiple emotions) is not contemplated by current emotional models.

The goal of this work is to give a first approach to a social emotional model including multiple emotions between humans and agents. Our model uses as base the *PAD* emotional model to represent the social emotion of a group.

2   Previous Approaches

This section presents an introduction to the emotional models *OCC* and *PAD*. The goal is to give a general view of both emotional models.

2.1   Ortony, Clore & Collins: OCC

The *OCC* model designed by Ortony, Clore & Collins is a model frequently used in applications where an emotional state can be detected or simulated. This has allowed to create applications to emulate emotions in virtual humans [8] and to create agents reacting to stress situations [9].

The OCC model specifies 22 emotional categories, which are divided into five processes: 1) the classification of the events, the action or the found object, 2) the quantification of the affected emotions intensity, 3) the interaction between the just generated emotion with the existing ones, 4) the cartography of the emotional state of one emotional expression and 5) is the one expressed by the emotional state [10]. In OCC model is observed. These processes define the whole system, where the emotional states represent the way of perceiving our environment (objects, persons, places) and, at the same time, influencing in our behaviour positively or negatively [11]. However, the OCC model utilization presents one complication due mainly to his high dimensionality.

2.2   PAD Model

The PAD is a simplified model of the OCC model. This model allows to represent the different emotional states using three values. These three values are usually normalized in $[-1, 1]$, and correspond to the three components conforming the emotional model (*Pleasure, Arousal, Dominance*). These components can be represented in a $\mathbb{R}^3$ space.

Each one of the components conforming the PAD model allow to influentiate the emotional state of an individual in a positive or negative way. This influence evaluates the emotional predisposition of such individual, modifying in this way his emotional state. The Pleasure-Displeasure Scale measures how pleasant an emotion may be. For instance both anger and fear are unpleasant emotions, and score high on the displeasure scale. However joy is a pleasant emotion. This dimension is usually limited to 16 specific values. ([12], pp. 39–53). The Arousal-Nonarousal Scale measures the intensity of the emotion. For instance while both anger and rage are unpleasant emotions, rage has a higher intensity or a higher arousal state. However boredom, which is also an unpleasant state, has a low arousal value. This scale is usually restricted to 9 specific values([12], pp. 39–53).The Dominance-Submissiveness Scale represents the controlling and dominant nature of the emotion. For instance while both fear and anger are unpleasant emotions, anger is a dominant emotion, while fear is a submissive emotion. This scale is also usually restricted to 9 specific values ([12], pp. 39–53).

As have been presented above, the existing emotional models are thought to detect and/or simulate human emotions for a lonely entity. That is, it is not taken into account the possibility of having multiple emotions inside an heterogeneous group of entities, where each one of such entities have the capability of detecting and/or emulating one emotion. The need of detecting the emotion of an heterogeneous group of entities can be reflected in the different applications that could be obtained. With the appearance of the different smart devices, ubiquitous computation and ambient intelligent, emotional states turn into valuable information, allowing to develop applications that help to improve the human being life quality. Therefore, it is needed to create a new model that allow to detect the emotion of a group.

At this point, the two emotional models are used in applications where MAS are is involved, allowing to determine the emotional model PAD is most appropriate for our model. This is mainly due to the emotional representation is performed with three normalized values and not 22 as the OCC model poses. So as obtaining the quantified emotion of each of the individuals, which allows obtaining total emotion of the agent group. It is for this reason that this work wants to pose a possible solution to this problem, pretending to give a first approximation of a social emotional model based on the PAD model on $SEPAD$.

3   Social Emotional Model Based on PAD

This section proposes a model of social emotion based on the PAD emotional model. This model will represent the social emotion of a heterogeneous group of entities capable of expressing and/or communicate emotions. To define a model of social emotion, it is necessary first to define the representation of an emotional state of an agent on the PAD model. The emotion of an agent ag_i is defined as a vector in a space $\mathbb{R}^3$, represented by three components that make up the PAD emotional model. The variation of each component allows to modify the emotional state of the agent (Equation 1).

$$E(ag_i) = [P_i, A_i, D_i] \qquad (1)$$

A first approach to of a social emotion representation of a group of n agents $Ag = \{ag_1, ag_2, ..., ag_n\}$ is obtained by averaging their P, A, D values (Equation 2). This average will enable us to determine where the central emotion (CE) of this group of agents and be visualized in the PAD space.

$$\bar{P} = \frac{\sum_{i=1}^{n} P_i}{n}, \bar{A} = \frac{\sum_{i=1}^{n} A_i}{n}, \bar{D} = \frac{\sum_{i=1}^{n} D_i}{n} \qquad (2)$$

The final result is a vector in the space $\mathbb{R}^3$ which is the core emotion or $CE(Ag)$ of a group of agents (Equation 3).

$$CE(Ag) = [\bar{P}, \bar{A}, \bar{D}] \qquad (3)$$

The $CE(Ag)$ by itself is not enough to represent the social emotion of a group of agents, since there may be different groups of agents with the same central emotion but in a very different emotional situation. Figures 1 and 2 [1], show two different situations where the central emotion is the same. In Figure 1 a group of agents is observed with $CE(Ag) = [0.0, 0.22, 0.45]$. In Figure 2 another group of agents is observed with completely different emotions, but generating the same central emotion of the agents shown in Figure 1.

Clearly, the $CE(Ag)$ is not enough to represent the social emotion of an agent group. As it can be seen in the previous example the emotions of an agents

---

[1] The red triangles represent the different agents, green triangle represents the central emotion $CE(Ag)$ and the blue point refers to (0,0,0).

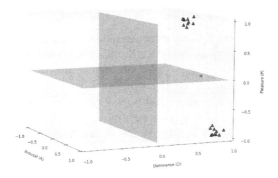

Fig. 1. Group of agents with two subgroups completely opposite

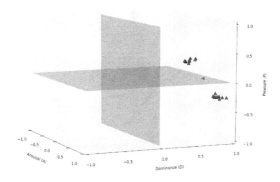

Fig. 2. Group of agents with two subgroups with more nearest emotions

group can be very different but have the same CE. This is why it is necessary to introduce some measurement about the distance of the agents with respect to the CE. To do this we include the definition of the maximum distances of agent emotions respect to $CE(Ag)$. In order to calculate the maximum distances, the Euclidean distance (Equation 4, 5, 6) is used as follows.

$$m_P(Ag) = max\left(\sqrt{(P_i - \bar{P}(Ag))^2}\right), \forall ag_i \in Ag \qquad (4)$$

$$m_A(Ag) = max\left(\sqrt{(A_i - \bar{A}(Ag))^2}\right), \forall ag_i \in Ag \qquad (5)$$

$$m_D(Ag) = max\left(\sqrt{(D_i - \bar{D}(Ag))^2}\right), \forall ag_i \in Ag \qquad (6)$$

The results of these equations can be represented as a vector of maximum distances (Equation 7).

$$m(Ag) = [m_P(Ag), m_A(Ag), m_D(Ag)] \qquad (7)$$

The $m(Ag)$ can indicate if there exist agents having their emotional state far away from the central emotion. From a graphical perspective it is also possible to use these maximum distances to plot an enveloping which encapsulates all emotions, allowing the limit of all the agents to be defined. To represent this enveloping shape of emotions an ellipsoid as a geometric figure was used. This ellipsoid (Figure 3) [2] can be adapted to represent different emotional states, which allows a dynamical way for displaying the social emotion of a group.

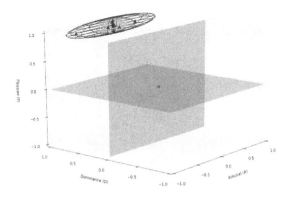

Fig. 3. Ellipsoid enveloping the emotions of a group of agents

Furthermore, considering $m(Ag)$ as a part of the definition of the social emotion of a group of agents, there may be situations in which $m(Ag)$ is not enough. In Figure 4 and 5 a group of agents is shown with similar $CE(Ag)$ and $m(Ag)$, but with completely different emotional situations. In order to solve this problem the notion of standard deviation (SD) is introduced. This SD allows the calculation of the level of emotional dispersion of this group of agents around the central emotion $CE(Ag)$ for each component of the PAD(Equation 8).

$$
\sigma_P(Ag) = \sqrt{\dfrac{\sum\limits_{i=1}^{n}(P_i - \bar{P}(Ag))^2}{n}}, \forall ag_i \in Ag
$$

$$
\sigma_A(Ag) = \sqrt{\dfrac{\sum\limits_{i=1}^{n}(A_i - \bar{A}(Ag))^2}{n}}, \forall ag_i \in Ag \qquad (8)
$$

$$
\sigma_D(Ag) = \sqrt{\dfrac{\sum\limits_{i=1}^{n}(D_i - \bar{D}(Ag))^2}{n}}, \forall ag_i \in Ag
$$

---

[2] This figure is a snapshot of the emotion of a group of agents in a specific time

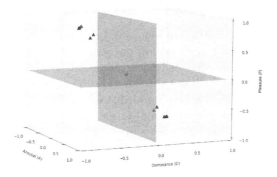

Fig. 4. Group of agents with two subgroups with central emotion different but equal maximum distances

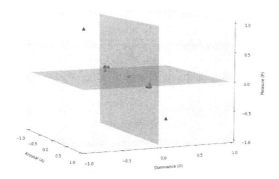

Fig. 5. Group of agents with two subgroups with central emotion different but equal maximum distances

The result of each of the above equations can be represented as a vector (Equation 9), which allow to determine the level of emotional dispersion.

$$\sigma(Ag) = [\sigma_P(Ag), \sigma_A(Ag), \sigma_D(Ag)] \tag{9}$$

From this definition, it can be deduced that:

1. **if** $\sigma(Ag) >> \mathbf{0}$, the group has a high emotional dispersion, i.e. the members of the group have different emotional states.
2. **if** $\sigma(Ag) \cong \mathbf{0}$, the group has a low emotional dispersion, this means that individuals have similar emotional states.

Adding the emotional dispersion in the definition of the social emotion of a group of agents, the social emotion of a group of agents $Ag = ag_1, ag_2, ..., ag_n$ can be defined by the following triplet (Equation 10).

$$SE(Ag) = (CE(Ag), m(Ag), \sigma(Ag)) \tag{10}$$

Where $CE(Ag)$ is the central emotion, $m(Ag)$ represents the maximum distances and $\sigma(Ag)$ represents the emotion dispersion of an agent group.

Based on this model it is possible to determine the emotional distance among different groups of agents or between the same group in different instants of time. This will allow to measure the emotional distance between the current social emotional group and a possible emotional target. This approach can be used as a feedback in the decision making process in order to take actions to try to move the social emotion to a particular area of the PAD space or to allow that the emotional state of a group of agents can be approached or moved away from other groups of agents. From an emotional point, of view these movements or actions are domain-dependent and are out of he scope of this model. In Equation 11 the profile of the emotional distance function is defined as the distance of the social emotions of two groups of agents.

$$\Delta_{SE} : SE(Ag^i), SE(Ag^j) \rightarrow [0,1] \tag{11}$$

According to this profile, Equation 12 shows how we calculate this emotional variation. The equation calculates three distances corresponding to the three components of the SE. Given two groups of agents Ag_i, Ag_j with social emotions $SE(Ag^i), SE(Ag^j)$ respectively, the emotional distance between these two groups is calculated as:

$$
\begin{aligned}
\Delta_{SE}(SE(Ag^i), SE(Ag^j)) = \frac{1}{2} \Big(& \omega_c \Delta(CE(Ag^i), CE(Ag^j)) \\
& + \omega_d \Delta(m(Ag^i), m(Ag^j)) \\
& + \omega_v \Delta(\sigma(Ag^i), \sigma(Ag^j)) \Big)
\end{aligned}
\tag{12}
$$

$$where \quad \omega_c + \omega_d + \omega_v = 1; \quad \omega_c, \omega_d, \omega_v \in [0,1] \tag{13}$$

and Δ calculates the vectorial distance between two vectors. As every dimension of the PAD space is bounded between $[-1,1]$, each Δ will give values between $[0,2]$. Therefore, Δ_{SE} will have a range between $[0,1]$.

Calculating the distance among social emotions allows the study of the behavior of emotional-based agents, either minimizing or maximizing the $\Delta_{SE}(SE (Ag^i), SE(Ag^j))$ function. This way, it can be achieved that an agent group approaches or move away of an specific emotional state. To do this it is necessary to modify through stimuli the individual emotions from each agent and therefore changing the social emotion. Nevertheless, how to maximize or minimize the emotional distance is domain-dependent and it is out of the scope of this paper.

4   Case Study

A practical application which uses the previously proposed model is presented in this section. This application example is based on how music can influence in a positive or negative way over emotional states [13], [14], [15].

The application example is developed in a bar, where there is a DJ agent in charge of play music and a specific number of individuals listening the music. The main goal of the DJ is to play music making that all individuals within the bar are mostly happy as possible. Each of the individuals will be represented by an agent, which has an emotional response according to its musical taste. That is, depending on the musical genre of the song, agents will respond varying their emotional state. Moreover, varying emotions of each agent will modify the social emotion of the group. The different scenarios have been designed in order to show how the social emotion can facilitate the decision making of the DJ. In each scenario the DJ agent plays a song. Once the song has ended, the DJ evaluates the social emotion of the group of listeners that are within the bar. In this way, the DJ agent can evaluate the effect that the song has had the song over the audience. This will help the DJ to decide whether to continue with the same musical genre or not in order to improve the emotional state of the group.

4.1 Scenario 1: Group of Agents with Low Emotional Dispersion

The first case analyzed is one in which the emotional states of the agents are close. This emotional difference may be due mainly because the agents have little differences in their musical tastes. The social emotion in this scenario has a $EC(Ag)$ very close to all the values of the agents and the $m(Ag)$ and $\sigma(Ag)$ values will be very small and in many cases close to zero. This provokes that the DJ will try to play songs of similar generes trying to maintain this situation, which is not the ideal situation but it can be considered as a very good situation. A graphical representation of this example can be seen in Figure 6 while Table 1 shows the different emotional states of each of the agents in this group.

Table 1. Individual emotion of each agent and its magnitude in the PAD space

Agents	P	A	D	Emotional State
ag_0	0.90	0.0	0.90	Happy
ag_1	0.70	0.0	0.91	Happy
ag_2	0.80	0.0	0.95	Happy
ag_3	0.85	0.0	0.99	Happy
ag_4	0.91	0.0	0.89	Happy
ag_5	0.93	0.0	0.86	Happy
ag_6	0.89	0.0	0.83	Happy
ag_7	0.79	0.0	0.81	Happy
ag_8	0.92	0.0	0.89	Happy
ag_9	0.81	0.0	1.0	Happy

As it can be see in the Figure 6 all the represented emotions in this group are around the emotion *Happy*, achieving a social emotion with these values of $SE(Ag) = ([0.85, 0.0, 0.9], [0.85, 0.0, 0.9], [0.07, 0.0, 0.06])$.

4.2 Scenario 2: Group of Agents with High Emotional Dispersion

In this second case it is represented the existence of a group of agents emotionally dispersed in the bar. These agents have completely different emotions

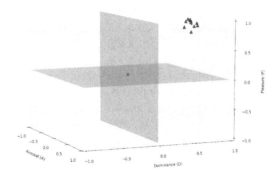

Fig. 6. Scenario 1: Group of agents with low emotional dispersion

Table 2. Individual emotion of each agent and its magnitude in the PAD space

Agents	P	A	D	Emotional State
ag_0	-0.9	-0.9	-0.9	Remorse
ag_1	-0.7	0.6	0.0	Anguish
ag_2	0.9	0.9	0.0	Joy
ag_3	0.9	-0.5	0.9	Satisfaction
ag_4	-0.7	0.8	-0.9	Hurt
ag_5	0.9	0.9	0.9	Admiration
ag_6	0.9	0.0	0.9	Happy
ag_7	-1.0	1.0	0.9	Anger
ag_8	1.0	1.0	-0.9	Love

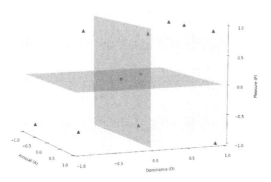

Fig. 7. Scenario 2: Group of agents with high emotional dispersion

distributed along the PAD space. The emotional values of each of the agents can be seen in Table 2. This high dispersion is reflected in the calculated values of the social emotion ($SE(Ag) = ([0.14, 0.42, 0.1], [1.14, 1.32, 1.0], [0.87, 0.67, 0.79])$). In this case, the social emotion is very different and more complicated to manage then the previous case. The central emotion is very far from the emotional states of each agent and the maximum distances and dispersion values are high too.

So, from the perspective of the DJ this scenario is very chaotic and unwished because it is difficult to choose which kind of music is the most appropriated. In this case the DJ should try to move the central emotion to a state close to "happy" testing different musical styles and analyzing carefully the effect of each song in the social emotion of the group.

5 Conclusions and Future Work

A new model for representing social emotions has been presented in this paper. The goal of this model is to give a first approach for the detection and simulation of social emotions in a group of intelligent entities. This social emotion model builds on the PAD emotional model, which allows the representation of individual emotions in intelligent entities. The proposed model of social emotion uses the individual emotions of each entity of a group, allowing us to represent the emotion of that group as a triplet consisting of three vectors $(EC(Ag), m(Ag) and \sigma(Ag))$. This definition allows us to represent the emotional state of a group of entities that are placed in a specific environment. Moreover, the model adds the mechanisms to compare the social emotional state of two groups of agents or the social emotion of a group in different time instants. The social emotion of a group of agents not only allows a global view of the emotional situation of the group, moreover it can be used as a feedback in order to change the emotional state of the group or only of a part of the agents. As future work we want to introduce the human within the model, adding their emotional state through the analysis of body gestures or through the face. To do this, specialized hardware must be used in order to obtain this information, helping to create environments in which humans interact in a transparent way with intelligent entities employing their emotional states.

Acknowledgments. This work is partially supported by the MINECO/FEDER TIN2012-36586-C03-01 and the FPI grant AP2013-01276 awarded to Jaime-Andres Rincon.

References

1. Tivatansakul, S., Ohkura, M.: Healthcare system design focusing on emotional aspects using augmented reality. In: 2013 IEEE Symposium on Computational Intelligence in Healthcare and e-health (CICARE), pp. 88–93 (2013)
2. Bos, D.O.: EEG-based emotion recognition. The Influence of Visual and Auditory Stimuli, 1–17 (2006)
3. Pham, T.D., Tran, D.: Emotion recognition using the emotiv EPOC device. In: Huang, T., Zeng, Z., Li, C., Leung, C.S. (eds.) ICONIP 2012, Part V. LNCS, vol. 7667, pp. 394–399. Springer, Heidelberg (2012)
4. Nogueira, P.A., Rodrigues, R., Oliveira, E., Nacke, L.E.: A hybrid approach at emotional state detection: merging theoretical models of emotion with data-driven statistical classifiers. In: 2013 IEEE/WIC/ACM International WI and IAT, vol. 2, pp. 253–260, November 2013

5. Meftah, I.T., Le Thanh, N., Amar, C.B.: Towards an algebraic modeling of emotional states. In: 2010 Fifth International Conference on Internet and Web Applications and Services (ICIW), pp. 513–518, May 2010
6. Ortony, A., Clore, G., Collins, A.: Cognitive Structure of Emotions. Cambridge University Press (1988)
7. Mehrabian, A.: Analysis of affiliation-related traits in terms of the PAD temperament model. The Journal of Psychology **131**(1), 101–117 (1997)
8. Becker-Asano, C., Wachsmuth, I.: Affective computing with primary and secondary emotions in a virtual human. JAAMAS **20**(1), 32–49 (2010)
9. Jain, D., Kobti, Z.: Simulating the effect of emotional stress on task performance using OCC. In: Butz, C., Lingras, P. (eds.) Canadian AI 2011. LNCS, vol. 6657, pp. 204–209. Springer, Heidelberg (2011)
10. Ortony., A.: The Cognitive Structure of Emotions. Cambridge University Press, May 1990
11. Ali, F., Amin, M.: The influence of physical environment on emotions, customer satisfaction and behavioural intentions in chinese resort hotel industry. In: KMITL-AGBA Conference Bangkok, pp. 15–17 (2013)
12. Mehrabian, A.: Basic Dimensions for a General Psychological Theory: Implications for Personality, Social, Environmental, and Developmental Studies. Oelgeschlager, Gunn & Hain, January 1980
13. Whitman, B., Smaragdis, P.: Combining musical and cultural features for intelligent style detection. In: Proc. of the 3rd International Conference on Music Information Retrieval (ISMIR 2002), pp. 47–52, Paris, France (2002)
14. van der Zwaag, M.D., Westerink, J.H.D.M., van den Broek, E.L.: Emotional and psychophysiological responses to tempo, mode, and percussiveness. Musicae Scientiae **15**(2), 250–269 (2011)
15. Scherer, K.R., Zentner, M.R.: Emotional effects of music: Production rules. Music and Emotion: Theory and Research, 361–392 (2001)

AgentDrive: Towards an Agent-Based Coordination of Intelligent Cars

Martin Schaefer$^{(\boxtimes)}$ and Jiri Vokrinek

Department of Computer Science,
Faculty of Electrical Engineering, Agent Technology Center,
Czech Technical University in Prague, Prague, Czech Republic
{martin.schaefer,jiri.vokrinek}@fel.cvut.cz
http://agents.fel.cvut.cz/agentdrive/

Abstract. Multi-agent approach to study coordination among intelligent cars is discussed. Intelligent cars are presented as a promising domain for multi-agent applications as modelling, simulations and coordination algorithms. AgentDrive coordination platform is introduced to illustrate possibilities in development of such applications. AgentDrive allows development of coordination algorithms and their validation via simulation. The coordination algorithms notion covers some of the following tasks: dynamic routing, trajectory planning, or collision avoidance and cooperation. Simulation can be performed in an arbitrary level of detail by using various external physics simulators.

Keywords: Multi-agent simulation · Autonomous vehicles coordination · Integrated driving and traffic simulation

1 Introduction

Development of intelligent cars and assistance systems is motivated by two main arguments. The first one is the safety of road traffic. There were about 26 000 deaths on roads in European Union in 2013[1]. Second argument is that the technologies can improve inefficient usage of resources. The most spelled resources in this context are road infrastructure and fuel.

In recent years, the research in the domain of autonomous vehicles is greatly accelerated. A lot of technologies for autonomous drive support or advanced driver assistance systems (ADAS) have been developed and deployed in production. The self-driving cars are already being tested in the real traffic, but the most of the technologies currently available are car-centric oriented. The research domain of connected cooperating vehicles faces difficulties of transfer the scientific results to the reliable production ready technology. Such research crosses the borders of the fields of telecommunication, information processing, robotics, distributed planning and control. While the development of vehicle-to-vehicle

---

[1] http://ec.europa.eu/transport/road_safety/specialist/statistics/index_en.htm

© Springer International Publishing Switzerland 2015
Y. Demazeau et al. (Eds.): PAAMS 2015, LNAI 9086, pp. 211–224, 2015.
DOI: 10.1007/978-3-319-18944-4_18

(V2V) communication standards almost reaches the wide-spread implementation in car production, the autonomous cooperative systems research domain is disconnected from this stream.

The assistance systems that rely on car mounted sensors are limited by the local knowledge. The connected (communicating) vehicles broaden the perception by information obtained via communication from other cars or infrastructure. Shared sensory information and V2V communication abilities enable to deploy effective coordination mechanisms. The coordination can vary from awareness of other cars to explicit cooperation or negotiation. Our interest is in mechanisms of coordination of cars, while we assume the vehicles are equipped with technologies providing perception of the environment.

The development of coordination mechanisms among intelligent vehicles is complex task. Let us assume we develop a theoretical coordination mechanism, then we need to validate it in realistic scenarios. Safety and economic reasons motivate usage of simulators for wide spectrum of applications where deployment of new technologies is risky or expensive. Coordination mechanism is a convenient technology to be simulated before deployment in real world. The simulation should cover realistic physical models of vehicles, realistic communication, and realistic sensor models. The simulation should be also scalable in size of scenario and number of cars. Scalability enables to study the influence of coordination mechanisms on traffic flows in congested areas.

2   Motivation for Development of AgentDrive Platform

The purpose of the AgentDrive platform is to support development of coordination mechanisms. It allows to deploy and to test coordination mechanisms in the various level of abstraction. The scalability in the terms of number of (heterogeneous) agents in the scenario with flexible level of simulation detail is essential for development of coordination mechanisms for future (semi-)autonomous vehicles in the everyday traffic situations. The traffic simulation and realistic driving simulation features are combined in the AgentDrive platform.

The multi-agent nature of the domain motivates usage of the agent-based modelling of car drivers. We consider drivers to be agents responsible for controlling physical car models. The coordination mechanism is to be designed among these agents. The development of coordination mechanisms is usually an iterative process. The methods are prototyped considering perfect execution in the first stage. Realistic execution with uncertainty and with more detailed models of vehicles is gradually incorporated into the development process. The agents – drivers are independent of the physical models of the related cars and the physics simulation detail can vary using various physics simulators – from perfect plan execution to realistic drive simulation.

The integration of realistic physical models of cars into the traffic simulation offers realistic interaction of cars with each other. Since driving simulators focus on believable realistic car physics, these can be integrated as a physics engine for traffic simulation. Various driving simulators exist and can provide the traffic simulation with realistic physics and visualization. The integration of human-in-the loop is natural in driving simulators, not in the traffic simulators. Integration of driving simulator into the traffic simulation brings the human factor into the traffic simulation. Therefore, mechanisms controlling vehicles in traffic simulator need to deal with human controlled vehicles.

From driving simulator perspective, the coordination mechanism among traffic can be seen as a module responsible for controlling traffic vehicles, thus it can provide realistic autonomous traffic in driving simulators. Such traffic autonomy is rare in driving simulators available on the market. Autonomous drive can be introduced into the driving simulation by implementing sophisticated sensors to sense and map the environment or by providing structured environment data. Structured road network is the base for most of the traffic simulations. The networks are commonly generated from real map data (e.g. OpenStreetMaps). Integration of the traffic simulation with driving simulation is beneficial for users of both driving and traffic simulators. Traffic simulation is confronted by challenges related to realistic physics and human-in-the-loop tests. Driving simulation is extended by interaction with autonomous traffic.

Additional technologies are needed to integrate driving and traffic simulators. The driving and traffic simulation is based on the common world model. The world model is based on the real world – real map data. The driving simulation requires physical model of the world, the traffic simulation requires the structured world description – road network. The unified approach to the world model and it's compatible representation in driving and traffic simulation is vital for successful integration.

The domain of the traffic simulators usually focusses on traffic scenarios with statistical measures. On the other hand the driving simulators usually targets on realistic user single-car experience. AgentDrive fills the gap between these two approaches – it is focused on many-car realistic (cooperative) drive in the realistic traffic situations.

3   Related Work

Simulation platforms related to traffic, driving, sensor and network simulations are discussed in this section. We focus on platforms or projects that are open to modification, integration and research.

The most used traffic simulator is called SUMO (Simulation of Urban MObility) [5]. It is an open-source simulation suite. SUMO is a microscopic traffic simulator enriched by a set of tools related to a preparation of simulation scenarios. SUMO is a well matured system that is widely used by research communities. Import or generation of both road network and mobility model are the key features of the tool. Similar to SUMO, MATSim [1] is a relevant open-source framework for large-scale agent-based traffic simulations.

Agent-based modelling of traffic allows to model individual heterogeneous drivers, also to study the influence of local interactions to the complex system. The emergent effect of the social behaviour to the overall system is generally discussed in [3]. A review of usage of agent-based for traffic simulation providing motivation and examples of the agent-based approach is in [2].

The main applications of driving simulators are in research of driver behaviour, training of drivers and entertainment. There is a wide range of features addressed by driving simulators. One of the most important features is a realistic human driver experience. There are high-end simulators in research laboratories of many manufacturers. Daimler[2], Toyota[3] or Ford[4] are just few examples. These high-end simulators are equipped with large motion platforms providing realistic accelerations. The main disadvantage of these simulators is the cost of acquisition and operation.

Professional simulation companies like Vires[5] or Oktal[6] provide usually a scale of solutions. High-end simulator with a cabin on a motion platform is the most advanced, realistic and expensive solution. Simpler solution is a static cabin or only seats equipped with visual projection. The basic solution is the simulation software without any special peripheries.

An interesting project in the area is OpenDS[7]. OpenDS is an open-source driving simulator open to modification and integration. OpenDS is based on a game engine jMonkeyEngine (jME)[8]. The jME provides the simulator with a 3D visualization and game-like physics. OpenDS uses a possibility of importing various 3D models in jME. All scenes can be prepared in advance and loaded. Individual models can also be added using related XML format settings files or loaded directly in source code. OpenDS also contains so-called Drive Analyser, which allows to replay a drive and to perform further analysis after the simulation run itself. OpenDS is a driving simulator aiming mainly on human-machine interaction community. There are several prepared scenarios and drive tasks in OpenDS, nevertheless creation of a new experiment in OpenDS is possible.

Vehicular communication (V2X) is a big step towards transportation safety. V2X communication brings new possibilities and challenges into the related research areas, but the evaluation of concepts with higher number of real cars is expensive. It motivates the experimentation in simulations. The vehicles with communication units and infrastructure units form VANET – vehicular ad-hoc network. The network simulation can be performed in dedicated simulators (e.g. ns-2, ns-3, OMNeT++, JiST/SWANS), but there is a need of providing a mobility model in addition to network simulation. The common way to provide the mobility model is usage of traffic simulators.

---

[2] http://www.mercedesclass.net/safety-2/driving-simulator-2/driving-simulator/

[3] http://www.toyota-global.com/innovation/safety_technology/safety_
measurements/driving_simulator.html

[4] http://www.extremetech.com/extreme/133549-inside-virttex-fords-amazing-
driver-distraction-simulator

[5] http://www.vires.com/products.html

[6] http://www.oktal.fr/en/automotive/simulators-operational-needs

[7] http://opends.eu

[8] http://jmonkeyengine.org

The communicated information by network simulation can have impact on traffic simulation e.g. rerouting in case of a reported accident, so the integrated closed-loop simulation is necessary for realistic scenarios.

TraNS [6] is one of the first simulator with bidirectional binding of mobility model and network simulation. TraNS combines ns-2 with SUMO traffic simulator. It seems to be no longer developed since 2008. iTetris [9] project is a successor of TraNS as it combines SUMO with ns-3. The project is funded by EU FP7 framework and aims to be compliant with European standard for V2X technologies.

Vehicles in Network Simulation (Veins) [7] is also using SUMO as a traffic simulator but for network simulation the OMNet++ is used. The project is actively maintained, its third version was released. The V2X Simulation Runtime Infrastructure (VSimRTI) [8][10] is a comprehensive framework that allows to couple different simulators in simulation. The tests were done with traffic simulators SUMO, VISSIM and network simulators ns-3, OMNeT++, JiST/SWANS.

The driving simulators enables simulation with 3D visualization, physics simulation and human-in-the-loop simulation. We converged to experiment mainly with OpenDS as it is open-source, it allows us to adapt it for our specific purposes. The integration process of OpenDS serves us to proof the concept of general driving simulator integration. The large community around SUMO generates numerous useful tools to work with maps or mobility models. The tools and data structures used by SUMO are convenient for our purposes. Network simulation is not yet integrated into AgentDrive platform. The binding of a network simulation with our simulation platform is discussed as a future work in the Section 7.

4 AgentDrive Architecture

AgentDrive simulation platform architecture is built on the top of two main components: a coordination module and a physics simulation. The decomposition of a car into a reasoning agent and a physical model is to be seen in Figure 1. The decomposition allows us to validate coordination methods on various level of simulation detail varying from simple mathematical movement model to a realistic physical drive simulation. The subset of modules needed for a basic setting with simplistic physics simulation is highlighted by red color in Figure 1. This subset represents a core of the AgentDrive platform. The core consists of a coordination module, interface to connect to physics simulation and simplistic physics simulator. The coordination module – traffic simulation environment and multi-agent coordination module – is described in Section 5.

The simulator with idealistic plan execution is useful for development of coordination mechanisms. A developer can see what exactly the coordination

---

[9] http://www.ict-itetris.eu/platform.htm
[10] http://www.dcaiti.tu-berlin.de/research/simulation/download/

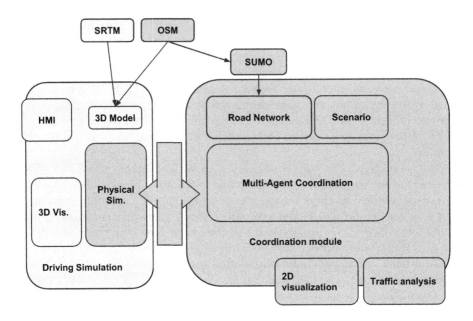

Fig. 1. AgentDrive architecture. Core of the AgentDrive platform is highlighted by red color. Coordination is to be implemented in multi-agent coordination module. The environment of the module – road network is generated using SUMO tools from OSM map data. Physics of the vehicles is simulated in external physics simulation. The physics simulation can be implemented by a driving simulator. In case the driving simulation is used, the blue modules are additionally available.

mechanism is proposing. When the developer is satisfied with functionality in the simulator with perfect execution then the challenge of imperfect execution in realistic physics is introduced.

The experiments with the realistic physics can be performed after replacement of the simple simulator by an advanced one. Advanced simulator can be used even for a single vehicle or a selected subset of vehicles. The specification of the interface between coordination module and physics simulation is crucial. Proper specification of the interface enables application of the coordination module in various simulators, while the development of the coordination methods within coordination module is independent from the specific physics simulation properties. Therefore, physics simulation module is described in Section 6.

We are proposing to use a realistic driving simulator as the physics simulation module. The extensions of the platform by using a driving simulator are illustrated in Figure 1 (blue modules). Driving simulator integration provides the platform with realistic simulation of physics, 3D visualization and possibility of the human-in-the-loop experiments.

5   Coordination Module

Purpose of the coordination module is to embrace individual agents that are responsible of controlling related individual cars. The module implementation is based on a simulation toolkit Alite [4]. The simulation environment is based on a road network model. The creation of the environment based on the real world data is important feature of the module.

5.1   Multi-agent Simulation

The coordination module is a multi-agent simulation environment itself where agents correspond to individual cars. The multi-agent simulation allows to use distributed coordination methods as well as the centralized ones. An agent in this context is specified as an entity that can perceive and act on the environment. The sensors and actuators respectively are used to provide interactions with the environment. We use a new agent implementation for each coordination method.

Implementing an agent in our context means to implement a mechanism to create a plan of the related vehicle(s) with respect to the sensed state of the environment. Our intention is to allow a user of the AgentDrive platform to use a wide spectrum of coordination mechanisms. Free-drive based methods for collision avoidance as well as methods based on structured road network can be implemented. Cooperative methods can be implemented by defining a communication protocol among agents.

The module provides environment representation that the agents operate in. An agent senses the environment including the related car state. The module synchronizes the environment with a physics simulator. The environment is updated by data from physics simulation. The physics simulation (particularly the car models) executes the plans received from the coordination module (i.e. related agents).

5.2   Environment Representation

The environment consists of the car representation and structured model of the world. The world is considered to be 2-dimensional in coordination module. The terrain is not considered, only the road network is taken into account. Obstacles are implicitly defined by border of the roads. It is sufficient if the navigation of the cars is based on road following methods. We can also explicitly specify the obstacles, that is used by methods that are based on a free ride and a collision avoidance.

Road Network. Realistic scenarios are more convenient than artificial road networks, so we decided to build our scenarios on real map data. We have chosen to use open data, particularly OpenStreetMaps[11] is the first choice.

---

[11] http://www.openstreetmap.org/

The representation of the environment in the coordination module corresponds to representation used in traffic simulators. Actually the scenario specifications are built on the SUMO data model [5]. We use SUMO tools to import XML-based road definition from OSM map data.

The structured road network is used for routing on the level of a city. The path is obtained by graph-based algorithms (e.g. A^*). Also waypoint navigation is based on the road network, the waypoints trace the shape of the roads.

The data model of roads also contains information about junctions and allows the coordination module to handle junctions. The features required to be available in the data model of the road network are enumerated and described in the following list.

1. Shape representation – the data is describing the particular shape of the road infrastructure
2. Routing – data allows to find sequence of road segments to get from segment A to segment B
3. Navigating – data considers lanes in segments (e.g. only right lane allows to turn right in junction)
4. Smooth/drivable – lanes that are structurally connected are also geographically connected (without discontinuities)

The road network representation is in general sufficient for coordination module, but there are several issues we needed to deal with. Although routing feature is usually satisfied, there are still anomalies in data that can cause unexpected behaviour. An example can be seen in Figure 2. The car in figure is routed to exit the main street and to join back the main street immediately. A bug in connection between two segments of main street caused that the cars are routed this strange way, potentially creating nontrivial problems in the driving simulation. Anomalies like this are hard to be detected automatically. But in case where a bug like this matters, it usually strongly affects a traffic flow, so it is not hard to detect it by observation of the visualization of the simulation.

Localization. Procedure of localization of a car in the road network is extendedly used. The reason is that a position of a car is obtained in coordinates and it is needed to be decided which of road network segments it corresponds to. It is a consequence of our design where dynamics of a car is simulated in physics module (possibly with human controlled free ride) and an agent reasoning on road network is in the coordination module. The complexity of the procedure is reduced by usage of kd-trees as a structure to store the road segments. Every vehicle is dynamically localized using the actual position mapped to the road network, so the error introduced by data, physics or human driver are a part of the simulation and provide a realistic noise for the coordination module (of course, it can be avoided by using the accurate data or simplified drive simulation with perfect execution of plans).

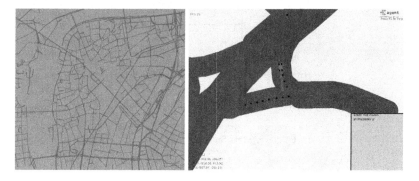

Fig. 2. Visualization of SUMO network data of Prague (left), the red and green image is also used for texturing of the terrain. An example of a bug in data is shown on right, the vehicle is routed to leave a main street to immediately join back instead of just following the main street.

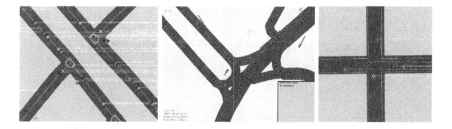

Fig. 3. Visualization layers in AgentDrive. The left image shows the graph visualization of the road network. Complex junction (city center of Prague) imported from OSM is in the middle image. The right image contains blue areas representing obstacle areas used by free-ride collision avoidance methods.

5.3 Visualization

The visualisation of coordination module results is a crucial component for the development. The visualization component is optional and can be easily switch off. The visualization is also easily expandable by new layers. New layers can be registered by for example an agent implementation. So any method used for coordination can provide a visualization specific for the method (e.g. planning graphs, velocity obstacles, potential fields, etc.). Examples can be seen in Figure 3.

6   Physics Simulation

Since the physics simulation is more tool than primary research topic for us, we focus on defining interface of such simulation rather than on its implementation.

The interface from coordination module to simulator is designed in three layers. The maneuver, waypoint and actuator layers are presented. The layers

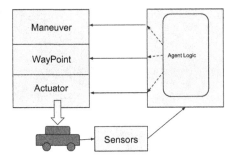

Fig. 4. Three layers architecture of physics simulation interface – maneuver, waypoint and actuator

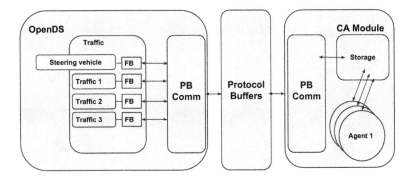

Fig. 5. Architecture of integration of AgentDrive and OpenDS

allow to implement the simulation in desired level of detail (see Figure 4). It means that the physical model of car is controlled by sequence of maneuvers, waypoints or actuator adjustments. The maneuver layer is the highest level. A maneuver is to be performed by several waypoints, waypoint can be reached by sequence of actuator adjustments.

An agent can operate in various level of abstraction and choose the interface level accordingly. Depending on the selected level of detail there is a need to translate the plan from higher level to lower one in the coordination module.

The usage of higher levels of the interface is desirable if the physics simulator implements the level of control of the models. The translation from higher level to lower one (e.g. maneuver to waypoints) is usually better to be performed in the physics simulator. There is more information about the physical model of the controlled cars available to implement effective control strategy. The choice of interface level depends on the level of abstraction of agent's reasoning and on the availability and quality of the controllers in physics simulator.

The proposed architecture is reflected in an already implemented solution. An example of the implementation of physics simulation module follows.

Fig. 6. Driver's view in OpenDS with integrated HMI for collision avoidance support. The system provides the driver with the visual representation of a proposed plan. The proposed lane to follow is highlighted by blue, the speed adjustment is proposed via green or red signal of appropriate intensity. There is an example of an instruction to change lane to left to overtake (left image). Second case shows how the red color informs the driver of proposal to slow down (right image) because of speeding in this case.

Particular integration of OpenDS in the role of physics simulator with coordination module is depicted in Figure 5. OpenDS is a driving simulator that supports control of traffic cars on the level of waypoints. There is a controller of cars that navigates cars to follow so called follow box. The coordination module then feeds the trajectory of the follow box with waypoints. Note that OpenDS is a driving simulator, so there is a car controlled by a human-driver available. The manually driven car has a related agent in coordination module as the other traffic cars. In contrast to traffic cars the driven car execution of plan is in responsibility of the human driver. The plan is presented to the driver by a human-machine interface (see Figure 6). In fact it can be seen by driver as a driver assistance system. The system using the coordination module as a back-end. Moreover the human driver potentially introduces a huge source of uncertainty and error in the plan execution that may help a lot in development of car-to-car coordination schemes.

We need to create scenarios in both physics simulation and coordination module. The structure of the world or road network is important in coordination module where we use the network to navigate cars. The graphical representation is needed mainly in physics simulation module where we have also 3D visualization (e.g. visualization of OpenDS). The representation of both modules should correspond.

3D World in Physics Simulation. We were then faced the problem how to generate 3D world in physics simulation based on the OSM data.

Unfortunately elevation data is in general not provided in OSM. We decided to model terrain from SRTM[12] height maps. The resolution of the raw data is about 90 meters in Europe. The precision is too low to be able to direct drive on

---

[12] https://lpdaac.usgs.gov/products/measures_products_table

Fig. 7. Terrain with high cross slope (left) and flattened terrain (right)

Fig. 8. Driving in 3D world. A generated world (Dresden, Germany) with flat terrain and buildings by OSM2World (left) and the same city but with terrain based on SRTM (right).

the surface, so the terrain is smoothed according the road network. Our aim was to eliminate too high cross slope of the roads. We flatten the terrain by equalizing elevation of area on the roads and applied blurring by Gaussian kernel on the height map. The difference between original and processed terrain data can be seen on Figure 7.

The visualisation of the road network is possible without creating 3D model of all the roads. The road can be visualized by texturing model of the terrain. An example of an alphamap of Prague city center is in Figure 2.

Another approach is to use a OSM2World[13] tool to generate 3D buildings directly from OSM. OSM2World can read OSM data and create 3D model for example in .OBJ format. The shape of a building is an optional tag in OSM. An example of a city where this additionally information is to be found in OSM is Dresden in Figure 8. The OSM2World can also generate a terrain but we decide to use only the buildings because the support of elevation in OSM2World is

---

[13] http://osm2world.org/

fragile – for instance we had troubles with z-fighting of multiple layers in one plane.

The combination of the presented approaches – OSM2World for the 3D building shapes and terrain data from SRTM combined with the road network given by SUMO – revealed to be the most progressive approach usable in majority of potential scenarios. One of the most important aspects for the proper integration of generated world data is to fit all the layers into common base and scale. It is necessary to harmonize all the transformations of the whole tool chain to get expected result.

7 Conclusion

We introduced the AgentDrive platform, its implementation architecture and main components. We described functionality and some lessons learned during development of the platform. The tools related to creation of scenario from real world data were presented. Their integration into the simulation platform was proposed. The presented simulation tool proved to be viable in various traffic scenarios and environment settings. The integrated drive and traffic simulation perspective enables to increase the validity of the experimental environment for testing a wide range of cooperative vehicles algorithm in the realistic traffic scenarios. The human in the loop experimental capabilities enable to perform experiments with a mixed deployment of future driver assistant systems. Presented cars modelling and simulation shows a promising potential not only for development of intelligent assistant systems, but also as an experimental platform for coordination algorithms and their validation via simulation. Examples of experiments with the AgentDrive platform including videos can be found at the project website[14].

Further extension of the platform will focus on following areas:

Network Simulation Integration. Next step towards more realistic simulation considering communication issues in V2V is to model network. The integration of network simulator seems to be the convenient option. We are experimenting with network simulators that we presented in Section 3. The bidirectional binding of mobility model with network simulation is required for most of the possible V2V application.

Sensor Simulation. The models of sensors used in AgentDrive are very simple. Usually we model only visibility range. The sensors are essential for perception of the world. The realistic simulation should consider limitations of the real sensors and noise in the data. One of the most suitable extension can be integration of specific sensor simulation tools developed for car manufacturers, such as PreScan[15].

---

[14] http://agents.fel.cvut.cz/agentdrive/
[15] PreScan, https://www.tassinternational.com/prescan

Empirical Evaluation. For further comparison of various coordination methods the metrics need to be specified. Measuring performance of the coordination methods would be beneficial for development. The measurement of performance could also serve as indicator of functionality of the coordination methods in case of testing during development on the AgentDrive platform. The platform is open for any specific metrics to be analyzed on the level of detail the model is implemented. So far, the implemented measures consist of traffic properties and car oriented measures (e.g. speed profile, fuel consumption, gear logging, etc.). Additional specific measures for particular scenarios will be introduced.

Acknowledgments. This work was supported by the Grant Agency of the Czech Technical University in Prague, grant No. SGS15/209/OHK3/3T/13 and by the Ministry of Education, Youth and Sports of Czech Republic within the grant no. LD12044.

References

1. Balmer, M., Rieser, M., Meister, K., Charypar, D., Lefebvre, N., Nagel, K., Axhausen, K.: Matsim-t: architecture and simulation times. In: Multi-agent Systems for Traffic and Transportation Engineering, pp. 57–78 (2009)
2. Bazzan, A.L.C., Klügl, F.: A review on agent-based technology for traffic and transportation. The Knowledge Engineering Review **29**(3), 375–403 (2013). http://journals.cambridge.org/article_S0269888913000118
3. Helbing, D.: Social self-organization: Agent-based simulations and experiments to study emergent social behavior. Understanding complex systems (2012)
4. Komenda, A., Vokrinek, J., Cap, M., Pechoucek, M.: Developing multiagent algorithms for tactical missions using simulation. IEEE Intelligent Systems **28**(1), 42–49 (2013)
5. Krajzewicz, D., Erdmann, J., Behrisch, M., Bieker, L.: Recent development and applications of SUMO - Simulation of Urban MObility. International Journal on Advances in Systems and Measurements **5**(3&4), 128–138 (2012)
6. Piórkowski, M., Raya, M., Lugo, A.L., Papadimitratos, P., Grossglauser, M., Hubaux, J.P.: Trans: Realistic joint traffic and network simulator for vanets. SIGMOBILE Mob. Comput. Commun. Rev. **12**(1), 31–33 (2008)
7. Sommer, C., German, R., Dressler, F.: Bidirectionally Coupled Network and Road Traffic Simulation for Improved IVC Analysis. IEEE Transactions on Mobile Computing **10**(1), 3–15 (2011)
8. Stanica, R., Chaput, E., Beylot, A.L.: Simulation of vehicular ad-hoc networks: Challenges, review of tools and recommendations. Computer Networks **55**(14), 3179–3188 (2011). http://www.sciencedirect.com/science/article/pii/S138912861 1001629, deploying vehicle-2-x communication

Multi-agent Based Flexible Deployment of Context Management in Ambient Intelligence Applications

Alexandru Sorici[1,2]([✉]), Gauthier Picard[1], Olivier Boissier[1],
and Adina Florea[2]

[1] Ecole Nationale Supérieure des Mines, FAYOL-EMSE, LSTI,
42023 Saint-Etienne, France
{sorici,picard,boissier}@emse.fr
[2] Department of Computer Science, University Politehnica of Bucharest,
313 Splaiul Independentei, 060042 Bucharest, Romania
adina.florea@cs.pub.ro

Abstract. Industry involvement in the Ambient Intelligence (AmI) domain together with openness and complexity expected from context-aware applications drive research into generic context management middleware (CMM) solutions. However, the variety of AmI scenarios requires flexibility in design-time and run-time deployment options, while existing CMM approaches do not sufficiently address the means to easily configure and engineer such mechanisms. In response to these challenges we propose a context management middleware with a design based on techniques and principles from the research fields of Multi-Agent Systems and the Semantic Web. We focus on showing how deployment principles based directly on the application context model and ontology-based configuration options offered by CONSERT lead to flexible development. We showcase the usage of our solution with a scenario from the area of smart university life management.

Keywords: Ambient Intelligence · Context management · Multi-agent systems · Semantic web · Deployment flexibility

1 Introduction

Ambient Intelligence (AmI) is nowadays a well recognized area of research with a clear sign of industry take-up in activity areas like home monitoring and automation or smart cities. As application space is rapidly increasing, ever stronger importance is placed on deployment flexibility and runtime adaptability of systems that handle information management within context-aware applications. While existing proposals for *context management middleware* (CMM) solutions in the literature present various methods for managing context information (in terms of acquisition and reasoning mechanisms, processing architectures, etc.), not much work seems to focus on concrete methods of easing application development by means of *specification* and *runtime control* of the deployment of their

© Springer International Publishing Switzerland 2015
Y. Demazeau et al. (Eds.): PAAMS 2015, LNAI 9086, pp. 225–239, 2015.
DOI: 10.1007/978-3-319-18944-4_19

context management approaches. Given that many AmI scenarios involve working with multi-dimensional and dynamic context models, we consider that an ease of usage in context management configuration becomes important. Let us introduce the following scenario to see the importance of the above issues.

Alice is a student, currently in a tram on her way to a CS master course taking place at the Computer Science Faculty at 10:00. It is currently 9:55 and Alice's smartphone receives an automatic notification from the tram's smart transportation system. It informs of an estimate of 7 minutes until Alice's stop. Knowing her walking speed, Alice's smartphone computes that she will be 5 minutes late for her class and automatically sends this information to a service managing teaching related activities at her university. Bob, the CS course professor, is subscribed to this same service and receives Alice's notification. Since Bob wants all students to be present when his course begins, he decides to start the class 5 minutes late. After the course, Alice meets with Cecille and the two decide to talk about their AmI course project. They get to the AmI laboratory and sit down to discuss their ideas. Upon arrival, their smartphones automatically connect to the system responsible for managing situations in the AmI-Lab. Using information about noise-level and body posture (e.g. Kinect camera), the AmI-Lab manager soon determines that Alice and Cecille are in an ad-hoc meeting and notifies their smartphones. Alice's personal manager than deduces that she is busy. Meanwhile, Dan, a friend of Alice who is in a separate room, wants to meet with her for lunch. He subscribes for Alice's availability status to the faculty building manager. When Alice and Cecille finish their meeting, Dan is notified that she is available, so he contacts her to grab lunch.

In response to challenges explained above, our objective is to create a flexible and configurable CMM, able to address different scenarios. To this end we build our solution based on techniques and principles from the Semantic Web and Multi-Agent Systems research fields. We propose an agent-based context management architecture where the functionality of units that make up the context information provisioning path (sensing, coordination, dissemination, usage) is carefully encapsulated within the behaviours of a designated agent. The initial and runtime deployment of agents that handle the management needs of a context-aware application is further guided by ontology-based specifications.

In this work, Section 2 presents the foundations of our proposed CMM. In Section 3 we explain how the deployment of context management agents can be specified based on characteristics of the application context model. Section 4 details deployment runtime management in terms of agent life cycle and interactions. A software-centric analysis of flexible context management deployment advantages and their exemplification on hand of the reference scenario is given in Section 5. We present related work in Section 6 and conclude the paper in Section 7.

2   CONSERT Middleware Foundations

CONSERT (an acronym formed from *CONtext asSERTion*) is our solution for a context management middleware offering support for expressive context modeling and reasoning, flexible deployment options and adaptable context provisioning mechanisms. Figure 1 presents a global view of the CONSERT CMM architecture and control relations. The application level creates an ontology-based context model, loaded and used at runtime by a reasoning component (CONSERT Engine) which is controlled by an agent-based context management logic. Interaction between the middleware and the application and sensing layers occurs through OSGi-based adaptor services.

2.1 Context Modeling and Reasoning

We use semantic web technologies as a uniform and expressive mean for context representation and reasoning. Applications build a *context model* using the CONSERT Ontology[1], which defines a context meta-model [1]. It contains three modules (core, annotation and constraint) able to express context content (i.e. *ContextAssertions* describing the situation of *ContextEntities*), context meta-properties (e.g. source and quality-of-context - QoC metrics) and context integrity, uniqueness or value constraints.

A context model developed with the CONSERT ontology is leveraged at runtime by the CONSERT Engine, a software component handling context updates, higher-level inference, constraint and consistency checking, as well as asynchronous query answering. The engine inference mechanism performs semantic event processing, employing a rule-based derivation approach using SPARQL CONSTRUCT queries coupled with ontology reasoning. The custom reasoning mechanisms of the CONSERT Engine are built using the Apache Jena and

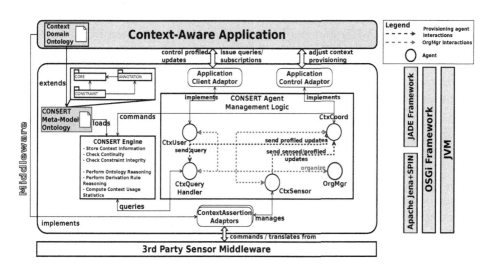

Fig. 1. Conceptual overview of the CONSERT Middleware

---

[1] http://purl.org/net/consert-core-ont, http://purl.org/net/consert-annotation-ont, http://purl.org/net/consert-constraint-ont

SPIN frameworks[2]. Its implementation as an OSGi-compliant service component allowing the developer to extend it with custom constraint resolution and inference scheduling services.

2.2 Multi-agent Based Management Architecture

The CONSERT Middleware uses a multi-agent system (MAS) based management architecture. The design principles from the MAS domain allow us to individually encapsulate each aspect of the context provisioning life cycle (sensing, coordination, dissemination, usage), thereby opening up the possibility for more flexible management (cf. Section 4). Our proposed CMM uses the set of agents shown in Figure 1. A `CtxSensor` agent interacts with sensors using adaptors to translate from sensor data into statements from the CONSERT Ontology. A `CtxCoord` agent manages the main life cycle of the CMM using the CONSERT Engine to control context reasoning and consistency. A `CtxQuery Handler` agent responds to actual dissemination requests, while a `CtxUser` agent provides the interface with the application specific code above it.

From an implementation perspective, the context management agents run over JADE[3]. The behaviour-based reasoning cycle and FIPA-compliant[4] interaction protocols are well suited for implementing the context provisioning logic. JADE distribution options (e.g. JADE containers, message transfer protocols), on the other hand, support the middleware distribution and configuration options we discuss in Section 3.

Figure 1 depicts a generic instance of the CONSERT Middleware. The set of agents deployed within an application (e.g. the AmI-Lab smart room) to serve its context production, management or consumption needs form a *Context Management Group* (CMG) and the lifecycle of a CMG is overseen by an `OrgMgr` agent. However, as we explore in Sections 3 and 4, an application can be structured to use one or more CMGs (e.g. like on Alice's smartphone), depending on the multi-dimensionality of the application context model. The way in which the composition and deployment of a CMG is configured is the subject of the next section.

3   Context Management Deployment Policies

In the scenario concerning Alice's academic activity management we saw that the application managing her interactions in the university was confronted with several types and dimensions of context information. From an engineering perspective, we can distinguish both elements that are fixed (e.g. the sensor control system within the AmI laboratory) as well as mobile ones (e.g. the smartphones of people in the university). Furthermore, reasoning with context information can take place both in a fixed node (e.g. deducing an ad-hoc meeting in the AmI

---

[2] https://jena.apache.org/,http://spinrdf.org/
[3] http://jade.tilab.com/
[4] http://www.fipa.org/

laboratory) or in a mobile one (computing and communicating Alina's availability status).

The conceptual and technical deployment options of the CONSERT Middleware are meant to address important concerns like the ones above, in the attempt to reduce application development effort. Specifically, we define a set of notions that a developer can use to design and specify the deployment structure of agents from the CMGs used in a context-aware application. These specifications are given as declarative *deployment policies* that use an ontology-based configuration vocabulary.

3.1   Context Management Structuring Elements

Following the application engineering analysis made above, a first element that influences the deployment of context management agents is *scale*. The CONSERT Middleware supports two deployment schemes: *centralized-local* and *decentralized-hierarchical*.

The first scheme represents an organization where there is a single application context model, with a centralized provisioning control and local consumption of context information. Examples where this setting could be used are applications providing smart document management on a device [3] or even all-in-one smart home platforms [10].

The *decentralized-hierarchical* scheme targets applications of larger scale, with a distributed context model, a decentralized provisioning control, mobile nodes and non-local context consumption. Our reference scenario provides a typical example of such an application.

Examples of this would range from the one in the scenario we presented to smart city applications.

To deployment structure can be further characterized by two key concepts which create a binding between CMGs and the application context model: *Context Dimension* and *Context Domain*.

ContextDimension. Let us note that, in literature, most applications (from medium to large scale ones) structure their context provisioning process along one privileged direction (e.g. space, user activity). Our notion of *Context Dimension* reflects this idea and is defined as a *binary ContextAssertion* (expressed using the CONSERT Ontology), belonging to one of the five categories which Zimmermann et al. [2] use to characterize the statements of an application context model: *individuality, space, time, activity* and *relations*. In examples from our scenario, the *ContextAssertion* `locatedIn(Person, UniversitySpace)` is a spatial *ContextDimension*. On the other hand, the information exchanged by Alice with the university system that manages the *CS Lecture ContextDomain* belongs to an `engagedIn(Person, TeachingActivity)` activity dimension. The purpose of *ContextDimensions* is to provide a means to distinguish between different contextual interactions. These interactions can be further refined and logically separated into *context interaction domains*, which are defined next.

ContextDomain. The subject part of a *ContextDimension* are *ContextEntities* which can be generally regarded as *consumers* of context information (e.g. a person). The objects, on the other hand, are instances of *ContextEntities* which define *values* along the *ContextDimension*. The values delimit *consumption domains* for context information related to them. This introduces our notion of a *ContextDomain*, representing the set of context statements *actively used* by an application, given a *ContextDimension* value.

Taking the example of `locatedIn(Person, UniversitySpace)`, the faculty building and the AmI laboratory are instances of the `UniversitySpace` *Context-Entity*. They represent different *ContextDomain* values along the `locatedIn` *ContextDimension*. Similarly the CS course represents a *ContextDomain* value on the `engagedIn(Person, Teaching Activity)` dimension. The *Person* instance is the entity that consumes context information produced in these *ContextDomains*.

By default, the *ContextDomains* created from a *ContextDimension* are federated with each other (i.e. they form a flat network). However, if the *Context-Entities* that give the values of a *ContextDimension* are characterized by inclusion-like *EntityDescriptions* (e.g. `partOf(AmI -Lab, FacultyBuilding)`), this fact can be exploited to create a *ContextDomain* tree-based hierarchy along that dimension. This option allows an application aware of the existence of several *ContextDomains* and their potential hierarchy to perform complex query mechanisms. Due to paper size limitations, we discuss these concerns in a technical report[5]. A *decentralized-hierarchical* deployment setting is therefore configured in terms of one or more *ContextDimensions* and the *ContextDomains* arising from them.

3.2   Context Deployment Policies

The CONSERT Middleware allows developers to make use of the previously defined concepts to structure the context management needs of their application. Such specifications are achieved through *context deployment policies*. A deployment policy defines a set of properties that declare the make up of the context model of a *ContextDomain* and the *composition* (in terms of agent types) of a CMG that is *assigned* to handle the context management needs of that particular domain. This is a distinguishing feature of the CONSERT Middleware. We envision a design model where a CMG is dedicated to the production, coordination or consumption of information from a given *ContextDomain* (i.e. a one-to-one mapping). More insight about this idea is given in Section 5, on hand of examples from the reference scenario.

To express a deployment policy, we create a configuration vocabulary defined by the CONSERT Deployment Ontology[6], which we detail next.

Platform Specifications. In Section 1 we mentioned that context management agents are implemented over JADE. The platform-specific vocabulary of

---

[5] http://aimas.cs.pub.ro/people/alexandru.sorici/consert-domain-based-query-report.pdf

[6] http://purl.org/net/consert-deployment-ont

the CONSERT Deployment Ontology specifies the JADE infrastructure-related options that setup the CMM platform for a given machine. Specifically, it configures the platform name, host and port number for the JADE main container and the address of the HTTP message transport protocol used for contacting agents remotely. The excerpt below shows an example of the container configuration for the AmI-Lab manager from our reference scenario (using Turtle[7] RDF syntax):

```
:Container_EF210 a orgconf:AgentContainer ;
  orgconf:containerHost "localhost" ;
  orgconf:containerPort 1099 ;
  orgconf:hasMTPHost "localhost" ;
  orgconf:hasMTPPort 7778 ;
  orgconf:platformName "AmI-Lab".
```

Context Domain Specifications. On a configured CONSERT Middleware platform, a developer can specify one or several *ContextDomains*, depending on the deployment scheme (*centralized-local* or *decentralized-hierarchical*) and context model structure he gives to the application. A *ContextDomain* is always characterized by a *context model document* and an applicationId, which serves to identify the particular context model managed on the platform. This would be a typical configuration in simple, centralized deployments where the context-aware application needs not consider multiple dimensions of context.

In decentralized settings however, a *ContextDomain* configuration can additionally specify the URIs of the *ContextDimension* and *ContextDomain value* for which the context model is provided. The example below shows the configuration given for the AmI-Lab domain from the reference scenario:

```
:AmILab_Domain  a  orgconf:ContextDomain ;
  orgconf:hasContextModel   :EF210_ContextModel ;
  orgconf:hasDomainDimension  person:locatedIn ;
  orgconf:hasDomainRangeEntity  space:Laboratory ;
  orgconf:hasDomainRangeValue  ami:AmILab .
```

The CONSERT Deployment Ontology defines further vocabulary that helps describe the composition of the context model used in a *ContextDomain*. This is done in terms of RDF documents that define the model content, annotations, constraints and inference rules using the CONSERT Ontology (cf. Figure 1). A last configuration option is the one indicating the *domain hierarchy document*. Remember from section 3.1 that *ContextDomain* may build hierarchies along a *ContextDimension* in a decentralized deployment scheme. This document holds the overview of this hierarchy and is exploited at runtime by the OrgMgr agent, as we detail in Section 4.

Agent Specifications. In the beginning of the section we explained that each *ContextDomain* is managed by a CMG. However, the composition of the CMG (i.e. what type of agents from Figure 1) depends on the required servicing or usage of the *ContextDomain* information on a given physical node.

For example, in applications using a *centralized-local* deployment, with a single context model, there will usually be one instance of CtxCoord, CtxQueryHandler

---

[7] http://www.w3.org/TR/turtle/

and `CtxUser` agents and one or more `CtxSensors`. In a *decentralized-hierarchical* setting, however, the type of agents deployed on a machine depend on whether it is a manager, or producer/consumer of the context model associated to the *ContextDomain*. On managing nodes, an instance of `CtxCoord` and `CtxQueryHandler` will usually be present, while on mobile consumers, one `CtxUser` and several `CtxSensor` instances may be possible.

Using the deployment ontology, a developer can create the specifications of required CMG agents. He can configure their address (i.e. name, container and *ContextDomain* they belong to), the assigned `OrgMgr` agent that manages their lifecycle and an optional *provisioning policy* which guides the behavior of the agents at runtime. We reported on methods of context provisioning adaptation in the CONSERT Middleware in other work [4]. In the example below we see a sample configuration for the coordinator agent of the AmI lab domain.

```
:CtxCoord_AmILab  a  orgconf:CtxCoordSpec ;
  orgconf:assignedOrgManager  :OrgMgr_AmILab_Address ;
  orgconf:hasAgentAddress  :CtxCoord_AmILab_Address ;
  orgconf:hasControlPolicy :CtxCoord_ProvisioningPolicy .
```

In the next Section we explore how the deployment specifications are bundled together and used at application runtime as well as how the lifecycle of the agents forming a CMG is dynamically managed.

4   Context Management Deployment

In Figure 1 we see that the CONSERT Middleware implementation is based on the OSGi service component specification. The code for the CONSERT Engine, management agents and different application adaptors is packaged as OSGi bundles. More importantly, however, the CMG deployment specifications themselves are packaged in the same way. In the following, we explore the advantages of this design choice.

4.1   Deployment Configuration Packaging

In Section 3.2 we presented three types of specification: platform-related, *ContextDomain*-related and agent-related. Platform configurations are included in a *platform-config* file, whereas specifications about *ContextDomain* information model and CMG agent composition are included in a *agent-config* file.

When using the CONSERT Middleware, an application developer will always create a *default* (or bootstrap) configuration bundle, identifiable by a pre-defined Bundle-Name attribute, which must contain the *platform-config* file. When the application launches this bundle, an activator service called *CMMPlatformManager* automatically creates the JADE platform according to the configuration given in the platform specifications. This service is accessible throughout the runtime of the application and allows the developer to manage (install, start, stop, uninstall) the lifecycle of CMGs on the platform.

In settings where the application uses only one *ContextDomain* (e.g. a *centralized-local* scheme) the bootstrap bundle can typically also include the *agent-config* file. In this case the *CMMPlatformManager* will automatically launch the configured context management agents, which will handle the defined context model. However, in more complex cases, like the one in our reference scenario (e.g. on Alice's smartphone), the application will require several CMGs, each one used for a specific *ContextDomain*. The *agent-config* files that configure the CMGs are each packaged in a corresponding bundle. The *CMMPlatformManager* can automatically track all bundles of this type and uniquely identify them using their `applicationId` specification. In this way, launching the CMG required for interacting with a particular *ContextDomain* becomes as easy as starting the corresponding bundle. We explore how the *CMMPlatformManager* manages the lifecycle of a CMG bundle in what follows.

4.2   Context Management Group Lifecycle

Figure 2 depicts the packaging mechanisms discussed previously. It also shows that when the application level launches a CMG bundle, it will first create the `OrgMgr` agents which oversees the lifecycle of the CMG agents. The `OrgMgr` reads

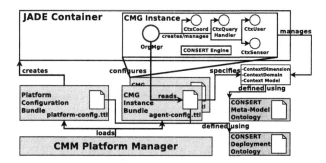

Fig. 2. CONSERT Middleware Deployment Engineering

the specifications contained in the *agent-config* file and deploys the configured agents in a well-defined order (*coordinator → queryhandler → sensors → user*). The agent is responsible for relaying all lifecycle-related commands (e.g. start, stop) from the application level to the managed CMG agents.

The `OrgMgr` also maintains the overview of existing *ContextDomain* hierarchies. In Section 3.2 we mentioned the optional specification of a *domain hierarchy document*. When a hierarchy exists, the `OrgMgr` uses this document to know which are the parent and child *ContextDomains* of the domain he manages. This information is essential in *decentralized-hierarchical* schemes, where an application can make domain-based queries or perform broadcasts of static or profiled context information along a *ContextDimension*. The `CtxUser` and `CtxQueryHandler` agents that handle such application requests interact with their respective `OrgMgrs` to ensure appropriate message routing. However, details of the agent protocols involved in federated queries and context information broadcasts are left out due to paper size restrictions.

A last responsibility of `OrgMgr` agents is in mobile node handling, more precisely in detecting when a node enters and leaves a *ContextDomain*. To handle automatic domain detection in the CONSERT CMM, an application has two possibilities. The first one implies mobile node proactivity and involves using the CMG from the *bootstrap* configuration bundle to detect the *ContextAssertion* informing about the current *ContextDomain*. The second one uses the `OrgMgr` of a *ContextDomain* to inform the `OrgMgr` of a mobile node of entering or leaving the domain. To do this the domain manager uses special deduction rule templates defined in the CONSERT Ontology that allow it to detect when *Context-Assertions* matching the *ContextDimension* of its domain are produced. From the subject part of that assertion, the domain `OrgMgr` can extract the necessary information to contact the `OrgMgr` of the mobile node.

5   Context Management Engineering Analysis

In recent technical reports we validated and discussed the runtime performance of the CONSERT Engine[8] and the benefits of a policy-based control of the context provisioning process within a CMG[9]. Results from both reports are based on a simulation of the ad-hoc meeting situation within the AmI laboratory that is part of our current reference scenario.

However in this work we want to perform an analysis of the support for engineering context-aware applications offered by CONSERT, given its design model, and report on how our middleware would potentially ease the development of the entire scenario given in the introduction.

5.1   Ease of Development Analysis

Component-Based Design. One of the strong feature of CONSERT Middleware is that it promotes a component-based design, both internally and at application level. Internally, both CONSERT Engine and context management agents are software units that encapsulate control-flow, providing a clearly defined context provisioning process. However, relevant aspects of this process (e.g. context model, sensing update modes, coordination policies) are entirely specifiable by the application. In this sense, CONSERT promotes *reuse by design*, as the agents and CONSERT Engine can be reused within many context-aware applications with different context management needs (see also Section 5.2).

A CONSERT Middleware instance provides however key *variation-points* by means of *service implementations* (most notably at reasoning level) that allow an application to adapt and extend the context management process. Specifically, the application can implement custom constraint resolution and inference scheduling services and configure their usage in the CONSERT Engine either through the *ControlAdaptor* or through *declarative configurations* which we discuss next.

---

[8] http://aimas.cs.pub.ro/people/alexandru.sorici/consert-engine-performance-report.pdf

[9] http://aimas.cs.pub.ro/people/alexandru.sorici/consert-provisioning-report.pdf

Configuration-Based Development. CONSERT defines configuration options for almost all context management aspects it supports. It uses semantic web technology to create vocabulary for *policies* that determine the deployment of context management units and control of the context provisioning process within a deployed context management group (sensing and coordination policies). Parameters controlling update modes, enabled inference rules, current inference scheduling services etc., are configurable at initialization and changeable at runtime by the application layer, leading to a very customizable context management process. Our experience in developing the AmI-Lab simulation of the reference scenario shows that declarative configuration options significantly lower programming effort. For example, each CMG in the simulation (AmI-Lab management, Alice and Cecille's smartphones, etc) requires the definition of a single *agent-config* file to specify both required agent types, connectivity information and context model elements. The ontology-based vocabulary means that these files can be edited using readily available semantic web IDEs (e.g. Protege, TopBraid) alleviating development effort even further.

Flexible Provisioning. A last strong feature we want to point out is the availability of clear application structuring elements (*ContextDimensions* and *ContextDomains*) which depend on the application context model itself. The fact that a CMG lies in a 1-to-1 mapping with a *ContextDomain* and that its configuration is packaged as an OSGi bundle means that its lifecycle can be directly tied to dynamic use of the context information within that *ContextDomain*. This mapping promotes *separation of concerns* and makes the CMG a unit of *control encapsulation*. This can furthermore be exploited as an extensibility mechanism for context management. It means that an application can define several CMG configurations that manage, provide or consume information from the same *ContextDomain*. Each configuration will however specify different provisioning instructions for the agents of the CMG using declarative policies and custom services as explained in the previous two paragraphs. The application can then use the CMG lifecycle management support to dynamically choose among defined CMGs that perform the same management but in different ways. For example, to reduce energy consumption when events are less dynamic in the AmI-Lab, a managing CMG that configures `CtxSensors` with lower update times and a `CtxCoord` with less complex inference rules can be dynamically swapped instead of a more demanding configuration.

5.2   Scenario Deployment Example

In what follows, we revisit the example scenario and explain how the presented application could benefit from the modularized development advantages discussed above.

The application managing Alice's university related activities handles context information from multiple domains. Figure 3 models the application in terms of *ContextDimensions* and *ContextDomains* and shows the composition of CMGs that manage the context models assigned to each *ContextDomain* on both fixed

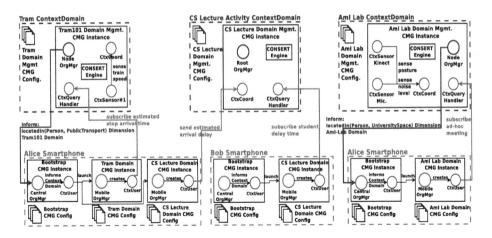

Fig. 3. *ContextDomain* view, CONSERT Middleware instance deployment and agent connections for analyzed scenario

and mobile nodes. Notice the *bootstrap* CMG on Alice's smartphone. It manages Alice's private information, but also acts as a receiver for notifications of entering / leaving a *ContextDomain*. Thus, using the CtxUser of the bootstrap instance, the application level is informed when Alice enters the tram and the AmI laboratory, or when it is time to take her CS lecture activity into consideration.

Upon entering the tram, the application level requests that the CMG instance responsible for the locatedIn(Person, PublicTransport) *ContextDimension* be installed. At the same time, seeing as Alice must attend her CS lecture, the application level requests a similar process for the CMG handling the engagedIn (Person, CourseActivity) *ContextDimension* and the CS_Lecture *Context-Domain*. The CtxUser from the tram CMG retrieves the estimated station arrival time. The application level transfers this information to the bootstrap instance, where Alice's private walking speed is factored in to compute her estimated delay. Then, the application level can use this information and the CtxUser from the CS lecture CMG to notify the CtxCoord on the node managing the CS lecture *ContextDomain* at the university of her delay.

When Alice steps out of the tram, the bootstrap CMG will be notified that she has left the Tram101 *ContextDomain*, so the application level will request the stop of the CMG responsible for the context information of that domain.

In the Ambient Intelligence laboratory, the node managing the *ContextDomain* contains a *CtxCoord* and *CtxQueryHandler*, as well as two *CtxSensors* that send updates about detected human postures (Kinect cameras) and noise levels (microphones) near each desk of the laboratory. When Alice enters the lab, the bootstrap CMG is informed that she entered the AmI_Lab *ContextDomain*. The CtxUser of the CMG that the application level launches on her smartphone for this *ContextDomain* connects to the CtxQueryHandler on the management node and subscribes for notifications of being in an ad-hoc meeting, to find out if Alice is busy.

The interactions above show the benefits of developing context-aware applications with the CONSERT Middleware. Creating CMG bundles for individual context domains of an application makes development of the specific context model easier, helps encapsulate the associated provisioning logic and provides support for management of CMG life cycle at application runtime.

6 Related Work

Many works from the AmI research field have discussed in recent years the idea of *context-driven* configuration, deployment and composition of component-based smart services [5–7]. However, the issue of flexible and configurable deployment of the context management solution *itself* has been explored to a much lesser extent.

SOLAR [8] defines a pervasive computing infrastructure built around a P2P network of processing nodes called Planets. Its strength lies in the extensive number of services provided by Planets (e.g. resource discovery, fault-tolerance, mobility management) as well as in its focus on reusable, distributed operators that use the filter and pipe paradigm to form DAG-like processing flows. Solar provides configuration options for internal communication services that underpin its functionality, as well as XML-based definitions of operator compositions. However, the available configurations only serve at infrastructure and operator deployment initialization. Support for lifecycle management of deployed provisioning services is limited and no mean is available to structure or group the operators required by an application according to the dimensionality of the context model. This leaves developers with a flat application design space, in contrast to options of the CONSERT CMM. Furthermore, the system envisions Planets as fixed high-performing computing nodes, in contrast to our agent-based CMM which, in its centralized-local deployment setting, can also be used in lighter-weight nodes (e.g. in smartphones).

COSMOS [9] and COPAL [10] are CMMs that adopt a component-based development and configuration approach, similar to our own. COSMOS uses the FRACTAL[10] architecture description language to configure its context nodes, while COPAL creates its own DSL to define the functionality and relationships of its processing components as well as their grouping into deployment artifacts. However, both COSMOS and COPAL use simple attribute-value based representations of context information and are thus limited in both representation expressiveness as well as provisioning structure capability. In contrast to our approach, the two works do not detail methods to dynamically control context management components at runtime and are limited to centralized deployments.

The ACAI [11] system proposes an agent-based context-aware infrastructure. However, the agent model used in ACAI differs from our own, as it is less

---

[10] http://fractal.ow2.org/fractaladl/

focused on providing individually deployable context provisioning units and more on building a dependable infrastructure for context-aware applications. The approach presents representation and reasoning capabilities similar to those of CONSERT and defines a custom wrapper over the SIP[11] protocol to provide discovery of remote ACAI management nodes. However, the work offers no configuration support and, as in the case of SOLAR, is very rigid in its infrastructure-focused deployment, being unsuitable for application scenarios that are lighter-weight or that require a different context model partitioning besides spatial.

Lastly, CoCA [12] and CROCO [3] are two CMM proposals having many points in common with our work (e.g. ontology-based content representation, meta-property processing, consistency management). However, neither of these works discusses means to structure the deployment of their context provisioning elements and they do not seem to offer any configuration support, thus leading to a much more demanding development effort compared to the CONSERT Middleware.

7   Conclusions

The CONSERT Middleware presented in this work proposes a component-based implementation and offers flexible deployment options. The engineering analysis on hand of the envisioned scenario highlights the offered development benefits. They stem from defining application structure by exploiting the dimensionality of a context model and by supporting declarative deployment specifications. Furthermore, the dynamics of mobile applications are addressed through a proper lifecycle management of deployed context management agents.

In future work we wish to create a toolkit exploiting our current application design paradigm. It will help developers specify context model structure and context management deployment configurations much more easily. In a parallel endeavour, we intend to use the increased autonomy potential offered by our agent-based context management architecture. We wish to introduce the ability of establishing context-level agreements (the context-awareness analogues of service-level agreements) that take into account specific goals set for each agent of a CMG. We consider such a feature to be of significant importance in future AmI applications.

Acknowledgments. This work has been funded by the Sectoral Operational Programme Human Resources Development 2007-2013 of the Romanian Ministry of European Funds through the Financial Agreement POSDRU/159/1.5/S/134398.

References

1. Sorici, A., Boissier, O., Picard, G., Zimmermann, A.: Applying semantic web technologies to context modeling in ambient intelligence. In: O'Grady, M.J., Vahdat-Nejad, H., Wolf, K.-H., Dragone, M., Ye, J., Röcker, C., O'Hare, G. (eds.) AmI 2013 Workshops. CCIS, vol. 413, pp. 217–229. Springer, Heidelberg (2013)

---

[11] http://www.voip-info.org/wiki/view/SIP

2. Zimmermann, A., Lorenz, A., Oppermann, R.: An operational definition of context. In: Kokinov, B., Richardson, D.C., Roth-Berghofer, T.R., Vieu, L. (eds.) CONTEXT 2007. LNCS (LNAI), vol. 4635, pp. 558–571. Springer, Heidelberg (2007)
3. Pietschmann, S., Mitschick, A., Winkler, R., Meißner, K.: Croco: ontology-based, cross-application context management. In: Third International Workshop on Semantic Media Adaptation and Personalization, SMAP 2008, pp. 88–93. IEEE (2008)
4. Sorici, A., Picard, G., Boissier, O., Florea, A.: Policy-based adaptation of context provisioning in AmI. In: 6th International Symposium on Ambient Intelligence (2015, in print)
5. Vallée, M., Ramparany, F., Vercouter, L.: Flexible composition of smart device services. In: International Conference on Pervasive Systems and Computing (PSC 2005), pp. 165–171 (2005)
6. Preuveneers, D.: Context-aware adaptation for Ambient Intelligence. LAP Lambert Academic Publishing (2010)
7. Gouin-Vallerand, C., Abdulrazak, B., Giroux, S., Dey, A.K.: A context-aware service provision system for smart environments based on the user interaction modalities. Journal of Ambient Intelligence and Smart Environments 5(1), 47–64 (2013)
8. Chen, G., Li, M., Kotz, D.: Data-centric middleware for context-aware pervasive computing. Pervasive and Mobile Computing 4(2), 216–253 (2008)
9. Conan, D., Rouvoy, R., Seinturier, L.: Scalable processing of context information with COSMOS. In: Indulska, J., Raymond, K. (eds.) DAIS 2007. LNCS, vol. 4531, pp. 210–224. Springer, Heidelberg (2007)
10. Li, F., Sehic, S., Dustdar, S.: Copal: an adaptive approach to context provisioning. In: Wireless and Mobile Computing, Networking and Communications (WiMob), pp. 286–293. IEEE (2010)
11. Khedr, M., Karmouch, A.: ACAI: Agent-Based Context-Aware Infrastructure for Spontaneous Applications. Journal of Network and Computer Applications 28(1), 19–44 (2005)
12. Ejigu, D., Scuturici, M., Brunie, L.: Hybrid Approach to Collaborative Context-Aware Service Platform for Pervasive Computing. Journal of Computers 3(1) (2008)

Multi-agent Multi-model Simulation of Smart Grids in the MS4SG Project

Julien Vaubourg[1,3]([✉]), Yannick Presse[1,3], Benjamin Camus[2,3],
Christine Bourjot[2,3], Laurent Ciarletta[1,3], Vincent Chevrier[2,3],
Jean-Philippe Tavella[4], and Hugo Morais[4]

[1] Inria, 54600 Villers-lès-Nancy, France
{Julien.Vaubourg,Yannick.Presse,Laurent.Ciarletta}@inria.fr
[2] Université de Lorraine, LORIA, UMR 7503, 54506 Vandœuvre-lès-Nancy, France
{Benjamin.Camus,Christine.Bourjot,Vincent.Chevrier}@loria.fr
[3] CNRS, LORIA, UMR 7503, 54506 Vandœuvre-lès-Nancy, France
[4] EDF - R and D MIRE/R44, 1 avenue du Général de Gaulle, BP 408,
92141 Clamart cedex, France
{Jean-Philippe.Tavella,Hugo.Morais}@edf.fr

Abstract. This paper illustrates how the multi-agent approach, or paradigm, can help in the modeling and the simulation of smart grids in the context of MS4SG (a joint project between LORIA-INRIA and EDF R&D). Smart grids simulations need to integrate together pre-existing and heterogeneous models and their simulation software; for example modeling tools of the power grids, of telecommunication networks, and of the information and decision systems. This paper describes the use of MECSYCO as a valid approach to integrate these heterogeneous models in a multi-agent smart grid simulation platform. Several use cases show the ability of MECSYCO to effectively take into account the requirements of smart grids simulation in MS4SG.

Keywords: Multi-agent · Smart grids · Multi-modeling · Co-simulation · DEVS

1 Introduction

The 2020 Climate and Energy Package of the European Union (20% renewable, 20% energy savings and 20% reduction in emissions of greenhouse gases) has led to the rapid development of production from intermittent energy sources (wind, solar photovoltaic -PV-). This is certainly the phenomenon the most significant of the evolution of electrical systems in the past five years. In France, the installed capacity of the wind farms increased from 3.5 GW in early 2009 to almost 8 GW in late 2013. In the same period, the installed PV capacity has been multiplied by 50 (4.5 GW in 2013). The emergence of renewable energy, but also of new uses of electricity (heat pumps, electric vehicles), the control of peak consumption and the desire to constantly improve the provision of quality

© Springer International Publishing Switzerland 2015
Y. Demazeau et al. (Eds.): PAAMS 2015, LNAI 9086, pp. 240–251, 2015.
DOI: 10.1007/978-3-319-18944-4_20

led to a necessity to develop more intelligent systems, especially in distribution networks. Such systems are usually called smart grids.

The French DSO (Distribution System Operator) ERDF operates distribution networks having a cumulative total length of 1,250,000 kilometers, mainly in rural areas with overhead power lines. To face these new challenges, ERDF opted several years ago to perform demonstrator systems in some regions of France (e.g. the demonstrator VENTEEA in Aube nearby Troyes which intends to test innovative technologies for the medium voltage grid where Enel Green Power France operates lots of wind farms) and in the French islands (e.g. the demonstrator MILLENER in La Reunion where the lack of interconnection of the grid increases the risk of failure during peak periods). However, despite the advantages of real prototypes, it is not easy to find a local area for experimentation and it is long and expensive to enroll industrial or residential customers. In this sense, the smart grid simulation is an attractive technological solution to test new distributed algorithms (e.g. advanced voltage management) or original operating mode (e.g. islanding) before their use in real prototypes and even in the real networks.

This paper illustrates how the multi-agent paradigm can help in the modeling and the simulation of smart grids in the context of MS4SG (Multi-Simulation for Smart-Grids), a joint project between LORIA-INRIA and EDF R&D. The main goal of the proposed platform is to model real systems, allowing the simulation of different domains of the smart grids at the same time, namely the electrical domain, the information domain and the decision domain. To demonstrate the capacity of the proposed platform to perform simulation with different domains, three case studies are proposed considering three distinct problems. In the first case, a real high voltage network of La Reunion Island is simulated and an agent is used to detect congestion situations. This agent will transmit the congestion information to the decision level which is responsible to find a best solution to solve the problem. The second case is focused in the MV network with two overhead feeders under a fault situation. The main goal is to show the interoperability between the electrical domain and the telecommunication domain under a very stressing scenario, namely a ground phase default. Finally, a third case study will be presented to show the interoperability of the three domains of a smart grid. In this example the system should determine the load shedding considering two house equipped smart-meter with bi-directional communication systems and equipments to control the equipments and appliances. The entire platform was developed considering complex scenarios, real operation situations and the future hierarchical decision structure.

In the next part, we explain the requirements of smart grids simulation especially the ability to design a system as a set of heterogeneous interacting subsystem (namely multi-modeling). We then introduce MECSYCO [1] (Multi-agent Environment for Complex SYstems CO-simulation) – formely based on AA4MM (Agents & Artefacts for Multi-Modeling) – a multi-agent approach for multi-modeling and multi-simulation, and explain how it enables to design a

---

[1] The MECSYCO library is available under the Affero General Public License v3 on http://mecsyco.fr.

multi-model and its execution. The next section details different use-cases of smart grid simulations developed in the MS4SG project, before discussing the examples and concluding.

2   Requirements in Smart-Grids Simulation

As stated in the previous section, modeling and simulating a smart grid system should integrate different domains of expertise; at least power grid, communication, information and decision systems. In MS4SG, each domain uses different tools. The electricity one uses executable Modelica [1] models exported from Dymola [2] or EMTP-RV (ElectoMagnetic Transient Program, Restructured Version [3]) as modeling tools of power grid components; the telecommunication network one may use NS-3 [4] or OMNeT++ [5] depending on the protocols requirements, and decision systems can be modeled with UML-oriented tools such as Enterprise Architect [6]. Moreover, operators such as ERDF already own heterogeneous business models designed on different simulation softwares, potentially non-interoperable together.

This state is our starting assumption: tools exist and they must be integrated together. The central problem is then the multi-simulation that intends to simulate the whole as the coordinated simulation of several heterogeneous and interacting simulators. Handling heterogeneity and enabling the interaction between components can be envisaged at different levels:

- software interoperability level: software exist in each domain and must interoperate even though they are not conceived with that purpose ;
- formalism level: each domain uses the most convenient formalism(s) for itself [7], ordinary and differential equations for power grids, event-based in telecommunication networks, etc ;
- time management level: as simulation of smart grids involves several simulators, the time management in each simulator is potentially different (with constant or variable time-step, event-based, ...);
- information representation level: each software uses its own representation and data exchanges imply an information mapping between tools ;
- programming languages level: API can be in different languages ;
- hardware level: basically, for legal reason (e.g. non-replicable licenses) some software must be executed on a specific machine. More generally, some software may need specific resources and require to use dedicated hardware ;
- co-simulation norms and standards integration level: as smart grids are in an industrial finality, standards should be used in the simulation.

Different solutions exist (for example HLA [8] for software interoperability) at the different levels but they are mainly conceived independently and taking into account all the requirements imposes to integrate all of these solutions [9]. For instance, [10], [11] and [12] are focused on the coupling between power grid models and communication models. Regarding the requirements listed above, they only try to bring solutions for the integration of the different formalisms used by these two kinds of models.

In addition to these requirements, the activity of modeling and simulation brings its own (classical) requirements (calibration, validation, etc.). Moreover, the integration of several heterogeneous components brings new requirements.

The first is about incremental system design: starting from simple use cases to more elaborate ones. This implies to be able to add new models (and then simulators) in the system, but also to remove or exchange components [9].

The second is about tools supporting modeling and simulation activity. As the activity gathers several domains [13], levels of concerns have to be separated: domain experts have to focus on the modeling phase, specialists of the theory of modeling and simulation will focus on formalism integration and computer scientists on software interconnection. As a consequence, there is a need of support for domain experts in modeling to fill the gap between system domains and the co-simulation of software.

In MS4SG, we chose the MECSYCO approach, that answers these requirements by using the multi-agent paradigm, to develop simulations of smart grids.

3 The MECSYCO Approach

MECSYCO proposes concepts and tools to describe a system and to simulate it as a set of interacting heterogeneous models/simulators. It relies on the multi-agent paradigm to envisage a multi-model as a set of interacting models/simulators: each couple model/simulator corresponds to an agent, and the data exchanges between the simulators correspond to the interactions between the agents. Originality compared to other multi-agent multi-model approaches is to consider the interactions in an indirect way within the Agents and Artifacts (A&A) paradigm [14,15].

Within this paradigm, artifacts support interactions between models as processes outside of the models and express them independently of the models' internal functioning. As a consequence, the simulators interoperability issue is managed by the artefacts. The information representation mapping issue is managed as a transformation service of the artefact in charge of the interaction between models.

MECSYCO proposes a meta-modelling approach based on the multi-agent metaphor to describe a heterogeneous multi-model. The MECSYCO multi-agent concepts are represented graphically and associated with semantic and syntactic constraints guaranteeing a non ambiguous description. These concepts are formalized with DEVS [16] (Discrete Event System Specification) operational specifications enabling to derive from a graphical representation to an executable multi-simulation. The DEVS formalism ensures the integration of different formalisms [17] with discrete and continuous dynamics [18], and include simulation algorithms. An example of the integration of equation based model with DEVS can be found in [17] and [19].

MECSYCO relies on four concepts to describe a multi-model. A **model** m_i is a partial representation of the target system implemented in a simulator

(Figure 1d). It has a set of input and output ports. The models are the pre-existing parts we want to interconnect to build a multi-model. An **m-agent** $\mathcal{A}_i$ manages a simulation model m_i and is in charge of interactions of this model with the other ones (Figure 1a). The behavior of an m-agent is specified by the DEVS simulation protocol to enable agent coordination. A **model artifact** $\mathcal{I}_i$ reifies interactions between a simulation m-agent $\mathcal{A}_i$ and its simulation model m_i (Figure 1c). An interaction from $\mathcal{A}_i$ to $\mathcal{A}_j$ is reified by a **coupling artifact** $\mathcal{C}_j^i$ (Figure 1b). A coupling artifact $\mathcal{C}_j^i$ that has two roles: for $\mathcal{A}_i$, it is an **output coupling artifact**, whereas for $\mathcal{A}_j$ it is an **input coupling artifact**. The coupling artifacts can transform the data exchanged between the models using **operations**.

(a)   (b)   (c)   (d)

Fig. 1. Symbols of the MECSYCO components for simulation (a) m-agent $\mathcal{A}_i$, (b) coupling artifact $\mathcal{C}_j^i$, (c) model artifact $\mathcal{I}_i$, (d) model m_i

In our implementation of MECSYCO , coordination between models is achieved in a fully decentralized way thanks to the m-agents behavior. This behavior corresponds to the parallel conservative DEVS simulator based on the Chandy-Misra-Bryant (CMB) algorithm [20]. Detail on the integration of the CMB algorithm in the multi-agent paradigm of MECSYCO can be found in [21].

4   Building a Multi-Model with MECSYCO

The key steps to build a multi-model with the MECSYCO approach assume the existence of the different simulators and of the MECSYCO library (see (a)). The starting point is to define the structure of the multi-model, that is how models are connected and what kind of information are exchanged between models. The

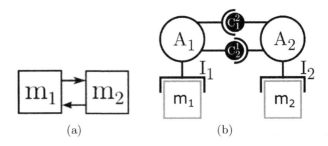

(a)   (b)

Fig. 2. (a) Graph of relations between models. (b) The corresponding MECSYCO diagram.

next step is to define the equivalent of the intuitive graph with the MECSYCO primitives (see Figure 2). Each model corresponds to an m-agent with its model artifact and its simulator. Each information exchange is reified by a coupling artifact. This implies two aspects to be defined: i) model artifacts (see (b)); ii) information types and transformation operations between types (see (c)). From the specifications of these components, it becomes possible to have the equivalent code and then to deploy the system (see (d)).

(a) **Existing Components: Simulators and MECSYCO library.** The approach assumes the existence of simulators corresponding to the different parts of the multi-model. In order to be compatible with MECSYCO , these simulators are supposed to be compliant with the DEVS formalism.

   Each concepts of MECSYCO has operational specifications. This enables to have each basic component to be programmed (currently either in Java or C++) by instantiating predefined classes with the right types and/or operations.

(b) **Connecting Simulators to MECSYCO.** This corresponds to the definition of a model artifact (that acts as a DEVS wrapper [19]) for each type of simulator and coupling used in the multi-model.

   Concretely, this means defining five functions corresponding to the primitives of the DEVS simulation protocol[2]:

   - $init()$ sets the parameters and the initial state of the model.
   - $processExternalEvent(e_{in}, t, x^k)$ processes the external input event e_{in} at simulation time t in the kth input port of the model.
   - $processInternalEvent(t)$ processes the model event scheduled at time t.
   - $getOutputEvent(y_k)$ returns e^k_{out}, the external output event at the kth output port of the model.
   - $getNextInternalEventTime()$ returns the time of the earliest scheduled internal event of the model.

(c) **Defining Operations.** Operations perform the information mapping between simulators. They have to be defined and attached to coupling artifacts. They can correspond to scale transformation (from meters to kilometres), information reduction (from a list of values to its mean), etc.

(d) **Software Deployment.** We developed several instantiations of the MECSYCO software that allow different deployment choices: from single process (in JAVA or in C++) to an hybrid (JAVA and C++), distributed (on several machines) execution thanks to a specific implementation of the coupling artifacts (with DDS middleware [23]).

5   Smart-Grids Multi-Simulation

This section describes different use cases based on real scenarios of smart grids simulation. It shows the ability of MECSYCO to effectively take into account the requirements of smard-grids simulation. Section 5.1 explains the integration of existing software in the MECSYCO framework. Next three cases (from simple to complete) are detailed and underline the kinds of requirements to meet.

---

[2] Details on the design of a new model artifact are given in [22].

5.1 Software Integration in MECSYCO : Defining Model Artifacts

Grid Domain The design of models in the electrical domain can be done with various tools such as Modelica-based simulators [1], EMTP-RV [3], Matlab, etc. A common characteristic of these tools is their compliance with the Functional Mock-up Interface (FMI) [24]. Such models are equation based (algebraic or differential).

FMI is a standard [25] to handle the coupling of models described by differential, algebraic, and discrete equations. It enables to export a set of equations with its solver as FMUs (Functional Mock-up Units). Simulating with a set of FMUs implies to design a master component; role played by MECSYCO.

EDF R&D made the choice to use this standard to develop their models. As a consequence, we had to define a model artifact for FMU simulators. Once defined any FMU can be connected to MECSYCO . As FMI standard has been conceived for coupling purpose, it was quite easy to design these model artifacts.

Communication Network Domain: Simulators in communication network domain are mainly event-based. The major tools are NS-3 [4] and OMNeT++ [5] that were not designed to interoperate together.

In the case of the NS-3 simulator we developed a model artifact with some efforts to have some genericity [22]. For OMNeT++, we re-use an existing (but more ad-hoc) possibility (see Section 5.3).

5.2 Single Domain Example

In electrical domain, we started with simple examples to demonstrate the integration of a model in MECSYCO. The aim of these examples was i) to show the technical feasibility, ii) to produce the same results as simulations with other approach (classical simulation), and iii) to manage real cases. For this use case, the Réunion island was simulated with a steady state case of the corresponding high voltage grid (modeled with an FMU). Basically, the simulation system involves an m-agent $\mathcal{A}_{REU}$ for simulating the Réunion island power grid and another m-agent $\mathcal{A}_{CHK}$ for detecting traffic congestions by checking the state variables. We were able to integrate this model by developing the FMI generic model artifact.

5.3 Power Grid and Communication Network

A second challenge in the electrical domain, was to design systems with different interacting sub-models. As smart grids simulation requires the use of IP network models for the communication network part (*Telecom*), we worked on an example coupling electrical models and communication network models.

This use case corresponds to a medium voltage (MV) grid with two overhead feeders. When a ground phase default occurs on a feeder, the theory says that it is possible to determine whether the default is upstream or downstream from the measuring point depending on the fact that the residual voltage and the

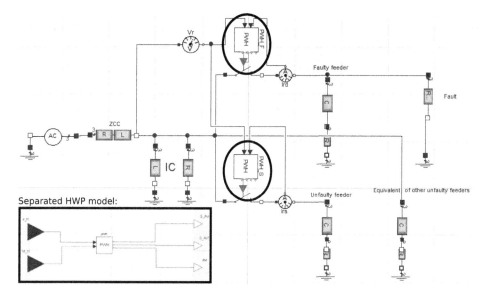

Fig. 3. The HWP use case to simulate. The HWP protections (highlighted in the diagram) are separately modeled as two FMUs connected to the MV power grid FMU.

residual current are in phase or in phase opposition. The system (named HWP meaning Homopolar Wattmetric Protection) is described in Figure 3.

Messages (e.g. "residual current", "residual voltage" or "breaker to open") are sent over a communication network including the protections and a Supervisory Control And Data Acquisition. From the perspective of the grid power modeling, the two protections in Figure 3 are represented by the same model. They both detect the default but only one is supposed to clear it. The template corresponding to this use case is shown in Figure 4a.

The communication network models are executed by OMNeT++ (m-agent $\mathcal{A}_{O++}$). Since a standard HLA ambassador was available for OMNeT++ [26], we exploited this possibility for integrating it in MECSYCO. We needed to develop a special model behaving as an HLA Federate. In this way, OMNeT++ is connected to the MECSYCO multi-simulation through a standard HLA RTI. The other models in this example are contained in FMUs (m-agents $\mathcal{A}_{HWP_1}$ & $\mathcal{A}_{HWP_2}$ corresponding to protections and $\mathcal{A}_{GRID}$ corresponding to the power grid). Simulation results for both protections are shown in Figures 4b and 4c.

This example was the opportunity to run a complete example in a decentralized manner. This example is multi-formalisms, with equation-based models for the protections and the grid, and event-based models for OMNeT++.

5.4   Power Grid, Communication and Information System Domains

The final example combines electrical models and communication network models with an information (and decisional) system model (*I.S.*). These three kinds of model correspond to the three main fields of smart grid. The template of this

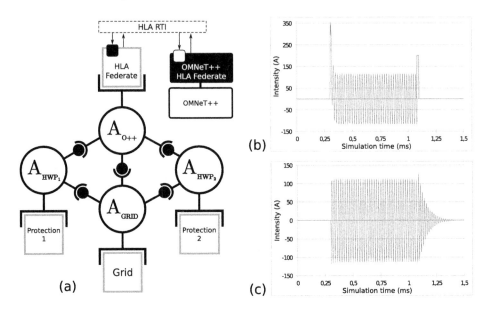

Fig. 4. (a) Template corresponding to the HWP use case. (b) Simulation results for the m-agent $\mathcal{A}_{HWP_1}$, corresponding to the protection detecting a ground phase default, with the fault signal in blue. (c) Simulation results for the m-agent $\mathcal{A}_{HWP_2}$.

use case is described in Figure 5. It corresponds to a load shedder with a cascado-cyclic algorithm and two consuming houses. Each house is equipped with a heat pump and an AMI (Advanced Metering Infrastructure) smart meter (m-agents $\mathcal{A}_{AMI_1}$ and $\mathcal{A}_{AMI_2}$). The heat pumps are always enabled, except in a time slot determined by the ALSF (Advanced Load Shedding Function) decisional system (m-agent $\mathcal{A}_{ALSF}$). This last sends a message to meters for indicating their time slot (specific to each house), and the meters are responsible for enabling or disabling the heat pump (thanks to the m-agent $\mathcal{A}_{GRID}$) during the simulation according to this information. Each meter has to confirm the consideration of the message received, by responding a boolean to the ALSF.

Each meter, the Power grid and the decisional system are modeled with FMUs and the communication network models are directly implemented with the NS-3 IP network simulator software. On the MECSYCO side, we used the generic model artifact for NS-3 (see Section 5.1). Each message exchanged between the decisional system and the grid or the meters is simulated by NS-3, through the m-agent $\mathcal{A}_{NS3}$.

This use case was tested with a real life demonstrator and five houses. We measured the voltage consumed by the group of houses, supposed to be reduced by the load shedding. We can then compare these measurements to the simulation results.

This example is multi-formalisms (FMUs are equation-based while NS-3 models are event-based), multi-languages (m-agents for FMUs are written in Java while the NS-3 m-agent is in C++) and multi-platforms (m-agents for FMUs are

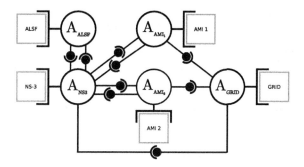

Fig. 5. The cascado-cyclic load shedder use case with only two AMI

executed on Windows while the NS-3 m-agent is on GNU/Linux). Moreover, the time-scale used for the FMUs is the minute while the time-scale used for NS-3 is the nanosecond. This issue was solved thanks to an operation at the coupling artifact level.

6   Discussion

The examples show the ability of MECSYCO to build multi-simulations that involve different domains of expertise, using different formalisms and different tools. Furthermore, they show its ability to integrate existing models developed on different tools and existing norms or standards. A summary of the challenges managed in the two previous examples is given in Tab. 1.

Table 1. Overview of the heterogeneity and interoperability challenges managed in the two multi-domain examples

Use Case	Model	Domain	Simulator	Platform	Language	Formalism	Time Scale
HWP	Protection 1 Protection 2 Grid	Electricity	FMU	Windows	Java	Equational	ms
	O++	Telecom	OMNeT++	GNU/Linux		Event	
Cascado-cyclic	AMI 1-5	Electricity	FMU	Windows	Java	Equational	s
	ALSF	I.S.	Ad-hoc			Automaton	
	NS-3	Telecom	NS-3	GNU/Linux	C++	Event	ns

We also wish to emphasize several aspects. The coordination of simulators and the formalisms integration is ensured by the DEVS formalization of MECSYCO. To design a new application, efforts are put on simulators integration into MECSYCO framework and on information representation and translation. There is no need to redesign a new coordination algorithm. A model artefact has to be built once for all (e.g. for FMUs) for a given kind of coupling.

Using a decentralized multi-agent paradigm and implementing its concepts with a decentralized coordination algorithm ease the deployment on several machines (with possibly different operating systems) and with different programming language. The step comes after the multi-model design: domain experts can focus on the multi-model design while computer scientists will focus on implementation stage.

7   Conclusion

The paper presented how the multi-agent paradigm through the MECSYCO approach can be successfully applied for the smart grids multi-model simulation. It demonstrated through examples developed in a joint project between LORIA-INRIA and EDF R&D how multi-agent can answer the requirements of the smart grids domain.

Three detailed examples showed a real use case (La Réunion island); a multi-domain, multi-formalism example; and finally described a complete use case under development. All these examples were developed in order to provide practical (multi-agent) solutions to EDF in the perspective of performing modeling and simulation based studies instead of experiments with real demonstrators.

As short term perspectives, we envisage to integrate business tools as pre and post processing of information: generating automatically the physical domain from CIM (Common Information Model[3]) as input of the multi-simulation and connecting business tools to visualize simulations.

Acknowledgments. This work is partially funded by EDF R&D through the strategic project MS4SG.

References

1. Fritzson, P., Engelson, V.: Modelica - a unified object-oriented language for system modeling and simulation. In: Jul, Eric (ed.) ECOOP 1998. LNCS, vol. 1445, pp. 67–90. Springer, Heidelberg (1998)
2. Dynamic Modeling Laboratory (Dymola). http://www.3ds.com/products-services/catia/capabilities/modelica-systems-simulation-info/dymola
3. Mahseredjian, J., Dennetière, S., Dubé, L., Khodabakhchian, B., Gérin-Lajoie, L.: On a new approach for the simulation of transients in power systems. Electric Power Systems Research **77**(11) (2007)
4. Henderson, T.R., Roy, S., Floyd, S., Riley, G.F.: NS-3 project goals. In: Proceeding of WNS2 2006, p. 13. ACM (2006)
5. Varga, A., Hornig, R.: An overview of the OMNeT++ simulation environment. In: Proceedings of ICST, p. 60 (2008)
6. Enterprise Architect. http://www.sparxsystems.com.au/products/ea/index.html
7. Vangheluwe, H., De Lara, J., Mosterman, P.J.: An introduction to multi-paradigm modelling and simulation. In: Proc. AIS2002, pp. 9–20 (2002)

---

[3] An IEC (International Electrotechnical Commission) standard to model data in the power grids.

8. 1516_WG - HLA Evolved Working Group: IEEE standard for modeling and simulation (M&S) high level architecture (HLA)- framework and rules. IEEE Std 1516–2010 (Revision of IEEE Std 1516–2000), pp. 1–38, August 2010
9. Siebert, J., Ciarletta, L., Chevrier, V.: Agents and artefacts for multiple models co-evolution: building complex system simulation as a set of interacting models. In: Proceedings of AAMAS 2010, pp. 509–516 (2010)
10. Hopkinson, K., Wang, X., Giovanini, R., Thorp, J., Birman, K., Coury, D.: EPOCHS: a platform for agent-based electric power and communication simulation built from commercial off-the-shelf components. IEEE T Power Systems (2006)
11. Nutaro, J., Kuruganti, P., Miller, L., Mullen, S., Shankar, M.: Integrated hybrid-simulation of electric power and communications systems. In: IEEE PES 2007, pp. 1–8 (2007)
12. Lin, H., Sambamoorthy, S., Shukla, S., Thorp, J., Mili, L.: Power system and communication network co-simulation for smart grid applications. In: 2011 IEEE PES (ISGT), pp. 1–6 (2011)
13. Galán, J.M., Izquierdo, L.R., Izquierdo, S.S., et al.: Errors and artefacts in agent-based modelling. JASSS 12(1), 1 (2009)
14. Omicini, A., Ricci, A., Viroli, M.: Artifacts in the A&A meta-model for multi-agent systems. AAMAS 17(3), 432–456 (2008)
15. Ricci, A., Viroli, M., Omicini, A.: Give agents their artifacts: the A&A approach for engineering working environments in MAS. In: Proc. AAMAS 2007. ACM (2007)
16. Zeigler, B., Praehofer, H., Kim, T.: Theory of Modeling and Simulation: Integrating Discrete Event and Continuous Complex Dynamic Systems. Academic Press (2000)
17. Vangheluwe, H.: DEVS as a common denominator for multi-formalism hybrid systems modelling. Proc. of CACSD 2000, 129–134 (2000)
18. Zeigler, B.P.: Embedding DEV&DESS in DEVS. In: Proc. of DEVS 2007 (2006)
19. Quesnel, G., Duboz, R., Versmisse, D., Ramat, É.: DEVS coupling of spatial and ordinary differential equations: VLE framework. In: Proc. of OICMS 2005 (2005)
20. Chandy, K.M., Misra, J.: Distributed simulation: A case study in design and verification of distributed programs. IEEE Trans. Software Engineering (1979)
21. Camus, B., Bourjot, C., Chevrier, V.: Combining DEVS with multi-agent concepts to design and simulate multi-models of complex systems (WIP). In: Proc. of TMS/DEVS 2015, SCS (TBP)
22. Vaubourg, J., Chevrier, V., Ciarletta, L.: Co-simulation of IP network models in the smart grids context, using a DEVS-based platform. Technical report, Inria, Université de Lorraine (2015)
23. OMG: (DDS), v1.2, January 2007. http://www.omg.org/spec/dds/1.2
24. Functional Mock-up Interface. https://fmi-standard.org/
25. Blochwitz, T., Otter, M., Arnold, M., et al.: The functional mockup interface for tool independent exchange of simulation models. In: 8th International Modelica Conference, pp. 20–22 (2011)
26. Galli, E., Cavarretta, G., Tucci, S.: HLA-OMNET++: an HLA compliant network simulator. In: 12th IEEE/ACM DS-RT 2008 (2008)

Demo Papers

iaBastos: An Intelligent Marketplace for Agricultural Products

Gonzalo A. Aranda-Corral[1]([✉]), Joaquín Borrego Díaz[2], and David Solís Martín[2]

[1] Depto. de Tecnologías de la Información, Universidad de Huelva, Crta. Palos de La Frontera s/n, 21819 Palos de La Frontera, Spain
garanda@us.es
[2] Depto. de Ciencias de la Computación e Inteligencia Artificial, Universidad de Sevilla, Avda. Reina Mercedes s/n, 41012 Sevilla, Spain

Abstract. In this paper we present a multi-agent platform designed to support p2p auctions on agricultural products. Experiments show that it could be feasible to integrate a platform, which is de-centralized by nature, into the current socioeconomic environment. The reason is that this market is managed by hard-centralized ecosystem, and experiments with our system show a significant reduction in marketing margins for the benefit of consumers and producers.

1 Introduction and Motivation

In Spain, the existence of some issues in the relation between producers and intermediaries in agricultural markets is well known. One can find a large number of news that reveal the significant price increase that takes place since the product leaves the production zone until it arrives to final consumers. This increase not only affects to final consumers, but also producers are warning about the low income that they get, which even could not cover production costs.

This rigid business ecosystem contrasts with the astonishing number of transactions through P2P auctions, applied to very different goods and services by means of Internet. For example, in 2001, eBay had 42 million users and it auctioned 1 million items per day. Internet auctions are available to anyone with a computer or mobile and an internet connection [2].

In this paper, we propose a Multiagent System (MAS), called *iaBastos*, to provide an infrastructure to support auctions between agricultural producers and final consumers (or retailers). More specifically, in this work we study if it is affordable to decentralize hard-centralized markets.

Within the scope of similar markets, the use of auctions in fish markets is well known. For example MASFIT [1] is a system where software agents live together with human agents in the auction process of fish. In the scope of agricultural products, it is usual to find only sites like http://www.arcocoag.org or http://www.naranjasyfrutas.com, where users can search producers for a specific product, which aims to bring that two profiles closer.

© Springer International Publishing Switzerland 2015
Y. Demazeau et al. (Eds.): PAAMS 2015, LNAI 9086, pp. 255–258, 2015.
DOI: 10.1007/978-3-319-18944-4_21

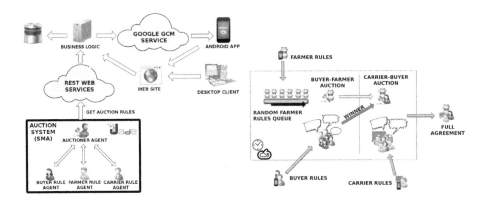

Fig. 1. left: MAS architecture, right: MAS ecosystem associated to iaBasto

2   iaBastos' Architecture

The iaBastos platform provides support to a system more complex than a simple contact directory between producers and consumers; it is a complete and autonomous auction system. Unlike MASFIT system, in this platform, there is not any integration between human and software agents within the auction process, in which only take part software agents (see Fig. 1).

The architecture has five main modules (see Fig. 1 left):

- Database: Django's ORM allows to abstract the database management.
- Business module: Implements business logic (user management, authoring and authentication) and interacts with the Database module.
- REST web services: allow the MAS to interact with the business module.
- MAS: Developed using JADE platform [5] (http://www.jade.tilab.com) and FIPA English Auction Interaction Protocol Specification (http://www.fipa.org/specs/fipa00031/). It performs the autonomous auction process.
- Web and Android app: provides an user interface where auction rules can be managed, and achieved contracts can be looked up. The android app also provides instantaneous notifications and warnings on smartphones and tablets.

Another key difference with respect to MASFIT -and other auction systems-is that in our case we have three target profiles, buyers, sellers and carriers (those providing logistics). To solve this issue we have to split the auction process in two semi-independent auctions as it is shown in Fig. 1 (right). When the auction system runs, it takes all rules, defined by different profiles, into the system. Randomly, it takes the first farmer rule and starts an auction to find a buyer. All buyers have to consider how much money they must save in order to find a transport. After the auction between the farmer and buyers finishes, if a deal is reached, the auction between the buyer and carriers starts. If an agreement is reached in both auctions, users will be notified and the system will continue with the next farmer. Otherwise, the previous deal between farmer and buyer will be dismissed. The auction system will continue working until any new deal can be found.

Therefore, we can find the following software agents:

- SynAgent: this agent is responsible for getting all available rules through the web appropriate service.
- BuyerRuleAgent: this agent represents a buyer rule and its mission is to buy a product taking into account the constraints.
- SaleRuleAgent: this agent is responsible for selling the farmer products.
- CarrierRuleAgent: this agent represents the carrier's behavior in order to get a transport contract.
- BuyerAndFarmerDeal: this agent tries to find transport after a buyer has achieved a deal with a farmer.

3   Experimentation

As we mentioned earlier, three profiles can be found in our system (see Figure 1). After the registration process, the user has to set the rules based on his profile. Farmers has to set products (from harvests) as well as sale rules (based on quality, minimum sale price, minimum weight for orders, etc.); buyers has to set the buyer rules (based on quality product, maximum buying price, kilogram range, ...) and carriers in the same way (maximum weight per order, maximum distance,etc.). Once the overall rule set is in the system the MAS dynamics starts.

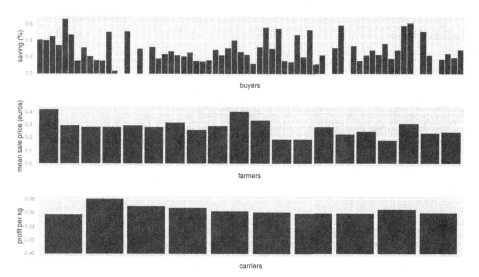

Fig. 2. up: savings obtained by each buyer, middle: mean sale price per kilogram by each farmer, down: total profit per kilogram obtained by each carrier

For demonstration purposes, we have created an experimental set of producers, consumers (or retailers) and carriers around the city of Seville. To be as realistic as possible, such agents have been geolocated in order to compute road distances. Farmer rules (what product, what quality and the minimum sale's price) are designed, taking minimum price a higher value than the current sale prices get by producers. Further, we have been created buyer and transport rules. We have considered 68 buyer rules, 20 farmer rules and 10 carrier rules.

When the system stops, it has got 61 deals. As shown in Figure 2, most buyers have obtained very good savings with a mean of 29%. Farmers are buying its products to a mean price of 0.27 cents. This price is very higher than the current mean market. Carriers offered transport to a mean of 6 cents per kilogram, with a very low standard deviation.

4 Conclusions

This work presents a MAS-based auction system oriented to agricultural market. The system is composed by a website, a mobile app and the multi-agent system. Actually, it is a beta version and we are studying different agent strategies to get a more advantageous system for all profiles (farmers, buyer and carriers) and adding new functionalities to the website. For example, to give carriers tools for managing his routes and deliveries.

On the initial question, whether is possible to decentralize hard-centralized markets, we think that it is truly possible, we have margin on buyer savings and on sale price. The only remaining doubt is if society is ready to take this system on.

References

1. Cuni, G., Esteva, M., Garcia, P., Puertas, E., Sierra, C., Solchaga, T.: MASFIT: Multi-Agent System for Fish Trading (2004)
2. Krishna, V.: Auction Theory. Academic Press (2009)
3. Weiss, G.: Multiagent systems. MIT Press (2013)
4. Poslad, S.: Specifying Protocols for Multi-Agent Systems Interaction (2007)
5. Bellifemine, F., Poggi, A., Rimassa, G.: JADE–A FIPA-compliant agent framework (1999)

TrafficGen: A Flexible Tool for Informing Agent-Based Traffic Simulations with Open Data

Alexandre Bonhomme, Philippe Mathieu$^{(\boxtimes)}$, and Sébastien Picault

Multiagent Team, CRIStAL UMR CNRS, University of Lille – Science
and Technology, 9189 Villeneuve d'Ascq, France
{philippe.mathieum,sebastien.picault}@univ-lille1.fr

Abstract. Multi-Agent Systems have been widely used for traffic simulation. The modeling of individuals allows indeed to introduce a behavioral diversity which is crucial to obtain realistic simulation outcomes. The recent growth of open geographical databases and related flow information provides an opportunity for enhancing traffic simulators with data automatically retrieved from the real world and updated regularly. We present here TrafficGen, a highly modular platform based on the integration of such open data within a library of rule-based behaviors, in order to provide a versatile decision support tool in traffic.

Keywords: Multi-agent simulation · GIS · Road traffic · Traffic generator · Decision support system

1 Introduction

Individual-based approaches proved very early their benefits in traffic simulation [1,2], especially to assess the outcome of individual decisions at a macroscopic scale. But the diversity of goals of such simulations, from flow prediction to immersive simulation to study car ergonomics, either in academic or industrial contexts, lead to the development of dedicated tools with a lack of reusability and adaptability. Yet, there is a growing need for simulation tools able to handle and compare various scenarios and hypotheses, so as to support decision in traffic management or public policies. More recently, the use of statistical data to tune the behaviors of driver agents has also become a growing issue [3,4]. The TrafficGen project, which is demonstrated here, is meant as an answer to this problematic by studying how to combine flexibility in behavior design and model revision, together with the use of geographical data and flow information in several open formats.

2 Main Purpose

Modular and flexible behavior modeling. In most traffic simulators, agents are in general limited to vehicles: cars, bicycles, buses, etc. and by extension, pedestrians. Those agents are in charge of modeling all the traffic complexity through

© Springer International Publishing Switzerland 2015
Y. Demazeau et al. (Eds.): PAAMS 2015, LNAI 9086, pp. 259–262, 2015.
DOI: 10.1007/978-3-319-18944-4_22

their behaviors, which are tightly dependent on the aims of the simulator. But, in order to test and compare various scenarios or assumptions, e.g. regarding intermodality, or drastic changes in transport policies, the key problem is rather to endow the user with the capability of accessing *explicitly* (and intelligibly) the behavioral models that reflect those assumptions, choosing those to use in a scenario, and easily redesigning the experiments, without being forced to rewrite any line of code.

To do so, we rely upon the "Interaction-Oriented Approach" (IODA) which handles each entity involved in the system as an agent [5] endowed with capabilites of interacting with the others [6]. Interactions are abstract condition/action rules which constitute the declarative part of the models, and are designed independently from the agents. Hence, they offer a modular and reusable way to build and test the behaviors of all agents in various contexts. Driver habits, path planning, scripted routes, environment learning, can be modeled through this unified, rule-based approach, and combined to build arbitrarily complex vehicle behaviors.

Exploitation of open data. Besides, we aim at using the growing amount of open data available both in geographical information systems and in transport, in order to enhance the realism of simulations. Regarding traffic path information, we tackled two formats: OSM, used in the *OpenStreetMap* participatory project[1] which provides exhaustive cartographic information, and *OpenDrive*[2], designed for describing road features.

Depending on the purpose of each experiment, data related to an interest area are retrieved, then filtered to keep only relevant information (e.g. highways, cycle lanes, or tram lines) which is also mapped to the corresponding kinds of vehicles. Besides, special transport items such as roads, crossroads, traffic lights, bus stops, tram stations, etc. are also represented by agents according to the IODA approach, so that they are endowed with a behavior (even simple) which can be modified interactively during the simulation (e.g. during market hours some roads are closed). This allows to reduce the complexity of driver agents by delegating part of their behaviors to infrastructure agents, in a way close to the affordances theory [7]. In order to generate realistic populations of vehicles, generator agents can be placed on ways and parameterized either through probability laws or real data. Finally, additional agents measure the characteristics of simulated vehicles (*probes*) so as to bridge the gap with the macroscopic level, or introduce specific events (such as a local speed reduction in response of pollution peaks) [8].

3   Demonstration

The TrafficGen platform demonstrated here has been built as a proof of concept in order to asses our approach (and not currently for competing in performances with industrial products). In this demonstration, we can select any interest area

---

[1] http://wwww.openstreetmap.org
[2] http://www.opendrive.org

from *OpenStreetMap*, apply the filtering to select part of the available ways within a few seconds, and run the simulation (see fig. 1). We give examples of interactive experiments that can be carried out (road closing, local speed reduction, etc.) and of the corresponding measurements. The level of detail can be tuned according to the needs (fig. 2), and depending on the aims of the experiments other transport modes can be studied within the same platform (e.g. metro, fig. 3), by changing the filter.

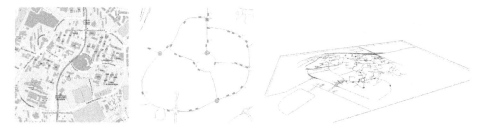

Fig. 1. From an extraction of OSM data (left), the relevant ways are imported in *TrafficGen* (middle) for building the appropriate environment for the simulation (right)

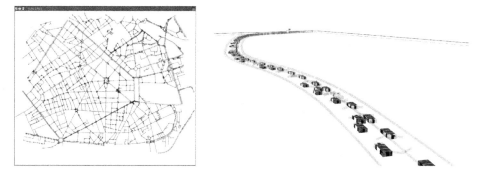

Fig. 2. Left: part of the city center of Lille (France) loaded in *TrafficGen*; right: Traffic on French highway A23

4   Conclusion

We have presented and demonstrated the TrafficGen platform, aimed at providing a multi-purpose approach to traffic simulation, by allowing the user to easily compare scenarios and hypotheses within actual geographical data and flow information. This tool has proven its efficiency to model road traffic (fig. 1, 2) as well as rail (fig. 3). Ongoing work on this project focus, on the one hand, on concrete case studies in the city of Lille (France) based on recorded traffic measures, and on the other hand, the extension of our model towards multi-level simulation, grounded on our previous work in this domain [9].

Fig. 3. A simulation of the subways of Lyon (left) and Paris (right) in *TrafficGen*

References

1. Espié, S., Saad, F., Schnetzler, B., Bourlier, F., Djemane, N.: Microscopic traffic simulation and driver behaviour modelling: the ARCHISIM project. In: Conf. Road Safety in Europe and Strategic Highway Research Program (SHRP), pp. 22–31 (1994)
2. Champion, A., Mandiau, R., Kolski, C., Heidet, A., Kemeny, A.: Traffic generation with the SCANER^{TM} simulator: towards a multi-agent architecture. In: Driving Simulation Conference, pp. 311–324 (1999)
3. Lacroix, B., Mathieu, P., Kemeny, A.: Formalizing the construction of populations in multi-agent simulations. J. Eng. App. of AI **26**(1), 211–226 (2013)
4. Darty, K., Saunier, J., Sabouret, N.: A method for semi-automatic explicitation of agent's behavior: application to the study of an immersive driving simulator. In: 6th Int. Conf. on Agents and AI (ICAART), pp. 81–91. SciTePress (2014)
5. Kubera, Y., Mathieu, P., Picault, S.: Everything can be agent! In: 9th Int. Joint Conf. on Auton. Agents and Multi-Agent Systems (AAMAS), IFAAMAS, pp 1547–1548 (2010)
6. Kubera, Y., Mathieu, P., Picault, S.: IODA: An interaction-oriented approach for multi-agent based simulations. J. of Auton. Agents and Multi-Agent Systems **23**(3), 303–343 (2011)
7. Gibson, J.: The Ecological Approach to Visual Perception, Hillsdale (1979)
8. Bonhomme, A., Mathieu, P., Picault, S.: A versatile description framework for modeling behaviors in traffic simulations. In: Proc. of the IEEE 26th Int. Conf. on Tools with AI (ICTAI), pp. 937–944. IEEE Press (2014)
9. Picault, S., Mathieu, P.: An interaction-oriented model for multi-scale simulation. In: Proc. of the 22nd Int. Joint Conf. on AI (IJCAI), AAAI, pp. 332–337 (2011)

Distributed Analytical Search

Subrata Das[✉], Ria Ascano, and Matthew Macarty

Machine Analytics, Cambridge, MA, USA
sdas@machineanalytics.com

Abstract. The main purpose of this research is to develop an agent-based Distributed Analytical Search (DAS) tool to search and query distributed data sources regardless of data's location, content or format from a natural language query.

1 Introduction

DAS allows end users to query distributed data sources in natural language without having to know the source formats and locations. DAS answers queries through the following stages:

- Accepts a search query from a user in natural language via a web interface.
- Automatically translates the query to a set of sub-queries by deploying a combination of planning and traditional database query optimization techniques.
- Generates a query plan represented in XML and guide the execution by spawning intelligent agents with wrappers as needed for distributed sites.
- Merges the answers returned by the agents and return them to the user.

The distributed query execution as described above therefore avoids downloading large volumes of Mobility and SALUTE (size-activity-location-unit-time-equipment) data records from these remote tables to the host site. An example query in this context that we will be using throughout the paper is "Show Salute platforms from NAIs with mobility no go."

SALUTE

NAI	FROM	ACTIVITY	EQUIPMENT	TIME	SIZE
47	JSTARS	Milling	Vehicles	14:20	40-60
65	UAV	Emplaced	BMP	18:12	?
91	LRS	Meeting	AK 47	10:30	100-200
20	IMINT	Digging	Truck	05:10	1
...	...	...	...	...	...

NAI-Mobility

NAI	Mobility
47	Slow Go
23	No Go
49	Go
43	Go
...	...

Fig. 1. SALUTE and Mobility tables stored in different remote DB with some example rows

2 Demonstration

Figure 2 depicts a screenshot that demonstrates the main webpage for the DAS tool. The left side shows the User Query input, the lower right side shows the optimized

© Springer International Publishing Switzerland 2015
Y. Demazeau et al. (Eds.): PAAMS 2015, LNAI 9086, pp. 263–266, 2015.
DOI: 10.1007/978-3-319-18944-4_23

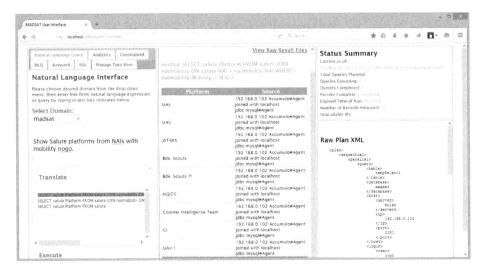

Fig. 2. DAS web-based use interface

plan in XML format, the upper right side shows the status, and the middle shows the merged results obtained from an Accumulo table and MySQL table.

The user will select a domain from a dynamic list. Once a domain is selected, the user will begin typing a query in the textbox below the domain selection. DAS automatically translates a natural language query to its equivalent SQL representation to be executed against structured data. We are making use of the publicly available Stanford parser and the dependency relations that it generates from a given sentence representing a user query in the context of a given database. The algorithm also makes use of the underlying database scheme and its content. The algorithm exploits the structure of the database to generate a set of candidate SQL queries, which we re-rank with a heuristics based ranking algorithm developed in-house. In particular we use linguistic dependencies in the natural language question and the metadata to build a set of plausible SELECT, WHERE and FROM clauses enriched with meaningful joins.

Once the translation is complete, possible SQL queries are returned to the user. The list of translated queries that the user is presented with is displayed in rank order as shown in Figure 2. However, the "correct" translation in terms of relevancy is not always ranked highest due to the ambiguity of natural language.

The user can select any translation by clicking on it and then click the execute button below the list of SQL translations. At this point DAS starts by preparing an execution plan whereby subqueries are created and optimized prior to execution. In the UI presentation layer, the user is presented with the XML-based plan that DAS will execute.

Once the plan has been created by DAS, we will know how many queries will be executed at a maximum, and this number will be presented to the user. In some instances the number of queries planned will not be the same as the number of queries executed. This is primarily due to the fact that some nodes may be unavailable when contacted by an agent. Since it is a basic assumption that nodes will be or become unavailable for querying, DAS can and does continue the execution on available nodes. The user is presented with a new statistic so s/he are alerted to the fact that not all queries will be executed and by extension that some nodes on the network are not available. However should unavailable nodes become available during the course of execution, they will be included in the execution.

The final step in carrying out a user's request for data is performed by the Query Execution module. The Query Execution module controls all aspects of agent creation, migration, data retrieval, and collaboration. The module receives a list of sub-queries from the Planning and Optimization systems and generates a series of mobile agents to carry out these sub-queries. For each agent, the module creates an itinerary of the various sites to be visited and the data retrieval and processing tasks to be executed at each site. Each mobile agent is then spawned and the system waits for the return of each agent with its associated data. Upon return, the system performs any required data joining, processing, and formatting before displaying the results to the user.

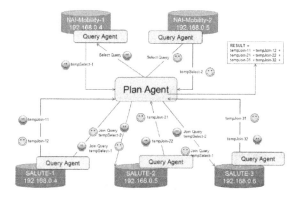

Fig. 3. Plan Agent spawning Query Agents processing information from several databases

Our mobile agent approach as shown in Figure 3 created multiple Plan Agents and Query Agents as part of the Query Execution module. These mobile agents were built on top of the Aglets 2.02 API along with Tahiti server running on the Java 1.8. But we now have the ability to replace Aglets with our in-house mobile agent platform. Aglets is a Java mobile agent platform and library. An aglet is a Java agent that is able to autonomously and spontaneously move from one host to another. The Plan Agents and Query Agents inherit the properties of an Aglet.

Figure 4 shows the DAS demo implementation environment that we have created. We have set up three database servers to emulate storing and serving big data from a variety of environments, including Hadoop-based cloud and a traditional database server. These servers are connected via a router providing fixed IP addresses to these servers, thus creating local area network. The servers are connected by a common maintenance terminal for configurations.

The table below shows a comparison between distributed and centralized database as well as direct parallel querying and sending the Agents to remote

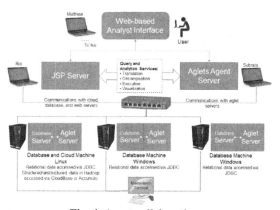

Fig. 4. Agent collaboration

locations. Centralized DB consisted of 2.1 million rows of data stored in a SALUTE table in MySQL. Distributed DB consisted of three remote Databases with 0.7 million rows of SALUTE data per remote database. It took less than half the time to retrieve 2.1 million records from three distributed databases than the same amount of records from one centralized database. There is not much difference between the direct parallel approaches as opposed to sending the mobile agents remotely.

	Direct	Mobile Agent
Centralized MySQL DB (2.1M rows of records returned)	7 min 43 sec	7 min 32 sec
Distributed in 3 remote MySQL DB (0.7M each) (2.1M rows of records returned)	3 min 22 sec	3 min 12 sec

Plan Agents and Query Agents have been configured to run on both Windows and Ubuntu Operating systems. Testing is being done on different machines to ensure that the DAS system can operate in a heterogeneous environment.

The ability to have multiple clients querying from different browsers or different machines has been designed and implemented. A unique session directory is created when a user chooses a particular translated query to execute. The plan XML document and all the other relevant documents that are related to this particular query will be contained in this unique session directory. Relevant files include the status XML file and the partial and merged results.

The limits of our system have been continuously subjected to stress testing by sending huge data results across the wires. Gigabytes of data have been loaded across several data sources. Up to 3 million result objects per remote data source have been sent through the wires. There were no issues with using the mobile Agents and we run into heap space issues with the direct approach. Major refactoring was implemented to accommodate the migration of huge data results into different machines. We continued to encounter heap space issues as we continue to increase the data and several steps were taken to improve performance. Memory management is continuously monitored and managed.

3   Conclusion

The paper presented an approach and an architecture of a distributed data base search system using mobile agents. DAS semantically analyzes natural language queries from a web-based user interface and automatically translates the queries to a set of subqueries by deploying a combination of planning and traditional database query optimization techniques. It then generates a query plan represented in XML and guide the execution by spawning intelligent agents with various types of wrappers as needed for distributed sites. The answers returned by the agents are merged appropriately and returned to the user. We have demonstrated DAS using a variety of data sources that are distributed and heterogeneous. The tool is the prime product of our company with big enterprises as our target market.

Situated Regulation on a Crisis Management Collaboration Platform

Maiquel De Brito[1]([✉]), Lauren Thevin[2], Catherine Garbay[2],
Olivier Boissier[3], and Jomi F. Hübner[1]

[1] PPGEAS/Federal University of Santa Catarina, Florianópolis, Brazil
maiquel.b@posgrad.ufsc.br
[2] LIG/Université de Grenoble, Grenoble, France
[3] Laboratoire Hubert Curien UMR CNRS 5516, Institut Henri Fayol,
MINES Saint-Etienne, Saint-Etienne, France

Abstract. Collaborative platforms are useful to mediate the interaction among the different actors involved on a crisis management. This paper demonstrates the grounding of the policies that regulate crisis management activities on the concrete environment where the collaborative platform is deployed. This grounded regulation is enabled by the abstractions and constructs of the Situated Artificial Institution model.

1 Introduction

Crisis management deals with disasters such as flooding, car crashes, etc. Given the inherent distributed and decentralized nature of crisis management, multi-agent systems (MAS) are a well suited approach to conceive collaborative management platforms to mediate the interaction among the different (and possibly distant) actors involved on this activity (e.g. police, firefighters, citizens, etc). A key issue on crisis management, that must be considered in the collaborative platforms, are the overall policies that regulate and coordinate the autonomous actions of the different actors. To be effective, the norms expressing the policies related to the crisis management must be anchored in the physical environment where the collaboration takes place. For example, a norm stating that the mayor is obliged to command an evacuation will be effective when an specific actor is identified as mayor and when a specific action is interpreted as a command to evacuation (Figure 1). This demonstration shows how a Situated Artificial Institution (SAI), as conceived in [1], anchors the norms regulating the crisis management on a collaborative platform deployed on a network of TangiSense tables [2,3].

2 Main Purpose

The collaborative crisis management platform conceived in [3] is deployed on a network of TangiSense tables [2]. This is the *environment* where the human actors act. They put tangible objects equipped with RFID tags on the table

© Springer International Publishing Switzerland 2015
Y. Demazeau et al. (Eds.): PAAMS 2015, LNAI 9086, pp. 267–270, 2015.
DOI: 10.1007/978-3-319-18944-4_24

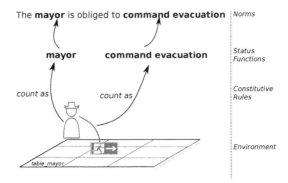

Fig. 1. SAI overview

to signal their intended actions on the crisis management. Since these tangible interactions do not have per se any meaning in the crisis management, it is necessary to *institutionalize* the facts occurring in the environment, giving them the proper meaning in the particular application (e.g. the tangible B in the position (C, D) counts as the evacuation of the downtown). Such institutionalization is important to the regulation of the scenario that is, ultimately, the regulation of the activities of the actors in the tangible equipments.

To provide this anchoring of the regulation in the environment, we turn to Situated Artificial Institution (SAI), as proposed in [1]. SAI provides the abstractions and constructs to ground the norms on the environment. Norms on SAI do not point to the concrete elements implementing the system. Rather, they refer to *status functions*, that are the institutional interpretation of environmental facts. This interpretation is specified through *constitutive rules*. The main purpose of this demonstration is to show norms, status functions and constitutive rules, as conceived and arranged in SAI, providing the regulation to the crisis management scenario based on facts that do not have, themselves, meaning in such scenario. The focus is on the SAI rather than on the tangible equipments. The SAI platform handles the informations coming from the environment and, according to the SAI specification, performs the *constitution* of status functions, i.e. relates the status functions to the environmental elements. The constitution determines then the activations, fulfilments, violations, etc, of the norms.

3   Demonstration

We consider a simplified use case where the goal is to evacuate a zone. The actors, in this activity, are (i) the *Mayor*, that in charge to evacuate (or to command it) a secure zone and (ii) the *Firefighters (FF)*, that are in charge to evacuate insecure zones.

This use case is realized in an environment composed of two tables, identified as *table_mayor*, and *table_fire_brigade*, used by the *mayor* and *FF* respectively. From the SAI perspective, the agents are also part of the environment.

The relevant events that may occur in the environment are (*i*) *checkin(AgentID, TableID)*, triggered when the agent *AgentID* checks into the table *TableID*, and (*ii*) *putTangible(TableID, TangiID, X, Y, AgentID)*, triggered when the agent *AgentID* puts a tangible *TangiID* on the coordinates (X, Y) of *TableID*. The relevant environmental properties that compose the environmental state, provided by databases, GIS, etc, are (i) *nbInhabitants(ZoneID,X)* holding when the *ZoneID* has X inhabitants and (ii) *security_phase(ZoneID, Phase)* holding when the *ZoneID* is on security phase $Phase \in \{preventive, emergency\}$.

The SAI specification that defines the situated regulation of the scenario is illustrated below:

```
status_functions:
  agents: mayor, firefighter.
  events: evacuate(Zone).
  states: secure(Zone), insecure(Zone), electric_risky(Zone).
norms:
  /*The mayor is permitted to evacuate secure zones*/
  1: secure(downtown): mayor permitted evacuate(downtown)
  /*The mayor is prohibited to evacuate insecure zones*/
  2: insecure(downtown): mayor prohibited evacuate(downtown).
  /*Firefighters are prohibited to evacuate secure zones*/
  3: secure(downtown): firefighter prohibited evacuate(downtown).
  /*The firefighter is obliged to evacuate insecure zones*/
  4: insecure(downtown): firefighter obliged evacuate(downtown).
constitutive_rules
          /*** Agent-Status Functions constitutive rules ***/
  /*Actors carry the status functions according to their check in the tables*/
  1: Actor count-as mayor
          when checkin(table_mayor,Actor) while not(Other is mayor)|Other==Actor.
  2: Actor count-as firefighter when checkin(table_fire_brigade,Actor).
          /*** Event-Status Functions constitutive rules ***/
  /*Mayor putting tangibleObject1 on (15,20) means the mayor evacuating the downtown*/
  3: putTangible(_,tangibleObject1,15,20,Actor) count-as evacuate(downtown)
          while Actor is mayor.
  /*FF putting tangibleObject2 on (15,20) means the FF evacuating the downtown*/
  4: putTangible(_,tangibleObject2,15,20,Actor) count-as evacuate(downtown)
          while Actor is firefighter.
              /*** State-Status Functions constitutive rules ***/
  /*A zone in preventive phase is secure if it does not poses electrical risks
    and if it has at most 500 inhabitants*/
  5: security_phase(Zone,preventive) count-as secure(Zone)
          while not(electric_risky(Zone)) &
              ((nbInhabit(Zone,X)& X<=500) | (phase(Zone,preventive) is secure(Zone)))
  /*A zone in preventive phase is insecure if it poses electrical risks*/
  6: security_phase(Zone,preventive) count-as insecure(Zone)
          while electric_risky(Zone).
  /*A zone in emergency phase is insecure*/
  7: security_phase(Zone,emergency) count-as insecure(Zone).
  /*The downtown is electric risky if the firefighter puts the tangible tangibleObject3 on (15,20)*/
  8: count-as electric_risky(downtown)
          when putTangiNote(_,tangibleObject3,15,20,Actor) while Actor is firefighter.
```

The norms define the expected behaviour of the agents on the crisis management. For example, the norm 1 states that, when the downtown is *secure*, the *mayor* is permitted to perform a tangible interaction that, from the institutional perspective, means the evacuation of the downtown. On other hand, it is prohibited to do that when the downtown is *insecure* (norm 2). Firefighters, on their turn, are prohibited to evacuate the downtown when it is considered *secure* (norm 3) but are obliged to evacuate it when it is considered *insecure* (norm 4).

Note that the norms do not refer to the concrete elements of the environment. They do not specify neither who is the mayor and the firefighter, nor which tangible interaction is considered an evacuation, nor when a zone is considered secure or insecure. These components of the norms are status functions that are constituted by environmental elements according to the specified constitutive rules. The constitutive rules 1 and 2 define that the actor that act on the tangible equipments producing the event *checkin(Actor, Table)* carries the status function of *mayor* or *firefighter*. They define, thus, who are the actors targeted by the norms. The constitutive rules 3 and 4 define the tangible interactions that mean, in the institution, the evacuation of the downtown, defining thus, what the actors must do or avoid to comply with the norms.

While the constitutive rules 1 to 4 define the concrete actors and tangible interactions related to the norms, the constitutive rules 5-8 define the concrete situations that, from the institutional perspective, mean that downtown is either secure or insecure. The constitutive rule 5 defines that the property *security_phase(downtown,preventive)* holding in the environment means, from the institutional perspective, that the *downtown* is *secure* if (i) the it does not pose electrical risks and (ii) if the it has, at most, 100 inhabitants. Note that while the number of inhabitants is a property of the environment, a *Zone* is electrical risky if the *firefighter* puts the tangible object *tangibleObject3* on the coordinates $(15, 20)$ of the table (constitutive rule 8). By the constitutive rules 6 and 7, the downtown is insecure either when the environment indicates that crisis management is on emergency phase or when it is considered electrical risky.

4 Conclusion

The policies referring to crisis management activities are not related per se to the concrete interaction on the tangible equipments. On other hand, the concrete elements involved on the tangible interactions do not have, per se, any meaning in the crisis management. This paper demonstrates how the SAI model, through its abstractions and constructs, conciliates these two dimensions, grounding the policies of crisis management on the environment where the collaboration takes place. SAI provides two levels of interpretation to the tangible interactions: first, they are interpreted as elements of the crisis management domain and, then, interpreted as either valid or invalid interactions on crisis management.

Acknowledgments. The authors acknowledge the support given by CAPES (PDSE process 4926-14-5), CNPq (grants 448462/2014-1 and 306301/2012-1) and ARC 6 Region Rhône-Alpes (ARC-13-009716-01).

References

1. de Brito, M., Hübner, J.F., Boissier, O.: A Conceptual Model for Situated Artificial Institutions. In: Bulling, N., van der Torre, L., Villata, S., Jamroga, W., Vasconcelos, W. (eds.) CLIMA 2014. LNCS, vol. 8624, pp. 35–51. Springer, Heidelberg (2014)
2. Kubicki, S., Lepreux, S., Kolski, C.: Rfid-driven situation awareness on tangisense, a table interacting with tangible objects. Personal and Ubiquitous Computing **16**(8), 1079–1094 (2012)
3. Thévin, L., Badeig, F., Dugdale, J., Boissier, O., Garbay, C.: Un système multi-agent normatif pour la collaboration et l'interaction mixte. JFSMA **18**, 1–10 (2014)

Demo Paper: AGADE
Using Communities of Agents to Provide Realistic Feedback in Business Simulations

Thomas Farrenkopf[1][(✉)], Michael Guckert[1], and Neil Urquhart[2]

[1] KITE - Kompetenzzentrum für Informationstechnologie,
Technische Hochschule Mittelhessen, Giessen, Germany
{thomas.farrenkopf,michael.guckert}@mnd.thm.de
[2] School of Computing, Edinburgh Napier University, Edinburgh, Scotland
n.urquhart@napier.ac.uk

Abstract. The need to provide realistic feedback against decisions made within business games is a requirement if business games are to continue to remain relevant in training towards increasingly complex business scenarios. We attempt to address this problem by using software agents to simulate individuals and to model their actions in response to business decisions. In our initial studies we use agent technologies to simulate consumers who will make buying decisions based on their own preferences and those within their social network. Other applications are search for structure in complex contexts, or verification of predicted values based on theoretical considerations. In this demo paper we present the tool set AGADE (Agile Agent Development Environment) which incorporates agent based and semantic technologies to address this. It is applied to simulate different market mechanisms in a mobile phone market.

Keywords: Multi-agent system · BDI · OWL ontology · Market simulation · Human behaviour

1 Introduction

Traditionally, business games attempt to model real world business scenarios. They are typically based on mathematical models where cause-and-effect relationships are basically represented in difference and differential equations. Agent-based systems are perfectly suited to describe individuals and their behaviour rather than effects through equations and thresholds. Behaviour can be modelled for each agent and its effects on the comprising environment can be determined by running simulations. The BDI software model (belief-desire-intention) provides a common well established approach for building multi-agent simulations. Moreover ontologies can be used to make world knowledge available to the agents which can then determine their actions in accordance with this knowledge. We demonstrate how ontologies can be integrated into the BDI concept namely into the popular agent framework Jadex [4]. Each agent will maintain its knowledge

© Springer International Publishing Switzerland 2015
Y. Demazeau et al. (Eds.): PAAMS 2015, LNAI 9086, pp. 271–274, 2015.
DOI: 10.1007/978-3-319-18944-4_25

in an individual ontology and then access this dynamically during runtime. The generic approach will allow the simulation of different scenarios which can easily be modelled by creating appropriate ontologies. The approach is implemented in an interactive round based multi-agent simulation tool (AGADE). It was applied to simulate different market mechanisms in a mobile phone market, which will be presented in this demonstration.

2   Main Purpose

AGADE aims at providing an integrated environment in which round based multi-agent simulations can be modelled and executed. Its emphasis lies on modelling individuals that are aware of their environment, have knowledge and are able to learn. A means for that is integrating ontologies and multi-agent systems so that the modelling of knowledge is shifted to writing OWL ontologies. Powerful inference engines are then available and can be exploited from within the BDI infrastructure.

3   Demonstration

AGADE is a round based multi-agent tool set designed to support the development and calibration of dynamic business scenarios. It is based on the Jadex framework which allows the definition of BDI agents. Agents are active parts of a complex social structure, allowing them to not only communicate but also to permanently learn from each other.

In our case study of a mobile phone market we have to distinguish between customer and seller agents. Therefore we have to define two types of agents and the number of agents each type that are to take part in the simulation. Before starting a simulation we have to define the social structure comprised of the mutual relations of all agents. We provide an adjacency matrix (see Fig. 1) in which we can manually define the *who knows whom* relations or calculate them using an appropriate algorithm such as Barabasi's preferential attachment [1]. Influence matrices quantify the mutual influence agents may have. Additionally other relational aspects (each with its own adjacency and influence matrix respectively) can be built e.g. random graph like structures. These matrices can be used to define the degree of technical understanding an agent a attributes to another agent b or the quantified degree to which one agent is affected by another.

Each agent is equipped with its own inference engine (reasoner) and private ontology which is accessed using the OWL API [3]. Social aspects and information about the agent's current state are mapped to the ontology. The simulation itself can be controlled using the GUI displayed in Fig. 2. On the top of the GUI the control buttons are located: Because of AGADE's round-based approach, between any two rounds a simulation can be halted so that further inspections of the current state of affairs are possible. Simulation data is displayed continuously.

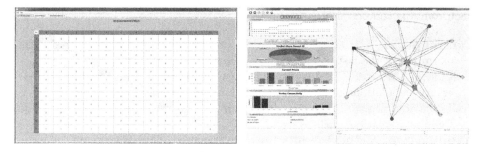

Fig. 1. Adjacency matrix setup   **Fig. 2.** AGADE simulation GUI

On the right hand side of the screen there is a graphical display of the social structure formed by all participating agents. The vertices of the graph represent the agents using different shapes for different agent types and different sizes to indicate the popularity (the amount of edges connected to them) of an agent. The agent types are visualised by different geometrical forms: squares represent sellers and consumers are represented by circles. The edges between the vertices depict the relations of the agents giving a precise description of each relation as they are labelled with the respective relation indices. The colours of the consumer vertices indicate the state of the respective agents e.g. the happiness with their current product.

On a very abstract level AGADE (see Fig. 3) knows two different kinds of BDI agents: A director type agent that acts as some kind of conductor for the simulation which triggers the beginning of each new round and participant type that comprises any kind of agent participating in the simulation (i.e. consumer and seller).

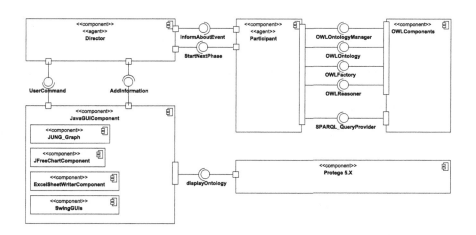

Fig. 3. Abstract view on the AGADE architecture

Each round is composed of four phases:

Control phase. The director processes commands issued by the user during execution of the last round. GUI components are updated.

Calculation phase. The director tells every single participant to make its necessary calculations (e. g. updating its happiness value).

Socialisation phase. Agents update their mutual relationships and possibly build new relationships.

Acting phase. The next agent actions are triggered. This depends on the individual state and the rules expressed in the agent's ontology.

Note that the ontology based belief base leads to a very flexible architecture, because important aspects of the agent do not have to be coded statically any more but may be expressed in the rules of the ontology.

4 Conclusion

The demonstration shows that multi-agent simulations can indeed be created by modelling agent behaviour through OWL ontologies and integrating that with the BDI concept. This reduces programming efforts as it is no longer necessary to code the complete agent logic in a programming language. Together with AGADE's ability to define social environments for the agents realistic simulations of real world scenarios can be built. Proof of concept was given in a case study with a scenario where agents are part of a typical social structure (small world network) [2]. The tool is designed to carry arbitrary simulations as long as the underlying structures of the scenario can be modelled by means of ontologies (individual aspect) and social structure.

References

1. Albert, R., Barabási, A.L.: Statistical mechanics of complex networks. Reviews of Modern Physics **74**(1), 47–97 (2002)
2. Farrenkopf, T., Guckert, M., Hoffmann, B., Urquhart, N.: AGADE. In: Müller, J.P., Weyrich, M., Bazzan, A.L.C. (eds.) MATES 2014. LNCS, vol. 8732, pp. 234–250. Springer, Heidelberg (2014)
3. Horridge, M., Bechhofer, S.: The OWL API: A Java API for OWL ontologies. Semantic Web **2**(1), 11–21 (2011)
4. Pokahr, A., Braubach, L., Jander, K.: The jadex project: programming model. In: Ganzha, M., Jain, L.C. (eds.) Multiagent Systems and Applications, Intelligent Systems Reference Library, vol. 45, pp. 21–53. Springer, Berlin Heidelberg (2013)

BactoSim – An Individual-Based Simulation Environment for Bacterial Conjugation

Antonio Prestes García and Alfonso Rodríguez-Patón[✉]

Departamento de Inteligencia Artificial,
Universidad Politécnica de Madrid, Campus de Montegancedo s/n,
Boadilla del Monte, 28660 Madrid, Spain
antonio.garcia2@gmail.com

Abstract. BactoSim is an agent-based platform for simulating the conjugation in spatially structured bacterial populations, which are the conditions typically found on naturally occurring colonies such as biofilms or in agar-based laboratory cultures. The model provides a set of key indicators which can be visualized in real time as the simulation evolves and saved as for further analysis.

1 Introduction

The bacterial conjugation is a natural process where bacterial cells interchange circular DNA fragments known as plasmids. Conjugative plasmids are the vehicles of antibiotic resistance spreading in hospitals and also may carry genes which are responsible for bacterial virulence and pathogenicity [2]. Therefore it is worth to understand how they are propagated and that is the key point where individual-based models come to help to shed light over the inner intricacies of the process. The most common strategy for modeling conjugation was some variation of differential equations with mass action kinetics using whole population data for model calibration. But one of the main drawbacks of this approach is that it fails to take into account local variations and assume well-mixed environments which clearly are not realistic assumptions. In order to produce a more structurally realistic representation for conjugation, a spatially explicit individual-based model is required where agents have their own individual internal state and interact only with their closest neighbors being the changes in spatial position of agents exclusively consequence of the shoving relaxation due to the colony growth process.The BactoSim code and binaries are available for download[1]. The simulator is part of project European project PLASWIRES which also includes the simulator BactoSim II [1].

2 Main Purpose

In this paper we provide a brief overview of the BactoSim simulation platform. The main objective of the software is to provide a computational workbench for

---

[1] http://goo.gl/TDGxNr

© Springer International Publishing Switzerland 2015
Y. Demazeau et al. (Eds.): PAAMS 2015, LNAI 9086, pp. 275–279, 2015.
DOI: 10.1007/978-3-319-18944-4_26

using bacterial plasmid as a "wiring protocol" for harnessing the power of bacterial cell-cell communication as a tool for multicellular synthetic biology. This is achieved using an integrative approach where molecular level and individual-based observations are incorporated within the simulation model. Hence all relevant data about the system under study is used as model parameters and to implement the model rule base. This is a bottom-up approach where we specify how agents must evolve thereby producing an emergent global behavior. That kind of models is also useful for producing new insights about the process being studied, suggesting sometimes counter intuitive ideas about what local processes are responsible for some global system comportment. The simulation software was developed using the Repast Symphony multi-agent simulation platform [3].

3   Demonstration

The simulation model is comprised by a discrete set of agents each of them representing a single bacterial cell $\beta_i, i = 1 \ldots N$ where N is the current population size at the simulated time t. The agents interact with other agents and with the environment which holds some amount of nutrient. The environment is implemented using a *value layer* of repast framework [3]. The β_i agents lives and evolve in a computational domain represented as a 1000×1000 discrete² grid, corresponding to a real surface of $1mm^2$. In approximately 20 minutes of wall clock, BactoSim is able to simulate 600 minutes of colony growth with a final population of 10^5 bacterial cells.

The bacterial cells evolve during the simulated time having their state variables updated by some processes representing the intra and intercellular behavior of every agent β_i. Hence, at a functional high level, the model have a set of processes $\mathcal{P} = (p_1 \ldots p_5)$ each of them standing respectively for the Uptake, Diffusion, Division, T4SS expression (a protein needed for plasmid conjugation), Shoving relaxation and finally the Conjugation. The execution of these processes is shuffled in order to avoid any bias and the state of agents and the value layer holding the nutrient particles are updated asynchronously. The bacterial cells have three different states, namely R, D and T standing respectively for plasmid free (or recipient cells), plasmid donors (cells originally infected by plasmid) and transconjugant cells which are those plasmid free cells that have been infected by a donor or transconjugant cell.

The model requires the input of two groups of parameters, the first group is related to the definition of virtual plasmid-host features which will be simulated and the second group allows the specification of the initial population sizes. The first group includes the parameters G which is the doubling time for plasmid free cells³, the point of cell cycle where conjugation is deemed most prone to happen [4], the T4SS expression and the conjugation cost. The value of γ_0 must be also introduced, that parameter tells the model how many conjugations, on average,

---

² Actually it is implemented as a repast *multiOccupancy2D* allowing cells to overlap in some extent, in the same way it really happens in a real bacterial colony.

³ The values of doubling time for D and T cells are both emergent properties of model.

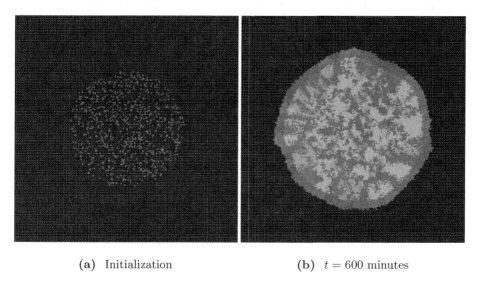

(a) Initialization   (b) $t = 600$ minutes

Fig. 1. The **BactoSim** Virtual Agar-Plate view for simulated version of *R1* plasmid. The color scheme used is green for R cells, red for D cells and blue for T cells. The light-green, light-read and light-blue colors are used to represent depleted nutrient zones where cells are no longer dividing.

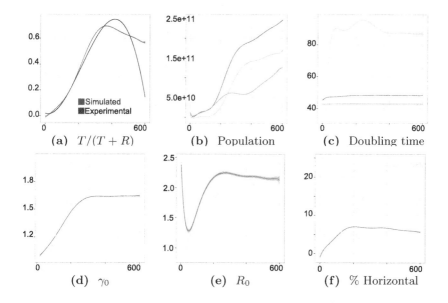

(a) $T/(T + R)$ (b) Population   (c) Doubling time

(d) γ_0 (e) R_0 (f) % Horizontal

Fig. 2. Sample of the output provided by the **BactoSim** model

are performed by bacterial cells. Model requires also two flags which allow the definition of repressed and conjugative plasmids.

The second group of parameters includes the value of N_0 or the initial population size which must be introduced in the model as a concentration in cells/ml and the initial proportion of donor cells as a percentage of N_0. Besides of these two groups the model has an optional parameter for a polynomial equation fitted to the experimental data which serve as a simple visual assessment of the quality of simulated data, an example of this can be seen in Figure 2a.

The model generates a lot of output with both quantitative and qualitative data about the evolution of the agents and the colony global outcomes. With respect to qualitative data a sample output is show in Figure 1 which represents, in some extent, a virtual agar-plate where bacterial agents interact and evolve during the simulated time.

The virtual-plate provides a simple visual tool to assess whether the colony is growing in a realistic pattern. Besides of the "plate view", BactoSim generates six performance indicators shown in Figure 2: the $T/(T + R)$ rate in Figure 2a, the population size and the doubling time in Figure 2b and 2c, the γ_0, R_0 (Basic Reproduction Number) and the ratio of new infections caused by horizontal transfers in Figures 2d, 2e and 2f respectively

4   Conclusions

In this paper we have presented the main features of BactoSim simulation environment and the master lines which have been used to implement the conjugation model and it is worth to mention that it is still an ongoing process. As has been outlined the objective of our model is twofold, on the one hand it is intended to be a predictive tool and on the other hand the model is a helpful tool to gather insights on the intra-cellular process which are building the global dynamics of the conjugation cell-cell communication at a whole colony level.

Acknowledgments. This work was supported by the European FP7 - ICT - FET EU research project 612146 and by MINECO research grant TIN2012-36992.

References

1. Beneš, D., Sosík, P., Rodríguez-Patón, A.: An Autonomous In Vivo Dual Selection Protocol for Boolean Genetic Circuits. Artificial life, 1–14, January 2015. http://view.ncbi.nlm.nih.gov/pubmed/25622012
2. Norman, A., Hansen, L.H., Sørensen, S.J.: Conjugative plasmids: vessels of the communal gene pool. Philosophical transactions of the Royal Society of London. Series B, Biological Sciences 364(1527), 2275–2289 (2009). http://dx.doi.org/10.1098/rstb.2009.0037

3. North, M., Collier, N., Ozik, J., Tatara, E., Macal, C., Bragen, M., Sydelko, P.:
   Complex adaptive systems modeling with Repast Simphony. Complex Adaptive
   Systems Modeling 1(1), 1–26 (2013). http://dx.doi.org/10.1186/2194-3206-1-3
4. Seoane, J., Yankelevich, T., Dechesne, A., Merkey, B., Sternberg, C., Smets, B.F.:
   An individual-based approach to explain plasmid invasion in bacterial populations. FEMS Microbiology Ecology 75(1), 17–27 (2011). http://dx.doi.org/10.1111/
   j.1574-6941.2010.00994.x

A Multimodal City Street and Entertainment Guide for Android Mobile Devices

David Griol$^{(\boxtimes)}$ and José Manuel Molina

Computer Science Department, Carlos III University of Madrid,
Avda. de la Universidad, 30, 28911 Leganés, Spain
{david.griol,josemanuel.molina}@uc3m.es

Abstract. Smart mobile devices have fostered new interaction scenarios that demand sophisticated interfaces. The main developers of operating systems for such devices have provided APIs for developers to implement their own applications, including different solutions for developing graphical interfaces, sensor control and voice interaction. In this paper, we describe a context-aware multimodal conversational agent for Android-based mobile devices that dynamically incorporate user specific requirements and preferences as well as characteristics about the interaction environment, in order to improve and personalize the service that is provided.

Keywords: Human-agent interaction · User interfaces · Conversational agents · Spoken and multimodal interaction · Mobile devices · Android

1 Introduction

Multimodal interactive systems offer the user combinations of input and output modalities for interacting with mobile devices, taking advantage of the naturalness of speech [1]. Different vendors offer APIs for the development of applications that use speech as a possible input and output modality, but developers have to design ad-hoc solutions to implement the interaction management.

Speech access is then a solution to the shrinking size of mobile devices (both keyboards to provide information and displays to see the results). Besides, speech interfaces facilitate the access to multiagent systems [2], especially in environments where this access is not possible using traditional input interfaces (e.g., keyboard and mouse). It also facilitates information access for people with visual or motor disabilities.

In this paper we describe a practical application showing how context-aware multimodal conversational agents can be easily integrated in hand-held Android mobile devices. The developed Android conversational agent uses geographical context in order to provide different location services to its users.

This work was supported in part by Projects MINECO TEC2012-37832-C02-01, CICYT TEC2011-28626-C02-02, CAM CONTEXTS (S2009/TIC-1485).

Y. Demazeau et al. (Eds.): PAAMS 2015, LNAI 9086, pp. 280–283, 2015.
DOI: 10.1007/978-3-319-18944-4_27

2   Main Purpose

Our proposal is focused on the development of multimodal conversational agents for mobile devices operating with the Android OS [3]. Our proposal integrates the Google Speech API to include the speech recognition functionality in a multimodal conversational agent. The development of multimodal systems involves user inputs through two or more combined modes, which usually complement spoken interaction by also adding the possibility of textual and tactile inputs provided using physical or virtual keyboards and the screen. In our contribution, we also model the context of the interaction as an additional valuable information source to be considered in the fusion process. We propose the acquisition of external context by means of the use of sensors currently supported by Android devices. The Android sensor framework (*android.hardware* package) allows to access these sensors and acquire raw sensor data.

The dialog manager of the system is based on a previously developed statistical methodology [4]. The visual structure of the user interface (UI) is defined by means of layouts, which are defined by declaring UI elements in XML or instantiating layouts elements at runtime. Finally, we propose the use of the Google TTS API to include the text-to-speech functionality. The *android.speech.tts* package includes the classes and interfaces required to integrate text-to-speech synthesis in an Android application.

3   Demonstration

We have developed a practical multimodal city street and entertainment guide for Android-based mobile devices. The app can be operated visually and orally. As a city guide, it is able to locate interesting sites near the current position of the user or a different starting point indicated by the user. It is able to locate sites such as banks, libraries or restaurants and to retrieve and display information about these sites, visualize their position in different maps, show routes and information, and navigate (Figure 1).

Also, the user can introduce and describe his own points of interest, which can be either permanent, e.g. preferred pub; or temporal, e.g. placed where he parked or a meeting point (Figure 2). As an entertainment guide, it also facilitates information about movies, theaters and other cultural activities. The information is provided in Spanish.

In order to provide the functionalities described, the system engages in a dialog with the user to retrieve different pieces of information that are complemented with the context-awareness capabilities of the system. This way, the system response is adapted taking into account the specific preferences and suggestions selected by the users, as well as to the context in which the interaction takes place.

The statistical models for the user's intention recognizer and dialog management modules were learned using a corpus acquired by means of an automatic dialog generation technique previously developed [5]. The application also allows

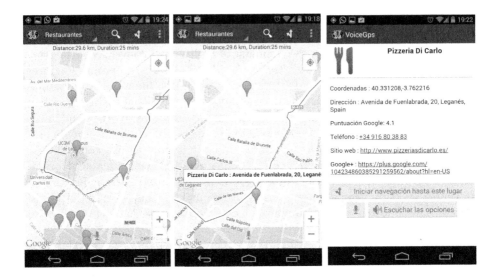

Fig. 1. System functionality to look for specific places and show the corresponding information

Fig. 2. "Where is my car?" functionality and configuration options for the agent

users to complete a profile corresponding to their preferences on the location of the initial maps, preferred travel facilities, preferred types of stores, and specific details for each one of them. With regard to cultural activities, the application collects user preferences (sports, movies, music, and museums) and film affinities (gender, country, year range, categories to be excluded, or favorite theaters).

The developed multimodal conversational agent uses Google Maps, Google Directions and Google Places. Google Maps Android API makes it possible to show an interactive map in response to a certain query. It is possible to add markers or zoom to a particular area, also to include images such as icons, highlighted areas and routes. Google Directions is a service that computes routes to reach a certain spot walking, on public transport or bicycle, and it is possible to specify the origin and destination as well as certain intermediate spots. Google Places shows detailed information about sites corresponding to number of categories currently including 80 million commerces and other interesting sites. Each of them include information verified by the owners and moderated contributors. The application also employs the *android.speech* libraries described in the previous section.

4 Conclusions

In this paper we have described a practical application of combining conversational agents and hand-held Android mobile devices to develop context-aware multimodal applications. The developed Android conversational agent uses geographical context in order to provide different location services to its users. To develop this system we have defined the complete requirements for the task and developed the different modules, and the necessary information to be incorporated in user profiles.

We are currently undergoing the next phases in the deployment of the application. We want to carry out a detailed study of the user rejections of system-hypothesized actions using the values extracted from the user profile, and study the benefits that could be derived from including additional features in the user intention recognition model related to the user emotional state. With the results of these activities, we will optimize the system, and make it available the in Google Play.

References

1. Pieraccini, R.: The Voice in the Machine: Building Computers that Understand Speech. The MIT Press (2012)
2. Corchado, J., Tapia, D., Bajo, J.: A multi-agent architecture for distributed services and applications. Computational Intelligence **24**(2), 77–107 (2008)
3. McTear, M., Callejas, Z.: Voice Application Development for Android. Packt Publishing (2013)
4. Griol, D., Hurtado, L., Segarra, E., Sanchis, E.: A Statistical Approach to Spoken Dialog Systems Design and Evaluation. Speech Communication **50**(8–9), 666–682 (2008)
5. Griol, D., Carbó, J., Molina, J.: An Automatic Dialog Simulation Technique to Develop and Evaluate Interactive Conversational Agents. Applied Artificial Intelligence **27**(9), 759–780 (2013)

EXPLAIN_MAS: An Agent Behavior Explanation System

Aroua Hedhili Sbaï[✉] and Wided Lejouad Chaari

National School of Computer Studies (ENSI), University of Manouba, Tunis, Tunisia
{aroua.hedhili,wided.chaari}@ensi.rnu.tn

Abstract. Agent-Based Simulations are well adapted to model complex social systems in various domains. The simulation is considered as an efficient way to predict, to explore and to test hypothesis for problems that cannot be reproduced in the real world. We are convinced and we fully believe that the simulation of complex systems requires the development and the execution of a complex Multi-Agent System (MAS). To face this complexity, users need to understand how such a complex MAS operates. This paper focuses on the explanation of agents' behaviors and their way to act and interact. For this purpose, we propose to associate the MAS with a Knowledge Based System for Explanation (KBSE) called EXPLAIN_MAS.

Keywords: Agent behavior · Reasoning explanation · Causal map · Simulation

1   Introduction

Multi-Agent Systems (MAS) have, on the one hand, the traditional advantages of the resolution of problems as modularity, parallelism and reliability. On the other hand, they inherit the attractive features of the artificial intelligence as the symbolic treatment of knowledge. In addition, they support sophisticated scenario of interactions (cooperation, coordination, negotiation). These aspects have classified MAS as complex systems marked by the lack of a global control. In fact, agents use their own knowledge, their environment perceptions and their interactions to reach their goals. So, we consider that it is crucial to elucidate, to interpret and to deal with the proceeding of the intelligent resolution of agents in a dynamic, complex, and open system. In order to deal with this issue, first, we focused on the explanation in knowledge based systems particularly expert systems. Second, we reviewed the existing works in MAS area. In this context, there are two directions that have underlined these works: The auto-explanation [1] and the modular one [2]. We think that the presented directions have limits. In fact, the auto-explanation starts with the design and the development of the MAS, so it could not be applied in already developed systems. Then, it affects the system performance by overloading the agent; each agent should resolve a problem and at the same time deal with the explanation process. The proposed approaches in the second direction depend on the application domain and the development platform. Furthermore, explanation mechanisms in expert systems cannot be applied directly in MAS considering their features (parallelism, interaction, etc.). In order to overcome

© Springer International Publishing Switzerland 2015
Y. Demazeau et al. (Eds.): PAAMS 2015, LNAI 9086, pp. 284–287, 2015.
DOI: 10.1007/978-3-319-18944-4_28

the above limits, we are realizing a separate modular explanation system. This system is dynamic and independent of the functionality of the system to explain, and the type of involved agents.

2   Main Purpose

We propose in this paper an intelligent approach. This approach consists in three principal modules: an observation module, a modeling module and an interpretation one. The observation module presents the knowledge acquisition phase. It detects agents' activities and collects their execution context in what we called an explanation structure presented as the tuple <K, A, G, R> (Knowledge, Action, Goal, Relation). The tuple attributes point out the explanatory knowledge. These knowledge describe the main reasoning concepts for each agent "i" at a moment "t" in the tuple $<K_i(t), A_i(t), G_i(t), R_i(t)>$ [3]. We consider that the explanatory knowledge could not reflect an explanation of agent performed actions, they are deprived of a clear and a semantic explanation. Consequently, we identify the causal links between these knowledge attributes to elucidate the cause/effect relationships among visualized events. So, we proceed according to different levels of construction in order to build connected causal maps in what we call an Extended Causal Map (ECM) [3]. These levels denote several types of causal links. The first level presents a **temporal** one. It describes a causal graph where the concepts are the reasoning states, RS_i. These concepts express the detected agents' behaviors while the graph arrows (t_i, t_{i+1}) show the alteration between behaviors. Each observed behavior depicted in the graph concept is represented in our case with the explanatory knowledge collected in the tuple <K, A, G, R>. Therefore, from this level we generate a second level, labeled **horizontal level**, that indicates the causal relations between the tuple attributes. Furthermore, we recognize additional causal links via the temporal relation depicted between RS_i and RS_{i+1} that refer to the detected behaviors of, on the one hand, the same agent, and on the other hand, of different agents. So, we consider that there are causal relations between explanatory knowledge collected at the moment t_i in the tuple $<K_i(t), A_i(t), G_i(t), R_i(t)>$ and the ones collected at the moment t_{i+1} in the tuple $<K_i(t_{i+1}), A_i(t_{i+1}), G_i(t_{i+1}), R_i(t_{i+1})>$ for the same agent. These relationships outline an **internal vertical level** in the ECM. This level indicates the causal relations between the actions performed by the agent and its satisfied goals. Then, we note that the relation between the behaviors of different agents of the MAS depends on the interaction process elaborated between these entities. We remind that each performed communication act is detected by the observation module, and its execution parameters are stored in the attributes R and A. So, we focus on these attributes for each agent at different moments to describe and analyze the established interactions. We create these causal maps in what we call an **external vertical level** based on the performatives of the agent communication language. This level presents the causal links between the explanatory knowledge acquired at the moment "t" of the agent "i", $<K_i(t), A_i(t), G_i(t), R_i(t)>$, and the ones acquired at a moment " t' "of the agent "j", $<K_j(t'), A_j(t'), G_j(t'), R_j(t')>$. Further, a knowledge representation model as a graph could provide a visual interpretation in terms of a set of relationships between concepts. Such interpretation is easier if the graph has a limited number of nodes and arrows. This is not the case of our ECM elaborated for complex systems like MAS. So, we propose to associate this causal map with an interpretation formalism to deduce a knowledge for explanation. We define the CAUMEL language [4] based on the first-order and the temporal logics.

3   Demonstration

Our work has been validated on a MAS simulation of large scale emergency rescue SimGenis [3].   The interface depicted in the figure 1 shows the required tabs to configure this application. When the simulation is launched, the explanation is triggered.

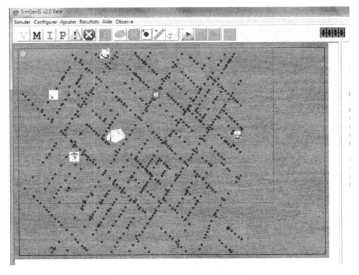

Fig. 1. SimGenis interface

First, each action performed by agents is observed and the explanatory knowledge are acquired in real time. The observation module is developed using the aspect-oriented programming with the AspectWerkz[1] tool.   Then, the appropriate causal map is built according to the different levels (temporal, horizontal, internal vertical, external vertical). We present in the figure 2 some 3D causal maps generated, during the SimGenis execution. Eventually, each produced map is interpreted and translated to predicates using CAUMEL. In the second part of the figure 2, we point out some of these predicates. The interface contains a narrator agent to report the explanation process.

---

[1]   http://aspectwerkz.codehaus.org/

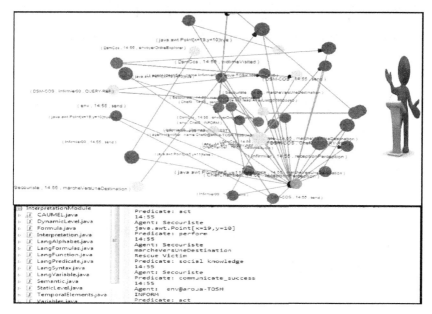

Fig. 2. Causal maps

4   Conclusion

In this paper, we dealt with an online explanation of agent behaviors during the MAS execution. For this purpose, we developed a knowledge based system composed of three modules. The observation module presents a knowledge acquisition phase. The modeling module describes the knowledge representation phase and the interpretation module corresponds to the interpretation phase. Our explanation system EXPLAIN_ MAS is validated using a large scale emergency rescue MAS.

References

1. Johnson, L.: Agents that explain their own actions. In: International Conference on Computer Generated Forces and Behavioral Representation (1994)
2. Lam, D.N., Barber, K.S.: Comprehending agent software. In: Proceeding of AAMAS, pp. 586–593 (2006)
3. Hedhili Sbaï, A., Lejouad Chaari, W.: Extended Causal Map for Explanation in Multi-Agent Systems. Special Issue on: "Intelligent Systems and Applications Using Knowledge and Agent-Based Technologies" of the Int. Journal of Intelligent Systems Technologies and Applications **12**(3/4), 301–315 (2013)
4. Hedhili Sbaï, A., Lejouad Chaari, W.: CAUMEL: a temporal logic based language for causal maps to explain agent behaviors. In: Jezic, G., Kusek, M., Lovrek, I., Howlett, R.J., Jain, L.C. (eds.) Agent and Multi-Agent Systems: Technologies and Applications. AISC, vol. 296, pp. 127–138. Springer, Heidelberg (2014)

A Fully Integrated Development Environment for Agent-Oriented Programming

Vincent J. Koeman[✉] and Koen V. Hindriks

Delft University of Technology, Delft, The Netherlands
{v.j.koeman,k.v.hindriks}@tudelft.nl

1 Introduction

When provided with the support of proper development and maintenance tools, programmers are more likely to work efficiently and produce high-quality software [1,2]. A mature and professional Integrated Development Environment (IDE) provides the required tools in an integrated manner and allows those tools to be easily adapted for use in new contexts as well [3].

Providing these capabilities for agent-oriented programming (AOP) is not trivial. Specific features of agents like decision cycles, rule-based evaluations, mental states, external environments, and embedded knowledge representation (KR) technologies pose specific challenges to the design and development of an IDE for AOP. These challenges significantly differ from object-oriented or functional programming for example, as those paradigms do not (inherently) deal with for instance distributed execution, database inspection, and logic inference.

In this paper, we present a mature and professional IDE for the multi-agent programming language GOAL[1] [4]. In contrast to other AOP development environments, our approach is novel, as we fully integrate all agent and agent-environment development tools within one environment. Other AOP development environments are generally composed of several standalone tools [5]. For instance, running or debugging an agent after editing its program code is usually performed in a separate application (pop-up).

2 Main Purpose: MAS Development Tool

In order to obtain the requirements for the design of a full-fledged development environment, the needs of a developer in all areas of the (agent) software development process have been identified. These design requirements can be split into three distinct areas of application, reflecting the three different phases of a software development process [2,6]: development, analysis, and debugging.

Debugging is especially important but also especially hard in a rule-based context [7]. A direct insight into the relationship between an agent's exhibited behavior and its program code should be provided whilst debugging. Moreover, the display of a mental state should have advanced features like sorting or

---

[1] https://ii.tudelft.nl/trac/goal
https://github.com/goalhub

© Springer International Publishing Switzerland 2015
Y. Demazeau et al. (Eds.): PAAMS 2015, LNAI 9086, pp. 288–291, 2015.
DOI: 10.1007/978-3-319-18944-4_29

searching, making them easier to use, especially when a large number of objects is present in such a state. To facilitate program development and analysis, the code-editor should be up-to-date with the latest industry-standards such as auto-completion and a source outline. In addition, the execution platform or mental state inspector should not be separated from the editing environment. This does not only prevent a developer from having to use (and thus familiarize with) different interfaces, but also ensures a developer is not forced to use a large amount of programs or windows simultaneously. Significant room for improvement exists [5], and the whole field of AOP might benefit from the creation of a mature and adaptable agent programming IDE that raises the standard.

3   Demonstration: Eclipse for GOAL

In this section, we will discuss the GOAL programming language, its new IDE in Eclipse, and the development of accompanying educational environments.

GOAL Agents. GOAL is a language for programming autonomous decision systems at the knowledge level with a rich set of language features. Knowledge, beliefs and declarative goals are used to specify the (desired) state of an environment. The programming language facilitates the specification of strategies or policies inspired by human common sense decision making. A strategy is specified as a set of condition-action rules where conditions are evaluated on an agent's mental state. Actions can be either internal or external. An external action is an action that is performed by the agent's corresponding entity in an environment, whilst an internal action only affects the agent itself. A KR language is used to represent the information agents have about such an environment in order to achieve their goals. GOAL does not commit to any particular KR language. A hierarchical structure can be imposed on the decision making processes by using modules, facilitating encapsulation and reuse.

Eclipse IDE. The presented IDE for GOAL uses the Eclipse platform to provide a full-fledged development environment for agent programmers, integrating all agent and agent-environment development tools in a single well-established setting. The Eclipse platform is based on an open architecture in which each plug-in can focus on a specific feature, adding new functionalities without impact to other tools [8]. This allows for building on top of well-known existing frameworks. By using Eclipse and the DLTK framework [9], for example, a state-of-the-art editor for GOAL has been created. Its features include syntax highlighting, auto-completion, a code outline, code templates, bracket matching, and code folding. By using a newly designed ANTLR 4 grammar [10], specifically its new 'lexical modes' feature for 'language islands', exchangeable support for embedded KR languages is provided. In addition, a testing framework for the validation of agents based on temporal operators has been created.

The debugger implementation makes use of the DBGP protocol [11]. By representing each agent as a thread, run, pause (break), and kill (stop) actions are automatically provided. A 'debug model' is used to customize the presentation of these threads, allowing a display of an agent's runstate. When a thread is in a paused state, the mechanisms provided by Eclipse and DBGP are used to display the mental state of an agent in a sortable and searchable manner. Finally, a code stepping mechanism is enabled for paused threads. This mechanism allows a developer to execute a program in a step-wise fashion, halting on specific instructions and thus facilitating the evaluation of the effects of specific code sections. The resulting debugger interface is illustrated in Fig. 1.

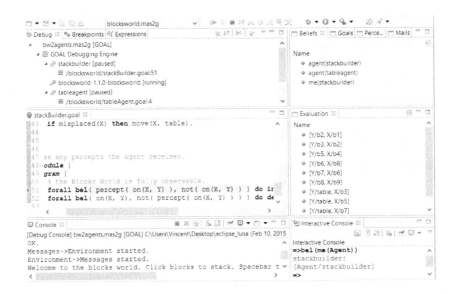

Fig. 1. A feature highlight of the debugging interface for GOAL agents in Eclipse

Agent Environments. The integration of all of these agent development tools within the Eclipse platform also facilitates the integrated development of both the agents and the environments they operate in. Changes to an environment's program code (in Eclipse) can be immediately used by and thus reflected in a corresponding agent program (in Eclipse). This is for example beneficiary for the development of the several educational environments[2] that are developed alongside the GOAL language as well, like the Blocks World for Teams (BW4T) [12] and Unreal Tournament [13].

Example. In order to demonstrate the complete set of agent development tools that our IDE offers, we will use the 'Hello World' toy-example. By default, an agent can instruct this environment to print some text. We will add some features to this (Java) environment, which the agent can directly implement through our feature-rich editor. However, as this might not work out as intended, we will

---

[2] https://github.com/eishub

need to debug the behavior of the agent by using our new code stepping tool. Besides demonstrating the stepping debugger with this example, we will use the first-person shooter Unreal Tournament 3 to illustrate an agent development process for a complex and real-time environment as well.

4   Conclusion

In this paper, we have presented a mature and comprehensive IDE for the multi-agent programming language GOAL, implemented as an Eclipse plug-in that provides both editing and debugging facilities. The development of agent environments is promoted by facilitating this in the same working environment. This implementation aims to raise the standard for the whole field of AOP, and facilitates future work on providing a better insight into an agent's behavior by for example a navigable mental state history and self-explaining agents.

References

1. Kline, R.B., Seffah, A.: Evaluation of integrated software development environments: Challenges and results from three empirical studies. International Journal of Human-Computer Studies **63**(6), 607–627(2005)
2. Ducasse, M., Noye, J.: Logic programming environments: Dynamic program analysis and debugging. The Journal of Logic Programming **19**, 351–384 (1994)
3. Ossher, H., Harrison, W., Tarr, P.: Software engineering tools and environments: a roadmap. In: Proceedings of the Conference on the Future of Software Engineering. ACM (2000)
4. Hindriks, K.V.: Programming rational agents in goal. In: Multi-Agent Programming, pp. 119–157. Springer, US (2009)
5. Bordini, R.H., et al.: A survey of programming languages and platforms for multi-agent systems. Informatica (Slovenia) **30**(1), 33–44 (2006)
6. Wasserman, A.I.: Tool integration in software engineering environments. In: Long, F. (ed.) Software Engineering Environments. LNCS, vol. 467, pp. 137–149. Springer, Heidelberg (1990)
7. Zacharias, V.: Development and verification of rule based systems — a survey of developers. In: Bassiliades, N., Governatori, G., Paschke, A. (eds.) RuleML 2008. LNCS, vol. 5321, pp. 6–16. Springer, Heidelberg (2008)
8. Geer, D.: Eclipse becomes the dominant Java IDE. Computer **38**(7), 16–18 (2005)
9. Gomanyuk, S.V.: An approach to creating development environments for a wide class of programming languages. Programming and Computer Software **34**(4), 225–236 (2008)
10. Parr, T.: The definitive ANTLR 4 reference (2013)
11. Caraveo, S., Rethans, D.: DBGP - a common debugger protocol for languages and debugger UI communication (2007)
12. Johnson, M., Jonker, C., van Riemsdijk, B., Feltovich, P.J., Bradshaw, J.M.: Joint activity testbed: blocks world for teams (BW4T). In: Aldewereld, H., Dignum, V., Picard, G. (eds.) ESAW 2009. LNCS, vol. 5881, pp. 254–256. Springer, Heidelberg (2009)
13. Hindriks, K.V., et al.: Unreal goal bots. In: Dignum, F. (ed.) Agents for Games and Simulations II. LNCS, vol. 6525, pp. 1–18. Springer, Heidelberg (2011)

Can Social Media Substitute Revolutionary Leaders? An Agent-Based Demonstration

Alessandro Moro[(✉)]

PhD Student, Department of Economics, Ca' Foscari University,
Cannaregio 873, 30121 Venice, Italy
alessandro.moro@unive.it

Abstract. This paper demonstrates in an agent-based framework that, in the presence of social media, it is possible to observe a revolution without the need of a strong political leadership.

Keywords: Political revolutions · Arab spring · Political leadership · Social network technology · Agent-based modeling

1 Introduction

One of the main aspects of the recent wave of revolutions in the so-called Arab Spring is the absence of a strong political leadership, substituted by an intensive use of social network technologies as a mean to obtain mass mobilization, as noted by Hussain and Howard (2013). This evidence is in sharp contrast with the previous historical experience: in fact, charismatic figures, like Robespierre, Lenin, Mao and Khomeini, have shaped the major revolutions in History.

2 Main Purpose

The present paper tries to provide an explanation for this radical change into an agent-based framework. In particular, this paper presents a model in which a subjugated population of agents decides to rebel or not against a central authority. This decision is made under two different settings: in the absence of a social network, with and without charismatic leaders, in one case; and in the presence of a social network, in the other case. The simulations of the model show that, without the use of social media, influential leaders are necessary to obtain a huge mass mobilization while, in the presence of a social network, it is possible to observe such a result without the need of a strong political leadership.

I am grateful to professor Paolo Pellizzari, my thesis supervisor, and to three anonymous referees for their extremely useful comments and suggestions.

Y. Demazeau et al. (Eds.): PAAMS 2015, LNAI 9086, pp. 292–295, 2015.
DOI: 10.1007/978-3-319-18944-4_30

3   Demonstration

The population of agents interacts in a bidimensional torus space and the results of this interaction are followed over time.

Each agent i is endowed with two time-invariant characteristics: a value for the grievance g_i, drawn from a uniform distribution on the $[0, 1]$ interval, and a value for the ability to persuade other agents to rebel, which measures the influential power of the agent, denoted by p_i and drawn again from a uniform distribution on the $[0, 1]$ interval.

Following Epstein (2002), at each time agents decide to be quiet or active, i.e., to rebel or not against the central authority, according to a threshold-based rule. In the present model, the activation rule involves: i) the level of grievance g_i; ii) the average persuasion agent i is exposed to, indicated with $\bar{p}_{it}$; iii) finally, a deterrence term represented by the probability of being arrested P_{t-1}, which is determined by the aggregate behavior of agents in the previous period.

Combining these quantities, the decision rule can be defined: agent i becomes active if and only if inequality

$$g_i + \beta \bar{p}_{it} - \gamma P_{t-1} > \tau \tag{1}$$

holds, where β, γ and τ are positive parameters.

The average persuasion each agent can be exposed to ($\bar{p}_{it}$) is the result of three potential sources. The first of them is the presence of already active agents in the neighboring positions. The second source is represented by the presence of revolutionary leaders in the neighborhood: this second type of players is characterized by an extraordinary high persuasion ability taking a much higher value compared to the average persuasion of the population of agents. Moreover, leaders are always active, except when they are in jail, as it will be explained below. Finally, the third source of propaganda is the social media technology: in some model simulations, it is assumed that a fraction of agents is connected to a social network and, consequently, it is subject to the persuasion of the other connected rebellious agents, no matter their geographical location.

In any period t the probability of arrest for a single active player is a decreasing function of the fraction of rebel forces to the overall population:

$$P_t = \frac{exp\left[-\phi\left(\frac{n_{A_t} + n_{L_t}}{n_a + n_l}\right)\right]}{1 + exp\left[-\phi\left(\frac{n_{A_t} + n_{L_t}}{n_a + n_l}\right)\right]} \tag{2}$$

where n_{A_t} is the number of active agents in the population, n_{L_t} is the number of active leaders, n_a and n_l are the numbers of agents and leaders, respectively, in the population, and ϕ is a positive constant. If an agent or a leader is arrested, he turns from active to quiet and the number of periods in jail is drawn from a uniform distribution on the $[0, j_{max}]$ interval, like in Epstein (2002).

Furthermore, it is assumed that at each time only a fraction θ of agents decides to change its status from quiet to active or vice versa. In order to start the revolution, at time t_0 a shock occurs and, starting from this period, a greater fraction of agents, equals to $\theta + \sigma$, decides to change or not its status. In the case of the Arab Spring, this shock may represent the Mohamed Bouazizi's self-immolation, which gave rise to the revolution in Tunisia.

Six simulations of the model have been performed to demonstrate the main thesis of the paper. For each of these simulations three graphs are reported: the time series of the number of quiet, active and jailed agents. These graphs are shown in Figure 1.

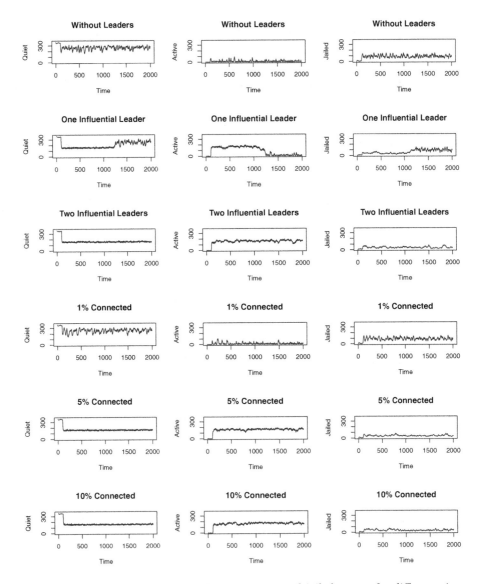

Fig. 1. Time series of the number of quiet, active and jailed agents for different simulations of the model

In all simulations, the period before the revolution is characterized by small episodes of rebellion involving very few agents because only a small fraction of the population takes into consideration the possibility of rebelling: these riots are immediately suppressed by the government. At time $t_0 = 100$, a shock happens and a considerable number of agents evaluates the decision to rebel or not against the central authority. The following situation depends strongly on the presence of influential political leaders and on the availability of a social network.

In the first simulation, without political leaders and social media, the rebel activity increases after the shock but it remains bounded geographically because the transmission mechanism of the rebellion is only local: this results in a modest turmoil after the start of the revolution, as shown in the first row of Figure 1.

Results change substantially with an influential leader. In this scenario, the number of active agents increases after the shock and it persistently remains at an high value for a long period of time (second simulation). With two influential leaders this effect is even reinforced: in fact, the number of active players is anchored to a very high value during the entire observed period after the start of the revolution, as can be seen by the graphs in the third row.

This last result can be equivalently reached without political leaders, introducing a social network technology connecting a sufficient number of agents. In fact, if the fraction of connected population is very low (1% in the fourth simulation), the rebel activity is very modest after the shock. On the contrary, if the number of connected agents is slightly higher (5% in the fifth simulation), the diffusion mechanism allowed by the social network is able to stimulate massive protests after the shock. The same is true for a percentage of connected agents equal to 10%, as presented in the last row.

4   Conclusions

The presence of a social network technology connecting a reasonable number of agents is able to generate massive protest movements by increasing the overall connectivity of the society. This mechanism explains why modern revolutions can be generated by social media without the need of a strong and influential political leadership, as happened in the Arab Spring uprisings.

References

1. Epstein, J.M.: Modeling Civil Violence: An Agent-Based Computational Approach. Proceedings of the National Academy of Sciences of the United States of America **99**, 7243–7250 (2002)
2. Hussain, M.M., Howard, P.N.: What Best Explains Successful Protest Cascades? ICTs and the Fuzzy Causes of the Arab Spring. International Studies Review **15**, 48–66 (2013)

Simulating the Optimization of Energy Consumption in Homes

Fernanda P. Mota[⊠], Plauto W. Filho, Jonas Casarin, Robledo Castro,
Vagner Rosa, and Silvia S. da C. Botelho

Centro de Ciências Computacionais, Universidade Federal do Rio Grande- Furg,
Av. Itália, S/N, Campus Carreiros, Rio Grande, Brazil
{nandapm2010,plauto.inf,jonas.casarin,bedocastro,
vsrosa,silviacb.botelho}@gmail.com

1 Introduction

According to Brazilian National Electric Energy Agency (ANEEL), the electric energy consumption is one of the main indicators of both the economic development and the quality of life of a society. However, the electric energy consumption data of individual home use is hard to obtain due to several reasons, such as privacy issues [1]. In this sense, the social simulation based on multiagent systems comes as a promising option to deal with this difficulty through the production of synthetic electric energy consumption data.

In the context of Artificial Intelligence, agents are defined as computational entities, embedded in an environment, which are able to perceive it and act on it. A computational agent has specific properties, such as: it operates under autonomous control, perceiving its environment, persists for a period of time, adapts to changes and it is able to accept goals [2]. There are several programming environments that are designed to work with agent-based modeling, however with different advantages, as shown in [3]. MultiAgent System (MAS) ofter a computing environment where programs that has a certain degree of autonomy (agents) interact with each pther in fulfillment of individual and collective goals [4].

The main categories that are associated with techniques for residential demand modeling are: top-down and bottom-up [5]. The top-down model uses total consumption of energy estimates of the residential sector, along with other relevant macro variables, for example, assigns the power consumption to the housing sector characteristics [5-7]. On the other hand, the bottom-up model identifies the contribution of each end-user consumption of total residential sector energy [8-9]. Bottom-up approaches refine the modeling of energy consumption, allowing the simulation of the effect of technological improvements and policy decisions in the household electricity consumption.

The authors [7, 10] have conducted studies aimed at reducing consumption by persuasion of residential consumers of electricity. About 20 years ago, there were few examples of persuasive technologies influencing the human decisions. The web was not ubiquitous, and the systems were not designed to change behavior, for they were more focused on data processing and increased productivity. Currently, experiments

© Springer International Publishing Switzerland 2015
Y. Demazeau et al. (Eds.): PAAMS 2015, LNAI 9086, pp. 296–299, 2015.
DOI: 10.1007/978-3-319-18944-4_31

with the persuasive technologies are emerging via the web (from e-commerce to social networks), video games (Wii Fit, Dance Dance Revolution), smartphones (applications in general) and specialized electronic devices (pedometers, smart TV), [11].

This paper proposes a multiagent bottom-up approach to model the behavior of residential energy consumers' in Brazil, the model's name is SapiEns. Consumers and their behavior household are modeled by multiagent techniques calibrated using data provided by the Brazilian Program of Household Estimate (POF), [12].

The authors chose to use the NetLogo simulator to implement the scenario analysis. Our approach differs from other methods on four main issues. First, some of the model parameters, which make the simulation, are easily calibrated by using the average data of the literature [12]. Second, the same system may be applied in different simulation environments involving degree of scalability (from several hundred million), the heterogeneity of individuals and home profiles. Thirdly, the MAS approach is responsible for simulating the complexity of the system by sharing use of the equipments and the relationship between the consumers. Finally, we used the concept of persuasion to optimize the power consumption by sending messages to the consumer when he leaves home and forgets connected equipment.

2   Main Purpose

The proposed of SapiEns system is to understand the triggers was sending to the user, and they can make decisions based on these messages. The system should select the message according to a classification created for each user (pre-defined according to the persuasion theory [13,14]) and send these triggers in order to obtain the best possible result, that is, the largest number of positive responses. If this happens, the system must understand that there is a repetitive behavior of the user, and thus developing into an autonomous system which is able to make decisions without consulting the user. However, if the triggers receive a greater number of negative responses, the system must understand that the user prefers leave equipment switched on during that time, so removing the trigger related to the equipment in question.

Our approach is to generate profiles based on the responses of electricity consumers for each message answered by the user. This paper simulates the final consumer and residential appliances through the energy consumption data of parameters obtained from the literature [12]. This will allow the consumer behavior analysis (cognitive agents) according to the equipment located in their homes (reactive agents). The consumer is defined at the beginning of the simulation, as a cognitive agent who can forget any connected equipment when you go out or asleep. For the construction of this method the following design decisions were taken:

- Users and equipments are modeled as computational agents. This decision was taken to make it possible to simulate the behavior of consumers in their homes and the interaction with each other household members. Thus, it becomes possible to analyze the complex behaviors that arise from the interactions of the agents;

- Each household has at least one and up to three people. This decision was based on the average number of people per household found in the literature [12];
- Sending of messages is done randomly, so there's not a predefined period for submission of messages;

3   Demonstration

The authors conducted a case study involving nine equipment on the Intelligent Automation Core Laboratory of the Federal University of Rio Grande (Nautec - Furg), among them: two refrigerators, two air conditioners and five computers. The equipments remain connected for up to eight hours in the laboratory, being under the use of researchers. Were performed twenty simulations over a period of 24 hours. In ten of these users answered the messages of triggers and another ten consumers did not respond.

The simulator allows to simulate one or more residences according to need user. In addition, it allows you to select the maximum number of consumers for each simulation. In addition, the tool saves the consumption and response messages every minute simulated in a text file, allowing a detailed analysis of the behavior of consumers throughout the simulation.

Simulating could persuade consumers to disconnect the equipment answering message of the triggers, there was a consumer 3,33kWh. We consider the price per kWh as R $ 0.47, so consumers spent on average R$ 1.57 per day. Furthermore, the simulations where users were not convinced to turned off the equipments there was a consumption of 4.64 kWh, doing the same analogy of the price per kWh, consumers spent an average of R$ 2.18 per day. From these two types of simulation we can conclude that persuaded users consumed around approximately 28% less than the others.

4   Conclusion

In this work we chose to POF data because it is a study that enables the analysis of various issues in Brazil. This proposal is based on data that were collected throughout the Brazilian territory (urban and rural) allowing the analysis of expenses, income and household consumption. However, we found a problem with the lack of data as the standard deviations for the means that were not provided, which limits the usefulness of the statistics. The objective is to build a simulation methodology for consumers of electricity, which is a simplification of the real world and on the basis of information obtained from the literature.

Thus, as can be seen from the presented results, the use of the agent paradigm and the NetLogo tool is a viable alternative for simulations of electric user profiles. This is due to the fact that many utility company behaviors inherent in this service may be mapped to different types of agents which are inserted respectively in a virtual environment. From the foregoing, the project is considered relevant and continuity can bring benefits to distributors, through better planning of distribution network, and for users, as an educational tool for better use of energy. Through the survey, the following topics were identified that could be realized as an extension to this work: Construction of fuzzy logic for the development and demonstration of consumer profiles; and improving communication between the tool and NetLogo database.

References

1. Aneel.: Energia no Brasil e no Mundo, Atlas de Energia Elétrica do Brasil (2002). Dis-ponível em www.aneel.gov.br (Acessado em Janeiro de 2014)
2. Russel, S., Norvig, P.: Artificial Intelligence: A modern approach, 2nd edition. Pearson Education (2003)
3. Dimuro, G.P., Costa, A.C.R., Palazzo, L.A.M.: Systems of exchange values as tools for multi-agent organizations. Journal of the Brazilian Computer Society 11(1), 3150 (2005)
4. Wooldridge, M.: An introduction to multiagent systems. Whiley, Chichester (2002)
5. Swan, L.G., Ugursal, V.I.: Modeling of end-use energy consumption in the residential sector: A review of modeling techniques. Renewable and Sustainable Energy Reviews 13, 1819–1835 (2009)
6. Hansen, A.M.D.: Padrões de Consumo de Energia Elétrica em Diferentes Tipologias de Edificações Residenciais em Porto Alegre. In: UFRGS, Porto Alegre (2000)
7. Picolo, L.S.G., Baranauskas, M.C.C.: Energy, environment, and conscious consumption: making connections through design. In: IHC Proceedings, Cuiabá, Brazil (2012)
8. Richardson, I., Thomson, M., Infield, D.: A high-resolution domestic building occupancy model for energy demand simulations. Energy and Buildings 40, 1560–1566 (2008)
9. Widen, J., Wackelgard, E.: A high-resolution stochastic model of domestic activity patterns and electricity demand. Applied Energy 87, 1880–1892 (2010)
10. Wood, G., Newborough, M.: Design and functionality of prospective energy-consumption displays. In: Proceedings of the 3rd International Conference on Energy Efficiency in Domestic Appliances and Lighting, pp. 757–70 (2003)
11. Kushiro, N., Suzuki, S., Nakata, M., Takahara, H., Inoue, M.: Integrated residential gateway controller for home energy management system. IEEE Transactions Consumer Electronics 49(3), 629–636 (2003)
12. POF. Pesquisa de orc amentos familiares 2008–2009. despesas, rendimentos e condições de vida. Instituto Brasileiro de Geografia e Física (Rio de Janeiro 2010)
13. Fogg, B. J.: Persuasive technology: using computers to change what we think and do. San Francisco, Calif. Oxford: Morgan Kaufmann; Elsevier Science (2003)
14. Cialdini, R.B.: Influence: The Psychology of Persuasion, revised edition. Harper-Collins (2007)

First Steps Toward an Auction-Based Traffic Signal Controller

Jeffery Raphael[1]([⊠]), Simon Maskell[2], and Elizabeth Sklar[1]

[1] Department of Computer Science, University of Liverpool, Liverpool, UK
{jeffery.raphael,e.i.sklar}@liverpool.ac.uk
[2] Department of Electrical Engineering and Electronics, University of Liverpool,
Liverpool, UK
s.maskell@liverpool.ac.uk

Abstract. As the cost of traffic congestion continues to rise traffic engineers have become more inclined to pursue Intelligent Traffic Systems to maximize the capacity of existing road networks. In this paper we demonstrate an auction-based traffic controller which exploits all the benefits of a market-based agent coordination system but it does not require vehicles to have any special software to utilize said system. Our auction-based traffic controller is better at reducing delay and increasing throughput in a simulated city, as compared to fixed-time signal controllers.

Keywords: Multi-agent systems · Auctions · Traffic signal control

1 Introduction

Traffic management focuses on improving the traffic flow of road networks using a variety of methods such as variable speed limits, road signs, traffic signals, lane management and ramp metering. Traffic signals are one of the most common means by which traffic flow is controlled. These simple devices are at the forefront of the fight against traffic congestion. Improving traffic performance through optimising traffic signal settings is more cost effective than making structural changes to roadways. Therefore there have been many attempts to develop algorithms to optimise traffic signal settings. Adaptive Urban Traffic Controllers (UTCs), such as RHODES [6], OPAC [3] and SCOOT[1] are systems that continually change traffic signal settings in order to prevent traffic congestion and maintain adequate traffic flow [7,11]. Adaptive UTCs use various road sensors to model traffic conditions and calculate the optimal traffic signal settings in real-time or offline. Adaptive UTC systems are difficult to develop, maintain and scale [11]. They often require expert knowledge in order to fine-tune their working parameters. Our long term goal is to develop an adaptive UTC that uses existing road sensors but provides a more flexible platform for managing traffic.

---

[1] http://www.scoot-utc.com

© Springer International Publishing Switzerland 2015
Y. Demazeau et al. (Eds.): PAAMS 2015, LNAI 9086, pp. 300–303, 2015.
DOI: 10.1007/978-3-319-18944-4_32

2   Main Purpose

Researchers have investigated many ways to cope with the complex and dynamic nature of traffic. We view traffic control as a coordination problem similar to those found in Multi-Robot Routing [4]. We propose using auctions to facilitate coordination behaviour amongst the traffic signals [2]. In our solution, traffic signal agents take part in auctions in order to manage the amount of time opposing vehicle manoeuvres have access to the intersection. This particular auction-based method of controlling the traffic signals is unique because it does not involve vehicles (or drivers) taking part in the auction. Using stationary agents in this manner offers many advantages over using vehicles as the focal point of the auction [9]. Other auction-based traffic controllers that rely on *vehicle agents* (software specifically designed to run on a vehicle that enables it to participate in the auction) [1,8,10] are entirely infeasible since such software (and prerequisite hardware) does not exist.

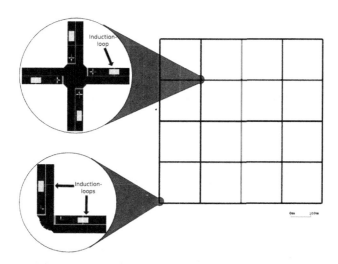

Fig. 1. Grid city (insets: SUMO junctions with vehicle detects (induction loops) labelled)

3   Demonstration

We demonstrate our auction-based traffic control method using *Simulation of Urban MObility (SUMO)* an open source microscopic traffic simulator [5]. We developed a client application to control the simulation using SUMO's Traffic Control Interface (TraCI) through a TCP socket. We demonstrate the effectiveness of our traffic control mechanism in a simulated Manhattan-style road network aptly named "Grid" city (shown in Figure 1).

Grid city contains 25 traffic signals, but only the 21 four-way junctions (the four corners do not have opposing traffic flows) have adaptive traffic signals.

At each intersection there are four induction-loops (vehicle detectors), one for each traffic flow entering the intersection, that provide data on the volume of traffic occurring at the intersection. The exact positions of the induction-loops are shown in the insets of Figure 1.

We examine two methods of traffic control (or traffic signal bidding rules): **Saturation (SAT)** and **Saturation with Queuing (SATQ)**.

SAT. In the SAT method, the traffic signal agents use the *saturation* (Equation 1) of their road segment as a bidding rule. The *saturation* of a road segment is the ratio of the volume of traffic (v) to its estimated capacity (c) (defined by the physical road network). Traffic signal agents are only concerned with the single block preceding the junction they manage. For example, the west/east traffic signal agent collects traffic data one block west and one block east of its location.

$$bid = v/c \qquad\qquad (1)$$

SATQ. The SATQ method functions similarly to the SAT method, except that its bidding rule (Equation 2) is augmented with road occupation (u) which is an indication of how "full" the road is. The road occupation provides vital information on the traffic behaviour of static vehicles or vehicle queues (which is not found in traffic volume measurements). A traffic camera could be used to obtain this data.

$$bid = (v/c) + u \qquad\qquad (2)$$

4 Conclusion

In this paper we present an auction-based traffic controller which does not use *vehicle agents*. Our approach takes advantage of road sensor devices (induction loops) that are currently available and in use by other adaptive UTCs such as SCOOT. Of particular interest is the ability of SATQ to reduce travel time even though the agents are acting locally. Our mechanism exhibits traits that make it ideal for a real-time adaptive traffic signal controller: it has minimal communications overhead, it is highly reactive to changing traffic conditions and its design is uncomplicated.

References

1. Carlino, D., Boyles, S.D., Stone, P.: Auction-based autonomous intersection management. In: Proceedings of the 16th IEEE Intelligent Transportation Systems Conference (ITSC) (2013)
2. Dias, M.B., Zlot, R., Kalra, N., Stentz, A.: Market-based multirobot coordination: A survey and analysis. Proceedings of the IEEE **94**(7), 1257–1270 (2006)

3. Gartner, N.H., Pooran, F.J., Andrews, C.M.: Implementation of the OPAC adaptive control strategy in a traffic signal network. In: IEEE Intelligent Transportation Systems. IEEE (2001)
4. Koenig, S, Tovey, C.A., Lagoudakis, M.G., Markakis, E., Kempe, D., Keskinocak, P., Kleywegt, A.J., Meyerson, A., Jain, S.: The power of sequential single-item auctions for agent coordination. In: Proceedings of the 21st National Conference on Artificial Intelligence, AAAI 2006, vol. 2, pp. 1625–1629. AAAI Press (2006)
5. Krajzewicz, D., Erdmann, J., Behrisch, M., Bieker, L.: Recent development and applications of SUMO - simulation of urban MObility. International Journal on Advances in Systems and Measurements 5(3&4), 128–138 (2012)
6. Mirchandani, P., Wang, F.-Y.: RHODES to intelligent transportation systems. IEEE Intelligent Systems 20(1), 10–15 (2005)
7. Mladenovic, M., Abbas, M.: A survey of experiences with adaptive traffic control systems in north america. Journal of Road and Traffic Engineering 59(2), 5–11 (2013)
8. Schepperle, H., Bhm, K.: Auction-based traffic management: towards effective concurrent utilization of road intersections. In: CEC/EEE, pp. 105–112. IEEE (2008)
9. Tumer, K., Agogino, A.: Distributed agent-based air traffic flow management. In: Proceedings of the Sixth International Joint Conference on Autonomous Agents and Multiagent Systems, pp. 330–337, May 2007
10. Vasirani, M., Ossowski, S.: A market-inspired approach for intersection management in urban road traffic networks. Journal Artificial Intelligence Research 43, 621–659 (2012)
11. Wang, F.-Y.: Agent-based control for networked traffic management systems. IEEE Intelligent Systems 20(5), 92–96 (2005)

Addressing Long-Term Digital Preservation Through Computational Intelligence

Jose Antonio Olvera[✉] and Josep Lluis de la Rosa

TECNIO - Centre EASY, Agents Research Lab, VICOROB Institute,
University of Girona, 17071 Girona, Spain
joseantonio.olvera@udg.edu, peplluis@eia.udg.edu

Keywords: Multi-agent system · Simulation · Digital preservation · Computational intelligence

1   Introduction

The challenge in long term digital preservation (LTDP) of complex objects – consisting of text, video, images, music, 3D information, sensor data, etc. generated throughout all areas of our society – is real and growing at an exponential pace. An already old study by the International Data Corporation (IDC) found that in 2012 the information created and replicated broke the zettabyte barrier growing by a factor of 9 in just five years [2]. The LTDP of such information will become a pervasive as well as ubiquitous problem that will concern everyone who has digital information to be kept for long time, implying a shift in at least a couple of software and hardware generations.

Currently the level of automation in DP solutions is low. The preservation process currently involves many manual stages but should be approached in a flexible and distributed way, combining intelligent automated methods with human intervention. The scalability of existing preservation solutions has been poorly demonstrated; and solutions have often not been properly tested against diverse digital resources or in heterogeneous environments [4]. These problems, together with the rapid obsolescence of software and hardware due to frequent update of private vendors, make DP one of the most challenging application areas for MAS.

As was explained at [3], the prevailing paradigm is centralized, top-down, where institutions are the main players. We propose studying a change of paradigm, mainly bottom-up, where the digital objects *self-preserve*.

Our research is based in studying what self-preservation behaviors need the digital objects (DOs), based in computation intelligence (CI), and related methods of cost management under their own budget, powered by a social network as an environment that enables their behavior under the policy that "preservation is to share". In this concept, DOs become active actors in their own LTDP, here named the Self-Preserving Digital Object (SPDO) [1], which has a DP budget devoted to funding the replication of the objects and other operations such as format migration or finding a safe storage within a social network of users; in all, an environment where they will "live".

© Springer International Publishing Switzerland 2015
Y. Demazeau et al. (Eds.): PAAMS 2015, LNAI 9086, pp. 304–307, 2015.
DOI: 10.1007/978-3-319-18944-4_33

2   Main Purpose

We focus on the migration strategy (ensure that the digital information is re-encoded in new formats before the old format becomes obsolete) to simulate DP activities of refreshing and migration while SPDOs sharing using different computational intelligence methodologies. We conceived the migration of SPDO formats as a replication (copies) of files in different formats and refreshing as a copy in the same format. The SPDOs will be distributed over a network of computers or devices as an environment that enables the behavior of the SPDOs in an attempt to preserve them.

Migrated copies of SPDOs are created in various formats following a migration strategy to ensure their survival against Software Adoption Waves (SAW), which occur regularly. SAW are defined as massive format changes that DOs suffer throughout their lifetime after the shifts of software and hardware, resulting in the likely "disappearance" of a percentage of the SPDOs when they become unreadable or inaccessible due to the accumulation of technological changes that provokes their obsolescence.

In our model, a network with nodes represents the users' computers (the sites) and the connections among nodes determine which users are friends with who else, resulting in a social network devoted to the DP.

In all the experiments, DOs travel through the network that is build up out of a social network and distribute copies of them for preservation. These copies maintain links to the parent SPDO because they correspond to a same object. Each node representing a user's computer might only be able to read a specific format of files after suffering a SAW. Formats range from *oldest* to *newest* to simulate the processing of files in a computer when these files can only be read by special software installed in the computer (the site). The files in older formats become *unreadable* when they are no longer compatible with the new software versions installed on a given computer after several migrations.

The following describes the three CI algorithms that have been implemented over the SPDO behaviors:

- Multi-Population Genetic Algorithm (MPGA),
- Ant Colony Algorithm (ACA),
- and Virus-Based Algorithm (VBA), approach that we implanted it similar to a computer *worm*. SPDOs try to move through the entire network selecting connections randomly but attempting to spread as far away as possible replicating themselves, with some limitations for not collapsing the system.

3   Demonstration

TiM simulations are deployed over 35-year period in which a SAW occurs every 5 years. After every SAW it is the time at which SPDOs show severe symptoms of obsolescence and an urgent need of DP or curation. We use the month as the temporal unit at every step for our simulations, and thus, there is a SAW every 60 steps (12 months × 5 years), and an execution has a total length of 420 steps (12 months x 35 years). The three CI algorithms as a SPDO behaviors have been simulated and Table 1 shows all the parameters of the simulations.

Table 1. Formulation of the parameters used for the TiM experiment

Parameters	MPGA	ACA	VBA
Total simulation time		35 years	
Equivalence of 1 simulation step		1 month	
Total waves		6 (for 35 years)	
Percentage of DOs involved in a SAW		72%	
# DOs associated to any user		Between 1 and 5	
Preservation service for each user		100%	
Percentage of statistical stability		99.3%	
Random seed		123456789	
Percentage of mutation	2% of the population		
Percentage of exchange	2% of the population		
Percentage of nodes of the network where ants can make copies		20%	
Period in which nodes are changed where ants can make copies		3 years	
Maximum number of copies that a DO can have at each site			1

The function watts.strogatz.game() from R package igraph was used to create the small-world graph of 1000 nodes. The graph was checked to ensure that it was simple and connected. The clustering coefficient (CC) resulting from the graph is 0.48 and the average path length (APL) is 4.41. It was added as default network that can be chosen with the simulator.

The results of the experiments are shown in Fig. 1, that show the evolution of the average entropy over the simulation period, where the X axis are the steps of the simulation (months) and the Y axis is the entropy value (measure that indicates the

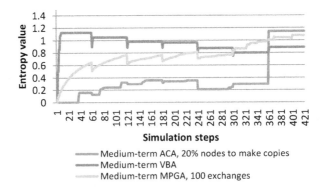

Fig. 1. Comparison of CI algorithms over 35-year period

preservability of the system). Looking the results obtained with this experiments, in the end of the simulation the highest entropy value is obtained with the ACA, but the period before is also of the same importance (SPDO must be accessible and reproducible by users at any time) and in that case both VBA and MPGA are better solutions than ACA. In this case is difficult to select the best because the three executions have positive entropy values during all the simulation, but the one that have higher entropy as a mean is VBA (high entropy value indicates high expected preservation).

4   Conclusions

In this paper we have presented an environment that simulates the digital assets onto the future and allows studying what self-preservation behaviors need the digital objects, based in computation intelligence, and related methods of cost management under their own budget, powered by a social network as an environment that enables their behavior under the policy that preservation is to share. The key differentiation feature of TiM is that digital objects become active actors in their own long term digital preservation. Then, TiM design considerations and implementation details are presented. Additionally, a demonstration illustrates some of the functionalities of our proposal.

Future work will follow in the direction of studying variations of the CI algorithms that we performed, adding electronic auctions of preservation and curation services for these objects to be preserved and use real social network topologies and make the topology varying with time to have more realistic simulation.

We hope that TiM evolves with the addition of new functionalities and that this software becomes a helpful tool for the digital preservation research community.

References

1. de la Rosa J.L., Olvera, J.A.: First Studies on Self-Preserving Digital Objects. Artificial Intelligence Research & Dev. In: Procs 15th Intl Conf. of the Catalan Assoc. for Artificial Intelligence, CCIA 2012, Alacant, Spain, vol. 248, pp. 213–222 (2012)
2. Gantz, J., Reisel, D.: The Digital Universe in 2020: Big Data, Bigger Digital Shadows, and Biggest Growth in the Far East (December 2012)
3. Olvera, J.A.: Digital Preservation: a New Approach from Computational Intelligence. In: Joint Conference on Digital Libraries 2013, JCDL Doctoral Consortium 2013, July 22-26, Indianapolis, Indiana, USA (2013)
4. Quisbert, H.: On Long-term Digital Information Preservation Systems – a Framework and Characteristics for Development. Ph D Thesis. Luleå University of Technology (2008)

Representing Social Emotions in MAS

J.A. Rincon[⊠], V. Julian, and C. Carrascosa

Departamento de Sistemas Informáticos y Computación (DSIC),
Universitat Politècnica de València, Camino de Vera s/n, Valencia, Spain
{jrincon,vinglada,carrasco}@dsic.upv.es

Abstract. This article aims to give an approach of a social emotional model, which allows to extract, calculate, represent and manage the social emotion of a group of intelligent entities. The emotional model is based on the PAD model allowing the representation of the emotion of a group of intelligent entities in a 3-D space. The social emotional model presented in this paper uses individual emotions of each one of the entities, which are represented in the emotional space PAD. The social emotional model allows the creation of simulations, in which the emotional states are used in the decision-making of the intelligent entities.

1 Introduction

Human beings manage themselves in different environments, either in the working place, at home or in public places. At each one of these places we perceive a wide range of stimuli, that interfere in our commodity levels modifying our emotional levels. For instance, the high levels of noise or the temperature conditions may produce stress situations. Before each one of these stimuli, humans answer varying our face gestures, body or bio-electrical ones. These variations in our emotional states could be used as information useful for machines. Nevertheless, it is needed that the machines will have the capability of interpreting or recognising such variations. This is the reason for implementing emotional models that interpret or represent the different emotions. Emotional models such as OCC [1] presented by *Ortony, Clore & Collins* and the PAD model [2] are the most used ones to detect or simulate emotional states. Nevertheless, these models don't allow to execute intelligent decisions based on the emotional state perception.

In this work we define a social emotional model which includes multiple emotions between humans and software agents. Our model is based on the PAD model to represent the social emotion of a group. Specifically, our proposal employs the emotional state of a group of agents (humans or not) in an AmI application. Concretely, we propose in this paper a system for controlling automatically the music which is playing in a bar. The main goal of the DJ is to play music making that all individuals within the bar are mostly as happy as possible. Each of the individuals is represented by an agent, which has an emotional response according to his musical taste. That is, depending on the musical genre of the song, agents will respond varying their emotional state. Moreover, varying emotions of the agents will modify the social emotion of the group.

© Springer International Publishing Switzerland 2015
Y. Demazeau et al. (Eds.): PAAMS 2015, LNAI 9086, pp. 308–311, 2015.
DOI: 10.1007/978-3-319-18944-4_34

2   Social Emotional Model

This section proposes a model of social emotion based on the PAD emotional model. To define a model of social emotion, it is necessary first to define the representation of an emotional state of an agent on the PAD model. The emotion of an agent ag_i is defined as a vector in a space $\mathbb{R}^3$, represented by three components that make up the PAD emotional model. The variation of each component allows to modify the emotional state of the agent (Eq. 1).

$$\vec{E}(ag_i) = [P_i, A_i, D_i] \qquad (1)$$

The social emotion representation of a group of n agents $Ag = \{ag_1, ag_2, ..., ag_n\}$ is composed by a triplet that allows us to define the social emotion (SE). This triplet is formed by a central emotional vector $\overrightarrow{CE}(Ag)$ (obtained by averaging the P, A, D values of the group of agents); the maximal distance vector $\vec{m}(Ag)$ (which is a measure of the maximum euclidean distance of the agents with respect to the $\overrightarrow{CE}$); and the standard deviation (SD) vector $\vec{\sigma}(Ag)$ (which allows the calculation of the level of emotional dispersion of the group of agents around the central emotion $\overrightarrow{CE}(Ag)$). This triplet can be expressed as follows (Eq. 2):

$$SE(Ag) = (\overrightarrow{CE}(Ag), \vec{m}(Ag), \vec{\sigma}(Ag)) \qquad (2)$$

Based on this model it is possible to determine the emotional distance among different groups of agents or between the same group in different instants of time. This will allow to measure the emotional distance between the current social emotional group and a possible emotional target. This approach would facilitate the decision making in order to take actions to try to move the social emotion to a particular area of the PAD space or to allow that the emotional state of a group of agents can be approached or moved away from other groups of agents. From an emotional point of view, these movements or actions are domain-dependent and are out of the scope of this model. In Equation 3 the profile of the function which calculates the emotional distance of two groups of agents is defined.

$$\Delta : SE(Ag^i), SE(Ag^j) \to [-1, 1] \qquad (3)$$

According to this profile, Equation 4 shows how we calculate this emotional variation. The equation calculates three distances corresponding to the three components of the SE. Given two groups of agents $SE(Ag^i), SE(Ag^j)$, the emotional distance between these two groups is calculated as:

$$\Delta(SE(Ag^i), SE(Ag^j)) = \frac{1}{2}\Big(\omega_c \Delta_c(\overrightarrow{CE}(Ag^i), \overrightarrow{CE}(Ag^j))$$
$$+\omega_d \Delta_d(\vec{m}(Ag^i), \vec{m}(Ag^j)) \qquad (4)$$
$$+\omega_v \Delta_v(\vec{\sigma}(Ag^i), \vec{\sigma}(Ag^j))\Big)$$

$$where \quad \omega_c + \omega_d + \omega_v = 1; \quad \omega_c, \omega_d, \omega_v \in [0, 1] \qquad (5)$$

Calculating the distance among social emotions allows the study of the behavior of emotional model based agents, either minimizing or maximizing the $\Delta(SE(Ag^i), SE(Ag^j))$ function. This way, it can be achieved that an agent group approaches or move away of an specific emotional state. To do this, it is necessary to modify through stimuli the individual emotions from each agent and therefore changing the social emotion. Nevertheless, how to maximize or minimize the emotional distance is domain-dependent and it is out of the scope of the paper.

3   Demo

A practical application which uses the previously proposed model is presented in this section. This application example is based on how music can influence in a positive or negative way over emotional states [3]. The application example is developed in a bar, where there is a DJ agent in charge of play music and a specific number of individuals listening the music. The main goal of the DJ is to play music making that all individuals within the bar are mostly happy as possible. Each of the individuals will be represented by an agent, which has an emotional response according to its musical taste. That is, depending on the musical genre of the song, agents will respond varying their emotional state. Moreover, varying emotions of each agent will modify the social emotion of the group. The different scenarios have been designed in order to show how the social emotion can facilitate the decision making of the DJ. In each scenario the DJ agent plays a song. Once the song has ended, the DJ evaluates the social emotion of the group of listeners that are within the bar. In this way, the DJ agent can evaluate the effect that the song has had the song over the audience. This will help the DJ to decide whether to continue with the same musical genre or not in order to improve the emotional state of the group.

As an example, we can see Figure 1, where we show a vitrual distribution of the bar where different entities represent humans that are in the real world. To build it we used Unity3D[1] to create the virtual representation, and we used free 3D models for the bar and human representation[2]. On the right of Figure 1 it can be seen the representation of the emotional states of the group of agents. In this case the emotional states of the agents are very close. This low emotional difference may be due mainly because the agents have little differences in their musical tastes. The social emotion in this scenario has a $\overrightarrow{CE}(Ag)$ very close to all the values of the agents and the $\overrightarrow{m}(Ag)$ and $\overrightarrow{\sigma}(Ag)$ values will be very small and in many cases close to zero. This provokes that the DJ will try to play songs of similar generes trying to maintain this situation, which is not the ideal situation but it can be considered as a very good situation.

As it can be see in the Figure 1 all the represented emotions in this group are around the emotion *Happy*, achieving a social emotion with these values of $SE(Ag) = ([0.85, 0.0, 0.9], [0.85, 0.0, 0.9], [0.07, 0.0, 0.06])$.

---

[1] http://unity3d.com/
[2] http://tf3dm.com/3d-model/vega-strike-starship-bar-economy-class-88446.html,
http://tf3dm.com/3d-model/alexia-89488.html,
http://tf3dm.com/3d-model/dante-33087.html

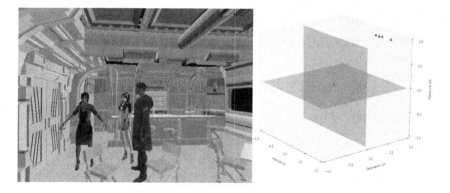

Fig. 1. An example scenario of the virtual bar and a graphical representation of the social emotion when the agents have similar musical tastes

4   Conclusions and Future Work

A new model for representing social emotions has been presented in this paper, giving a first approach for the detection and simulation of social emotions in a group of intelligent entities. The proposed model uses the individual emotions of each entity of a group in order to calculate and represent the emotional state of that group. Moreover, the model adds the mechanisms to compare the social emotional state of two groups of agents or the social emotion of a group in different time instants. The social emotion of a group of agents not only allows a global view of the emotional situation of the group, moreover it facilitates the group decision making in order to change the emotional state of the group or only of a subgroup of the agents. The paper introduces also a demo about how to calculate, represent and use the social emotion of a group of persons which are in a pub.

Acknowledgments. This work is partially supported by the MINECO/FEDER TIN2012-36586-C03-01 and the FPI grant AP2013-01276 awarded to Jaime-Andres Rincon.

References

1. Ortony, A.: The Cognitive Structure of Emotions. Cambridge University Press, May 1990
2. Mehrabian, A.: Analysis of affiliation-related traits in terms of the PAD temperament model. The Journal of Psychology **131**(1), 101–117 (1997)
3. Whitman, B., Smaragdis, P.: Combining musical and cultural features for intelligent style detection. In: Proc. of the 3rd International Conference on Music Information Retrieval (ISMIR 2002), pp. 47–52, Paris, France, October 2002

Developing Agent-Based Driver Assistance Systems Using AgentDrive

Martin Schaefer[✉] and Jiri Vokrinek

Agent Technology Center, Department of Computer Science, Faculty of Electrical Engineering, Czech Technical University in Prague, Prague, Czech Republic
{martin.schaefer,jiri.vokrinek}@fel.cvut.cz
http://agents.fel.cvut.cz/agentdrive/

Abstract. We demonstrate how AgentDrive platform can be used to develop agent-based driver assistance systems. We expect that new V2X technologies penetrating automotive industry can lead to more sophisticated coordination mechanisms among road vehicles. Driver assistance system that is enabled to communicate with other vehicles promises safer and more efficient future of road traffic. AgentDrive allows to prototype agent-based coordination mechanisms. The developer using our platform is provided with a tool to prepare realistic simulation scenarios. The scenarios are based on real world data generated from OpenStreetMap. The development of the sophisticated multi-agent coordination algorithms is supported by possibility to evaluate the algorithms in arbitrary level of simulation detail. Human-in-the-loop simulation is enabled by integrating a driving simulator. Developers are empowered to challenge multi-agent coordination algorithms by the presence of a human driver in the control loop.

Keywords: Multi-agent simulation · Autonomous vehicles coordination · Integrated drive and traffic simulation · Advanced driver assistance system

1 Introduction

Road safety and comfort of the drivers motivate development of Advanced Driver Assistance Systems (ADAS). All of the key players in automotive industry equip new models with various assistance systems, e.g., adaptive cruise control, emergency braking system or parking assist.

Nowadays the ADAS technology is based on single robot principles. Data is collected by sensors, fusion and interpretation of sensory data precede reasoning. The systems in most cases present the result of the reasoning to the driver, in some cases directly apply actuation.

The concept of connected vehicles based on the V2X technologies opens the field to new approaches. Communication between vehicles or communication of vehicles and road infrastructure enables applying more advanced coordination mechanisms. There is possibility of distributed sensing among vehicles. Moreover, explicit cooperation of vehicles can solve conflicting situations in traffic.

© Springer International Publishing Switzerland 2015
Y. Demazeau et al. (Eds.): PAAMS 2015, LNAI 9086, pp. 312–315, 2015.
DOI: 10.1007/978-3-319-18944-4_35

2   Main Purpose

AgentDrive is a multi-agent simulation platform for development of advanced coordination mechanisms of road vehicles [2]. The platform supports prototyping of advanced driver assistance systems. AgentDrive provides a developer with a realistic simulation. The scenarios are generated from real world maps – OpenStreetMaps[1] (OSM). The architecture of AgentDrive is depicted in Figure 1.

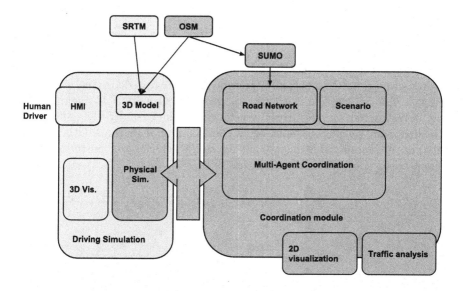

Fig. 1. AgentDrive architecture. Core of the AgentDrive platform is highlighted by red color. Coordination is to be implemented in multi-agent coordination module. The environment of the module – road network is generated using SUMO tools from OSM map data. Physics of the vehicles is simulated in external physics simulation. The physics simulation can be implemented by a driving simulator. In case the driving simulation is used, the blue modules are additionally available.

The architecture is modular, for example simulation of physics is performed in several levels of realism. Built-in idealistic simulation with perfect execution is used for initial experiments with algorithms. Later, an integration of realistic driving simulation offers validation in more realistic environment. Integration with various external simulators and a HMI devices is possible, e.g., for cooperative drive on highway [4].

---

[1] http://www.openstreetmap.org/

3 Demonstration

Lane merging assistant is a particular ADAS to increase road safety mainly on highways. We demonstrate on this example how AgentDrive platform can be used:

1. to prepare a simulation scenario,
2. to prototype the ADAS logic using agent technologies,
3. to perform proof-of-concept simulations,
4. to evaluate usability by introducing Human-in-the-loop simulation.

Simulation scenario in AgentDrive is generated from chosen OSM area. Extracted road network is used for navigation of the vehicles by controlling mechanisms in coordination module (see Figure 1). Physics simulation, 3D visualization and Human-machine interaction is provided by integrated driving simulator – OpenDS[2]. The interaction with human driver is visualized in Figure 2. The driver is instructed by the driver assistance system visually. The suggestions for the driver are outputs of multi-agent coordination algorithms. Other vehicles (traffic) are autonomous. It means that the traffic vehicles are controlled directly by agent-based coordination mechanism.

Fig. 2. Driver's view in OpenDS with integrated HMI for collision avoidance support. The system provides the driver with the visual representation of a proposed plan. The proposed lane to follow is highlighted by blue, the speed adjustment is proposed via green or red signal of appropriate intensity. There is an example of an instruction to change lane to left to overtake (left image). Second case shows how the red color informs the driver of proposal to slow down (right image) because of speeding in this case.

The core of the implementation of the ADAS functionality is in the Multi-Agent Coordination module (see Figure 1). Each vehicle is represented by an agent in the coordination module. An agent's reasoning is based on the sensed state of the environment. Considering the example of the lane merging assistant, the agent needs to consider vehicles around and to decide how to adjust the speed and whether it is desirable to change the lane or not. There is variety

---

[2] http://opends.de

of approaches that can implement such a coordination mechanism in the Agent-Drive platform. We already experimented with reactive methods [1] or cooperative planning [3].

4 Conclusions

AgentDrive platform supports development of agent-based driver assistance systems. The agent-based approach for such application is motivated by vehicular communication and its consequence of need for sophisticated coordination mechanisms in road traffic domain. Realistic simulations with human drivers, real world based scenarios and agent-based coordination framework offer a wide range of applications. Multi-agent coordination prototyping, user acceptability or studies of impact of the novel coordination approaches on the traffic flow are examples of the topics that can be addressed by AgentDrive platform. Development of an advanced driver assistance system need to cover all of the mentioned steps.

Acknowledgments. This work was supported by the Grant Agency of the Czech Technical University in Prague, grant No. SGS15/209/OHK3/3T/13 and by the Ministry of Education, Youth and Sports of Czech Republic within the grant no. LD12044.

References

1. Schaefer, M.: Collision Avoidance of Highway Traffic, Czech Technical University in Prague (2014)
2. Schaefer, M., Vokrinek, J.: AgentDrive: towards an agent-based coordination of intelligent cars. In: Advances in Practical Applications of Agents, Multi-Agent Systems, and Sustainability. The PAAMS Collection (2015)
3. Vokrinek, J., Janovsky, P., Faigl, J., Benda, P., Tango, F., Pinotti, D.: A cooperative driver model for traffic simulations. In: 2013 11th IEEE International Conference on Industrial Informatics (INDIN), pp. 756–761, July 2013
4. Vokrinek, J., Schaefer, M., Pinotti, D.: Multi-agent traffic simulation for human-in-the-loop cooperative drive systems testing. In: Proceedings of the 2014 International Conference on Autonomous Agents and Multi-agent Systems. International Foundation for Autonomous Agents and Multiagent Systems, pp. 1691–1692 (2014)

Demonstration of Realistic Multi-agent Scenario Generator for Electricity Markets Simulation

Francisco Silva[✉], Brígida Teixeira, Tiago Pinto, Gabriel Santos,
Isabel Praça, and Zita Vale

GECAD – Knowledge Engineering and Decision-Support Research Center,
Institute of Engineering – Politechnic of Porto (ISEP/IPP), Porto, Portugal
{fspsa,bccta,tmcfp,gajls,icp,zav}@isep.ipp.pt

1   Introduction

Worldwide electricity markets (EM) have undertaken a great revolution with the emergence of the liberalized market [1]. The restructuring of the constituent sectors of EM (production, marketing, transportation and distribution) turned EM into a more competitive environment, which in turn led to increased decision-making difficulty. In order to overcome the complexity and unpredictability of this sector, simulation tools began to be a great investment area. EM simulators are tools that help clarifying the functioning of markets in order to create profiles of the participant players through the analysis, study and forecast of different scenarios [2]. The profiles of participant players allow the understanding of the type of strategies taken by them and support their decision-making processes.

The emergence of simulation platforms has been a huge added value since it revolutionized the understanding of the markets operation. Additionally, simulation platforms allow the testing of different participants' behaviors as well as new rules and operations of regulators and market participants [3-5].

However, simulators of multi-agent energy markets face some problems when it comes to apply the simulated results in reality. In order to create realistic scenarios it is necessary to consider all the real information about the characteristics and behaviors of the players, as well as markets' specifications. This information is available on web platforms of market operators (e.g. MIBEL market data is available in [6]); however, it is not easily interpreted or extracted, which brings many limitations to the process of generating realistic scenarios. Once this limitation is surpassed and the necessary information is obtained, the main problem becomes the treatment of this information in order to create simulations of realistic scenarios.

In order to overcome the difficulty that EM simulators face to create realistic scenarios, the Realistic Scenarios Generator (RealScen) has been developed [7]. RealScen uses real data gathered from diverse sources to define the amount, characteristics and behavior of the software agents used in EM simulations, depending on the simulation requirements and on each EM specifications.

© Springer International Publishing Switzerland 2015
Y. Demazeau et al. (Eds.): PAAMS 2015, LNAI 9086, pp. 316–319, 2015.
DOI: 10.1007/978-3-319-18944-4_36

2   Main Purpose

RealScen has been developed with the purpose of providing EM simulators with adequate means to create realistic scenarios [7]. In particular, RealScen allows obtaining and processing real data and using this data to create the desired scenario. RealScen also allows managing the dimension of the created scenario taking into account possible limitations of processing resources and execution time required to perform simulations, given that usually thousands of players participate in real EM.

In order to accomplish its purpose, the scenario generation process, presented in Fig. 1, starts with the selection of real data to consider for the scenario. It is possible to indicate what market types to consider (e.g. Day-Ahead Market and Balancing Market), or even consider market types originating from different markets (e.g. Day-Ahead Market of MIBEL and Balancing Market of EPEX).

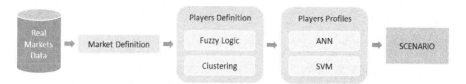

Fig. 1. RealScen scenarios generation process

After selecting the desired data, RealScen allows reducing the dimension of the scenario through data mining techniques, in order to facilitate the study of the generated scenario. Fuzzy logic is applied in order to support the determination of the best dimension for the scenario by combining the desired size (indicated by the user) with the amount of existing data, resulting in the most appropriate value of scenario dimension. In order to create the desired amount of agents from a larger source of data concerning all real market players a clustering technique is used. This technique enables grouping real players by the similarity of the characteristics chosen by the user. The players' characteristics that are used for the clustering process may have different weights to indicate their impact on the clustering process. Once this process is completed, the limited amount of created agents is able to represent a summarization of the larger quantity of real players that has been initially read. Thus, RealScen allows obtaining scenarios with smaller dimensions, which represent lower simulation times and resource consumption without losing the quality of the data.

After the definition of the size of the picture, RealScen allows creating Virtual Power Players (VPP) [8]. VPPs are entities that manage aggregations of lower dimension agents that, by themselves, cannot compete on equal terms on the market with larger dimension agents.

Finally, in order to be able to simulate the desired EM with the obtained agents, a price and energy forecast is performed for the selected day based on their historical energy transactions. RealScen uses three forecasting methods: Artificial Neural Networks (ANN), Support Vector Machines (SVM) and simple averages. Considering several methods allows the user to choose between a better quality forecast, but with a longer runtime or a much faster forecast yet with not so good prediction abilities.

3   Demonstration

The process of generating a scenario consists of several sequential steps. Therefore, in order to facilitate their creation process, a wizard has been implemented (see Fig. 2). The wizard allows the user to track the steps of scenario creation by following the current step in the side menu. If the user wants to go back and make any changes, he/she can do so by clicking the button for the corresponding step.

Fig. 2. RealScen's wizard to create a new scenario

The first step of the scenario generation is the choice of the markets from which data concerning real players will be considered. The user can specify one or more market types originating from the same market and mix market types originating from different markets. The following step features another selection of market types, but this time referring to the market types for which the created scenario is intended.

After the selection of markets, it is possible to indicate the date from which real data will be considered. In addition to the initial date, the user can also specify a target date, which concerns the date for the created scenario, for which the forecast of energy and prices offers for the selected agents will be performed. For that purpose, the desired forecast method and the corresponding parameters must be indicated.

The following step relates to the clustering process, and it is composed of two parts: the specification of the characteristics by which agents will be grouped together and the assignment of weights to these characteristics. If the user wishes to consider VPPs, he/she can create them by selecting the agents that constitute the VPP. Otherwise he/she can move on to the next and final step.

The wizard of scenario generation ends with the options to save the results and the profile of the scenario. The scenario profile consists of the set of user-chosen configurations during the scenario creation. Saving the scenario profile allows the user to repeat the creation of the same scenario, or to create a similar scenario based on the core characteristics of a previously defined scenario.

4   Conclusion

Due to the constant changes that EM are subject to and the increasing complexity in these environments, EM simulators are, more than ever, essential for the study and comprehension of EM. EM simulators are tools with the ability to study the characteristics, behavior, rules and other specifications of the markets in order to support players in their participation in these markets and operators and regulators in foreseeing market behavior and experiment potential changes and alternative market solutions. The projection of simulated results into the reality is however a difficult task due to the huge number of participant entities and the dynamism and unpredictability of the EM sector.

In order to increase the potential of EM simulators, RealScen generates realistic simulation scenarios through real transaction data, being able to represent participants in a smaller sample, in order to simplify the study of their behavior and help them in the decision-making process. In addition, new markets with unique characteristics can be studied and compared due to the possibility provided by RealScen of combining market types from different markets, hence diversifying the study range and potential.

Acknowledgements. This work is supported by FEDER Funds through COMPETE program and by National Funds through FCT under the projects FCOMP-01-0124-FEDER: PEst-OE/EEI/UI0760/2015 and PTDC/EEA-EEL/122988/2010; and by the SASGER-MeC project no. NORTE-07-0162-FEDER-000101, co-funded by COMPETE under FEDER Programme

References

1. Meeus, L., et al.: Development of the Internal Electricity Market in Europe. The Electricity Journal **18**(6), 25–35 (2005)
2. Pinto, T., et al.: Adaptive learning in agents behaviour: A framework for electricity markets simulation. Integrated Computer-Aided Engineering **21**(4), 399–415 (2014)
3. Li, H., Tesfatsion, L.: Development of Open Source Software for Power Market Research: The AMES Test Bed. Journal of Energy Markets **2**(2), 111–128 (2009)
4. Koritarov, V.: Real-World Market Representation with Agents: Modeling the Electricity Market as a Complex Adaptive System with an Agent-Based Approach. IEEE Power & Energy Magazine, 39–46 (2004)
5. Praça, I., et al.: MASCEM: A Multi-Agent System that Simulates Competitive Electricity Markets. IEEE Intelligent Systems **18**(6), 54–60 (2003)
6. MIBEL data files. http://www.omie.es/aplicaciones/datosftp/datosftp.jsp?path=/. (last accessed January 2014)
7. Teixeira, B., et.al.: Data Mining Approach to support the Generation of Realistic Scenarios for Multi-Agent simulation of Electricity Markets. In: IA 2014 – Intelligent Agents (IA) at the IEEE SSCI 2014 (IEEE Symposium Series on Computational Intelligence), Orlando, Florida, USA, December 09–12 (2014)
8. Pinto, T., et al.: A new approach for multi-agent coalition formation and management in the scope of electricity markets. Energy **36**(8), 5004–5015 (2011)

Smart Grids Simulation with MECSYCO

Julien Vaubourg[1,3,4](✉), Yannick Presse[1,3,4], Benjamin Camus[2,3,4],
Christine Bourjot[2,3,4], Laurent Ciarletta[1,3,4], Vincent Chevrier[2,3,4],
Jean-Philippe Tavella[3,4], Hugo Morais[3,4], Boris Deneuville[3,4],
and Olivier Chilard[3,4]

[1] Inria, 54600 Villers-lès-Nancy, France
{julien.vaubourg,yannick.presse,laurent.ciarletta}@inria.fr
[2] Université de Lorraine, LORIA, UMR 7503, 54506 Vandœuvre-lès-Nancy, France
{benjamin.camus,Christine.Bourjot,vincent.chevrier}@loria.fr
[3] CNRS, LORIA, UMR 7503, 54506 Vandœuvre-lès-Nancy, France
[4] EDF - R&D MIRE/R44, 1 avenue du Général de Gaulle, BP 408,
92141 Clamart cedex, France
{jean-philippe.tavella,Hugo.Morais,Boris.Deneuville,
Olivier.Chilard}@edf.fr

Keywords: Multi-agent · Smart grids · Multi-modeling · Co-simulation ·
DEVS

1 Introduction

These demonstrations show the current results of the DEVS-based platform
called MECSYCO (Multi-agent Environment for Complex SYstems CO-simulation), formerly named AA4MM (Agents & Artifacts for Multi-Modeling[1]), in
the context of smart grids simulation with different use cases based on real
scenarios.

This work (described in [2]) results of MS4SG (Multi-Simulation for Smart-
Grids), a joint project between LORIA-INRIA and EDF R&D which aims at
providing attractive technological solutions to test new distributed algorithms
(e.g. advanced voltage management) or original operating mode (e.g. islanding)
before their use in real prototypes and even in the real networks.

2 Smart Grid Simulation

The modeling and simulation of a smart grid system should integrate different domains of expertise (at least: power grid; communication; and information
and decision systems). In MS4SG, each domain uses different tools; and, in
the same domain, several different tools may have to cohabit. For example, the
electricity domain uses executable Modelica[3] models exported from Dymola
[4] or EMTP-RV (ElectoMagnetic Transient Program, Restructured Version[5])
as modeling tools of power grid components; the telecommunication network

© Springer International Publishing Switzerland 2015
Y. Demazeau et al. (Eds.): PAAMS 2015, LNAI 9086, pp. 320–323, 2015.
DOI: 10.1007/978-3-319-18944-4_37

domain may use NS-3[6] or OMNeT++[7] depending on the protocols requirements; and decision systems can be modeled with UML-oriented tools such as
Enterprise Architect [8].

The central problem is then the multi-simulation that intends to simulate
the whole as the coordinated simulation of several heterogeneous and interacting simulators. Handling heterogeneity and enabling the interaction between
components can be envisaged at different levels such as the one of formalisms,
of time management, of information representation, etc.; with the constraint of
integrating co-simulation norms and standards.

The solution we adopted is based on a meta-modeling approach with multi-
agent concepts (Agents and Artifacts [9]) to describe a heterogeneous multi-model.
These concepts are formalized with DEVS[10] (Discrete Event System Specification) operational specifications. The DEVS formalism ensures the integration of
different formalisms with simulation algorithms. We chose as simulation algorithm
the parallel conservative DEVS simulator based on the Chandy-Misra algorithm
[11] that enables a decentralized execution. We exploited its possibility by implementing the concepts either in C++ or in Java.

The resulting middleware, MECSYCO, is able to integrate the different kinds
of heterogeneity of the smart grid use cases and to simulate the whole in a
decentralized way.

3   The Concept-Grid Use Case

The demonstration is a use case, Concept-Grid, that combines electrical models
and communication network models with a decisional system model. These three
kinds of model correspond to the three main fields of smart grids. This use case
was tested with a real life demonstrator stated at EDF Lab Les Renardières and
named Concept-Grid. This demonstrator includes an MV/LV electrical grid with
five real houses enabling measurements to compare with the simulation results.

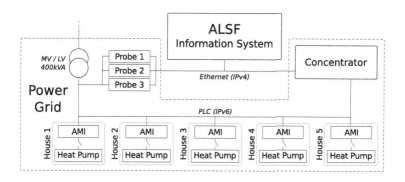

Fig. 1. Overview of the Concept-Grid use case

A general overview of the use case is described in Fig. 1. It corresponds
to a load shedder with a cascado-cyclic algorithm and five consuming houses.

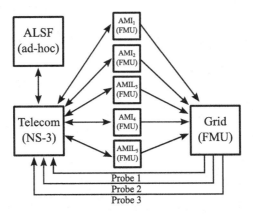

Fig. 2. The Concept-Grid use case with the different simulators interactions

Each house is equipped with a heat pump and an AMI (Advanced Metering Infrastructure also known as Linky) smart meter. The heat pumps are always enabled, except in a time slot determined by the ALSF (Advanced Load Shedding Function) decisional system. This last sends a message to meters to indicate their shedding time slot (specific to each house); the meters are responsible for enabling or disabling the heat pump during the simulation according to this information.

This use case involves different types of heterogeneity:

- multi-domain: ALSF corresponds to a decisional model, communications between equipments correspond to two communication network models (PLC and Ethernet) and power grid to electrical models;
- multi-simulator: communication models are simulated with NS-3, power grid components and AMI as FMUs[1] and decision system is currently simulated in an ad-hoc Java automaton;
- multi-formalism: FMUs are equation-based, NS-3 models are event-based;
- multi-language: FMU wrappers and decision system are in Java language, NS-3 is in C++;
- multi-platform: FMUs are executed on Windows while NS-3 is on GNU/Linux.

Implementation involves several different existing simulators: the power grid (one FMU), the AMIs (one FMU for each), the communication network (NS-3) and the decision system (an automaton in Java). Each simulator is managed by an agent (namely m-agent) in charge of the interactions of its model with the other ones. Interactions are reified through artifacts. M-agents and artifacts are provided by the MECSYCO middleware. Wrappers of simulators are specific to

---

[1] Each FMU (Functional Mock-up Unit) corresponds to a set of equations with its solver, exported from tools compliant with FMI (Functional Mock-up Interface), a standard [12] to handle the coupling of models described by differential, algebraic, and discrete equations.

the simulation software (we only developed one FMU-wrapper, not one for each simulator). Fig. 2 corresponds to the interactions between the simulators.

Demonstrations show the results provided by the simulation. In addition, they are completed by pedagogical proof of concepts focusing on each specific issue solved by MECSYCO.

4 Conclusion

The demonstrations show a use case based on smart grid real scenarios as an example of complex system. They demonstrate the ability of the MECSYCO simulation middleware to handle different kinds of heterogeneity in a homogeneous, multi-agent oriented point of view with a fully decentralized execution.

Acknowledgments. This work is partially funded by EDF R&D through the strategic project MS4SG.

References

1. Siebert, J., Ciarletta, L., Chevrier, V.: Agents and artefacts for multiple models co-evolution: building complex system simulation as a set of interacting models. In: Proceedings of AAMAS 2010, pp. 509–516 (2010)
2. Vaubourg, J., Presse, Y., Camus, B., Bourjot, C., Ciarletta, L., Chevrier, V., Tavella, J.P., Morais, H.: Multi-agent multi-model simulation of smart grids in the ms4sg project. In: Proc. of PAAMS 2015 (2015)
3. Fritzson, P., Engelson, V.: Modelica – a unified object-oriented language for system modeling and simulation. In: Jul, E. (ed.) ECOOP 1998. LNCS, vol. 1445, pp. 67–90. Springer, Heidelberg (1998)
4. Dynamic Modeling Laboratory (Dymola). http://www.3ds.com/products-services/catia/capabilities/modelica-systems-si
5. Mahseredjian, J., Dennetière, S., Dubé, L., Khodabakhchian, B., Gérin-Lajoie, L.: On a new approach for the simulation of transients in power systems. Electric Power Systems Research **77**(11) (2007)
6. Henderson, T.R., Roy, S., Floyd, S., Riley, G.F.: NS-3 project goals. In: Proceeding of WNS2 2006, p. 13. ACM (2006)
7. Varga, A., Hornig, R.: An overview of the OMNeT++ simulation environment. In: Proceedings of ICST, p. 60 (2008)
8. Enterprise Architect. http://www.sparxsystems.com.au/products/ea/index.html
9. Ricci, A., Viroli, M., Omicini, A.: Give agents their artifacts: the A&A approach for engineering working environments in MAS. In: Proc. AAMAS 2007. ACM (2007)
10. Zeigler, B., Praehofer, H., Kim, T.: Theory of Modeling and Simulation: Integrating Discrete Event and Continuous Complex Dynamic Systems. Academic Press (2000)
11. Chandy, K.M., Misra, J.: Distributed simulation: A case study in design and verification of distributed programs. IEEE Trans. Software Engineering (1979)
12. Blochwitz, T., Otter, M., Arnold, M., et al.: The functional mockup interface for tool independent exchange of simulation models. In: 8th International Modelica Conference, pp. 20–22 (2011)

Author Index

Printed in the United States
By Bookmasters